Proposed Language Reform for Ethiopia

Volume I: Orthography

PROPOSED LANGUAGE REFORM FOR ETHIOPIA

VOLUME I
— ORTHOGRAPHY —

LOU T.M. KAHSSAY

Three Qua Publishing
Selesitu Qua

Published by Three Qua Publishing.
First published in December 2016.

For more information about the publisher, including current contact information, visit threequa.com.

The 3Q! logo—which is made up of elements resembling the numeral 3 and the traditional Ethiopic character ቋ (qua) or the letter Q and the exclamation point on overlapping black and white frames—is a mark of Three Qua Publishing.

Library and Archives Canada Cataloguing in Publication

Kahssay, Lou T. M., author

Proposed language reform for Ethiopia / Lou TM Kahssay.

Includes bibliographical references and index.

Contents: Volume I. Orthography.

ISBN 978-0-9950911-0-8 (v. 1 : paperback)

1. Amharic language--Reform. 2. Tigrinya language--Reform. 3. Amharic language--Orthography and spelling. 4. Tigrinya language--Orthography and spelling. I. Title.

PJ9217.K34 2016 492'.87 C2016-902614-0

ISBN 978-0-9950911-1-5 (Volume II, paperback)

To my wife, Misrak W. Kahssay
And our precious, Eliana B. Kahssay

And

In memory of Prime Minister Meles Zenawi (May 9, 1955 – August 20, 2012),
Probably the greatest leader Africa has ever produced

"Meles Zenawi … emerged as perhaps the most original and intelligent African ruler of the last 50 years."

—Christopher Clapham,
Professor Emeritus at the Centre of African Studies,
University of Cambridge

"A thousand years from now, when Ethiopians gather to welcome the fourth millennium, they shall say that the eve of the third millennium was the beginning of the end of the dark ages in Ethiopia. They shall say that the eve of the third millennium was the beginning of the Ethiopian Renaissance."

—PRIME MINISTER MELES ZENAWI
From a speech the late premier delivered on September 10, 2007, which was the eve of Mesikerem 1, 2000 E.C.—the beginning of the third Ethiopian millennium

Eulogies for Prime Minister Meles Zenawi

"We join you in the mourning and paying tribute to a great man and a great son of Ethiopia, who is also ours as a continent. But we also celebrate his rich life that has touched millions of people in Africa. His was a life of immense courage, vision and enterprise which he devoted to the advancement of his fellow citizens in this country and across Africa. We gather here to recognize his remarkable achievement that has made us all proud–Ethiopians, Africans and beyond. ... He was a man of such a high caliber, royal talent and selflessness that we all feel the magnitude of the gap he has left. The late Prime Minister Meles Zenawi did not court greatness–he led a humble and simple but meaningful life. He was an unassuming person, but his sharp intellect and tremendous courage to face any kind of challenge made him a formidable presence. ... It is these qualities that he used to charge in the transformation of his country and that of our continent restoring the dignity of Ethiopians and Africans as a whole.

"Friends and foe alike recognized and respected Meles as a man of strong convictions, principles and long-term vision. Where some could have been compromised for short time profits or gains or easily succumbed to pressures, he was steadfast and always took a definite stand on issues of right and wrong and, more often than not, he was on the side of right. ... [H]e was sometimes misunderstood not because he was wrong but because he was ahead of many... For Meles, the benefits of freedom and prosperity were best [cherished] if shared with other African countries... The people of Rwanda will always remember with immense gratitude the people of Ethiopia gave our country at the time of need in the immediate aftermath of the Genocide. Ethiopians did this even when Ethiopia just started in its own transition. Meles led from the front with other leaders in working for the stability of this region in mediating in Sudan and Somalia. And in everything he did, he spared no effort, and he did not shy away from taking tough but right decisions to bring peace and security to our region. ...

"Prime Minister Meles Zenawi's legacy has deep roots in the rich heritage of independence and dignity that this great nation of Ethiopia has inspired on our continent. He was a true heir and fierce champion of that tradition and sought to share it with the rest of Africa. He was a very able voice for Africa in leading NEPAD [and in] climate change, agriculture, and food security [issues], to mention just a few. ... The most befitting tribute we can pay him is to consolidate and to carry on with the work and the vision he was associated with for our continent–to make a better future for Africa. His legacy to us does not lie in the past, but in the future. There is no doubt that the ideals Meles lived for [and] the courage he showed in facing many challenges will live on and be carried forward by the millions of young energetic and motivated Ethiopians and other Africans.

"May his soul rest in peace."

—Rwandan President Paul Kagame, 2012

"[W]e mourn the passage of one of the most distinguished leaders of his generation whose immense contributions to national development, regional and continental stability will be celebrated forever. History will record that Prime Minister Zenawi used his immense gift of intellect, eloquence and vision to [bring about] remarkable good and transformation for Ethiopia. Unfazed by difficulties and challenges, he spoke to the issues of his time with candor, courage and conviction. He was a truly visionary African leader who was sincerely and steadfastly committed to socio-economic development of not only the people of Ethiopia but all of Africa. Prime Minister Meles Zenawi fought ... on the global stage on the issues of sustainable development, equity, international financial management and climate change. When he spoke on these issues, he spoke not only for Ethiopia, but for the entire continent of Africa. Africa owes Meles a huge depth of gratitude for his service as Chairman of the New Partnership for African Development (NEPAD) Heads of State and Government Orientation Committee [HSGOC] and Chairman of the African Union [Committee of African] Heads of State and Government on Climate Change [CAHOSCC]. In his immense remarkable performance in these capacities, Meles truly became the spokesman on the major issues which have become the focal point of the continent's socio-economic and transformation agenda. I was honoured indeed to count this good son of Africa amongst my personal friends. ... My country Nigeria will miss you as a great friend of our nation and all Africa will miss you as a truly selfless, forthright and an extremely dynamic leader."

—Nigerian President Goodluck Jonathan, 2012

"The 20th of August 2012 was a sad day on the calendar of the African Union and Africa. As we lost one of the greatest sons of the continent–His Excellency Prime Minister Meles Zenawi. ... With Prime Minister Zenawi at the helm, a generation of Ethiopians have seen their country emerge from hunger and destitution to be a fast growing economy. The polices of his party and government have delivered a sustained double digit economic growth rate. ... His ideas were framed around the need to achieve social justice for his people and conquer poverty not just in Ethiopia but in all of Africa. As an African leader, we are proud of Meles Zenawi and the leadership he provided on issues affecting the continent around the globe. He took a leading role on African negotiations on climate change, in peace making in Sudan, and in the fight to bring stability back in Somalia. Prime Minister Meles ascendancy as a liberation fighter and later as a leader of Ethiopia was due to the force of his intellect, which not many could match. He was ready to engage and debate with policy makers, diplomats, and scholars from around the world. He was invited to groups of powerful nations such as the G8 and G20 not only due to the size and history of his country, but mainly due to the size of his ideas. Meles was a builder of institutions. He played a prominent role in the NEPAD Heads of State and Government [Orientation] Committee and formed a solid alliance ... to promote the African Renaissance. ...Undeniably, our colleague, friend and comrade has left a lasting impression in Ethiopia and on the continent as a whole. We should, as a collective [body], within the institution whose headquarters he generously hosted, advance his achievement in honour of his contribution and leadership.

"Farewell my dear brother and comrade. May your soul rest in eternal peace."

—South African President Jacob Zuma, 2012

"It was with sadness that I learned of the passing of Prime Minister Meles Zenawi of Ethiopia. Prime Minister Meles deserves recognition for his lifelong contribution to Ethiopia's development, particularly his unyielding commitment to Ethiopia's poor."

—United States President Barack Obama, 2012

"[A]n inspirational spokesman for Africa ... [Prime Minister Meles Zenawi's] personal contribution to Ethiopia's development, in particular by lifting millions of Ethiopians out of poverty, has set an example for the region... Our thoughts are with his family and with the nation of Ethiopia. He will be greatly missed."

—United Kingdom Prime Minister David Cameron, 2012

"Ethiopia, one of the poorest countries in the world, made more progress in education, health and economic development under his leadership than at any time in its history, and it is a tragedy for the Ethiopian people that they have lost a committed leader and a champion of children at such a young age... When I last saw him earlier this year we held meetings about how we would ensure every child would be in school in Ethiopia by 2015. His passion was in abolishing poverty and our hope is that he will inspire a new generation of men and women who will champion the cause of eradicating poverty."

—Former United Kingdom Prime Minister Gorden Brown, 2012

"The problem of Africa has not been resources–it has been vision–the lack of it. ... Meles [and his] generation, those who chose the option of struggle, have created new conditions for the people of Africa. ... [B]y the time Meles came to the government, Ethiopia was generating 300 megawatts [of electricity]. ... What is the situation now? You are now generating 2,100 megawatts and by 2015 after the Millennium Dam [is completed] you will be generating 10,000 megawatts. ... The economic growth in Ethiopia has been in double digits in recent days. If you look at the infrastructure here in Addis Ababa, it has changed so much. So that is the historic role of Meles and his colleagues. ... So you are here. Meles has shown you the vision. ... Please carry out that vision. This vision is the correct vision. The vision of electricity, the vision of factories, the vision of modern agriculture, the vision of an educated society. ... Move forward with the vision of Meles. If you do that he would not have suffered in vain.... May his soul rest in eternal peace."

—Ugandan President Yoweri Museveni, 2012

"We gather to mark a profoundly sorrowful lose for Ethiopia, for Africa and for the entire world. ... I suspect we all feel it deeply unfair to lose such a talented and vital leader so soon when he still had so much more to give. Meles ... was selfless, tireless and totally dedicated to his work and family. ... [A]mong Prime Minister Meles's many admirable qualities, above all was his world class mind. ... But he wasn't just brilliant. ... He was uncommonly wise–able to see the big picture and the long game even when others would allow immediate pressures to overwhelm sound judgment. Those rare traits were the foundations of his greatest contributions. ... I was always struck by two things: Meles was consistently reasoned in his judgment and thoughtful in his decisions. And he was driven not by ideology, but by his vision of a better future for the land he loved. ...

Prime Minister Meles was ... both the son of Ethiopia and a father to its rebirth. Passionately proud to be Ethiopian, Meles was determined that you, its people, conquer your history of poverty, hunger and strife. Meles was profoundly shaped by the memory of fragile young lives snuffed out in the 1980's by folly induced famine and despair. The torment of that terrible time spurred him to join in driving out the strongman who would turn Ethiopia into a parched field of sorrow. It spurred him to remake himself overnight from gorilla to statesman. It spurred him to make sustainable development both a personal passion and a national priority. And it spurred him to resolve that Ethiopians will claim and maintain your rightful place as peace makers and generous contributors on the world stage.

"Of course, Meles's vision and impact never stopped at Ethiopia's borders. Across Africa fellow leader looked at Prime Minister Meles to help them make peace and jump start their economies. He was instrumental in building the African Union. He made IGAD [Inter-governmental Agency for Development] deliver. He confronted terrorism directly and countered violent extremists bent on undermining the state and the region he did so much to build. He worked vigorously to end bitter conflicts from Burundi to Liberia. He was crucial in the negotiation and implementation of the comprehensive peace agreement that ended Sudan's tragic civil war.

"I can also testify personally, how much Ethiopia, under Prime Minister Meles's leadership has given to the UN and its life saving efforts from preventing and resolving conflict to striving to meet the Millennium Development Goals; from combating climate change to serving in UN peacekeeping operations, most recently in Abyei. These contributions remind us even nations facing their own challenges can make vast contributions to our shared security. ...

"Prime Minister Meles was uncommon leader–a rare visionary and a true friend to me and many. We all, we all, my friend, will miss you mightily. May you rest well. And true to your memory, may your beloved Ethiopia know a future of prosperity, hope and peace.

"Thank you and God bless."

—Susan Rice, United States Ambassador to the United Nations, 2012

The Great Leader Prime Minister Meles Zenawi, who laid the foundation for this critical stage of the beginning of Ethiopian renaissance and who gave us the vision for a bright future, was Ethiopia's beloved patriot. ... He was a master builder who built a strong foundation for a developmental state. Because of the sacrifices he made, our institutions are solid... Today, even faced with such a loss, our people have, unambiguously, vowed once again to carry on Meles's vision [and] shown their respect with their tears. ... Our leader was a beloved son of Africa, who not only laboured for the renaissance of Ethiopia, but also for the renaissance of African as well. The respect he had for the peoples of Africa was without match. He was a hero who represented our continent in global arenas and fought for the rights of its peoples. And in our neighbourhood, the volatile region of the Horn of Africa, he followed a policy of good neighbourliness and economic ties, which we will continue to promote. Prime Minister Meles Zenawi was a great leader who worked hard to make [hydroelectric] energy a win-win-win solution between Addis Ababa, Khartoum, and Cairo. ...

"Eternal glory for our Great Leader. I thank you."

—Acting Prime Minister Haile Mariam Desalegn (now Prime Minister), 2012

You can't build a monument for a hero–his legacy is the monument. The message I have for all Ethiopians is to finish the good work that Meles started.

—Haile Gebrselassie, the greatest distance runner in history, 2012

Brief Contents

Table of Contents

PART III. Proposed Orthographic Reforms 91

Preface

In January 2011, I tried to look up a word in an Amharic-English dictionary after I found out that my wife and I had different ideas about the meaning of the word. Although I have since forgotten the word, I do remember being baffled to have not been able to find the word in the dictionary. Consequently, I began to look for other relatively common words just to see if I could find them. To my dismay, it was not easy to find many of the words mainly because they were entered following complicated, counterintuitive, or illogical sequences or were not entered at all. Many Ethiopic dictionaries show words like ማቋረጫ <maquarecxa> (exit), ተቆራጭ <teqoracx> (per diem), ተቋራጭ <tequaracx> (contractor), and አቋራጭ <aquaracx> (shortcut), for example, listed under the main entry word ቆረጠ <qoretxe>, which is a verb and means *to cut* (lit., *he cut*), rendering the alphabetical order useless. You would have to know that the root word for all the above words is ቆረጠ to look for them under that main entry, which means that you would have to have a substantial knowledge of Ethiopic to make use of an Ethiopic dictionary. Even then there would still be many words you may not easily find, even if you are a native Amharic speaker as I am. This conundrum led me to start, on the same day, a research work into the nature of Ethiopic words and the Ethiopic writing system—research that spanned for more than five years eventually leading to the publication of the work in this first of two volumes.

Due to the Ethiopic alphasyllabic script and the fusional nature of Ethio Semitic languages, it is difficult to maintain alphabetical order for the majority of word derivatives and inflections without reforming the orthography to some degree. The existence of too many word derivatives, widespread spelling inconsistencies, and a large number of characters in the Ethiopic writing system means that only a small fraction of words in Ethio Semitic languages can be entered in any dictionary let alone to be ordered alphabetically. For example, the Amharic word ማጠብ (to wash) has three times more derivatives than the entire number of word entries in the Amharic-English Dictionary by Amsalu Aklilu (1986). Moreover, Ethiopic dictionaries list all verb entries only in the third-person-singular-male (3PSM) past-tense form of the verb—just one of the thousands of derivatives any verb can have. Such lexicographical problems are reflective of the nation's challenges in the areas of language and communication with the adverse consequences to society discussed in this book. The solution, I propose, is a reform of the Ethiopic writing system as presented in this book (Volume I) and a better understanding of the Ethiopic grammar (Volume II). The aim of this book, therefore, is to call for a comprehensive language reform that will improve communication in Ethiopia. Improved communication will provide Ethiopia with the tools it needs for an unprecedented social and economic advancement in its history.

This book will be best utilized and understood if read end to end. The components of the book are laid out sequentially, but due to the many proposed reforms that are affected by each other, one will need to go back and forth between chapters. Volume I discusses the proposed orthography and some grammar while Volume II almost exclusively discusses grammar. (In some ways, Volume I is incomplete without Volume II.) You will frequently find a word or phrase in SMALL CAPS, which is a technical term or new concept defined previously or within the next sentence or sentences. To not bog down the average reader with unfamiliar linguistic terms (since my intention is to reach a wider audience), I have mostly used simple-to-understand terms. A date in the Ethiopian calendar is indicated with the initials 'E.C.' and is sometimes followed by a Gregorian calendar date in parenthesis for clarity. Transliteration of Ethiopic words follows the new standard proposed in the book except when referring to names of historic places or historical personalities that have already been widely known by one of the traditional transliteration systems. With regards to the names of Ethiopic writers whose works I have cited, I have used the proposed system of romanization, except where the writer has already provided his or her name in the Latin script. All citations from Ethiopic sources, with or without the original Ethiopic text, are my translations unless noted otherwise. In-text citations for Ethiopian sources are shown with each author's first name or full name, rather than his or her last name alone since Ethiopian tradition does not recognize the use of the last name as a single identifier.

This book has been written in English for three reasons. First, the comprehensive nature of the proposed reform—ranging from orthography to grammar—meant that it would be unnecessarily too complicated to discuss the matter using the very script and languages considered for reform. Second, since both Tigirinya and Amharic have not yet been seriously used as mediums of instruction beyond elementary schools, except for individual Tigirinya and Amharic courses, there are no readily available linguistic terms and sometimes even concepts that can be used to write a book such as this one. Third, writing a book on two languages needed the use of a third language to switch between topics and discussions relevant to one or both languages quickly and flawlessly.

While I am convinced that implementing all the reforms proposed in this book as soon as possible will have immense benefits for the advancement of Ethiopia, I have no illusion that everyone will accept all the reform ideas at once. Rather, Government should take the lead in making the case for the reform and put in place the necessary legislation for it. For a smooth implementation, the proposed reforms can be phased in through a transition period the length of which will depend on national capacity. Although some of the reforms such as the proposed standard method for the romanization of Ethiopic may be universally accepted with little effort, others may need a concerted effort for their acceptance by everyone. I hope this generation is ready to adopt all the proposed reforms within a few years.

Lou Kahssay

December 2016

LIST OF TABLES

List of Figures

PART I

INTRODUCTION

Chapter 1

Introduction

Encompassed on all sides by the enemies of their religion the Æthiopians slept near a thousand years, forgetful of the world, by whom they were forgotten

—Edward Gibbon (1737 – 1794),
English historian and Member of Parliament

Ethiopia has ignited the imagination of Americans for generations. Before African Americans won their civil rights, many of them were inspired by this country—a nation that never suffered the indignities of colonialism, people who defended their freedom and their right in self-determination.

—United States President Barack Obama, 2015

IN THIS CHAPTER

This is a proposal for a comprehensive language reform for Ethiopia by taking Tigirinya (Tigrinya) and Amharic, two of the country's most popular languages, as examples and early candidates for reform. Through a scientific approach to the grammars and orthographies of Tigirinya and Amharic (and to some extent Giiz), I propose reform of these languages in a manner that can be applied to other Ethiopian languages. Ethiopia is home to 90 languages and dialects including those in the Semitic language group—such as Giiz (Ge'ez), Tigirinya, and Amharic—which use the Ethiopic script developed by the ancient Axumites. Today, Tigirinya and Amharic need to reform to survive and serve the modern needs of their users, particularly in the areas of technology and communication. Hence, the overriding goal of the proposed reform is a grammatical and orthographic simplification, standardization, and codification of the languages and their orthographies to ensure effective communication for generations to come.

BACKGROUND

Truly Ethiopia is a sleeping African giant in the process of being awakened. A cradle of civilization and the source of the human race,[1] today Ethiopia finds its destiny tangled in its distant glorious past, troubled recent history, and an immense potential for a bright future. Ethiopia's history begins around 900 B.C., but its golden age was during the first millennium after Christ when the Kingdom of Axum was one of the great powers in the world before its decline in the seventh century. After centuries of national decline, the Zagiwei (Zagwe) dynasty rose in the 11th century and ruled the nation for more than 200 years. Ethiopia again fell into centuries of decline after the Zagiwei dynasty ended in the 13th century.[2] Weakened by multiple wars with regional and foreign aggressors such as the Ottoman Empire and Arab invaders, central authority started to wane eventually leading to infighting between local kings and noblemen in one of the darkest eras in Ethiopian history—called Zemene Mesafinit (Era of Judges)—that lasted from 1769 to 1855. Having become the first African nation to defeat a modern European power at the Battle of Aadiwa (Adwa) against the Italians in 1896, Ethiopia once again maintained its sovereignty. Never colonized in its millennia-old history—except for a brief occupation by Fascist Italy from 1936 to 1941 following the asymmetrical Second Ethio-Italian War—Ethiopia had been a beacon of hope for Africans and peoples of African origin who were oppressed by European powers. Ethiopia's more recent troubled history occurred during the time of the brutal Derig (Derg) regime and was crowned by the most humiliating famine of 1984 that cut the lives of an estimated 400,000 people.[3]

The Kingdom of Axum, which had relations with Rome and other ancient powers, was one of the most powerful civilizations on earth.

In 1991, a coalition of freedom fighters under the umbrella of the Ethiopian Peoples’ Revolutionary Democratic Front, which was led by who later became Prime Minister Meles Zenawi, overthrew the Derig and ushered in one of the most important political changes in Ethiopian history. For the first time in Ethiopia, a multi-party political system was established and a new constitution came into effect in 1995 guaranteeing the rights of nations, nationalities, and peoples, including their rights for self-administration using their native languages. Since then the socio-economic and political change that has taken place in Ethiopia is just short of a miracle. Rapidly growing economy, political stability (in a troubled region), and developments in the education and health sectors are making Ethiopia a model for other developing countries. Dubbed the fastest growing economy in Africa, for almost fourteen years since 2002, the Ethiopian economy grew by more than 10% each year helping more than quadruple the nation’s per capita income. The country was a strong performer on at least six of the eight Millennium Development Goals set out by the United Nations at the turn of the century.[4]

Ethiopia’s mega projects that include massive electric power generation plants, thousands of kilometers of cross-country rail lines and paved roads, strategic industrial parks, and many new universities show the country’s increasing confidence in itself not only to manage complex projects but also to be able to fund many of them. Africa’s first light rail system that came to service in Addis Ababa in 2015 and Africa’s largest hydroelectric dam under construction in the Gamibeilla (Gambela) Region are signs of a rising Ethiopia dubbed an ‘African Lion.’[5] The remarkable progress Ethiopia is showing in lifting its people from the quagmire of poverty and leading Africa in socio-economic as well as global endeavours has continued to improve Ethiopia’s image internationally.[6] Ethiopia is a major stabilizer in East Africa thanks to its highly efficient and formidable military, which is the backbone of peacekeeping activities throughout Africa as well as constituting the largest contingent of troops in UN peacekeeping operations in the world.[7] In a 2014 bilateral meeting with His Excellency Prime Minister Haile Mariam Desalegn, United States President Barack Obama delivered remarks to the media admiring the massive socio-economic progress taking place in Ethiopia and Ethiopia’s contribution to global security, both of which made the country a leader in Africa.[6] Due to its policy of green economy and fight against environmental degradation, Ethiopia’s expertise in green initiatives has been cited as a model for other nations including industrialized ones.[9]

Unfortunately, these developments have not been matched by improvements in the use of Ethiopian languages, such as Tigirinya and Amharic, as mediums of communication. In fact, Ethiopian languages seem to be regressing rather than progressing, and this may be even more true with Amharic, the language used at the national level, than with any other Ethiopian languages. Ironically, Ethiopia needs accurate communication now more than ever before since it is trying to lay the foundation for a modern, prosperous society. The unprecedented confluence of economic, technological, and sociopolitical changes in today’s Ethiopia require well-developed domestic languages for accurate communication to function optimally and to protect and promote public safety and wellbeing. Accurate communication or lack thereof can, for example, have a huge impact on commercial activities, manufacturing processes, healthcare, the promulgation and observance

The recent economic progress in Ethiopia is not matched by progress in use of language—the most important medium of communication

of laws and regulations, environmental protection, and product and chemical labeling, among others. The use of four languages, such as including English and Chinese as reported in some of the newly set up factories in Ethiopia,[10] requires a sophisticated language policy to allow for accurate and efficient communication at the same time protecting domestic languages and ensuring public safety. In the absence of an effective language policy and a commitment to bring Ethiopian languages on par with international standards for communication for an industrial economy, ineffective communication and often miscommunication will continue to hamper progress in Ethiopia. Lacking commonly accepted standards and reference materials for domestic languages, it has proven almost impossible to use the languages as mediums of communication in endeavours that require sophisticated, high level, or exacting information such as in technological, medical, military, or manufacturing activities and processes. Tigirinya and Amharic are, for example, exceptionally weak when it comes to the collection, processing, storage, and retrieval of words as part of the processing of information.

Such weaknesses necessitate a coordinated effort for the development of the languages. According to Ethnologue, language development is the "result of the series of on-going planned actions that language communities take to ensure that they can effectively use their languages to achieve their social, cultural, political, economic, and spiritual goals." Charles Ferguson (1968) defined language development as to include three major themes: graphization, standardization, and modernization, which respectively are the development of a writing system, the development of a standard that overrides regional differences, and the development of the use of language especially suitable for "industrialized, secularized, structurally differentiated, 'modernized' societies" (as quoted by Ethnologue).[11]

Ethiopia's language assets are being squandered due to lack of proper attention; and considering the state of language usage in Ethiopia, they will not particularly be suited for an industrialized, 21st-century economy Ethiopia aims to become. Graduates of the country's tertiary educational institutions are, for example, mostly unable to properly use anyone of Ethiopia's languages for accurate written or spoken communication.[12] Nor is it possible to find a sample literature of highly sophisticated scientific or technical nature that is written entirely in any one of the Ethiopian languages. As of 2016, for example, the websites of the Ethiopian Commodities Exchange and the Central Statistical Agency provided very little information, if any, in any Ethiopian language. Even the Ethiopian Airlines, which serves more Ethiopians than nationals of any other single country, has no information on its website in any Ethiopian language, although, it provides information in foreign languages including Chinese, Korean, Italian, Spanish, and English.

Interestingly, and perhaps as an early sign of Ethiopia's "rise from the ashes," there seems to be a growing interest in learning Amharic and other Ethiopian languages, especially by the growing number of expatriates in the country.[13] However, we know that Ethiopian languages have some of the most difficult grammars in the world both for native speakers and foreigners.[14] It is, therefore, urgent that Government help develop standardized languages based on a modern language policy that will help propel the nation to achieve its stated goal of becoming a middle-income country by 2025 and eventually become a high-income country of highly literate and sophisticated society.

Language development is key for the overall socio-economic progress in Ethiopia.

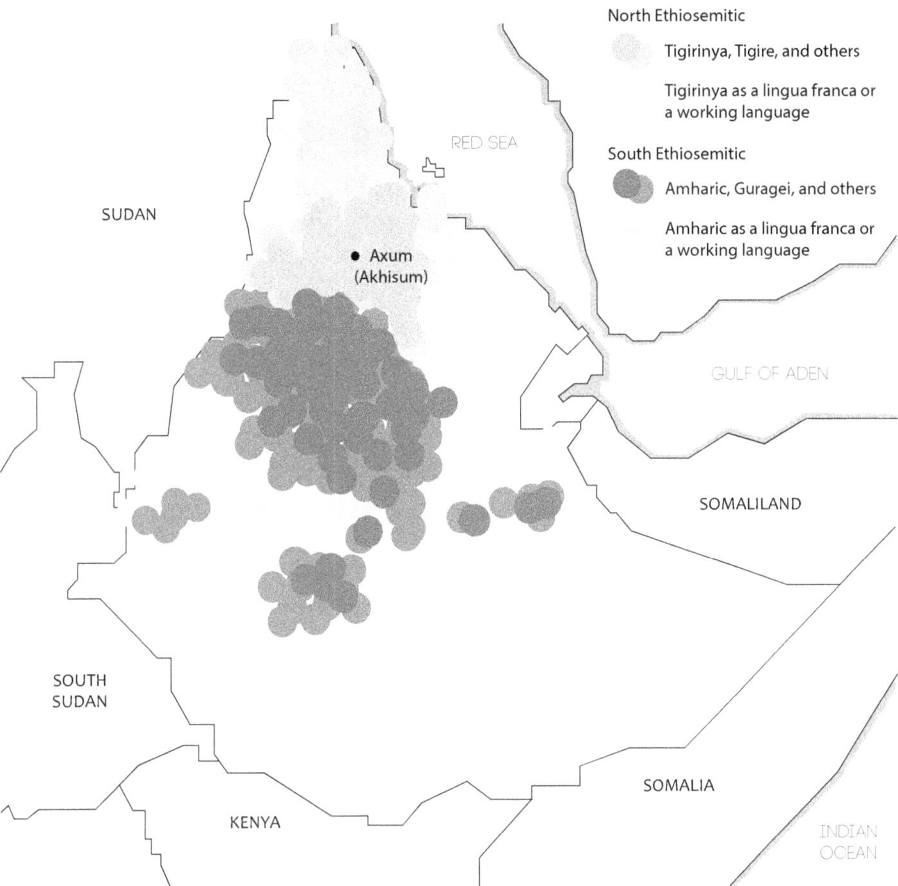

Figure 1.1: Geographic distribution of Ethiosemitic languages

The Ethiopian Semitic Languages

Also known as Ethiopic, Ethiosemitic is a branch of the Semitic languages. The term can be extended to refer to all Semitic languages in Ethiopia, including ancient Giiz and its most popular descendants Tigirinya and Amharic, almost all of which are found in Ethiopia (**Figure 1.1**). Ethiopic shows strong characteristic similarities to other Semitic languages, such as Arabic, in its grammatical structure. Dillmann and Bezold (2005) argued that Ethiopic, "[i]n its sounds and laws of sounds, in its roots, inflectional expedients and word-forms, in all that is reckoned the structure and essence of a language, it bears throughout a genuine and uncorrupted Semitic stamp."[15] The oldest written languages and urban civilizations in the Middle East and Ethiopia are attributed to Semitic populations, and some estimates indicate that Semitic originated in the Levant more than 5700 years ago. Kitchen, Ehret, et al. (2009) proposed the introduction of early Ethiosemitic to Africa via southern Arabia around 800 B.C.,[16] However, this has been disputed by Girma Demeke (2013) and other Ethiopianists.

Giiz was the official language of the ancient Kingdom of Axum. Also known by its variant spelling Aksum, the UNESCO World Heritage ruins of the ancient city of Axum are found in Tigiray (Tigray) Region, Ethiopia. Axum was the center of an ancient civilization and at that time the "most powerful state between the Eastern Roman Empire and Persia" according to UNESCO World Heritage Centre. The Kingdom of Axum lasted between the first and 13th centuries and at its peak in the fourth century stretched as far as most of southern Yemen.[17] Immigration and contacts with areas across the Red Sea that lasted for at least two millennia before the fourth century A.D. had, no doubt, made Axum the melting pot of cultures and races and may have shaped Giiz as we know it today.[18]

A major trading power with ancient Greece, Egypt, and Asia, the city of Axum existed for several centuries before Christ. Axum supplanted an even older civilization—the DEMT (D'mt) kingdom—which came into existence sometime between 1000 B.C. and 500 B.C.[19] While there is no agreement in academic circles as to whether or not the DEMT kingdom was established or influenced by the Sabaeans of southern Arabia, latest research indicates that Giiz was not derived from Sabaean.[20]

Giiz, which ceased to exist as a spoken language around the beginning of the 14th century (Leslau, 1946), remains one of the most prominent Ethiosemitic languages (**Table 1.1**) and still used by the Ethiopian Orthodox Church for liturgy. Amharic has been the dominant language in Ethiopia even at times when Ethiopia was ruled by rulers based outside of the Amhara hinterland. For example, Emperor Yohhannis (Yohannes) IV, who rose from Tigiray, used Amharic extensively in his administration and promoted it very well.[21] (Ethiopia remains one of the few countries in Sub-Saharan Africa which do not use a European language as their national language, although the use of English as a mandatory medium of instruction in Ethiopia is threatening to change this fact.)

Table 1.1: Summary of the three historically most prominent Ethiosemitic languages

LANGUAGE	ISO 639-3 CODE	SCRIPT	NUMBER OF SPEAKERS*	OFFICIAL LANGUAGE STATUS
Giiz	gez	Ethiopic	-	The ancient Kingdom of Axum
Tigirinya	tir	Ethiopic	10,000,000	Tigiray and Eritrea
Amharic	amh	Ethiopic	32,000,000	Amhara, Southern Nations, Beinishangul & Gumuz, Gamibeila, Addis Ababa, Direi Dawa, and Ethiopia

Note: Estimated number of speakers includes native speakers and non-native speakers in Ethiopia and speakers who live in other countries

The Ethio-Semitic languages constitute the South portion of the Semitic group of languages within the Afro-Asiatic language family. The following grouping adapted from Ethnologue shows the Ethiosemitic languages and their connection to Afro-Asiatic language family. As a sign of the diversity of the Ethiopian Semitic languages, and depending on how language is defined in contrast to dialect, there may be more living Semitic languages within Ethiopia than in any other country in the world.

Afro-Asiatic (376 languages and dialects) [22]
- Semitic (78)
  - South Semitic (21)
    - Ethio-Semitic (15)
      - North Ethiosemitic (4)
        - Giiz (Ge'ez)
        - Tigirinya (Tigrigna)
        - Tigire (Tigré)
        - Dahalik
      - South Ethiosemitic (11)
        - Transversal (6)
          - Amharic-Arigobba (Argobba) (2)
            - Amharic (or Amarinya)
            - Arigobba
          - Hareree (Harari)-East Guragei (East Gurage) (4)
            - Hareree
            - Silitxei (Silt'e)
            - Welanei (Wolane)
            - Zay
        - Outer (5)
          - n-Group (1)
            - Kisitanei (Kistane)
          - tt-Group (4)
            - Enor (Inor)
            - Mesimes (Mesmes)
            - Mesiqan (Mesqan)
            - Sebat Beit Guragei (Sebat Bet Gurage)

Tigirinya, the most popular cousin of Amharic, is widely used in the north as the statutory official language of the regions of Tigiray and Eritrea. Ninety-five percent of Tigiray's population of 5,310,000 and one-half of Eritrea's population of 5,228,000 are native speakers of Tigirinya.[23] There are also hundreds of thousands of native speakers of Tigirinya outside of the geographical areas of Tigiray and Eritrea. Tigirinya is also used as a second language by as many as 180,000 people in Ethiopia.[24] All in all, there may be as many as 10 million Tigirinya speakers in the world today—making it the third most popular Semitic language in the world just ahead of Hebrew. This number will continue to increase due to Ethiopia's relatively high rate of population growth and the government's constitutional policy of encouraging linguistic and cultural pluralism.

There may be more Semitic languages in Ethiopia than in any other country in the world.

The more popular Amharic, which became the lingua franca in Ethiopia sometime in the 17th century (Leslau, 2000), is the statutory working language of the Federal Democratic Republic of Ethiopia, four regional states—Amhara, Debub (SNNP), Beinishanigul & Gumuz (BG), and Gamibeilla—and two special city administrations—Addis Ababa (AA) and Dire Dawa (DD). Not including Amharic speakers who reside outside Ethiopia, Amharic has 26,600,000 native speakers[25] and 5,000,000 non-native speakers[26] in Ethiopia, which make it the language with the most speakers in Ethiopia and the second most popular Semitic language in the world after Arabic.

Unique in Africa, Ethiopia has been in continues official use of its script, called Ethiopic, for millennia. Today Ethiopic is used as the writing system for at least a dozen languages in addition to Tigirinya and Amharic. However, the necessity of a comprehensive language reform for Tigirinya and Amharic—and by extension for all Ethiosemitic languages—cannot be overemphasized. Today these languages suffer from multiple malaises ranging from bad grammar and lack of robust vocabulary to spelling inconsistencies and lack of standard reference materials, such as efficient dictionaries suitable for a modern society. As languages, they are increasingly becoming inadequate for communication in the modern world. The inexistent or minimally existent writing standards, reference materials, dictionaries, and grammar books for Tigirinya and Amharic means that much needs to be done to systematically collect, catalog, analyze, and disseminate linguistic information for public use.

Language as a Means of Communication

Language as a form of communication can refer to speech or writing. While speech is as old as humanity, writing is a relatively recent development in human history. Humans have used at various times four major types of information recording—pictograms, word-signs, syllabic signs, and the alphabet. Writing was invented around 3200 B.C. by the Sumerians in Mesopotamia.[27] All the world's writing systems, which were created afterwards, have greatly enhanced human communication. Language, in general, and writing, in particular, are two of the greatest communication tools that humanity has. Thomas Astle succinctly stated that "[t]he noblest acquisition of mankind is *speech*, and the most useful art is *writing*" as cited in Ullman, 1980.[28] Writing, in fact, is one of humanity's greatest inventions. It is inconceivable to think of highly civilized societies without well-developed language and some form of writing system no matter how rudimentary it may be. As cited in Ullman (1980), James Breasted, in *The Conquest of Civilization,* stated that,

> "The invention of writing and of a convenient system of records on paper has had a greater influence in uplifting the human race than any other intellectual achievement in the career of man. It was more important than all the battles ever fought and all the constitutions ever devised."[29]

Axum was the birthplace of Ethiopian civilization including its writing system—Ethiopic.

Coulmas (1989, 1991) also argued that "[w]riting is the single most important sign system ever invented on our planet."[30]

Modern societies depend on effective, accurate, and timely communication to support many of their intricate activities such as in the medical, social, economic, political, and security areas of a modern world. As human knowledge and interactions increase, accurate communication or lack thereof will continue to have a profound impact on society. Just as accurate communication is important for a sophisticated society, poor language use, which is inaccurate communication, is a stumbling block in the development of society. A pervasive culture of inaccurate communication, such as is the case in Ethiopia, will continue to negatively impact the socio-economic status of the nation because it creates a disconnect between what is said by the speaker and what is understood by the listener in almost every communication. All communications, written or spoken, rely on a set of conventions to be clearly understood. When those conventions are no longer understood or are broken, the potential for communication failure arises. Dye (2010) argued that "[i]n order for language to work, speakers and listeners have to have the same idea about what things mean, and they have to use words in similar ways." Dye further argued that if children were not wired to learn language by conventionalizing most commonly occurring patterns, "language, as a system, would become less conventional," and that what "words meant and the patterns in which they were used would become more idiosyncratic and unstable, and all languages would begin to resemble pidgins."[31]

Poor Language Use in Ethiopia

In spite of the fact that Amharic has been used as the lingua franca in Ethiopia for centuries, it may be one of the least studied and standardized major languages of the world. The average literate adult speaker of either Tigirinya or Amharic is unable to identify the primary personal pronouns in a sentence, for example, because both Tigirinya and Amharic are highly inflectional and primary pronouns are always attached to a verb, a noun or an adjective. The spelling inconsistencies and ignorance of the basic rules of grammar among users of these languages continues to be a great barrier to effective communication.

In a sign of a recognition of the poor state of Amharic, Desita Tekile Welid (1970) stated that *Ras* Teferee Mekonnin (Teferi Mekonnen), who later became Emperor Haile Selassie, ordered a linguist to help prepare a dictionary for the language by reminding him of "ያገራችንን የቋንቋ ድኽነት (our country's poverty of language)" in a 1921 E.C. (c. 1929) royal letter.[32] Despite its long history and ancient civilization, Ethiopia did not have a very good literary culture that would have prevented the nation's "poverty of language." It would not be an exaggeration to state that the average book written in Amharic will not pass a standard quality test for language. Regarding political publications in Ethiopia, Kibirom (2013) argued that "although it would be incorrect to lump all books published to date [in the same category], most have not only been written below the minimum level of literary quality but also show too much emotionalism."[33]

Ethiopic literature is replete with grammatical and orthographic problems in addition to problems related to style and accuracy. The main problems associated with grammar and orthography are a poor use of grammatical tenses, inconsistent spelling, inconsistent use of grammatical gender, excessive or unnecessary use of foreign words, lack of rules for adopting foreign words and their deriva-

The precarious state of Ethiopian languages is a threate to the 21st century communication needs of Ethiopia.

tives, double pluralization, no pluralization, and inconsistent pluralization, among others. Other problems are a lack of conciseness, redundancy, lack of clarity of argument, too many typographical errors, lack of flow, lack of focus, lack of references, inability to clearly identify the target audience, self-contradiction, and informal or casual writing style, among others. Unfortunately, even highly educated individuals and those in higher positions of authority, such as professors and politicians, are no less immune to the poor use of language in both the written and spoken forms.

The Amharic used in urban areas is in an even more precarious situation. (Ironically, speakers of Amharic in rural Amhara, who are generally less literate than their urban counterparts, use the language more correctly and efficiently.) Urban speakers of the language, often make erroneous sentences that are only partly effective in communicating the intended message or information. It is not uncommon to hear people say something when they mean something slightly or entirely different. The use of what we shall refer to as Ethiopic *bado* words, which are words that are supposed to act as placeholders, add to the pervasive poor communication because they are used too frequently (Chapter 5). As a result, it takes more effort to exchange information between a speaker and a listener. Often, the listener has to ask the speaker several questions until he or she understands the intended message because the speaker does not provide sufficient information at once. For example, an Amharic speaker could say to a listener: እንትትን ጨርሰውና ለንትና አቀብለው, which can be translated roughly as, "Finish whatchamacallit and pass it over to whatshisface," without finishing or clarifying the thought. If the listener is diligent, he or she would ask the speaker to provide the missing information. However, since diligence in such situations can be exhaustive, often a listener simply ignores the missing information. Alternatively, he or she tries to guess what the missing information is or simply hopes it will be revealed in the end. Such poor communication not only wastes time and energy but also causes errors that are often difficult to trace.

Similarly, the chronic use of incorrect grammatical tenses is a major cause of miscommunication in Ethiopia. For example, consider the Amharic sentence ልጅ እያለች፣ በበሽታ በጣም ነው የምትጠቃው, a grammatical construction commonly used and means, "*When she being a child, it is badly she suffers from disease." However, the intended message is ልጅ እንደ ነበረች፣ በበሽታዎች በጣም ትጠቃ ነበር (When she was a child, she used to suffer from diseases badly). Once I heard a native Amharic speaker say እጇን በላች, pointing to a baby who was *sucking* her thumb. Translated into English, the sentence means, "She *ate* her hand." Although the speaker was neither joking nor trying to be rude, both the verb and the grammatical tense used to describe the action are incorrect. The speaker's description of the action is just as shocking in Amharic (at least for me) as it is in English, but there should be no doubt that the speaker uttered those words simply because inaccuracy in communication is extremely tolerated by Ethiopians even for native speakers. Accuracy requires a conscious choice of words from the limited Ethiopic vocabulary, which can be laborious in a society that neither demands it nor appreciates it. In fact, those who use proper Ethiopic vocabulary and grammatical tenses are viewed as provincial (interestingly, not as snobs) and are often teased and, therefore, the effort can be taxing to those who try to employ effective communication.

Given the level of tolerance for inaccuracy, it is no wonder that these kinds of casual and erroneous conversations take place on a regular basis. By comparison, I would argue that few illiterate native English speakers would show such a poor language skill, while many literate Amharic speakers have similar if slightly less shockingly poor language skill, which is a sign of the fact that Ethiopic languages are gradually losing their power to convey accurate information. (This is especially true of Amharic.) Television and radio broadcasters often make too many grammatical and stylistic errors, in addition to failing to deliver a coherent message, especially when they report live. Even government communiqués and official statements often lack robust reviews and edits before they are released to the public. The use of loanwords, especially English words, is very common, even though often equivalent words in local languages already exist or should have been created using normal rules of grammar. In what may be referred to by the Ethiopic word *Guramayilei*—a Tigirinya or Amharic conversation characterized by excessive use of English words, phrases, or even sentences—is increasingly becoming a chronic problem with severe consequences for the grammars of the languages. More and more people have become accustomed to inserting English words in their conversation even in ordinary conversations requiring simple words. As some Ethiopians sarcastically say to shame those who use English words as a badge of honour, *The English word 'water' describes H2O more accurately than the Ethiopic word* may *or* wiha.* Some people find it convenient to insert English words in their otherwise Ethiopic conversations as a show of their knowledge of English, which indirectly is intended to show their academic achievement since English is the medium of instruction in Ethiopia from middle school onwards.

The Stakes

Research by Anderson and Harrison (2007) shows that almost 80% of humanity speaks only the 83 biggest languages of the world, which comprise 1.1% of the total number of languages; while only 0.2% of people speak the 3,586 smallest languages of the world, which comprise 51.2% of all languages. Rymer (2013) warned that every two weeks one of the world's languages dies and as a result "by the next century nearly half of the roughly 7,000 languages spoken on Earth will likely disappear, as communities abandon native tongues in favor of English, Mandarin, or Spanish."[34] While it is unlikely that Tigirinya or Amharic will disappear in the next century, they will probably become almost unusable and unrecognizable within a few decades unless reckless language use is kept in check. The Ethiopian media should be in the vanguard of the protection of Ethiopian languages—protection against the unnatural and sudden displacement of native vocabulary by invading foreign words that move in with the help of technology and globalization—but so far it has miserably failed with devastating consequences for society. Globally, the gradual disappearance of small languages is not new, but the rate of the loss of languages has increased exponentially in recent years[35] mainly due to modern social interactions and globalization. Although Tigirinya and Amharic, like all other languages, had developed naturally through the slow acquisition of words from other foreign and domestic languages, currently these languages are in a particularly vulnerable situation in their history unable to resist the onslaught of English.

*Note: 'May <ma-yi>' and 'wiha <wi-ha>' are the exact equivalents of the word 'water' in Tigirinya and Amharic, respectively.

I propose that the main causes of the poor state of these languages are the lack of a strong literary culture, the lack of a robust language policy to protect and develop domestic languages, the use of English as the official medium of instruction, and more recently the Internet and the effects of globalization. Yacob (2005-2006) argued that the "pervasiveness of electronic communication technology is forcing societies world wide to face the challenge of cultural preservation with an immediacy never before seen," and that societies should respond to technological innovations in a way that will guarantee the survival of their culture.[36] The century-long diminished role of the Ethiopian languages in education and science and technology where accuracy could be nurtured meant that the languages missed the opportunity to become effective communication tools by now. Perhaps as a result of this, Ethiopians, particularly speakers of Amharic, became lax with their use of accurate communication and developed a low expectation for communication leading to the prevalent language crisis in the nation today (Chapters 5 and 13). In his Amharic poetic prelude to his book *Adees Yamarinya Mezigebe Qalat (New Amharic Dictionary)*, Desita Tekile Welid (1970) lamented some people's attitude toward Ethiopic as follows:

> ያገሩን ፡ ቋንቋ ፡ ተምሮ ፡ ንባብ ፡ ከጽፈት ፡ ሳያውቅ ፡
> ያማርኛን ፡ ግስ ፡ በማቃለል ፡ ግእዝን ፡ ደግሞ ፡ በመናቅ ፡
> የፈረንጅ ፡ ፊደል ፡ አጥንቶ ፡ ምንም ፡ ቢያስተውል ፡ ቢራቀቅ ፡
> የሰው ፡ ወርቅ ፡ አያደምቅ ፤ አያደምቅ ፡ የሰው ፡ ወርቅ ።
>
> Not studying his country's language to be skilled in reading and writing,
> Belittling Amharic grammar and scorning Giiz,
> Even if [one] becomes learned and sophisticated in foreign script,
> Foreigners' heritage cannot be our heritage,
> Foreigners' heritage cannot be our heritage.[37]

Further, I propose that the problem is amplified by the fusional nature of the Ethiopic languages and their unique orthography which makes the study of grammar and the development of language materials, such as dictionaries with proper, alphabetically listed words very difficult. A verb in Tigirinya and Amharic can have tens of thousands of derivatives (**Appendix C**) making it virtually impossible for dictionaries to list them in any order, let alone to alphabetically list and define more than one or two of the derivatives (Chapter 3: Overview of Ethiopic Grammatical and Orthographic Problems). While there are many languages with a lot fewer speakers who have had their scripts supported by most of the major computer operating systems for many years now, Ethiopic has a long way to go. Texts in scripts of many languages with fewer speakers than Amharic or Tigirinya are more readily available on the Internet as well as on product labels, books and other mass produced items. For example, by 2015, Google Translate did not recognize either Tigirinya or Amharic but recognized the following languages, all of which have fewer speakers than Amharic, and many have fewer speakers than Tigirinya: Afrikaans, Albanian, Armenian, Basque, Bosnian, Croatian, Finnish, Greek, Hebrew, Latin, Lithuanian, Somali, Swedish, Yiddish, and Zulu.*

---

*Note: When last checked in September 2016, Google Translate had included Amharic.

Historically, the Ethiopian languages have been denied the development they need because they are used neither as mediums of instruction in higher education nor as languages for technical literature by public and private agencies.

There is no doubt that the general level of poverty and illiteracy in the Ethiopian society have denied Tigirinya and Amharic (and other Ethiopian languages) their proper place in the international language arena. However, the insignificant grammar studies done on these languages and the lack of a robust scientific approach in the studies may have hindered the languages even more. The fact that an Ethiopic verb can have thousands of derivatives is something that will stunt the development of these languages for generations to come unless language reforms, such as those proposed in this book, are implemented as soon as possible.

The overall lack of materials of any quality has been a great challenge for users of these languages. Native speakers did not even prepare the first Ethiopic grammars. Europeans prepared the first Ethiopic grammars in the 17th century. Desita Tekile Welid (1970) and Baye Yimam (2000 E.C.) stated that, for a long time, many of the materials available for teaching Amharic grammar were prepared by foreigners who wrote about the language using foreign languages. Leslau (1946) stated that Hiob Ludolf published the first Giiz grammar in 1661 and then the first Amharic grammar in 1698. Other noted works of Ethiopic grammar by foreign scholars of the 19th and 20th centuries include an Amharic grammar by Praetorius (1879), *Traite de langue amharique* by Marcel Cohen (1936), and C.H. Dawkin (1960) (see Leslau, 2000). However, according to Baye Yimam (2000 E.C.), until recently, about the only Ethiopic grammars available for Ethiopian students were those prepared by native speakers like Bilata Merisiei Hazen Welide Qeeriqos and Tekilemariyam Fanitayei, whose contents and arguments are now said to be outdated.

Leslau (1973) argued that students of Amharic had not been provided with the necessary practical tools to master the language despite the fact that Amharic had been scientifically studied since the 17th century. Similarly, Yimam (2000 E.C.) made the observation that one of the reasons for the problems of Amharic grammar is a lack of well-trained instructors and appropriate textbooks. Yimam further stated that "there is not a book that qualifies as a regular text or guide book or reference material" for Amharic written by Ethiopians despite the fact that Amharic grammar instructions have been given in colleges for many years now.[38] It is also important to note that the general attitude of the education system toward the teaching of Ethiopian languages, including Amharic, has not been positive for a long time. The mandatory Amharic lessons are considered by many as a waste of time, and the teachers are not esteemed in the same way as other teachers. This attitude has discouraged the educators and made them unable to provide lessons appropriate to their students. According to Yimam,

> In the old time[s], [Amharic] lessons [emphasized] grammar, poetry and reading. However, the role of grammar dwindled as emphasis shifted to practice. ... when language teachers grade their students' works, ... the strength of the argument, sequential arrangement, choice of words, clarity, etc., are not given due attention. ... Without teaching proper construction of phrases, it is inappropriate to [fail] students. ... [On the other hand,] the belief that, as long as an idea is expressed in a sentence, the correctness of the sentence is not important is a disastrous concept that makes the student unqualified to compete in the job market.[39]

A sign of the failing education system in Ethiopia, this has resulted in embarrassingly ill-equipped graduates who are not only unable to identify most basic features of the Ethiopic grammar but also are unable to make accurate communication in writing be it in a job application letter or a professional report. Baye Yimam (2000 E.C) lamented that even the upper echelons of the education system could not produce students who can distinguish between a subject and a predicate in a sentence and that,

> [Many] a student who graduate[s] from the secondary [school system], is becoming unable to write an ordinary letter properly, let alone a good job application letter. .... Employers frequently complain that graduate students at all levels lack the skills to prepare ordinary reports. They are unable to formulate their thoughts and express them using correct sentences.[40]

CHAPTER 2

THE ETHIOPIC SCRIPT: AN INTRODUCTION

Almost 3,000 years ago, the ruler of Sheba, which spanned modern-day Ethiopia and Yemen, arrived in Jerusalem with vast quantities of gold to give to King Solomon...Sheba was a powerful incense-trading kingdom that prospered through trade with Jerusalem and the Roman empire....[T]he queen's image inspired medieval Christian mystical works in which she embodied divine wisdom, as well as Turkish and Persian paintings, Handel's oratorio *Solomon*, and Hollywood films. Her story is still told across Africa and Arabia, and the Ethiopian tales are immortalised in the holy book the Kebra Nagast. Hers is said to be one of the world's oldest love stories. The Bible says she visited Solomon to test his wisdom by asking him several riddles. Legend has it that he wooed her, and that descendants of their child, Menelik—son of the wise—became the kings of Abyssinia.

—THE GUARDIAN

IN THIS CHAPTER

The Ethiopic writing system was originally developed during the Kingdom of Axum for use with the Giiz (Ge'ez) language. Today, Ethiopic is used as the writing system for all Ethiosemitic (Ethio-Semitic) languages and, until the 1990's, for Ethio-Cushitic and other Ethiopian languages. The Ethiosemitic languages are part of the South Semitic language group, which intern is a subgroup of the Afro-Asiatic language group in which the Ethiocushitic languages, such as Oromiffa, Affarinya, and Somaleenya are included.

THE BEGINNING OF WRITING IN ETHIOPIA AND THE DEVELOPMENT OF THE ETHIOPIC SCRIPT (*FEEDEL*)

Writing in what is today Ethiopia dates back to the first millennium before Christ with the earliest stone inscription in the Proto-Ethiopic (or Proto-Giiz) script dating back to the 9th century B.C.[1] As with other alphabetic scripts of the Middle East and Europe, the origins of the Proto-Ethiopic script goes back to the Semitic proto-alphabet developed in the Levant in the 2nd millennium B.C. The Proto-Ethiopic script (**Figure 2.1**), was used in an area that later gave rise to the Kingdom of Axum. Inscriptions found in Tigiray (Tigray or Tigrai)—the bastion of Ethiopian history, architecture, and literature for millennia[2]—indicate that variants of Proto-Ethiopic emerged in the 7th and 6th centuries B.C. These variants eventually led to the Ancient Ethiopic script, which was used to write the Giiz language before the end of the first century A.D. Proto-Ethiopic and its descendant Ancient Ethiopic, both of which are unvocalized, are considered by linguists to be abjads—writing systems consisting of consonants only. Ancient Ethiopic inherited twenty-four of its twenty-six letters from Proto-Ethiopic with some modifications, which became the basis for the traditional Ethiopic writing system (**Table 2.1**).

The concept of writing, which was invented in Mesopotamia more than 5000 years ago, influenced the development of other ancient writing systems, which through time evolved to writing systems used today including Ethiopic.

Table 2.1: The Old Ethiopic script (in the Noto Sans Ethiopic font) and its comparison to Proto-Ethiopic

	1	2	3	4	5	6	7	8	9	10	11	12	13	14	15	16	17	18	19	20	21	22	23	24	25	26
LETTER NAME	hoy	lewei	hhewit	may	sxewit	riis	sat	qaf	beit	tewei	hxarim	nehas	elif	kaf	wewei	eeyin	zey	yeman	denit	gemil	txeyit	pxeyit	xedey	xseppe	ef	pisa
OLD ETHIOPIC	ሀ	ለ	ሐ	መ	ሠ	ረ	ሰ	ቀ	በ	ተ	ኀ	ነ	አ	ከ	ወ	ዐ	ዘ	የ	ደ	ገ	ጠ	ጰ	ጸ	ፀ	ፈ	ፐ
PROTO-ETHIOPIC	𐩠	𐩡	𐩢	𐩣	𐩦	𐩧	𐩪	𐩤	𐩨	𐩩	𐩭	𐩬	𐩱	𐩫	𐩥	𐩲	𐩸	𐩺	𐩵	𐩴	𐩷		𐩮	𐩳	𐩰	
IPA	h	l	ħ	m	ɬ	r	s	q	b	t	x	n	ʔ	k	w	ʕ	z	j	d	g	tˤ	p'	sˤ	ɬˤ	f	p
TRADITIONAL TRANSLITERATION	h	l	ḥ	m	ś	r	s	ḳ	b	t	ḫ	n	'	k	w	'	z	y	d	g	ṭ	p̣	ṣ	ṣ́	f	p
PROPOSED TRANSLITERATION	h	l	hh	m	sx	r	s	q	b	t	hx	n	e	k	w	ee	z	y	d	g	tx	px	x	xs	f	p

Note: The Old Ethiopic characters are shown in the Noto Sans Ethiopic Bold font. By the time Old Ethiopic was fully developed, its characters became more curved than proto-Ethiopic, perhaps formed by speedy writing. Dillmann and Bezold (2005) stated that the older an Ethiopic text the thicker the strokes forming individual glyphs. For an image of a 15th century Ethiopic text with such a feature, see Figure 7.2.

Figure 2.1: "Ancient Blocks With Sabean [Proto-Ethiopic] Inscriptions, Yeha, Ethiopia," by A.Davey. Source: Wikipedia. Licensed under CC BY 2.0. Desaturated and background removed from original.

Indicating the script's links to South Arabian languages, Proto-Ethiopic has commonalities with scripts from the region. However, the location where Proto-Ethiopic, also called South Arabian script, originated is disputed by some Ethiopianists who argue that it was first developed in D'mt (DEMT) in what is today Ethiopia and migrated to South Arabia in what is today Yemen. The script was in use in both locations for centuries until it was replaced by the Arabic script in Yemen, while it eventually evolved into the traditional Ethiopic script still in use in Ethiopia.

The Ethiopic script is unique among the Semitic scripts, such as the Arabic and Hebrew scripts.

Like many ancient writing systems, early Proto-Ethiopic might have been written in alternating directions from one line to the next in what is called boustrophedon text, although, later inscriptions found in Axum were written from right to left. However, ever since Ancient Ethiopic emerged, it has been written left to right, which is unlike other Semitic writing systems.[3] Nakanishi (1980) stated that ancient Phoenician and Aramaic scripts were written only from right to left and today their descendants, which include the Hebrew and Arabic scripts, follow the same writing direction.

Since the development of the consonantal Ancient Ethiopic writing system, which expected the reader to guess the vowels for each word based on context, the last time Ethiopic went through a major reform was during the reign of King Ezana with the introduction of vowel notations to represent the seven basic vowel sounds in Ethiopic. At a time when writing was not a major tool for communication, not providing the vowels in words probably posed little problem. However, following the conversion of King Ezana and his kingdom to Christianity early in the fourth century, writing as a means of communication became increasingly more useful[4] necessitating vowel notations by adding diacritics to copies of each of the original consonantal characters. Hetzon (1997) stated that the

> Ethiopic script was thus the first Semitic script to notate vowels consistently, and it does so in a way unique within the Semitic sphere: it uses the technique followed in India, of taking a basic consonantal shape to represent the consonant followed by *a* [e] and modifying that shape to represent the consonant followed by the other vowels (or no vowels).[5]

Vowel notations probably occurred during the process of translating the Bible[6] from the Septuagint—the original version of the Bible in Greek—perhaps as a result of the influence of the use of vowels in the Greek alphabet. Hetzon (1997) further stated that vowel notations started to appear in the middle of the king's reign around 350 A.D. Creating a vocalized script, the reform produced seven syllables for every consonantal character family reflecting the seven basic vowelic sounds inherent in Ethiosemitic. By doing so, the writing system effectively became an alphasyllabary or abugida (ebugeeda)—a term adopted from the vocalization of the first four characters of the Ethiopic writing system in its alternative letter order (discussed later in this chapter)—which is to say that every character fuses a consonant and a vowel. (I propose 'dissecting' every character to separate the embedded consonant and vowel for a full-fledged Ethiopic alphabet, which, if implemented, will be the first in the history of Ethiopic.)

Dillmann and Bezold (2005) stated that Giiz continued to play a significant role as the preferred language for literature and official documents even after the seat of government moved to areas outside of Tigiray, and Amharic grew to become the spoken language in the court and official circles. Dillmann and Bezold further stated that Giiz eventually died out in the 17th century following political instability and fragmentation of the nation. Ethiopia's formidable terrain meant that people of the same culture and language were isolated in groups of settlements over vast territories leading to separate dialects which eventually became full-blown languages like Tigirinya and Amharic.[7] Tigirinya's rise to prominence was marked when it became a written language even when Giiz was still used officially. Tigirinya became a written language by inheriting and later slightly modifying the

Giiz script with the earliest written material in Tigirinya dating back to the 13th century.[8] From its humble beginnings in the southern fringes of the Kingdom of Axum, Amharic became a written language in the 14th century and eventually grew to be one of the most dominant languages in Ethiopian history. Beiminet Gebire Amilak (1947) stated that there are documents that indicate the use of Amharic by kings as a spoken language dating back to the fall of the Zagiwei dynasty and the restoration of the Solomonic line around 1272 as cited by Baye Yimam (2000 E.C.). Leslau (2000) stated that the 14th-century texts of Imperial songs were the earliest written documents in Amharic and that the language was used for religious writing by Portuguese missionaries in the early 17th century. Leslau further stated that the "first royal chronicles were written in the 19th century at the time of Emperor Theodoros II."[9]

Before Giiz was completely uprooted by its descendants, writing in Amharic, instead of the holy language of Giiz, was a capital offence punishable by death.

In contrast to Ancient Ethiopic—which is an abjad or consonant-only script—what we shall refer to as the TRADITIONAL ETHIOPIC script is an alphasyllabic script still in official use in modern Ethiopia, and is the subject of the orthographic reforms proposed in this book. Known as *feedel* by its Ethiopic name and consisting of a MAIN SET of characters and an EXTENSION SET of characters, the script is also referred to simply as 'Ethiopic' and sometimes less accurately as an alphabet. The script became vocalized soon after the introduction of the vowel notations in the fourth century. It also acquired *kenifer* (plosive) sounds from Greek represented by the character sets ጰ <px> and ፐ <p>, although the Ethiopic *px* may be another rendition of the Greek *p*. These sounds were exclusively used for loanwords borrowed from classical Greek, such as ጴሪጋሞን <Pxerigamon> (Ancient Greek: τὸ Πέργαμον (to Pergamon)). Today, the ጰ character set is a collection of uniquely arrested graphemes with very few new words ever utilizing it since classical Giiz. In contrast, the ፐ character set somewhat continues to be utilized albeit for loanwords borrowed from European languages with the phonemes having never been used in the Ethiopic verb system to this day (a litmus test I propose in Chapter 6 for determining the NATURALIZATION of phonemes).

When first used for Giiz, the Ethiopic main set of characters consisted of a 26-row-high by 7-column-wide grid layout with the rows representing consonantal values inherited from Ancient Ethiopic and the columns representing vowelic values for a total of 182 characters (**Table 2.2**). The vowelic columns are referred to as orders. The 1st order, also called *giiz*, consists of the original, unmodified letterforms of Ancient Ethiopic. The following are the names of the seven orders:

ግዕዝ <giiz> (1st order)
ካዕብ <kaiib> (2nd order)
ሣልስ <salis> (3rd order)
ራብዕ <rabiii> (4th order)
ኃምስ <hamis> (5th order)
ሳድስ <sadis> (6th order)
ሳብዕ <sabiii> (7th order)

The Ethiopic extension set as used for Giiz contains characters that combine a consonant and two consecutive vowels, all of which are derived from the main set. Each vowelic order in the main set contains the same vowel sound, which is indicated as a diacritic or other modification on the consonantal character. In other words, at the intersection of every row and column is a glyph representing

Table 2.2: The main set of the Giiz *feedel*

	TRANSLITERATION & PRONUNCIATION			TRADITIONAL GIIZ VOWELIC ORDER						
	IPA	INFORMAL*	PROPOSED	1ST ORDER	2ND ORDER	3RD ORDER	4TH ORDER	5TH ORDER	6TH ORDER	7TH ORDER
	IPA			ə	u	i	a	e	ɨ	o
	INFORMAL*			e/a	u	i	a	e/ie	-/e	o
	PROPOSED			e	u	ee	a	ei	i	o
1	h	h	h	ሀ	ሁ	ሂ	ሃ	ሄ	ህ	ሆ
2	l	l	l	ለ	ሉ	ሊ	ላ	ሌ	ል	ሎ
3	ħ	H	hh	ሐ	ሑ	ሒ	ሓ	ሔ	ሕ	ሖ
4	m	m	m	መ	ሙ	ሚ	ማ	ሜ	ም	ሞ
5	ɬ	s	sx	ሠ	ሡ	ሢ	ሣ	ሤ	ሥ	ሦ
6	r	r	r	ረ	ሩ	ሪ	ራ	ሬ	ር	ሮ
7	s	s	s	ሰ	ሱ	ሲ	ሳ	ሴ	ስ	ሶ
8	k'	k	q	ቀ	ቁ	ቂ	ቃ	ቄ	ቅ	ቆ
9	b	b	b	በ	ቡ	ቢ	ባ	ቤ	ብ	ቦ
10	t	t	t	ተ	ቱ	ቲ	ታ	ቴ	ት	ቶ
11	ḫ	h	hx	ኀ	ኁ	ኂ	ኃ	ኄ	ኅ	ኆ
12	n	n	n	ነ	ኑ	ኒ	ና	ኔ	ን	ኖ
13	ʔ	-	-	አ	ኡ	ኢ	ኣ	ኤ	እ	ኦ
14	k	k	k	ከ	ኩ	ኪ	ካ	ኬ	ክ	ኮ
15	w	w	w	ወ	ዉ	ዊ	ዋ	ዌ	ው	ዎ
16	ʕ	-	-	ዐ	ዑ	ዒ	ዓ	ዔ	ዕ	ዖ
17	z	z	z	ዘ	ዙ	ዚ	ዛ	ዜ	ዝ	ዞ
18	j	y	y	የ	ዩ	ዪ	ያ	ዬ	ይ	ዮ
19	d	d	d	ደ	ዱ	ዲ	ዳ	ዴ	ድ	ዶ
20	g	g	g	ገ	ጉ	ጊ	ጋ	ጌ	ግ	ጎ
21	t'	T	tx	ጠ	ጡ	ጢ	ጣ	ጤ	ጥ	ጦ
22	p'	P	px	ጰ	ጱ	ጲ	ጳ	ጴ	ጵ	ጶ
23	sˤ	ts	x	ጸ	ጹ	ጺ	ጻ	ጼ	ጽ	ጾ
24	ɬˤ	ts	xs	ፀ	ፁ	ፂ	ፃ	ፄ	ፅ	ፆ
25	f	f	f	ፈ	ፉ	ፊ	ፋ	ፌ	ፍ	ፎ
26	p	p	p	ፐ	ፑ	ፒ	ፓ	ፔ	ፕ	ፖ

Note: The International Phonetic Alphabet (IPA) is a "notational standard for the phonetic representation of all languages" devised by the International Phonetic Association. The table shows the values for the IPA, a traditional transliteration, and the transliteration proposed by this book. (For more on the romanization of Ethiopic and giizization of English, refer to Chapters 9 and 10.)

the phonemes of one of the original consonantal letters and one of the seven Ethiopic basic vowel sounds. Such a glyph is one of six copies of each of the original 1st order consonantal characters that were modified variously including by using diacritical marks mostly in a similar fashion within an individual order.

A base character is any one of the Ethiopic characters in the 1st order or column of the Ethiopic *feedel gebeta* (chart) and represents the family of characters within its row.

The 1st order character ሀ, for example, has the values of the Ethiopic abstract consonant *h* and the Ethiopic abstract vowel *e* (**Table 2.2**). Similarly, the character ሁ has the values of the Ethiopic abstract consonant *h* and the Ethiopic abstract vowel *u*. All characters in the main set fuse only one consonant and one vowel. Giiz makes use of several consonant-vowel-vowel fusions for its extension set. The extension set contains a total of 40 characters (**Table 2.3**) with four consonantal rows and five columns that we shall refer to as COMBINATION ORDERS. Combination 4th order, which is made up of the 2nd and 4th orders from the main set, is the most utilized order in the extension. Combinations 2nd and 7th orders do not exist; and the velar consonants ቀ <q>, ኀ <hx>, ከ <k>, and ገ <g> from the main set are the base characters for the extension set which is labialized.

Table 2.3: The extended set of the Giiz *feedel* (consisting of labiovelars)

			TRADITIONAL GIIZ EXTENDED VOWELIC ORDER					NOTES
			COMB. 1ST ORDER	COMB. 3RD ORDER	COMB. 4TH ORDER	COMB. 5TH ORDER	COMB. 6TH ORDER	
			ʷə	ʷi	ʷa	ʷe	ʷɨ	IPA
			ue	uee	ua	uei	ui	PROPOSED TRANSLITERATION
1	k'	q	ቈ	ቊ	ቋ	ቌ	ቍ	
2	ḫ	hx	ኈ	ኊ	ኋ	ኌ	ኍ	
3	k	k	ኰ	ኲ	ኳ	ኴ	ኵ	
4	g	g	ጐ	ጒ	ጓ	ጔ	ጕ	

Note: The most used and, therefore, most transliterated order in the Ethiopic extension set is Combination 4th Order, the vowels of which are most often transliterated as 'ua' or 'wa' informally.

The diacritics are not always the same in a given order, although often they are. Consider how the character ሁ from the 2nd order compares to its base character ሀ in the 1st order. The only difference between the two glyphs is the little projection or diacritic ⁻ on the right side of the 2nd order glyph. Almost all characters in the 2nd order use this diacritic to modify the base character (**Table 2.2**). The only exceptions are ረ/ሩ, and ፈ/ፉ , which modify their 2nd order characters by adding a diacritic at the bottom. On the other hand, the sixth order, which has the weakest vowel in Ethiopic, has the least consistency. (For more on the Ethiopic glyphs and use of diacritics, refer to Chapters 6 and 7.) Traditional Ethiopic has since been adopted by all Ethiosemitic languages, such as Tigirinya and Amharic, as well as by other Ethiopian languages with millions of speakers, which makes Ethiopic one of the oldest most widely used writing systems of the world.

The Ethiopic Script as Used for Tigirinya and Amharic

The use of the Ethiopic writing system for Tigirinya and Amharic is similar to the way the scrip is used for Giiz except that some graphemes have been added. Both Tigirinya and Amharic are descendants of Giiz, and as such have inherited the Ethiopic script as used for Giiz along with much of the vocabulary and grammar of Giiz. However, there are significant differences between the ancestral language and its descendants. Not only do Tigirinya and Amharic have more sophisticated grammar that removed some of the weakness of Giiz—such as the lack of a definite article (or definite articles)—but they have also lost some of the Giiz sounds while acquiring new ones. As a result, the traditional Ethiopic script as used for Tigirinya and Amharic has been changing ever since Giiz ceased to be the official medium of communication in the nation. Contacts between speakers of Semitic languages and Cushitic languages brought about the incorporation of sounds into Tigirinya and Amharic that were not present in Giiz. Moreover, some linguists have argued that the influence from Cushitic languages extended to grammar including, to some extent, sentence structure. Since such influence is two-directional (see Krapf and Isenberg, 1840), it may explain the strong socio-cultural and socio-linguistic bonds between the various language groups in Ethiopia.

Tigirinya inherited all but two of the characters in the Giiz script, while Amharic inherited the entire set of characters. Both Tigirinya and Amharic added new characters complete with the seven Ethiopic vowelic orders. The new characters or letterforms are modified forms of preexisting Ethiopic letterforms with the addition of a crown or horizontal stroke across the top of each character with some or no resemblance to the original phonemic value.

The *giiz* or 1st order of these family of characters are:

Palatal characters: ሸ <sh>, ቸ <c>, ኘ <ny>, ዠ <jz>, ጀ <j>, ጨ <cx>

Glottalic characters: ቐ <qh>, ኸ <kh>,

Characters representing borrowed phonemes: ቨ <v>

The letterforms are based on the following Giiz letterforms, respectively:

Palatal characters: ሰ <s>, ተ <t>, ነ <n>, ዘ <z>, ደ <d>, ጠ <tx>

Glottalic characters: ቀ <q>, ከ <k>,

Characters representing borrowed phonemes: በ <b>

It appears that the *gororo* (glottalic) characters ኸ <kh>[10] and ቐ <qh> were probably developed outside of the Cushitic influence. Amharic has several redundant characters, which add to the size and complexity of its writing system. A redundant character is a grapheme that represents the same phoneme that is also represented by another character or characters. Tigirinya, which is more closely related to Giiz, has been able to keep more Giiz sounds and, having dropped some unneeded Giiz characters, has no redundant characters now.

The groups of characters with the same or almost the same phonemes in Amharic are:

ሀ, ሐ, ኀ, and ኸ; ሰ and ሠ; አ and ዐ; and ጸ and ፀ.

Due to continuous changes to the script resulting from the addition of new glyphs or characters custom made to represent new sounds and new pronunciation, there are several versions of the Tigirinya and Amharic forms of the *feedel* even today with variations ranging from alphabetical order to the total number of base characters. The Ethiopian Languages Academy proposed dropping redundant characters in the Amharic form of the *feedel* as quoted by Haregeweyin Kebede et. al (1993 E.C.). For example keeping the character family ሀ <h> and dropping its phonetically equivalent and thus redundant character family ሐ. The proposal aimed at reducing the size of the *feedel* and avoiding spelling inconsistencies. At the same time, there has always been *feedels* in circulation that are modified by using various methods of streamlining the script and its letter order.

The phonology of Tigirinya and Amharic as well as their writing systems are heavily influenced by Ethiocushitic languages.

Some show the sequencing of characters with similar typeface to follow each other regardless of their phonemic value (example በ <b> followed by ቨ <v>), while others show characters representing a similar phoneme to be placed sequentially. Some show the modern Amharic 1st order glyph ኧ <ex> in the feedel without its family (i.e. characters in the 2nd to 7th orders). Still, others show the ቨ family of characters at the bottom of the main set or even separately, since it is one of the newest characters to enter into the script. The Tigirinya *feedel* is sometimes shown with one or more of the characters ሠ <sx>, ኀ <hx>, and ፀ <xs>, which have no use in modern Tigirinya, but are present probably because they are part and parcel of the Giiz and Amharic *feedels*. And yet, others show a combination of two or more of the above. By contrast, while Amharic makes no phonemic distinction between ሀ, ሐ, and ኀ, for example, all of them are considered to form part of the Amharic *feedel* because each of them is almost always used in written documents. Moreover, Ethiopic has an alternative letter order called *ebugeeda* (abugida)—a letter order that closely matches those of the other Semitic scripts, particularly that of the Hebrew script (see **Tables 2.10** and **2.11**). In the face of such inconsistencies, I have tried to present what could be considered the most typical or the most acceptable version separately for Tigirinya and Amharic based on actual use of the characters in written documents.

The Traditional Ethiopic Script as Used for Tigirinya

Tigirinya, like Amharic and other Ethiopian languages, has adopted the traditional Ethiopic script or *feedel* as its writing system with the addition of new characters. However, while the Amharic *feedel* has kept all of the Giiz characters, the Tigirinya *feedel* has eliminated some Giiz characters whose phonemes were no longer required in Tigirinya. The result is a total of 32 consonantal rows by seven vocalic columns in the Tigirinya alphabetic chart for a total of 224 characters in the main set (**Table 2.4**). Tigirinya has also inherited most, but not all, of the characters in the Giiz alphabetic extension set and added some of its own, as well as inheriting the Giiz numerals and punctuation. The Tigirinya alphabet extension set is a product of the characters in the main set. As with the main set, the extension set also has rows and columns. The Ethiopic extension set consists only of five vowelic orders. Every character in the extension set merges a consonantal value with two vocalic values (**Table 2.5**), which can be shown as CVV, where C stands for a consonant and V for a vowel. Note that each of the six rows has a C value, while each of the five columns contains two vowels. The total number of characters in the Tigirinya extension set is 26.

Table 2.4: The main set of the Tigirinya *feedel*

TRANSLITERATION & PRONUNCIATION				TRADITIONAL GIIZ VOWELIC ORDER						
	IPA	INFORMAL*	PROPOSED	1ST ORDER	2ND ORDER	3RD ORDER	4TH ORDER	5TH ORDER	6TH ORDER	7TH ORDER
1	h	h	h	ሀ	ሁ	ሂ	ሃ	ሄ	ህ	ሆ
2	l	l	l	ለ	ሉ	ሊ	ላ	ሌ	ል	ሎ
3	ħ	H	hh	ሐ	ሑ	ሒ	ሓ	ሔ	ሕ	ሖ
4	m	m	m	መ	ሙ	ሚ	ማ	ሜ	ም	ሞ
5	r	r	r	ረ	ሩ	ሪ	ራ	ሬ	ር	ሮ
6	s	s	s	ሰ	ሱ	ሲ	ሳ	ሴ	ስ	ሶ
7	ʃ	sh	sh	ሸ	ሹ	ሺ	ሻ	ሼ	ሽ	ሾ
8	k'	k	q	ቀ	ቁ	ቂ	ቃ	ቄ	ቅ	ቆ
9	ʁ'		qh	ቐ	ቑ	ቒ	ቓ	ቔ	ቕ	ቖ
10	b	b	b	በ	ቡ	ቢ	ባ	ቤ	ብ	ቦ
11	v	v	v	ቨ	ቩ	ቪ	ቫ	ቬ	ቭ	ቮ
12	t	t	t	ተ	ቱ	ቲ	ታ	ቴ	ት	ቶ
13	tʃ	ch	c	ቸ	ቹ	ቺ	ቻ	ቼ	ች	ቾ
14	n	n	n	ነ	ኑ	ኒ	ና	ኔ	ን	ኖ
15	ɲ	gn	ny	ኘ	ኙ	ኚ	ኛ	ኜ	ኝ	ኞ
16	ʔ	-	-	አ	ኡ	ኢ	ኣ	ኤ	እ	ኦ
17	k	k	k	ከ	ኩ	ኪ	ካ	ኬ	ክ	ኮ
18	x		kh	ኸ	ኹ	ኺ	ኻ	ኼ	ኽ	ኾ
19	w	w	w	ወ	ዉ	ዊ	ዋ	ዌ	ው	ዎ
20	ʕ	-	-	ዐ	ዑ	ዒ	ዓ	ዔ	ዕ	ዖ
21	z	z	z	ዘ	ዙ	ዚ	ዛ	ዜ	ዝ	ዞ
22	ʒ		jz	ዠ	ዡ	ዢ	ዣ	ዤ	ዥ	ዦ
23	j	y	y	የ	ዩ	ዪ	ያ	ዬ	ይ	ዮ
24	d	d	d	ደ	ዱ	ዲ	ዳ	ዴ	ድ	ዶ
25	dʒ	j	j	ጀ	ጁ	ጂ	ጃ	ጄ	ጅ	ጆ
26	g	g	g	ገ	ጉ	ጊ	ጋ	ጌ	ግ	ጎ
27	t'	T	tx	ጠ	ጡ	ጢ	ጣ	ጤ	ጥ	ጦ
28	tʃ'	CH	cx	ጨ	ጩ	ጪ	ጫ	ጬ	ጭ	ጮ
29	p'	P	px	ጰ	ጱ	ጲ	ጳ	ጴ	ጵ	ጶ
30	s'	ts	x	ጸ	ጹ	ጺ	ጻ	ጼ	ጽ	ጾ
31	f	f	f	ፈ	ፉ	ፊ	ፋ	ፌ	ፍ	ፎ
32	p	p	p	ፐ	ፑ	ፒ	ፓ	ፔ	ፕ	ፖ

Table 2.5: The extended set of the Tigirinya *feedel*

			TRADITIONAL TIGIRINYA EXTENDED VOWELIC ORDER					NOTES
			COMB. 1ST ORDER	COMB. 3RD ORDER	COMB. 4TH ORDER	COMB. 5TH ORDER	COMB. 6TH ORDER	
			wə	wi	wa	we	wɨ	**IPA**
			ue	uee	ua	uei	ui	**PROPOSED TRANSLITERATION**
1	k'	q	ቈ	ቊ	ቋ	ቌ	ቍ	based on the character ቀ
2	ʁ'	qh	ቘ	ቚ	ቛ	ቜ	ቝ	based on the character ቐ
3	b	b			ቧ			based on the character በ
4	k	k	ኰ	ኲ	ኳ	ኴ	ኵ	based on the character ከ
5	x	kh	ዀ	ዂ	ዃ	ዄ	ዅ	based on the character ኸ
6	g	g	ጐ	ጒ	ጓ	ጔ	ጕ	based on the character ገ

The Traditional Ethiopic Script as Used for Amharic

Amharic, like Tigirinya and other Ethiopian languages, has adopted the Traditional Ethiopic script or *feedel* as its writing system with the addition of new characters. However, while the Tigirinya has dropped some of the Giiz characters that it does not need, Amharic has kept all of them even though, phonetically, it can do well without some of them. The result is a total of 34 consonantal rows by seven vocalic columns in the Amharic alphabetic chart for a total of 238 characters in the main set (**Table 2.6**). Amharic has also inherited all the characters in the Giiz alphabetic extension set and added more of its own, as well as inheriting the Giiz numerals and punctuation.

Amharic seems to be in the process of eliminating the glottal sounds originally represented by many of its characters inherited from Giiz, by assigning them their corresponding non-glottal sounds, which resulted in the duplication and even quadruplication of the number of characters representing the same phoneme. Examples of such characters are ሐ and ዐ and their families. In the Amharic *feedel*, the character families ሀ, ሐ, ኀ, and ኸ represent the same phoneme with the arguable exception of the first-order character ኸ <kh>.[9] This is also true for ሠ and ሰ, አ and ዐ, and ጸ and ፀ.

The Amharic alphabet extension set (**Table 2.7**) is a product of the main set. As with the main set, the extension set also has rows and columns. The Ethiopic extension set contains only five vowelic orders. Every character in the extension set fuses a consonant with two vowels, which can be shown as CVV, where C stands for a consonant and V for a vowel. Note that each of the six rows has a C value, while each of the five columns contains two vowels. The columns shall be referred to as combination orders because they combine vowels or orders of Ethiopic. The total number of characters in the Amharic extension set is 38.

Table 2.6: The main set of the Amharic *feedel*

	TRANSLITERATION			TRADITIONAL GIIZ VOWELIC ORDER						
	IPA	INFORMAL	PROPOSED	1ST ORDER	2ND ORDER	3RD ORDER	4TH ORDER	5TH ORDER	6TH ORDER	7TH ORDER
1	h	h	h	-	ሁ	ሂ	ሃ/ሀ	ሄ	ህ	ሆ
2	l	l	l	ለ	ሉ	ሊ	ላ	ሌ	ል	ሎ
3	h	h	h	-	ሑ	ሒ	ሓ/ሐ	ሔ	ሕ	ሖ
4	m	m	m	መ	ሙ	ሚ	ማ	ሜ	ም	ሞ
5	s	s	s	ሠ	ሡ	ሢ	ሣ	ሤ	ሥ	ሦ
6	r	r	r	ረ	ሩ	ሪ	ራ	ሬ	ር	ሮ
7	s	s	s	ሰ	ሱ	ሲ	ሳ	ሴ	ስ	ሶ
8	ʃ	sh	sh	ሸ	ሹ	ሺ	ሻ	ሼ	ሽ	ሾ
9	k'	k	q	ቀ	ቁ	ቂ	ቃ	ቄ	ቅ	ቆ
10	b	b	b	በ	ቡ	ቢ	ባ	ቤ	ብ	ቦ
11	v	v	v	ቨ	ቩ	ቪ	ቫ	ቬ	ቭ	ቮ
12	t	t	t	ተ	ቱ	ቲ	ታ	ቴ	ት	ቶ
13	tʃ	ch	c	ቸ	ቹ	ቺ	ቻ	ቼ	ች	ቾ
14	h	h	h	ኀ	ኁ	ኂ	ኃ	ኄ	ኅ	ኆ
15	n	n	n	ነ	ኑ	ኒ	ና	ኔ	ን	ኖ
16	ɲ	gn	ny	ኘ	ኙ	ኚ	ኛ	ኜ	ኝ	ኞ
17	ʔ	-	-	አ	ኡ	ኢ	ኣ/አ	ኤ	እ	ኦ
18	k	k	k	ከ	ኩ	ኪ	ካ	ኬ	ክ	ኮ
19	h	h	h	ኸ	ኹ	ኺ	ኻ	ኼ	ኽ	ኾ
20	w	w	w	ወ	ዉ	ዊ	ዋ	ዌ	ው	ዎ
21	ʔ	-	-	-	ዑ	ዒ	ዓ/ዐ	ዔ	ዕ	ዖ
22	z	z	z	ዘ	ዙ	ዚ	ዛ	ዜ	ዝ	ዞ
23	ʒ		jz	ዠ	ዡ	ዢ	ዣ	ዤ	ዥ	ዦ
24	j	y	y	የ	ዩ	ዪ	ያ	ዬ	ይ	ዮ
25	d	d	d	ደ	ዱ	ዲ	ዳ	ዴ	ድ	ዶ
26	dʒ	j	j	ጀ	ጁ	ጂ	ጃ	ጄ	ጅ	ጆ
27	g	g	g	ገ	ጉ	ጊ	ጋ	ጌ	ግ	ጎ
28	t'	T	tx	ጠ	ጡ	ጢ	ጣ	ጤ	ጥ	ጦ
29	tʃ'	CH	cx	ጨ	ጩ	ጪ	ጫ	ጬ	ጭ	ጮ
30	p'	P	px	ጰ	ጱ	ጲ	ጳ	ጴ	ጵ	ጶ
31	s'	ts	x	ጸ	ጹ	ጺ	ጻ	ጼ	ጽ	ጾ
32	s'	ts	x	ፀ	ፁ	ፂ	ፃ	ፄ	ፅ	ፆ
33	f	f	f	ፈ	ፉ	ፊ	ፋ	ፌ	ፍ	ፎ
34	p	p	p	ፐ	ፑ	ፒ	ፓ	ፔ	ፕ	ፖ

It is interesting to note that Amharic's combination 4th order (in the extended set) characters are needed almost exclusively because of word inflection with the third-person singular female (3PSF) possessive pronoun. For example, the word ልጅ <lij> (child) is inflected to ልጇ <lijua> (her child) with the last consonant changing from ጅ to combination 4th order character ጇ. Comparison of the various Ethiopic alphabets (**Table 2.8**) shows that Amharic has the most number of characters while Giiz has the least.

Table 2.7: The extended set of the Amharic *feedel*

			TRADITIONAL TIGIRINYA EXTENDED VOWELIC ORDER					NOTES
			COMB. 1ST ORDER	COMB. 3RD ORDER	COMB. 4TH ORDER	COMB. 5TH ORDER	COMB. 6TH ORDER	
			ʷə	ʷɨ	ʷa	ʷe	ʷɨ	IPA
			ue	uee	ua	uei	ui	PROPOSED TRANSLITERATION
1	l	l			ሏ			based on the character ለ
2	m	m			ሟ			based on the character መ
3	r	r			ሯ			
4	s	s			ሷ			
5	ʃ	sh			ሿ			
6	k'	q	ቈ	ቊ	ቋ	ቌ	ቍ	
7	b	b			ቧ			
8	t	t			ቷ			
9	tʃ	c			ቿ			
10	h	h	ኈ	ኊ	ኋ	ኌ	ኍ	
11	n	n			ኗ			
12	ɲ	ny			ኟ			
13	k	k	ኰ	ኲ	ኳ	ኴ	ኵ	
14	z	z			ዟ			
15	ʒ	jz			ዧ			
16	d	d			ዷ			
17	dʒ	j			ጇ			
18	g	g	ጐ	ጒ	ጓ	ጔ	ጕ	
19	t'	tx			ጧ			
20	s'	x			ጿ			
21	f	f			ፏ			
22	p	p			ፗ			

The Giiz 'Vowel Shift'

An irregularity unique to Amharic is the loss of true *giiz* or first-order vocalized values for the family of characters ሀ, ሐ, ኀ, አ, and ዐ. In both Giiz and Amharic, the 1st order characters ሐ, ኀ, ዐ, and አ are often vocalized inaccurately with the 4th order vowel 'a' rather than the Ethiopic 1st order vowel 'e' (**Table 2.6**)—a phenomenon that may be referred to as the Giiz vowel shift. While Amharic has created the glyph ኧ to compensate for the loss of the 1st order vocalized value for አ, it did not do so for the rest of the characters with irregular 1st order vowelic values. Often አ occurs at the beginning of a word and rarely inside or at the end of a word. When it occurs inside or at the end of a word, it often has a value equivalent to the vowel 'e'. It is unlikely that this shift happened when Giiz was still in popular use, although today Giiz text is read by vocalizing አ as being the same as the vowel 'a'. The shift may be a spillover effect from Amharic, which routinely vocalizes the five irregular characters with the vowel 'a.' This phenomenon does not affect Tigirinya.

Table 2.8: Comparison of the number of characters in various alphabets

ALPHABET	NUMBER OF CHARACTERS		
	MAIN SET	EXTENSION SET	TOTAL
Giiz	182	20	202
Tigirinya	224	26	250
Amharic	238	38	276
English	26	-	26

The Ethiopic Punctuation

The Ethiopic punctuation, which has evolved since classical times, includes newer punctuation marks as well as some punctuation marks adopted from European orthographies.

The Ancient Giiz Punctuation

The original Giiz punctuation consisted only of the word separator ፡ and the full stop (period) ።. The 1513 first ever Ethiopic book published by a printing press rendered Psalm 1:1 using the ancient Giiz language as shown below on the left,[11] while a more modern version of the same verse in Giiz is shown on the right with an additional punctuation ፤ and more space between words.

ብፁዕ፡ብእሲ፡ዘኢሖረ፡በምክረ፡ረሲዓን።	ብፁዕ ፡ ብእሲ ፡ ዘኢሖረ ፡ በምክረ ፡ ረሲዓን ፤
ወዘኢቆመ፡ውስተ፡ፍኖተ፡ኃጥኣን።	ወዘኢቆመ ፡ ውስተ ፡ ፍኖተ ፡ ኃጥኣን ፤
ወዘኢነበረ፡ውስተ፡መንበረ፡መስተሳልቃን።	ወዘኢነበረ ፡ ውስተ ፡ መንበረ ፡ መስተሳልቃን ።

Notice that the ancient text is shown in what could be described in modern writing as consisting of three separate sentences because of the three Ethiopic full stops (።); while the text on the right shows two Ethiopic semicolons (፤) and only one full stop. As a matter of comparison, the same verse in the original first printing of the 1611 King James Version of the English Bible shows the text as follows (notice the two commas and one full stop):

> Blessed is the man that walketh not in the counsell of the vngodly, nor standeth in the way of sinners, nor sitteth in the seat of the scornefull.

The Modern Ethiopic Punctuation

In addition to inheriting the Giiz punctuation, Tigirinya and Amharic have added more punctuation marks including those from European orthographies, which are necessitated by modern communication (**Table 2.9**). The ancient word separator (፡) has almost entirely been supplanted by white space, except with stylistic writings and liturgical text, while the three dot (፧) question mark seems to be gaining more ground, especially with Tigirinya literature.

Table 2.9: List of the most prominent Ethiopic punctuation

	GLYPH	FUNCTION	ETHIOPIC NAME	SOURCE	REMARKS
1	፡	word separator	nequtx	Ancient Ethiopic	being phased out
2	፣	comma	netxela serez	Ethiopic	
3	፤	semicolon	dirrib serez	Ethiopic	
4	።	period (full stop)	aribaiitu netxib	Ancient Ethiopic	
5	፡-	preface colon		Ethiopic	
6	፥	colon		Ethiopic	
7	፠	section mark		Ethiopic	
8	፧	question mark		Ethiopic	
9	፨	paragraph separator		Ethiopic	
10	?	question mark		European	used more than ፧
11	!	exclamation mark		European	
12	()	parenthesis		European	
13	“ ” ‹‹ ››	quotation marks		European	
14	/	slash		European	often used for contraction of words, especially with proper names

The Ethiopic Numerical Characters

The Ethiopic numerals are a separate set of numerical characters originally developed for Giiz. The numerals are easily recognizable by the horizontal strokes at the top and bottom of every character. The characters are believed to have been influenced by scripts of other languages, especially Greek. There are striking similarities between the Giiz numerical characters and the Greek alphabet both in alphabetic (or numerical) order and the letterforms. Lambdin (1978) stated that the Greek alphabet was adapted for use in numerical forms by framing each letter with lines at the top and bottom. Lambdin further asserted that "the numerical values are the same as those known from Greek sources."[12] It is possible that Coptic letterforms were borrowed bringing in the Greek influence.[13] A comparison of the Giiz numerals with the Greek and Hebrew alphabetic numeral systems (**Table 2.10**) shows a strong similarity of glyphs and numeric values, although

Table 2.10: Comparison of the Ethiopic numerals to the Greek and Hebrew alphabetic numeral systems

DECIMAL	ETHIOPIC NUMERALS	GREEK ALPHABETIC NUMERALS		HEBREW ALPHABETIC NUMERALS (GEMATRIA)		ETHIOPIC EQUIVALENTS	
1	፩	Α α	(alpha)	א	(alef)	አ	(elif)
2	፪	Β β	(beta)	ב	(bet)	በ	(beit)
3	፫	Γ γ	(gamma)	ג	(gimel)	ገ	(gemil)
4	፬	Δ δ	(delta)	ד	(dalet)	ደ	(denit)
5	፭	Ε ε	(epsilon)	ה	(he)	ሀ	(hoy)
6	፮	ς	(stigrma)	ו	(vav)	ወ	(wewei)
7	፯	Ζ ζ	(zeta)	ז	(zayin)	ዘ	(zey)
8	፰	Η η	(eta)	ח	(heth)	ሐ	(hhewit)
9	፱	Θ θ	(theta)	ט	(teth)	ጠ	(txeyit)
10	፲	Ι ι	(iota)	י	(yud)	የ	(yeman)
20	፳	Κ κ	(kappa)	כ	(kaf)	ከ	(kaf)
30	፴	Λ λ	(lambda)	ל	(lamed)	ለ	(lewei)
40	፵	Μ μ	(mu)	מ	(mem)	መ	(may)
50	፶	Ν ν	(nu)	נ	(nun)	ነ	(nehas)
60	፷	Ξ ξ	(xi)	ס	(samekh)	ሠ	(sxewit)
70	፸	Ο ο	(omicron)	ע	(ayin)	ዐ	(eeyin)
80	፹	Π π	(pi)	פ	(pe)	ፈ	(ef)
90	፺	ϟ	(koppa)	צ	(tsadi)	ጸ	(xedey)
100	፻	Ρ ρ	(rho)	ק	(qof)	ቀ	(qaf)
10000	፼						

Note: While Giiz has a separate set of numeric characters, Greek and Hebrew employ alphabet numeric systems, i.e. the letters of their alphabets have pre-assigned numeric values.

some Ethiopianists disagree with the suggestion that the Ethiopic numerals were influenced by either. It is interesting to note that the Cyrillic numerals also happen to have some resemblance to and may have been influenced by the Giiz or Greek numerals. Giiz never used the modern Hindu-Arabic numerals, which arrived long after Giiz was sidelined by Tigirinya, Amharic, and other Ethiopian languages.

The Ethiopic numeric system is a system of ones and tens not unlike those of Hebrew and Greek numerals. The concept of zero is absent in the Ethiopic numeric system. Moreover, the system is not based on digital-positional notation and can only be used to represent natural numbers. A unique character represents each natural number between one and nine. Similarly, each tens from 10 to 90 are represented by a unique character. Moreover, the numerical value 100 is represented by a unique character as is the numerical value 10000. Other natural numbers are represented by combining two or more of the characters in a set order. For example, the number 22 is written by placing ፳ <20> before ፪ <2> as follows: ፳፪. The number 239 is written as follows: ፪፻፴፱ <[2] [100] [30] [9]>. (For more on the Ethiopic numeral system, refer to Chapter 11: Proposed Giizization of Mathematical Terms).

Although Tigirinya and Amharic have inherited the Ethiopic numerals from Giiz with little or no modifications, the Hindu-Arabic numerals have almost completely supplanted them in modern times as they have done to the Roman numerals. Not only are Ethiopic numerals no longer used on a regular basis, but are also unfit for complex mathematical operations, much like their Roman equivalents. Few people in Ethiopia are literate in Ethiopic numerals, which have for decades been relegated to liturgical documents. However, with some legislative support they can be used across a vast array of mediums including on signage, public artwork, and even jewellery.

The Two Ethiopic Letter Orders

The standard letter order of the Ethiopic script, which at least in part dates back to its Proto-Ethiopic roots in the first millennium B.C., is the ሀለሐመ <helehheme> order,[14] which is so named from the vocalization of the first four characters in the 1st vowelic order *he-le-hhe-me*. (I propose to refer to the *helehheme* series as *hoy-lewei*, based on the Ancient Ethiopic letter names of the first two letters (Chapter 8: Other Proposed Orthographic Reforms.) However, even the supposed standard *hoy-lewei* order has never been entirely fixed due to continuous addition of new characters through the centuries and reorganization of the sequence of the letters for various reasons by various authors without a central authority. **Tables 2.2, 2.4**, and **2.6** show what I believe are the most representative letter orders of the Ethiopic script in the Giiz, Tigirinya, and Amharic *feedels*, respectively.

Ethiopic also has an alternative letter order, which is called አበገደ <ebegede> from the vocalization of the first four characters in the 1st vowelic order *e-be-ge-de*, or አቡጊዳ <ebugeeda> by vocalizing the first four characters in the first consonantal row *e-bu-gee-da* (**Table 2.11**). (Abugida, which is a transcription of the Amharic name for the alternative letter order, was proposed by Peter T. Daniels (1990) to also refer to other alphasyllabaries, such as the Brahmic scripts of India.)

Table 2.11: The Ethiopic alternative alphabetical order

	TRADITIONAL GIIZ VOWELIC ORDER						
	1ST ORDER	2ND ORDER	3RD ORDER	4TH ORDER	5TH ORDER	6TH ORDER	7TH ORDER
1	አ	ቡ	ጊ	ዳ	ሄ	ው	ዞ
2	በ	ጉ	ዲ	ሃ	ዌ	ዝ	ዦ
3	ገ	ዱ	ሂ	ዋ	ዜ	ዥ	ሖ
4	ደ	ሁ	ዊ	ዛ	ዤ	ሕ	ጦ
5	ሀ	ዉ	ዚ	ዣ	ሔ	ጥ	ጮ
6	ወ	ዙ	ዢ	ሓ	ጤ	ጭ	ዮ
7	ዘ	ዡ	ሒ	ጣ	ጬ	ይ	ኮ
8	ዠ	ሑ	ጢ	ጫ	ዬ	ክ	ኾ
9	ሐ	ጡ	ጪ	ያ	ኬ	ኽ	ሎ
10	ጠ	ጩ	ዪ	ካ	ኼ	ል	ሞ
11	ጨ	ዩ	ኪ	ኻ	ሌ	ም	ኖ
12	የ	ኩ	ኺ	ላ	ሜ	ን	ኞ
13	ከ	ኹ	ሊ	ማ	ኔ	ኝ	ሶ
14	ኸ	ሉ	ሚ	ና	ኜ	ስ	ሾ
15	ለ	ሙ	ኒ	ኛ	ሴ	ሽ	ዖ
16	መ	ኑ	ኚ	ሳ	ሼ	ዕ	ፎ
17	ነ	ኙ	ሲ	ሻ	ዔ	ፍ	ጶ
18	ኘ	ሱ	ሺ	ዓ	ፌ	ጵ	ቆ
19	ሰ	ሹ	ዒ	ፋ	ጴ	ቅ	ቖ
20	ሸ	ዑ	ፊ	ጳ	ቄ	ቕ	ሮ
21	ዐ	ፉ	ጲ	ቃ	ቔ	ር	ሦ
22	ፈ	ጱ	ቂ	ቓ	ሬ	ሥ	ቶ
23	ጰ	ቁ	ቒ	ራ	ሤ	ት	ቾ
24	ቀ	ቑ	ሪ	ሣ	ቴ	ች	ኆ
25	ቐ	ሩ	ሢ	ታ	ቼ	ኅ	ጾ
26	ረ	ሡ	ቲ	ቻ	ኄ	ጽ	ፆ
27	ሠ	ቱ	ቺ	ኃ	ጼ	ፅ	ፖ
28	ተ	ቹ	ኂ	ጻ	ፄ	ፕ	ጆ
29	ቸ	ኁ	ጺ	ፃ	ፔ	ጅ	ኦ
30	ኀ	ጹ	ፂ	ፓ	ጄ	እ	ቦ
31	ጸ	ፁ	ፒ	ጃ	ኤ	ብ	ጎ
32	ፀ	ፑ	ጂ	ኣ	ቤ	ግ	ዶ
33	ፐ	ጁ	ኢ	ባ	ጌ	ድ	ሆ
34	ጀ	ኡ	ቢ	ጋ	ዴ	ህ	ዎ

The *ebugeeda* letter order is reminiscent of the scripts of other Semitic languages. There is not sufficient information to ascertain the period this particular order was adopted, but it appears that it derives directly from the letter order of the Phoenician script. The relationship is particularly evident in the fact that the *ebegede* order shows striking similarities to the Hebrew (**Table 2.10**) and the Old Arabic scripts, which descended from the Phoenician script. Desta Tekile Welid (1970) stated that the *ebegede* series, and not the *hoy-lewei* series, was the original series. Desta further stated that this was attested by Isenberg (1806–1864) who found an ancient stone inscription in Tigiray with the *ebegede* letter order, which proved that it was the older series. However, this position does not seem to be supported by more recent evidence.[15]

For alphabetical order, the consonantal component of a character is the primary determinant, while the vowelic component is a secondary determinant. Characters from the top row come first in alphabetical order before any other characters from the second row, etc. This ordering may be referred to as a vertical alphabetical order. The vowelic component of a character is determinant in alphabetical order only within the same consonantal family. Therefore, the first character in a row comes first in alphabetical order, followed by the second character in the same row, etc.; and this may be referred to as a horizontal alphabetical order. As with the more common *hoy-lewei* order, the *ebegede* order is often laid out in a grid layout so that every column consist of the same vowelic value while the consonantal value in a given row changes at every column and row intersection where a consonantal value steps up by one character spot compared to a preceding column, which means that no row contains the same consonantal value. (The consonantal value remains the same in an imaginary diagonal line connecting contiguous cells). Probably deliberately designed to challenge learners, this order has been almost exclusively used to teaching the *feedel*.

PART II

OVERVIEW OF THE ETHIOPIC PROBLEMS AND THE CONCEPT OF MODULARIZATION

CHAPTER 3

OVERVIEW OF ETHIOPIC GRAMMATICAL AND ORTHOGRAPHIC PROBLEMS

Of course you know our country's poverty of language...

—EMPEROR HAILE SELASSIE I (1892 – 1975)

Ethiopians do respect foreigners who learn their complicated languages and attempt to fathom the wax and gold of their culutre.

—STEPHEN PETERSON, 2015

The trouble with doing something right the first time is that nobody appreciates how difficult it was.

—ANONYMOUS

IN THIS CHAPTER

The Ethiopic script is unique among the scripts of other living Semitic languages—such as the Hebrew and Arabic alphabets or abjads (consonant only scripts)—in not only being written from left to right but also because its characters have features to indicate vowels, which makes the writing system an alphasyllabary. However, the Ethiosemitic languages are synthetic languages like all Semitic languages and many other languages of the world. The combination of a synthetic language and an alphasyllabic script, at least as far as Ethiopic is concerned, provides a unique set of challenges that are discussed in this chapter and whose solutions are proposed in subsequent chapters. I believe that these challenges must be addressed head-on to remove the obstacles to the progress of a modern society dependent on simple, fast and accurate communication more than ever before in human history.

The Ethiopic Grammatical Challenges

Declension, conjugation and the problem of personal pronouns and other grammatical elements, such as the Ethiopic definite articles, sandwiched between other morphemes is characteristics of synthetic languages like Giiz, Tigirinya, and Amharic (GTA). A synthetic language may be defined as one that has a high morpheme-per-word ratio. A morpheme is the smallest unit in a language that has a semantic meaning. Synthetic languages are intern divided into inflecting languages and agglutinative languages. Inflecting languages use affixes to show grammatical, syntactic or semantic changes. The affixes often do not carry a unit of meaning independently. By contrast, agglutinative languages use affixes which often carry a unit of meaning independently to create complex words. As can be demonstrated with the Tigirinya single-word sentences ክንሓጽበልኩምኢና <Kinihaxibelikumeena> (We will wash [it] for you) and its Amharic equivalent እናጥብላቹሃለን <Inatxibilacuhalen>, the GTA languages are examples of inflecting languages. However, like many inflecting languages, they also share some features of agglutinative languages. As highly inflected languages, Tigirinya and Amharic exhibit the morphological features of CONJUGATION and DECLENSION that increase word derivatives to such an extent that they have effectively become impediments to communication. Combined with the weaknesses of the Traditional Ethiopic writing system, conjugation and declension have made it practically impossible to manage the massive number of word derivatives in the GTA languages.

The Challenges with Ethiopic Grammatical Declension

Grammatical declension occurs when nouns, pronouns, and adjectives are inflected following certain rules of grammar to express number, case, and gender. Tigirinya and Amharic use affixes (prefixes or suffixes) or internal inflection or both to express these grammatical categories. Declension provides a challenge for modern communication in Ethiosemitic languages because of the sheer number of word derivatives it produces for every noun, adjective, or pronoun. For example, consider the Tigirinya word ድሙ <dimmu> (cat), which has a large number of word derivatives including the following:

ደማሙ	<demamu>	cats
ድሙን	<dimmun>	cat and
ትድሙ	<tidimmu>	the cat [male], that cat [male]
ታድሙ	<tadimmu>	the cat [female], that cat [female]
ዝድሙ	<zidimmu>	this cat [male]
ድሞይ	<dimmoy>	my cat
ድሙዓ	<dimmua>	her cat

I conservatively estimate the total number of word derivatives for the Tigirinya word ድሙ to be about 64 (**Appendix A**). For the equivalent Amharic word ድመት <dimet>, on the other hand, I conservatively estimate the inflected forms or word derivatives to be a whopping 550 or more (**Appendix B**), which is typical for a noun in Amharic. (For comparison, the English word *cat* has—not including words with different meanings like *catlike, cathead, catface* and *catfish* with possible etymological connection to it—only the plural derived form *cats*.) The following are some of the word derivatives of ድመት:

The fact that Ethiosemitic nouns can have as many as hundreds of derivatives is a great obstacle for effective communication in Ethiopia.

ድመቶች	<dimetoc>	cats
ድመትና	<dimetina>	cat and...
ድመቱ	<dimetu>	the cat [male], his cat
ድመቷ	<dimetua>	the cat [female], her cat
የድመት	<yedimet>	a cat's
ድመቴ	<dimetei>	my cat
ድመታቸው	<dimetacew>	their cat, his [polite] cat, her [polite] cat

In both Tigirinya and Amharic, I estimate that adjectives have fewer derivatives than nouns, while pronouns have even fewer derivatives than adjectives. Tigirinya has proportionally fewer word derivatives in each category because many of its grammatical elements, such as prepositions and definite articles, are free standing and do not appear as affixes as their Amharic equivalents do. Fewer affixes make the Tigirinya word derivatives slightly more manageable. Both in Tigirinya and Amharic, derivatives of nouns, pronouns and adjectives are created by adding prefixes, suffixes, or by internal changes in the words, or by any combination thereof. When internal changes occur, they occur to show plural forms or forms that indicate repetitiveness. For example, consider the Tigirinya noun ብዕራይ <biiiray> (cow) and the Amharic adjective ቆንጆ <qonijo> (beautiful, girl). The plural forms of the words are ኣዋዑር <awauur>, and ቆነጃጅት <qonejajit> respectively, and are created by changes in the internal structure of the words and a suffix in the case of the Amharic word.

The Challenges with Ethiopic Grammatical Conjugation

Grammatical conjugation, on the other hand, is the creation of derivatives of a verb by inflecting the root word of the verb. If declension provides a challenge for modern communication in Ethiosemitic languages because of the sheer number of word derivatives it generates, conjugation provides an even more severe challenge. Conjugation is a more complicated form of inflection as it involves the verb, which is affected by grammatical person, number, gender, tense, aspect, mood, and voice. In Tigirinya and Amharic, conjugation creates a lot more word derivatives than declension. In fact, as mind-boggling as it may be, almost every verb in both languages has tens of thousands of derivatives. This is because Ethiosemitic conjugation often fuses several grammatical elements, such as pronouns and negative markers, in addition to inflecting the root word or verb. Consider the Tigirinya infinitive verb ምሕጻብ <mihhixab> (to wash), which is made up of two morphemes: the single character ም <mi> (to) and the base verb form ሕጻብ <hhixab> (wash). The following are some of the derivatives of the verb.

ሓጸብኩዎ	hhaxebikuwo	I washed it
ኣይሓጸብናዮምን	ayihhaxebinayomin	We didn't wash them
እናሓጸበቶዒያ	inahhaxebetoeeya	She is washing it
ክትሓጽብንኦ	kitihhaxibinio	You ... going to wash it
ሓጻጺቤዮም	hhaxaxibeiyom	I having washed [repetitive action] them ...
ንተሐጻጸብ	nitehhexaxeb	Let's wash each other
ተሓጺቡሎ	tehhaxeebulo	It has been washed
ኣይተሓጸበትን	aytehhaxebetin	She did not get washed

Similarly, consider the Amharic equivalent ማጠብ <matxeb>, which is also made up of two morphemes fused together: the single character መ <me> (to) and the infinitive verb form አጠብ <atxeb> (wash). The following are some of the derivatives of the verb.

አጠብሁት	atxebihut	I washed it
አላጠብናቸውም	alatxeninacewim	We didn't wash them
እያጠበችው	iyatxebeciw	She … washing it
ሊታጥቡት	litatxibut	You [plural] … going to wash it
አጣጥቤያቸው	atxatxibeiyacew	I having washed [repetitive action] them …
እንተጣጠብ	initetxatxeb	Let's wash each other
ታጥቧል	tatxibual	It has been washed
አልታጠበችም	alitatxebecim	She did not get washed

Both Tigirinya and Amharic eliminate the first morpheme from their verb derivatives but often add one or more prefixes or one or more suffixes or any combination thereof. Note that it is difficult to determine the root word or verb in the above examples for anyone who is not intimately familiar with the languages and their grammar. This problem is more evident with text in the Ethiopic script where there are no separate letters for vowels and consonants. As an alphasyllabary, the Ethiopic script shows inflection within the base verb by changing the glyph for a given consonantal family.

In the Amharic examples above, the first verb derivative has its base verb unaltered (አጠብ[ሁት]); the second verb derivative does not show the first character of the base verb because it had been fused with the preceding consonant ([አላ]ጠብ[ናቸውም]); and the third (እያጠበችው), fourth (ሊታጥቡት), seventh (ታጥቧል) and eighth (አልታጠበችም) verb derivatives have their first character assimilated by a preceding consonantal character; and the rest of the characters have different glyphs indicating internal inflection almost obliterating the original or base verb. The verb has a mind-boggling 50,000 or so inflected forms (**Appendix C**) that are created by affixing morphemes and sometimes what would otherwise be free standing words. By contrast, the English verb "wash" has three inflected forms—washes, washed, and washing.

Most transitive verbs in Tigirinya and Amharic have at least 20,000 derivatives, which has made Ethiopic grammar an enduring mystery to many. In fact, most reference materials on Ethiopic grammar are embarrassingly shallow and often erroneous. Ethiopic dictionaries almost without exception show only one entry for every verb and its derivatives, which is represented by the third person singular male (3PSM) past tense form of the verb to the exclusion of every other form. Moreover, this approach excludes the definition for every grammatical affix which affects the meaning and grammatical function of verb derivatives. In the introduction to its Amharic dictionary, the then Ethiopian Languages Research Centre (1993 E.C.), the nation's presumed language authority, stated that with regards to verb derivatives, it followed the example set by previous influential Ethiopic dictionaries. Further, it stated that,

The fact that Ethiosemitic verbs can have as many as tens of thousands of derivatives through conjugation is an even greater obstacle for effective communication in Ethiopia when compared to the effects of declension.

> የመነሻ ግሱ ከሚኖረው ፍቺ ተጨማሪ ሌላ ፍቺ ወይም ፅንሰ ሃሳብ የሌላቸው ውልድ ቃላት በአብዛኛው አልተፈቱም። ይህንንም አሰራር መከተል ያስፈለገው የመዝገበ ቃላቱ ተጠቃሚ በመነሻ ቃሉ በተሰጠው ፍቺ መሰረት የውልድ አእማድ ቃላቱን ፍቺ መገመት ይችላል በሚል እምነት ነው።
>
> For the most part, no verb derivatives that do not fundamentally alter the definition of the base verb are provided. The reason it was needed to take this approach is in the belief [sic.] that the user of the dictionary can guess the definition of [all] verb derivatives based on the entry word.[1]

Unfortunately, this means that the odds of anyone learner of Ethiosemitic finding a definition in an Ethiopic dictionary for a randomly picked verb derivative are, on average, one in tens of thousands. In effect, this makes Ethiopic dictionaries almost irrelevant in the development of Ethiosemitic languages as far as grammar and verb derivatives are concerned. It is rare to find anyone who uses an Ethiopic dictionary, such as a Tigirinya dictionary or an Amharic dictionary, probably because very few people can browse through it, let alone to benefit from it in any significant way.

The Challenges with Identifying Primal Personal Pronouns

The concept of personal pronouns is almost inexistent in the minds of the speakers of Ethiosemitic languages—except for the grammatically less important but more visible SECONDARY PRONOUNS—resulting in poor communication skills. Two of the possible reasons for this may be the synthetic nature of Tigirinya and Amharic, which often attach primal pronouns with other morphemes making them less readily recognizable; and the nature of the Ethiopic writing system, which assimilates single-vowel/single-letter pronouns.

There are two major categories of personal pronouns in Ethiosemitic: PRIMAL PRONOUNS and SECONDARY PRONOUNS. In Tigirinya grammar, primal pronouns are the Tigirinya primary pronouns in all their applications. In Amharic grammar, the primal pronouns consist of the Amharic primary subject pronouns, object pronouns, and possessive pronouns. (See **Tables 9.9** and **9.10** in chapter 9; and Part II: Personal Pronouns in Tigirinya and Amharic in Volume II, for a more complete discussion on the Ethiopic personal pronouns.) In the traditional Ethiopic writing system, primal pronouns are morphemes that are always affixed to the main verb or to an auxiliary verb, while secondary pronouns are almost always shown as independent words. Consider the following Tigirinya single-word sentence: ገዛእኹዎ* <Gezaikhuwo> (I bought it). The sentence contains two morphemes representing a subject and a direct object, which are affixed to the main verb ገዛእ <gezai> (~bought). The morphemes are ኹ <khu> (I) and ዎ <wo> (it), which are primary pronouns in Tigirinya. Similarly, the Amharic single-word sentence ገዛሁት <Gezahut> (I bought it) contains two morphemes representing a subject and a direct object, which are affixed to the main verb ገዛ <geza> (~bought). The morphemes are ሁ <hu> (I) and ት <ti> (it), which are primary subject pronouns in Amharic.

Secondary pronouns are so called because they do not fundamentally change the meaning of sentences. Consider the following Tigirinya sentence: ኣነ ገዛእኹዎ* <Ane gezaikhuwo> ("I bought it," or more literally, "I, I bought it"); and its Am-

---

*Note: The informal way of saying, "I bought it" in Tigirinya is "ገዚኤዮ" <Gezeeeiyo>. However, it is grammatically incorrect since it is an incomplete sentence of Division 2. For more information refer to *Part I: The Ethiopic Grammatical Divisions* in Volume II.

haric equivalent እኔ ገዛሁት <Inei gezahut>. The Tigirinya and Amharic secondary pronouns are the first person singular (1PS) pronouns አነ <ane> and እኔ <inei>, respectively, which do not alter the meaning of the sentences when removed.

Primal pronouns in Ethiosemitic languages are some of the most important but least known grammatical elements.

The traditional Ethiopic writing system provides challenges for clearly representing the primary pronouns because most pronouns are made up of single vowel sounds. To illustrate this, let's apply the same verb we used in the first Tigirinya sentence above to the third person singular male (3PSM) pronoun as follows: ገዚኦ <Gezio> (He bought it). The sentence contains two pronouns – one for the subject and another one for the object. However, the Ethiopic syllabic writing system is such that both pronouns have seemingly disappeared and the only indication they exist is in the way the last character (part of the base verb) is modified. The Amharic equivalent ገዛው <gezaw> contains both pronouns, but only the object pronoun ው <it> is unambiguously represented in the text.

The most important, if negative, effect of the Ethiopic primary pronouns on Ethiopic grammar is their affix-ability to verbs which increases the number of derivatives for any given verb exponentially. In Ethiopic grammar, derivatives of some 'fertile' verbs can number up to 50,000 (**Appendix C**). To explain this, consider the following: There are ten primary subject pronouns in each of the four Ethiopic DIVISIONS (discussed later in the book), which make roughly a total of forty pronouns (4 x 10 = 40). Each of these subject pronouns can be paired with one of the ten object pronouns in Ethiopic, which means that there can be up to 400 (10 x 40 = 400) unique pairing of pronouns. (The actual pairings may be slightly fewer (a) because Ethiopic grammar does not allow any of the second person subject pronouns to pair with any of the second person object pronouns, regardless of the verb used and (b) for semantic reasons, which is dependent on the particular verb used.)

Now, consider that there are at least ten different kinds of prepositions which are often affixed to verbs, which can make the number of verb derivatives multiplied by a factor of ten to become 4,000 (10 x 400 = 4,000). These then need to be multiplied by the number of other grammatical elements, such as negative markers, some auxiliary verbs, causative makers, and the Ethiopic passive voice maker, which we will assume to collectively number about ten. Therefore, the total possible verb derivative for an average Ethiopic transitive verb becomes 40,000 (10 x 4,000 = 40,000).

THE NEGATIVE EFFECT OF CONJUGATION AND DECLENSION ON ETHIOPIC LITERATURE

Conjugation and declension, which often hide essential grammatical elements, have had adverse effects on the quality of Ethiopic literature unbeknownst to many Ethiopic writers, authors, and scholars. Conjugation, in particular, affects both prose and poetry because it crowds out nouns and adjectives and produces verb derivatives of multiple syllables complicating communication without adding much value (e.g. የሚያምር rather than ውብ), creates uninspiring wordiness, and is informal. It also affects poetry because of what we shall refer to as INFLATED RHYMING or CHEAP RHYMING—a situation in which the same suffix (such as the same PRIMAL PERSONAL PRONOUN or the same definite article) is applied to create derivatives of adjectives, nouns, or verbs that are used as rhyming words.

In addition to their negative effects on written communication, conjugation and declension have negatively affected Ethiopic literature for generations.

In such situations, the rhyming is achieved because of the repeated use of the same suffix regardless of whether or not the original words rhyme without the suffix. A surefire way to get words to rhyme, the use of the same word (suffix or not) repeatedly is inherently too pedestrian. Consider, for example, the suffix ኒ in the following stanza from a Tigirinya poem by Ge/E Gorifu (n.d.) and which occurs at the end of each of the five lines creating inflated rhyming. ኒ <nee> (me) is the Tigirinya first person singular pronoun in the objective case.

ኣክብኒ፣ ሓዳርኪ ግበርኒ፣
ከም ማዕተብ ክሳድኪ እሰርኒ፣
ከም መንዲል ኣብ ጉለኺ ኣእትውኒ፣
ሓደራ'ሞ ሻላ ኣይትበልኒ፣
ከም መርዓት ዓይንኺ ረኣይኒ...[2]

Isolating the morpheme ኒ as follows betrays the fact that the verse lacks the qualities of a poetic piece in the way the author intended it because of the use of the same word (or morpheme) at the end of more than one line.

ኣክብኒ [ኒ] ፣ ሓዳርኪ ግበር [ኒ] ፣
ከም ማዕተብ ክሳድኪ እሰር [ኒ] ፣
ከም መንዲል ኣብ ጉለኺ ኣእትው [ኒ] ፣
ሓደራ'ሞ ሻላ ኣይትበል [ኒ] ፣
ከም መርዓት ዓይንኺ ረኣይ [ኒ] ...

In the following examples of Amharic poem that I composed using deliberately repeated instances of the same suffix to demonstrate the problem, the text on the left is written in the traditional orthography while the one on the right shows a detached morpheme ኡ. ኡ could be one of Amharic's definite articles or the third person singular male pronoun, depending on the context. The negative effects of inflated rhyming are evident in the absence of rhyming words with the exclusion of the morpheme ኡ. Notice that due to elision, the last morpheme is traditionally shown as ው on the left (which creates the illusion of rhyming) but the correct form (ኡ) is shown on the right.

በብዙ ድካም የአመረተው፣	በብዙ ድካም የአመረተ [ኡ] ፣
የእርሱ ነውና አዝመራው፣	የእርሱ ነውና አዝመራ [ኡ] ፣
አፍርቶ አብቦ ተውቦ ቢአየው፣	አፍርቶ አብቦ ተውቦ ቢአየ [ኡ] ፣
ከአድማስ ወዲህ ከተንጣለለው፣	ከአድማስ ወዲህ ከተንጣለለ [ኡ] ፣
ከቆመበት ከዚያው ከማሳው፣	ከቆመበት ከዚያው ከማሳ [ኡ] ፣
ደምጹን ከፍ አድርጎ ክብርን ሰጠ ለፈጣሪው፣	ደምጹን ከፍ አድርጎ ክብርን ሰጠ ለፈጣሪ [ኡ] ፣
'ተመስገን' አለ፤ 'እልል' አለ፤ ተደሰተ ገበሬው።	'ተመስገን' አለ፤ 'እልል' አለ፤ ተደሰተ ገበሬ [ኡ] ።

The Amharic example is even more dramatic than the Tigirinya example, because once the suffix ኡ is detached, very few of the last syllables rhyme. The transliteration of the last words less the suffix ኡ in their order of appearance is as follows: *yeamerete, azimera, beeaye, ketenitxalele, kemasa, lefetxaree,* and *geberei.*

One of the adverse effects of cheap rhyming is that it deprives Ethiopic of vocabulary because poets are not encouraged to seek existing, forgotten, or rarely used words or use neologisms due to the ease of finding inflated rhyming words. (Despite the patriotic denial by some people, the GTA languages or at least their contemporary speakers are of course stricken with poor vocabulary—which is evident, among other things, by the unwarranted wholesale use of English words in Tigirinya and Amharic (see Chapters 5 and 13). This problem is something that every concerned citizen needs to work on to turn the tides.) Whereas Ethiopic poetry is otherwise unique because of its *qinei* and *sem* and *weriq* traditions, the repeated use of the same words or suffixes to create rhyming is its Achilles' heel. Even the laziest of Ethiopic poets can easily arrange rhyming words simply because of the fusional nature of Ethiopic and its alphasyllabic script. As Chris Beckett (2016) argued, all Ethiopic "poetries seem to rhyme" because it is easier to find rhyming words "in an inflected language like Amharic than it is in English."[3] To be sure, a good Ethiopic poem is one whose lines do not end with the same verb, verb derivative, personal pronoun, or definite article; and therefore is not a product of inflected or cheap rhyming. For an Ethiopic poem, I propose that a good practice is to minimize the use of a verb at the end of a line unless it is a gerund, which is the infinitive form of the Ethiopic verb. In the following example of an Amharic poem that I composed, notice that I have avoided the use of a verb at the end of each line.

Inflated or cheap rhyming is one of the negative effects of conjugation and declension.

ልክ እንደ ለየቻት፣
ልጃገረዷን ገና ከርቀት፣
የእናት ነገር፣
ልብዋ ተሞላ በሃሴት፣
'የኔ ፍቅር' አለች በለሆሳስ፣
አቅፎ-ለመሳም በዝግጅት፣
ዓይኖቿም አልቻሉ፣ ዘረገፉ የፍቅር እንባዎች፣
በድንገት፣ በዛች ቅጽበት፣
የባለቤታቸውን ተመሳሳይ ልጅነት፣
በመዘከር አይነት፣
ሊመሰከሩ ስለ የብላቴናዋ ታናሽነት፣
ከማህጸን እስከ ውልደት፣
ከውልደት እስከ እግር-ተከልነት፣
ተለይታ በዋለችባት በዛሬዋ የሕይወቷ የመጀመሪያ የትምህርት ዕለት፤
ወይ እናት!

Orthographic Challenges

The orthographic challenges in the GTA languages are just as important as the grammatical challenges, and more interestingly, the solution to the grammatical challenges lies in resolving the orthographic problems.

The Problem of Large Number of Characters in the Writing System

There are hundreds of characters in the Ethiopic writing system with too many confusingly visually similar characters. Such a large number of characters does not come without a price. To begin with, few literate people can recite the entire alphabet, including the characters in the extension set, from memory. In their early years, children spend a disproportionately large amount of time learning and identifying the individual characters in the alphabet instead of learning words that the alphabet is used to write. Ethiopian children, as well as foreigners who want to learn Tigirinya or Amharic, can easily get discouraged by this 'first great obstacle' to learning the languages and their writing systems.

The problem associated with computers, smartphones, and other devices that use keyboards for typing is one that will continue to stifle progress in literacy, particularly computer literacy, at a time when the country is struggling to re-establish itself in the economic and human development areas. The fact that it is technically impractical to provide a key for each character on a computer keyboard, as was the case with typewriters in a previous generation, is one problem among many.[4] Another problem associated with a large number of characters in each alphabet is the difficulty in working with and memorizing the alphabetical order. The consonantal layers are complicated by the seven vowelic orders so much so that the idea of arranging words in alphabetical order is almost foreign to users of the Ethiopic script.

The Inability to Mark Gemination

One of the most important features of Ethiosemitic languages, gemination or consonant elongation is a phenomenon in which a consonant is pronounced slightly longer than usual. Gemination can be contrasted to vowel length, which is absent in Ethiosemitic but present in other languages of Ethiopia, such as Oromiffa. Ethiopic does not have a means to indicate gemination, which means that the reader has to identify a geminated consonant based on context resulting in inaccurate communication. Consider the following Tigirinya proverb:

> ሓሳዊስ ይምሳሕ እምበር ኣይድረርን <Hhasawees yimisahh imiber ayidirerin>
> (A fraud may eat lunch but will not eat dinner)

The first, second and last words have at least one geminated consonant each, which are indicated by underlining the geminated characters for clarity as follows:

> ሓሳዊስ ይምሳሕ እምበር ኣይድረርን
> <Hhas·sawees yimis·sahh imiber ay·yidir·rerin>

The inability to mark gemination is one of the shortcomings of the traditional Ethiopic writing system. Not marking gemination on the right word can result in the wrong pronunciation with little or no semantic effect. However, the meanings of many words are altered by gemination even when the spelling remains the same. Sometimes context does not immediately indicate required gemination or lack thereof and a reader can misunderstand the intended message. For example, consider the Amharic single-word sentence **ተሰማ** <tesema>. Without gemination, the word means, "Be heard!", as in "Speak up! Be heard!". However, with gemination of the second character, it carries the meaning, "It was heard."

Gemination in Ethiosemitic is more prominent with verbs and verb inflections than with other words. The prevalence of gemination in Ethiosemitic verbs is so much so that almost every verb shows gemination at least in one of its four basic verb inflections or divisions. As a result, words whose meaning is altered by the presence or absence of gemination but are spelled alike are common in Ethiosemitic, especially in Amharic (**Table 3.1**).

The Inability to Represent New Sounds

One of the difficulties associated with the traditional Ethiopic writing system is its inability to represent a new sound or phoneme without creating a corresponding new glyph. In a truly alphabetic script, digraphs are used to represent sounds

Table 3.1: Examples of Amharic words with identical spelling but different meanings and use of gemination[5]

ETHIOPIC	ROMANIZATION 1	TRANSLATION	ROMANIZATION 2	TRANSLATION
መልስ	melis	answer, Ethiopian traditional reception after a wedding day	mel-lis	answer!
መተው	metew	to abandon, to drop an issue	met-tew	to be abandoned, to be left
መካድ	mekad	to deny, to disown, to defect, to act treasonably	mek-kad	to be disowned
ሳድስ	sadis	the Ethiopic 6th order	sad-dis	"when I [was/am/will be] renovating"
ርቀት	riqet	distance	riq-qet	sofistication
በራ	bera	bold	ber-ra	"it lit up"
አለ	ale	"...said"	al-le	"... is present"
አስር	asir	I tie...	as-sir	ten
አጠባ	atxeba	washing, laundry	atxeb-ba	"he fed [someone from a bottle]"
አዳኝ	adany	savior, rescuer	ad-dany	hunter, predator
ይበላ	yibela	"he may eat..."	yibel-la	"let it be eaten"
ዋና	wana	swimming	wanna	main
ገና	gena	not yet	Genna	Christmas

that cannot otherwise be represented using one of the letters in the alphabet. However, in an alphasyllabary like the Ethiopic writing system, it is not possible to create such digraphs and, as a result, new characters are needed for new sounds. While it is ingenious that Ethiopic has, throughout its history, developed new glyphs or characters to represent new phonemes that were borrowed as part of loanwords from other languages, it is impractical to accommodate every new sound that is not an integral component in Ethiosemitic.

ቨ <v> and its seven orders are some of the most recent glyphs or characters in Ethiopic that were created to represent such new phonemes, which are encountered during transliterating foreign documents into Ethiopic or when used with loanwords such as virus and Venus. The Unicode Standard code charts for Ethiopic—which include Ethiopic, Ethiopic Supplement, Ethiopic Extended, and Ethiopic Extended-A—contain hundreds of glyphs from the original as well as recent entrants to the Ethiopic family. Recently minted glyphs have simply made the script bulkier than ever before (**Table 3.2**), which illustrates the need to curb the rising number of the Ethiopic characters.

The problems associated with handling new phonemes is cited as one of the reasons that non-Ethiosemitic languages, such as Oromiffa, opted out of the Ethiopic writing system following the liberalization of the Ethiopian sociopolitical atmosphere in 1991. Before the early 1990's, Oromiffa was written using Ethiopic by inventing new characters to represent sounds that did not exist in Ethiosemitic for whom the alphabet was originally developed. New characters were added by taking an existing character for a closely related phoneme and modifying it by adding diacritic markers (**Table 3.2**). For example, the glyph ጰ̍ was created for Oromiffa by attaching a vertical stroke over the Ethiopic character ጰ. While,

Table 3.2: The numerically increasing characters of the Ethiopic script (with the Type 2 set being historically the most recent entrant into the script[6])

7TH ORDER	ሆ	ሎ	ሖ	ሞ	ሦ	ሮ	ሶ	ሾ	ቆ	ቖ	ቦ	ቶ	ቾ	ኆ	ኖ	ኞ	ኦ	ኮ	ኾ	ዎ	ዞ	ዦ	ዮ	ዶ	ጆ	ጎ		ጦ	ጮ	ጶ	ጾ	ፆ	ፎ	ፖ
6TH ORDER	ህ	ል	ሕ	ም	ሥ	ር	ስ	ሽ	ቅ	ቕ	ብ	ት	ች	ኅ	ን	ኝ	እ	ክ	ኽ	ው	ዝ	ዥ	ይ	ድ	ጅ	ግ		ጥ	ጭ	ጵ	ጽ	ፅ	ፍ	ፕ
5TH ORDER	ሄ	ሌ	ሔ	ሜ	ሤ	ሬ	ሴ	ሼ	ቄ	ቔ	ቤ	ቴ	ቼ	ኄ	ኔ	ኜ	ኤ	ኬ	ኼ	ዌ	ዜ	ዤ	ዬ	ዴ	ጄ	ጌ		ጤ	ጬ	ጴ	ጼ	ፄ	ፌ	ፔ
4TH ORDER	ሃ	ላ	ሓ	ማ	ሣ	ራ	ሳ	ሻ	ቃ	ቓ	ባ	ታ	ቻ	ኃ	ና	ኛ	ኣ	ካ	ኻ	ዋ	ዛ	ዣ	ያ	ዳ	ጃ	ጋ		ጣ	ጫ	ጳ	ጻ	ፃ	ፋ	ፓ
3RD ORDER	ሂ	ሊ	ሒ	ሚ	ሢ	ሪ	ሲ	ሺ	ቂ	ቒ	ቢ	ቲ	ቺ	ኂ	ኒ	ኚ	ኢ	ኪ	ኺ	ዊ	ዚ	ዢ	ዪ	ዲ	ጂ	ጊ		ጢ	ጪ	ጲ	ጺ	ፂ	ፊ	ፒ
2ND ORDER	ሁ	ሉ	ሑ	ሙ	ሡ	ሩ	ሱ	ሹ	ቁ	ቑ	ቡ	ቱ	ቹ	ኁ	ኑ	ኙ	ኡ	ኩ	ኹ	ዉ	ዙ	ዡ	ዩ	ዱ	ጁ	ጉ		ጡ	ጩ	ጱ	ጹ	ፁ	ፉ	ፑ
	↑	↑	↑	↑	↑	↑	↑	↑	↑	↑	↑	↑	↑	↑	↑	↑	↑	↑	↑	↑	↑	↑	↑	↑	↑	↑		↑	↑	↑	↑	↑	↑	↑
BASE	ሀ	ለ	ሐ	መ	ሠ	ረ	ሰ	ሸ	ቀ	ቐ	በ	ተ	ቸ	ኀ	ነ	ኘ	አ	ከ	ኸ	ወ	ዘ	ዠ	የ	ደ	ጀ	ገ		ጠ	ጨ	ጰ	ጸ	ፀ	ፈ	ፐ
	↓	↓	↓	↓	↓	↓	↓	↓	↓	↓	↓	↓	↓	↓	↓	↓	↓	↓	↓	↓	↓	↓	↓	↓	↓	↓		↓	↓	↓	↓	↓	↓	↓
									ቈ	ቘ				ኈ				ኰ	ዀ							ጐ								
TYPE 1		ሏ	ሗ	ሟ	ሧ	ሯ	ሷ	ሿ	ቋ	ቛ	ቧ	ቷ	ቿ	ኋ	ኗ	ኟ	ኧ	ኳ	ዃ		ዟ	ዧ		ዷ	ጇ	ጓ		ጧ	ጯ	ጷ	ጿ		ፏ	ፗ
EXTENSION									ቌ	ቜ				ኌ				ኴ	ዄ							ጔ								
SET									ቊ	ቚ				ኊ				ኲ	ዂ							ጒ								
									ቍ	ቝ				ኍ				ኵ	ዅ							ጕ								
				ᎀ		ፘ		ⶠ	ⷀ		ꬨ		ⶨ					ⷈ	ⷐ			ⶰ		ዸ		ጘ	ⷘ		ⶸ		[illegible]		ᎈ	ᎌ
				ᎁ			ꬁ	ⶡ	ⷁ		ꬩ		ⶩ					ⷉ	ⷑ		ꬑ	ⶱ		ዹ		ጙ	ⷙ		ⶹ		[illegible]		ᎉ	ᎍ
				ᎂ			ꬂ	ⶢ	ⷂ		ꬪ		ⶪ					ⷊ	ⷒ		ꬒ	ⶲ		ዺ		ጚ	ⷚ		ⶺ		[illegible]		ᎊ	ᎎ
TYPE 2				ᎃ			ꬃ	ⶣ	ⷃ		ꬫ		ⶫ					ⷋ	ⷓ		ꬓ	ⶳ		ዻ		ጛ	ⷛ		ⶻ		[illegible]		ᎋ	ᎏ
(NEWER)							ꬄ	ⶤ	ⷄ		ꬬ		ⶬ					ⷌ	ⷔ		ꬔ	ⶴ		ዼ		ጜ	ⷜ		ⶼ		[illegible]			
EXTENSTION				ፙ			ꬅ	ⶥ	ⷅ		ꬭ		ⶭ					ⷍ	ⷕ		ꬕ	ⶵ		ዽ		ጝ	ⷝ		ⶽ		[illegible]		ፚ	
SET							ꬆ	ⶦ	ⷆ		ꬮ		ⶮ					ⷎ	ⷖ		ꬖ	ⶶ		ዾ		ጞ	ⷞ		ⶾ		[illegible]			
(NON-GTA																								ዿ		ጟ			ꬠ					
LANGUAGES											ᎄ													ꬉ		ⶓ			ꬡ					
ONLY)											ᎅ													ꬊ		ⶔ			ꬢ					
											ᎆ													ꬋ		ⶕ			ꬣ					
																								ꬌ		ⶖ			ꬤ					
																								ꬍ					ꬥ					
																								ꬎ					ꬦ					
											ᎇ													[illegible]										
	ሇ	ⶀ		ⶁ		ⶂ	ⶃ		ቇ		ⶅ	ⶆ	ⶇ	ኇ	ⶈ	ⶉ	ⶊ	ኯ		ዏ	ⶋ		ዯ	ⶌ	ⶎ	ጏ		ⶏ		ⶑ		[illegible]		ⶒ

this method may still be considered in adopting the proposed reformed Ethiopic writing system for various languages, it will not be the only way nor the best way to do so. With the Reformed Ethiopic, new phonemes can be created as digraphs using two or more consonants or combinations of consonants and vowels.

Ethiosemitic languages are notorious for spelling inconsistency.

The problems associated with the sheer number of characters resulting from the seven Ethiopic vowelic orders also makes Ethiopic less attractive than a true alphabet. Since Ethiopic is an alphasyllabary and it has no free standing vowels, every newly minted consonantal character would have to come in a set to account for the abstract Ethiopic vowels which must be fused to the base character. Furthermore, the traditional script is unable to show vowel elongation, just like it is unable to show consonant elongation. Unlike Ethiosemitic languages, Ethiocushitic languages have different vowel lengths which play important grammatical roles in those languages. In a truly alphabetic script, such as the Latin alphabet, which is now used to write many Ethiocushitic languages, vowel length can easily be shown by doubling a given vowel.

The Problem of Chronic Spelling Inconsistency

A great hindrance to effective communication, the chronic spelling problem in Ethiosemitic and the absence of a spelling standard is attested by many. For example, in a Journal of Ethiopian Studies article titled *The Standardisation of Amharic Spelling*, Cowley (1967) argued that a standard Ethiopic orthography is desirable because "variation in spelling is a hindrance to all readers."[7] Desita Tekile Welid (1970) and Leslau (1973) stated that due to the prevalence of redundant characters representing identical phonemes, Ethiopic spelling is inconsistent. Similarly, Wright (1964) argued that the phonetic character of the Ethiopian script, although makes spelling easy,

> [G]ives rise to certain difficulties, for local and even individual varieties of pronunciation can - and are apt to - be reflected in the spelling. No Ethiopian Academy or other body exists which is in a position to set an example, much less to enforce the use, of standardized spelling.[8]

The damage caused by inconsistent spelling on Ethiopic literature and communication due to lack of standard spelling is staggering. One of the greatest damage to communication arising from inconsistent spelling, for example, is the adverse effects it has on Ethiopic lexicography. Ethiopic lexicography is almost irrelevant because of the difficulty of finding words in a list, such as in a dictionary. Geez-experience.com, one of the most popular Tigirinya online dictionaries, stated on its Tigirinya keyboard map page that "there is no formal spelling in Tigirinya and many people [have] issues finding the right word,"[9] which is also true for Amharic. Ethiopic dictionaries have so far failed to fully satisfy a dictionary's main purpose, which is to provide logically ordered list of words with their meaning. The failure is causing cascading damaging effects to society as people start to use English and the Latin alphabet as a way to circumnavigate the problems of Ethiopic lexicography, which has become a national disease (Chapter 13: More on the Ethiopian Language Crisis and Recommended Solutions).

There are various reasons for spelling inconsistency in Ethiopic, which include the historically poor literacy levels in the nation, the fusional nature of the languages, and the traditional orthography. In the traditional Ethiopic orthography, words, including compound words, are spelled almost exactly as they sound, which means that spelling can be affected by pronunciation variation between regions in the country. Asker and et al (n.d.) argued that,

> The Amharic writing system uses multitudes of ways to denote compound words and there is no agreed upon spelling standard for compounds. As a result of this—and of the size of the country leading to vast dialectal dispersion—lexical variation and homophony is very common.[10]

Spelling inconsistency is not a problem observed only in documents written by different individuals, but even the same person can and often does spell differently even within the same document (see, for example, Leslau (1973)). Moreover, Ethiopian scholars and their language materials do not have agreement on what is proper spelling. Leslau (1973) stated that

> Abba Yohannəs Gäbrä Egzi'abəher in his መዝገበ ፡ ቃላት ፤ ትግርኛ—አምሐርኛ (a Tigrinya-Amharic dictionary) spells the Amharic verbs አበረ [...], አደረ [...], [and] አለፈ [...], all with አ, whereas Kidanä Wäld Kəfle in his መጽሐፈ ፡ ሰዋሰው ፡ ወመዝገበ ፡ ቃላት ፡ አዲስ (A Geez-Amharic dictionary) spells the Amharic words with ዐ; thus, ዐበረ [...], ዐደረ [...], and ዐለፈ [...]. Incidentally the word for 'Amharic' is spelled አማርኛ (with አ) by Abba Yohannəs Gäbrä Egzi'abəher, but ዐማርኛ (with ዐ) by Käsate Bərhan Täsämma in his የዐማርኛ ፡ መዝገበ ፡ ቃላት (Amharic-Amharic dictionary), p. 979. On the basis of this evidence it seems to me it is not practical to follow the normal accepted spelling.[11]

The spelling problem in Ethiosemitic can be divided into three categories—spelling inconsistency due to redundant characters; inconsistent use of grammatical elements, including inconsistent use of wrongly applied grammatical elements; and inconsistent elision.

Spelling inconsistency due to redundant characters:

> Inconsistent spelling attributed to the use of different characters of the same phoneme (in the case of Amharic) or of a closely related phoneme (in the case of Tigirinya) is a chronic problem. Although the problem of redundant characters does not affect Tigirinya since it does not have more than one character representing the same phoneme, sometimes the Tigirinya *eyin* and *elf* characters, as well as characters representing closely related sounds are interchanged for the same word. Inconsistent spelling in Amharic is even more prevalent due to Amharic's use of many 1st order Ethiopic characters with the same phonemic value as their 4th order counterparts. The following lists show some examples of inconsistent spelling due to the use of redundant or phonemically similar characters with each line showing the various ways a word can be spelled, mostly wrongly, with the most common or least incorrect spelling shown at the beginning of the line.

Tigirinya:

- ድካ, ድኻ
- መወዳእታ, መወዳዕታ
- ከማይ, ኸማይ
- ሃጎስ, ሓጎስ

Amharic:

- ፀኃይ, ፀኀይ, ጸሐይ, ጸሓይ, ጸሀይ, ጸሃይ, ጸኀይ, ጸኃይ, ፀሐይ, ፀሓይ, ፀሀይ, ፀሃይ,
- መጽሓፍ, መጽሐፍ, መጽሀፍ, መጽሃፍ, መፅሀፍ, መፅሃፍ, መፅሐፍ, መፅሓፍ,
- ህፃን, ህጻን, ሕጻን, ሕፃን
- ሃገር, ሀገር, አገር, ኣገር, ሐገር, ሓገር,
- ሃርነት, ሀርነት, አርነት, ሓርነት, ሐርነት, ኣርነት
- ኣማራ, አማራ, ዐማራ, ዓማራ
- ዓለም, ዐለም, አለም, ኣለም
- ዘለዓለም፣ ዘለአለም፣ ዘልዓለም፣ ዘልአለም
- ሐሳብ, ሂሣብ, ሂሳብ, ሒሣብ

Spelling inconsistency due to inconsistent use of some grammatical elements:

Inconsistent spelling due to inconsistent use of some grammatical elements and wrong grammatical elements, such as adding redundant morphemes (unnecessary demonstratives or definite articles in Tigirinya and unnecessary pronouns in Amharic) and bad pluralization, especially in Amharic, (inconsistent application of pluralization modes and double pluralization). The following are examples of such inconsistent spelling in both languages:

Tigirinya:

- ካባኩም, ካባኹም, ካባታትኩም, ካባታትኹም, ካባትኩም, ካባትኹም
- ምስአም, ምሳቶም, ምስኣቶም, ምሳታቶም
- ንሰን, ንሳተን

Amharic:

- ኣመሰግናለሁ, አመሰግናለው, አመሰግናለውኝ, አመሰግናለሁኝ,
- ፈለግሁ, ፈለኩ, ፈለኩኝ
- ሃገራት, ሃገሮች, *ሃገራቶች
- ህፃናት, ህፃኖች, *ህፃናቶች
- ዓመታት, ዓመቶች, *ዓመታቶች
- ኣማልክት, *ኣማልክቶች
- መላእክት, *መላእክቶች
- ኣሕዛብ, *ኣሕዛቦች
- ኣዛውንት, *ኣዛውንቶች

Spelling inconsistency due to inconsistent elision:

Inconsistent elision, which is the omission of sounds, is prevalent in Ethiosemitic languages with the phenomenon directly affecting the orthography. During verb derivation and compound-word formations, spelling is inconsistently affected by the omission of vowels and consonants often resulting in the inconsistent use of diphthongs. The written word often mirrors the spoken word due to the Ethiopic alphasyllabic characters that assimilate some consonant or vowel sounds to the extent that the basic morphophonemic elements responsible for the forms of words are often difficult to be reconstructed, which makes the grammars of these languages mysterious to many speakers and learners alike. This phenomenon affects Amharic more than Tigirinya, which employs fewer affixes. The following are Amharic examples:

- የኣማርኛ, ያማርኛ
- ዘለዓለም, ዘላለም
- መጥቶኣል, መቷል, መጥቷል, መቱዋል, መቶዋል
- ቢያጥቡኣት, ቢያጥቧት, ቢያጥቡዋት
- ወሰደውብዎትኣል, ወሰደውብዎታል, ወሰደውቦታል

One of the possible three solutions previously recommended to standardize spelling in Ethiosemitic is the adoption of commonly accepted orthography (Leslau 1973). However, to this day, there is no commonly accepted orthography satisfactory for adoption and the problem has continued unabated. The use of etymology is another method that had been recommended to establish correct spelling for Amharic, which, unlike Giiz and Tigirinya, uses redundant characters that add to the chronic spelling inconsistency in the language. Etymology provides the Amharic word commonly spelled as እውቀት (knowledge), for example, to be spelled as ዕውቀት from the original Giiz word ዖቀ. Unfortunately, standardization of spelling through etymology is not a new idea (see, for example, Leslu 1973) but, for various reasons, has not worked as it is evidenced in the prevalence of chronic spelling inconsistency in contemporary as well as old Ethiopic literature.

The third possible solution and perhaps the most viable one, which I fully support, is a comprehensive reform of the Ethiopic script. Leslau (1973) argued that with a comprehensive reform of the script, only one of the characters with the same phonemic value would be retained regardless of how the original root word was spelled so that

> [I]f in the case of አ and ዐ, one were to choose, say, the letter አ, one would have to write አሰረ 'imprison', አወቀ 'know', አይን 'eye', all with the አ, even though አወቀ goes back to Geez ዖቀ (with ዐ), and አይን likewise goes back to Geez ዐይን (cognate with Semitic '*ayn*). Similarly, if between ሠ and ሰ one were to choose ሰ, one would have to spell ተሳለ 'vow' and ተሳለ 'be painted' both with ሰ, even though etymologically ተሳለ 'vow' goes back to Geez ሰአለ, and ሣለ 'paint' goes back to Geez ሠዐለ.[12]

Other Challenges

Other problems include the challenges with sounding out the spelling of words, the challenges with accurate and quick reading, the challenges with stemming, the challenges with developing computer handwriting recognition and optical character recognition (refer to *Benefits of the Proposed Alphabetic Reform* in Chapter 8 to learn how these problems can be addressed).

The Difficulty with Sounding Out the Spelling of Words

Another problem associated with the traditional Ethiopic script is the problem of sounding out the spelling of words. Since traditional Ethiopic is a vocalized script, the alphasyllabic characters do not have names other than the sound they represent. As a result, it is not possible to read the spelling of a word without also reading the word at the same time, which creates a major problem for clarity both for the student who would like to study Ethiopic spelling and for the general public's communication needs.

The Difficulty with Accurate and Speedy Reading

Notwithstanding the general problems of the Ethiopian education system, reading skills of people who use the Ethiopic script seem to be extremely low, often regardless of the individuals' level of education. Many people are slow readers or routinely stumble on words.[13] Shortage of reading materials, the general level of illiteracy in the society, and the failure of the education system may be some of the reasons for the low levels of reading skills in the country. However, the traditional orthography with its phonemic spelling may have an even more negative impact for the following reasons:

- The large number of the characters in the Ethiopic script makes it difficult to register the subtle differences between characters at a glance in a written material such as a news article. Unless one is familiarized with a particular written material, or has excellent reading skills, making errors is often avoided only by reading slowly.
- The mind-boggling number of word derivatives—which are combinations of nouns, pronouns, verbs, and other grammatical elements—means that there are almost infinite subtle variations of words that are difficult to recognize at a glance (**Appendices A, B,** and **C**)—which makes efficient reading a formidable task.

The Difficulty with Stemming

Stemming is crucial for language processing and information retrieval among many of its benefits. It is practically impossible to perform stemming with the traditional Ethiopic script because it does not have separate consonants and vowels. Stemming with Ethiosemitic words is often done first by converting the text into another (alphabetic) script, Latin, to expose the hidden consonants and vowels that make up the different parts of a given word or word derivative. The need to depend on a foreign alphabet to perform a simple task is a sign of the failure of traditional Ethiopic to be self-sufficient. As Madessa (2012) argued "such problems make designing information retrieval system for [Ethiopic] difficult and challenging, and it needs lots of work [by] experts so as to develop a better IR system..."[14]

The Difficulty with Optical Character Recognition

Computer handwriting recognition and optical character recognition technologies rely on the suitability of the characters as much as on technology. In that regard, the traditional Ethiopic script, like other little-known indigenous African scripts, suffers from a large number of similar and complicated characters which are difficult for machine reading (Meshesha and Jawahar, u.d.).

Chapter 4

Overview of Ethiopic Morphology and Proposed Modularization

ኣጼ ዮሓንንስ ሞኘ ነ ኣችቸው፣
እኘኛ ም ሁልል ኣችችን ናቅ ን ኣችቸው፤
ንጉሥ ቢል ኡ ኣችቸው በ መኻል ኡ፣
ወሰን ጠብባቂ ል ሁን ኣል ኡ።

The innocence of Yohhannis the Emperor
Whom we didn't honour
Although he was named Ruler
With his life did he defend the boarder

—Anonymous

IN THIS CHAPTER

Being highly synthesizing, WORD DERIVATIVES of nouns in Ethiosemitic can number up to a few hundred and those of verbs can number, in some cases, as high as 50,000 (**Appendices A, B,** and **C**). A word derivative is created when one or more grammatical units, such as prefixes and suffixes, are attached to a root word or NUCLEUS in a process called derivation. A root word is the most basic form of a word without any affixes. A nucleus, on the other hand, shall be defined as a root word or a minimal derivative of a root word—such as one made by rearranging or duplicating parts of a root word—that acts as a root word because of its unique form and role within in a larger derivative. A nucleus can be a pluralized noun or adjective, a verb showing reduplicative or reciprocal action, or a TYPE "A" CAUSATIVE VERB (Volume II: Chapter 11: Types of Verbs in Tigirinya and Amharic).

THE PROPOSED MODULARIZATION OF ETHIOPIC WORDS

Modularization may be defined as the process of creating or establishing a modular system. A modular system is one that has independent parts that form a coherent whole in more than one way. In *Modular America*, Blair (1988) argued that modular "[p]arts are conceived as equivalent and hence, in one or more senses, interchangeable and/or cumulative and/or recombinable."[1] The great advantage of a modular system, therefore, is its efficiency in forming almost limitless types of wholes with only a very few types of individual parts that can be arranged or rearranged as needed. Modularization in the context of Ethiopic grammar and orthography is a new concept that refers to deconstructing every word derivative into its individual parts—the root word (or nucleus) and one or more morphemes (prefixes or suffixes)—that can be used as modular elements without being attached to each other. Modularization will dramatically reduce the number of unique occurrences of word derivatives.

Modularization contrasts with crasis and synthesization, which assimilates as many as six or more word elements into a single bloated word called a word derivative. Many Ethiopic sentences consist of a single word derivative. Modularization, therefore, is the opposite process of separating such grammatical units—in what may also be referred to as reverse-derivation, deconstruction, or DE-SYNTHESIZATION—and using them to form phrases and sentences as free-standing elements. The idea behind de-synthesization is to systematically expose the stem or core of the word (i.e. noun, adjective, or verb) through word separation, for example, so that the reader knows the root word or nucleus. Word separation will make the written word systematic, easy to learn and easy to manipulate—and will enable efficient storing, categorizing, searching, retrieving, and processing of information for a modern society. For the purpose of the proposed language reform, a nucleus shall be considered indivisible and will not be further de-synthesized.

Modularization is a new concept for Ethiopic and will undoubtedly enable efficient storing, categorizing, searching, retrieving, and processing of information like never before in the history of writing in Ethiopia.

In theory, de-synthesization will only affect the written word, although the spoken word may be affected minimally over time. In other words, morphology, syntax, and phonology will not be directly affected by de-synthesization, although the orthography will show the morphology differently. A more developed system of writing will lay the foundation for an accurate and efficient medium of communication in Ethiopia. Given the large number of word derivatives in Ethiosemitic languages, the benefits of de-synthesizing cannot be overemphasized. The social cost of hyperinflation of words due to uncontrolled word derivation is colossal and is a major part of the current language crisis in the country.

The Ethiopic Morphology and De-Synthesization of Derived Words

The Ethiopic morphology is characterized by the roots of most Ethiopic words, like other Semitic languages, which have three characters or radicals and are known as 'triliteral' words. Before the development of vowel indications, Ancient Ethiopic and its predecessor proto-Ethiopic consisted of only consonants, leaving the reader to guess the necessary vowels to pronouns words. Triliteral words, therefore, were written using three consonants only. In the traditional Ethiopic script, which includes vowel indicators on each character except those in the 1st vowelic order, triliteral Ethiopic words are shown, for example, as ንጉስ <nigus> (king) and ሰማይ <semay> (sky or heaven) in all the GTA languages. Most Ethiopic words derive from their respective triliteral root words and account for 85% of words in Tigirinya, for example. Kasa G. (2004) argued that the rest of the Tigirinya words derive from quadliteral, en-literal, or hexa-literal words as cited in Yonas (2011). Amanuel (1998), on the other hand, stated that "compounding, affixation, and reduplication" are some of the morphological operations that are used to create word derivatives as cited in Yonas (2011).[2] There are four categories of affixes: Prefixes, suffixes, infixes, and circumfixes. According to Beyen (2013) examples of Tigirinya affixes are:

> [P]refixes that come at the beginning of the root, such as ን, ዝ, እንተ, ም, [and] ብም; suffixes that come at the end of the root, such as ና, ታት, ት, ነት, [and] ን; infixes that come inside the root, such as ባ in ሰባበረ, ላ in በላልዐ, [and] ታ in ሰታተየ; and circumfixes that are attached before and after the base form at the same time.[3]

To avoid dealing with all forms of an inflected verb and its derivatives (which make up a lexeme), the basic verb form (lemma) used by Ethiopic dictionaries is the past tense form of the verb as used with the third person singular male (3PSM) pronoun. The 3PSM past tense form of the verb is the least inflected form of the verb in all Semitic languages. Examples of triliteral verbs are the Tigirinya verb ሓጸበ <hhaxebe> and its Amharic equivalent አጠበ <atxebe>,[4] both of which are single word sentences and are translated as "He washed." The first character in the Amharic word in the above example is a vowel. However, it represents a single phoneme on its own and therefore is considered as one of the radicals required to make it a triliteral word.

Every word derivative in both languages is made up of at least two morphemes, including the Ethiopic infinitive verb form, which is a word derivative. The infinitive forms of the above verbs are ምሕጻብ <mihhixab> and ማጠብ <matxeb> (to wash) for Tigirinya and Amharic respectively. The two morphemes of the Tigirinya derivative are the single character morpheme ም <mi> (to) and ሕጻብ < hhixab> (wash), and the ones for the Amharic word are the single character morpheme መ <me> (to) and አጠበ <atxebe> (wash). Other examples are the Tigirinya single-word sentence በሊዓ <beleeaa>, and its Amharic equivalent በላች <belac>,

Table 4.1: Some derivatives of the Tigirinya verb ምብላዕ <mibilaii> (to eat)

SENTENCE TYPE 1 (I ate)			SENTENCE TYPE 2 (I ate it)			SENTENCE TYPE 3 (I ate them)		
	ORIGINAL CONSTRUCTION	DE-SYNTHESIZED CONSTRUCTION		ORIGINAL CONSTRUCTION	DE-SYNTHESIZED CONSTRUCTION		ORIGINAL CONSTRUCTION	DE-SYNTHESIZED CONSTRUCTION
1	በላዕኹ	በላዕ ኹ	11	በላዕኹዎ	በላዕ ኹ ኦ	21	በላዕኹዎም	በላዕ ኹ ኦም
	belaiikhu	belaii khu		belaiikhuwo	belaii khu o		belaiikhuwom	belaii khu om
2	በላዕና	በላዕ ና	12	በላዕናዮ	በላዕ ና ዮ	22	በላዕናዮም	በላዕ ና ዮም
	belaiina	belaii na		belaiinayo	belaii na yo		belaiinayom	belaii na yom
3	በላዕኻ	በላዕ ኻ	13	በላዕኻዮ	በላዕ ኻ ዮ	23	በላዕኻዮም	በላዕ ኻ ዮም
	belaiikha	belaii kha		belaiikhayo	belaii kha yo		belaiikhayom	belaii kha yom
4	በላዕኹም	በላዕ ኹም	14	በላዕኹምዎ	በላዕ ኹም ኦ	24	በላዕኹምዎም	በላዕ ኹም ኦም
	belaiikhum	belaii khum		belaiikhumiwo	belaii khum o		belaiikhumiwom	belaii khum om
5	በላዕኺ	በላዕ ኺ	15	በላዕኺዮ	በላዕ ኺ ዮ	25	በላዕኺዮም	በላዕ ኺ ዮም
	belaiikhee	belaii khee		belaiikheeyo	belaii khee yo		belaiikheeyom	belaii khee yom
6	በላዕኽን	በላዕ ኽን	16	በላዕኽንኦ	በላዕ ኽን ኦ	26	በላዕኽንኦም	በላዕ ኽን ኦም
	belaiikhin	belaii khin		belaiikhinio	belaii khin o		belaiikhiniom	belaii khin om
7	በልዐ	በላዕ አ	17	በልዖ	በላዕ አ ኦ	27	በልዖም	በላዕ ኦ ም
	beliee	belaii e		belioo	belaii e o		belioom	belaii o m
8	በልዑ	በላዕ ኡ	18	በልዑዎ	በላዕ ኡ ኦ	28	በልዑዎም	በላዕ ዑ ኦም
	beliuu	belaii u		beliuuwo	belaii u o		beliuuwom	belaii u om
9	በልዐት	በላዕ አት	19	በልዐቶ	በላዕ አት ኦ	29	በልዐቶም	በላዕ አት ኦም
	belieet	belaii et		belieeto	belaii et o		belieetom	belaii et om
10	በልዓ	በላዕ ኣ	20	በልዓኦ	በላዕ ኣ ኦ	30	በልዓኦም	በላዕ ኣ ኦም
	beliaa	belaii a		beliaao	belaii a o		beliaaom	belaii a om

which mean "She ate". The Tigirinya word is made up of two morphemes: the root word በሊ <belee> (ate) and the pronoun ዓ <aa> (she). The Amharic word is also made up of two morphemes: the root word በላ <bella> (ate) and the pronoun ች <c> (she). The infinitive form of the root word in Tigirinya is ምብላዕ <mibilaii> (to eat), which is made up of two morphemes: the single character morpheme ም mi (to) and ብላዕ <bilaii> (eat). The infinitive form of the word in Amharic is መብላት <mebilat> (to eat), which is also made up of two morphemes: the single character morpheme መ <me> (to) and ብላት <bilat> (eat). **Tables 4.1** and **4.2** illustrate how de-synthesizing can help with reducing the large numbers of word derivatives.

The Ethiopic Orthography and Modularization of Words

In **Table 4.1**, some derivatives of the Tigirinya verb ምብላዕ <mibilaii> for the simple past tense form are shown in three random sentence types applied for each of the ten grammatical persons in Tigirinya. For example, the single-word sentence በላዕኹ <belaiikhu> (I ate) becomes a two-word sentence (በላዕ ኹ) when de-synthesized into its individual morphemes. While in **Table 4.2**, some derivatives of the Amharic verb መብላት <mebilat> for the simple past tense form are shown in three random sentence types applied for each of the ten grammatical persons in Amharic. For example, the single-word sentence በላሁ <belahu> (I ate) becomes a two-word sentence (በላ ሁ) when de-synthesized into its individual

Table 4.2: Some derivatives of the Amharic verb መብላት <mebilat> (to eat)

SENTENCE TYPE 1 (I ate)			SENTENCE TYPE 2 (I ate it)			SENTENCE TYPE 3 (I ate them)		
	ORIGINAL CONSTRUCTION	DE-SYNTHESIZED CONSTRUCTION		ORIGINAL CONSTRUCTION	DE-SYNTHESIZED CONSTRUCTION		ORIGINAL CONSTRUCTION	DE-SYNTHESIZED CONSTRUCTION
1	በላሁ	በላ ሁ	9	በላሁት	በላ ሁ ት	17	በላኋቸው	በላ ሁ አቸው
	belahu	bela hu		belahut	bela hu ti		belahuacew	bela hu acew
2	በላን	በላ ን	10	በላነው	በላ ን ኧ ው	18	በላናቸው	በላ ን አቸው
	belan	bela n		belanew	bela ni e wi		belanacew	bela ni acew
3	በላህ	በላ ህ	11	በላኸው	በላ ህ ኧ ው	19	በላሃቸው	በላ ህ አቸው
	belah	bela hi		belahxew	bela hi e wi		belahacew	bela hi acew
4	በላሽ	በላ ሽ	12	በላሽው	በላ ሽ ው	20	በላሻቸው	በላ ሽ አቸው
	belash	bela shi		belahut	bela shi wi		belashacew	bela shi acew
5	በላችሁ	በላ አችሁ	13	በላችሁት	በላ አችሁ ት	21	በላችኋቸው	በላ አችሁ አቸው
	belacihu	bela acihu		belahut	bela acihu ti		belacihuacew	bela acihu acew
6	በሉ	በላ ኡ	14	በሉት	በላ ኡ ት	22	በሏቸው	በላ ኡ አቸው
	belu	bela u		belahut	bela u ti		beluacew	bela u acew
7	በላ	በላ ኧ	15	በላው	በላ ኧ ው	23	በላቸው	በላ ኧ አቸው
	bela	bela e		belahut	bela e wi		belacew	bela e acew
8	በላች	በላ ች	16	በላችው	በላ ኧች ው	24	በላቻቸው	በላ ች አቸው
	belac	bela c		belahut	bela ec wi		belacacew	bela c acew

Ethiopic dictionaries, like other Semitic dictionaries, use the past tense form of verbs inflected for the third person singular male (3PSM) pronoun as the headwords or lexemes.

morphemes. This exercise is significant because the Tigirinya triliteral በላዕ and its Amharic equivalent በላ can now be paired with (but not affixed to) each of their respective other pronouns as well as other grammatical elements—which is what the concept of modularization stands for—to create more sentences without increasing the number of word derivatives.

On the other hand, consider the Tigirinya single-word sentence በላዕኹዎ <belaiikhuwo> (I ate it), which becomes በላዕ ኹ ዎ <belaii khu wo> when de-synthesized. Notice that the last example has an additional pronoun (ዎ), which is a direct object, otherwise, the same verb is used in both Tigirinya single-word sentences. This object is different from the object in the word በላዕኹዎም <belaiikhuwom> (I ate them), which when de-synthesized becomes በላዕ ኹ ዎም. Similarly, consider the Amharic single-word sentence በላሁት <belahut> (I ate it), which becomes በላ ሁ ት <bela hu ti> when de-synthesized. Notice that the last example has an additional pronoun (ት), which is a direct object, otherwise, the same verb is used in both Amharic single-word sentences. This object is different from the object in the word በላኋቸው <belahuacew> (I ate them), which when de-synthesized becomes በላ ሁ አቸው. This exercise is significant because, the student of Tigirinya and Amharic can now clearly understand the relationship between a verb, a subject, and an object. Moreover, once the student masters the pronouns, he or she can easily make more sentences by combining the same verbs with the various pronouns.

Table 4.1 shows only thirty of the tens of thousands of derivatives of the verb ምብላዕ under the 'Original Word' columns. If we use the prefix ምስ- <mis->, which may mean "as soon as" depending on the context, for each of the verb derivatives in the table, we will effectively double the total number of word derivatives to sixty. For example, በላዕኹ becomes ምስበላዕኹ, በላዕና becomes ምስበላዕና, etc. Similarly, if we use the prefix እና- <ina-> (also alternately spelled እንዳ- <inda->) which is indicative of progressive action (Volume II: Chapter 2: The Ethiopic Grammatical Division One in Tigirinya), we will effectively triple the total number of word derivatives to ninety. For example, በላዕኹ becomes እናበላዕኹ, በላዕና becomes እናበላዕና, etc. If we use the prefix ም <mi>, which could mean 'would' as in 'I would eat,' we quadruple the total number of word derivatives to 120.

The number of word derivatives will continue to increase into the tens of thousands if we continue to add other affixes (**Appendix D**). However, by de-synthesizing these words as shown in the 'De-Synthesized Words' columns in **Table 4.1**, we can avoid the excessive number of word derivatives. By de-synthesizing or separating the basic components of the original words, we get one verb, ten subject pronouns and two object pronouns – a total of fourteen words rather than thirty derivative words. And, instead of adding a prefix that immediately doubles the number of word derivatives, a word would be used without adding any more derivatives. For example, instead of ምስበላዕኹ, we will have ምስ በላዕ ኹ.

Table 4.2 shows only twenty-four of the tens of thousands of derivatives of the verb መብላት under the 'Original Word' columns. As with the Tigirinya verb above, if we use prefixes and suffixes, the number of word derivatives for this verb will continue to increase into the tens of thousands. However, by de-synthesizing these words as shown in the 'De-Synthesized Words' columns in **Table 4.2**, we can avoid the excessive number of word derivatives.

On the other hand, consider a more complex word in Tigirinya ክምዘይተኻቲዕናልኩም and its Amharic equivalent እንዳልተሟገትንላችሁ, which when loosely translated into English make the clause: As if we did not advocate for you… The Tigirinya word is made up of six morphemes: ክም (as if), ዘይ ([negation]), ተኻቲዕ (advocate – *main verb*), ና (we), ል (for, in favour of), and ኩም (you). The Amharic word also is made up of six morphemes: እንደ (as if), ኣል ([negation]), ተሟገት (advocate – *main verb*), ን (we), ል (for, in favour of), and ኣችሁ (you). Such complex verb derivatives are common in both languages and are only two of the tens of thousands of verb derivatives possible for these verbs.

Careful observation of the words indicates that there are only a handful of affixes that are responsible for so many word derivatives. These are ሰ, ብ, ል, እንድ, ኣል ...., if these grammatical elements are separated, for the most part only the personal pronouns and the tenses will be left (the remaining being a little modification of the root word for gender and quantity).

Verb Inflections

One of the benefits of de-synthesizing of Ethiopic is the breaking up of verb derivatives so that the verb in its various inflected forms of its own is isolated from the rest of the component parts thereby providing the opportunity to identify the verb inflections and to reduce the massive number of verb derivatives. The proposed de-synthesizing of Ethiopic will also isolate the morpheme at the beginning of the infinitive forms of all verbs in the form of the prefixes ም <mi> in Tigirinya and መ <me> in Amharic from the actual verb. For example, the Tigirinya infinitive verb ምሕጻብ <mihhixab> (to wash) and its Amharic equivalent ማጠብ <matxeb> become ም ሕጻብ <mi hhixab> and መ ኣጠብ <me atxeb> respectively when de-synthesized. This exercise provides three consonantal characters or radicals for the base verb, which is the most common situation in Ethiopic grammar. The following are additional examples:

ምስራሕ <misirah> = ም ስራሕ <mi sirah>

ምድላይ <midilay> = ም ድላይ <mi dilay>

መስራት <mesirat> = መ ስራት <me sirat>

መሻት <meshat> = መ ሻት <me shat>

Often, verb inflections consist of all or most of the radicals with some modifications to one or more of them which indicates the influence of a vowel or vowels. However, since the current Ethiopic writing system does not have separate characters for vowels and consonants, such modifications are shown by changing the vowelic order of a given consonantal family. For example, ሓጸብ <hhaxeb> as in ሓጸብ ኩ ኦ <hhaxeb ku o> (I washed it) is one of the inflections of the Tigirinya base verb ሕጸብ or ም ሕጸብ discussed above. Similarly, ኣጥብ <atxib> as in እ ኣጥብ ኣለ ሁ <i atxib ale hu> (I wash) is one of the inflections of the Amharic base verb ኣጠብ or መ ኣጠብ discussed above.

In Tigirinya and Amharic, verb inflections are one of the most important features of Ethiopic grammar. Verbs are inflected to express variations in grammatical tense, voice, and (to some extent) person.

Verb Inflections Due to Grammatical Tense

Except for auxiliary verbs, all Ethiopic verbs have four verb inflections to indicate grammatical tense. While a single verb inflection can be used to express multiple tenses simply by employing different auxiliary verbs, the number of verb inflections can number as many as four in the active voice and another four in the passive voice. For example, each of the Tigirinya base verbs ም ብላዕ <mi bilaii> and ም ሕጻብ <mi hhixab> have four inflected forms and have the same number of characters or radicals as the corresponding base verb (**Table 4.3**). ም ብላዕ has three radicals—ብ-ላ-ዕ <bi-la-ii>—which is the same as the number of radicals in each of its inflections. However, the first character of the first inflection በ <be> is different from the corresponding character in the base verb ብ <bi>, even though they are both from the same consonantal family.

The dissimilarity is a result of a change in the underlining vowel with the underlining consonant remaining the same. This can be referred to as a change in the Ethiopic vowelic order (horizontal position) within the same consonantal family (vertical position). The second and third inflections have their first two characters assume different vowelic orders, while the last inflection incidentally shows no change. By contrast, all of the inflections of ም ሕጻብ have at least one character different from any other one. Similarly, the Amharic base verbs መ ብላት <me bilat> and መ አጠብ <me atxeb> have verb inflections that are sometimes dissimilar to the base verb (**Table 4.4**). Except for TYPE "ET" VERBS (Volume II: Chapter 11: Types of Verbs in Tigirinya & Amharic), such as the verb መ ብላት, most verb inflections keep the basic triliteral form.

Table 4.3: Examples of Tigirinya verb inflections due to grammatical tense

INFINITIVE VERB FORM	VERB INFLECTION (ACTIVE VOICE ONLY)			EXAMPLE	
1 ም ብላዕ	1	በላዕ	belaii	በላዕ ና	belaii na (We ate)
mi bilaii	2	በሊዕ	beleeii	በሊዕ ና ኢ. ና	beleeii na ee na (We have eaten)
(to eat)	3	በልዕ	beliii	ን በልዕ ኢ. ና	ni beliii ee na (We eat)
	4	ብላዕ	bilaii	ን ብላዕ	ni bilaii (Let's eat)
2 ም ሕጻብ	1	ሓጸብ	hhaxeb	ሓጸብ ና	hhaxeb ku (We washed)
mi hhixab	2	ሓጺብ	hhaxeeb	ሓጺብ ና ዮ ኢ. ና	hhaxeeb na yo ee na (We have washed it)
(to wash)	3	ሓጽብ	hhaxib	ን ሓጽብ ኢ. ና	ni hhaxib ee na (We wash)
	4	ሕጸብ	hhixeb	ን ሕጸብ	ni hhixeb (Let's wash)

The Ethiopic auxiliary verbs, on the other hand, are the most irregular of all verb types consisting less than four verb inflections each. The verb inflections of each irregular verb often show dissimilarities in the number and types of radicals or characters to the extent that most do not appear to be verb inflections of the same base verb.

Table 4.4: Examples of Amharic verb inflections due to grammatical tense

	INFINITIVE VERB FORM		VERB INFLECTION (ACTIVE VOICE ONLY)		EXAMPLE	
1	መ ብላት	1	በልላ	bella	በላ ን	bella ni (We ate)
	me bilat	2	በልተ	belite	በልተ ን ኣል	belite ni al (We have eaten)
	(to eat)	3	በላ	bela	እን በላ ኣለ ን	in bela ale ni (We eat)
		4	ብላ	bila	እን ብላ	in bila (Let's eat)
2	መ ኣጠብ	1	ኣጥጠብ	atxxeb	ኣጥጠብ ን	atxxeb ni (We washed)
	me atxeb	2	ኣጥበ	atxibe	ኣጥበ ን ኧ ው ኣል	atxibe ni e wi al (We have washed it)
	(to wash)	3	ኣጥብ	atxib	እን ኣጥብ ኣለ ን	in atxib ale ni (We wash)
		4	እጠብ	atxeb	እን እጠብ	in atxeb (Let's wash)

Verb Inflections Due to Grammatical Voice

Grammatical voices create parallel sets of verb inflections for transitive verbs mirroring the influence of grammatical tenses. Verb inflections due to grammatical voice affect the infinitive form of the verb as well as the rest of the verb forms. All phrases, clauses, and sentences can be constructed using Ethiopic infinitive verbs, such as the Tigirinya verbs ም ብላዕ <mi bilaii> and ም ሕጻብ <mi hhixab> (**Table 4.5**) and the Amharic verbs መ ብላት <me bilat> and መ ኣጠብ <me atxeb>, or one of their corresponding verb inflections. The proposed de-synthesization means that all grammatical features, including grammatical voice, will be marked by free standing morphemes or words along with the appropriate verb inflection and, therefore, there will be few or no verb derivatives. In other words, by de-synthesizing verb derivatives, it is possible to virtually eliminate tens of thousands of derivatives that each base verb used to have under the traditional orthography.

The implications of this exercise are far-reaching—not only will this make it easier to understand Ethiopic grammar better, but it will also open up the opportunity to systematically collect, catalog, analyze, and disseminate linguistic information thereby ushering in a golden age for Ethiopic grammar. As part of a transitional step to a full-blown Ethiopic alphabet (Chapters 6, 7, and 8), gemination in a verb inflection shall be shown by placing a *sadis* (6th order) copy of the geminated character in front of the same geminated character (**Tables 4.5** and **4.6**).

Applications of and Exceptions to the Proposed De-Synthesization

In addition to Tigirinya, Amharic, and other Ethiosemitic languages, the proposed de-synthesization is meant to be applied to Giiz. Even though it is no longer in popular use, Giiz continues to serve vital roles for liturgical purposes by the Ethiopian Orthodox Church and for the study of Ethiopian linguistics, history, and culture. Applying the reform to Giiz grammar, just like the Tigirinya and Amharic grammars, will help unlock the keys to understanding Giiz and make it more accessible to future generations.

Table 4.5: Examples of Tigirinya verb inflections due to grammatical voice

ACTIVE VOICE				PASSIVE VOICE				
INFINITIVE FORM	VERB INFLECTION			INFINITIVE FORM	VERB INFLECTION		EXAMPLE	
ም ብላዕ (mi bilaii)	1	በላዕ	belaii	ም ብብላዕ (mi bbilaii)	ተ በልዕ	te beliii	ቲ ሕብስቲ ተ በልዕ አ	tee hhibisiti te beliii e
	2	በሊዕ	beleeii		ተ በሊዕ	te beleeii	ቲ ሕብስቲ ተ በሊዕ ኡ ኣለ ዎ	..... te beleeii u ale wo
	3	በልልዕ	beliii		ብልላዕ	bellaii	ቲ ሕብስቲ ከ ብልላዕ ኢ ዩ	..... ki billaii ee u
	4	ብላዕ	bilaii		(ተ) በላዕ	(te) belaii	ቲ ሕብስቲ ዩ በላዕ	..... yee belaii
ም ሕጻብ (mi hhixeb)	1	ሓጻብ	hhaxeb	ም ትት ሕጻብ (mi tti hhixab)	ተ ሓጻብ	te hhaxeb	ተ ሓጻብ አ	te hhaxeb
	2	ሓጺብ	hhaxeeb		ተ ሓጺብ	te hhaxeeb	ተ ሓጺብ ኡ ኣለ ዎ	Te hhaxeeb u ale wo
	3	ሓጽጽብ	hhaxxib		ሕጽጻብ	hhixxeb	ዩ ሕጽጻብ ኢ ኡ	Yee hhixxeb ee u
	4	ሕጻብ	hhixeb		ተ ሓጻብ	te hhaxeb	ዩ ተ ሓጻብ	Yee te hhaxeb

Table 4.6: Examples of Amharic verb inflections due to grammatical voice

ACTIVE VOICE				PASSIVE VOICE				
INFINITIVE FORM	VERB INFLECTION			INFINITIVE FORM	VERB INFLECTION		EXAMPLE	
መ ብላት (me bilat)	1	በልላ	bella	መ ብበላተ (me bbelat)	ተ በልላ	te bella	ዳቦ ዉ ተ በልላ ኧ	dabo wu te bella e
	2	በልተ	belite		ተ በልተ	te belite	ዳቦ ዉ ተ በልተ አ አል	dabo wu te belit o al
	3	በላ	bela		በልላ	bella	ዳቦ ዉ ል ዩ በልላ ነው	dabo wu li yee bella new
	4	ብላ	bila		(ተ) (ብ)በላ	(te) (b)bela	ዳቦ ዉ ዩ ብበላ	dabo wu yee bbela
መ አጠብ (me atxeb)	1	አጥጠብ	atxxeb	መ ትተ አጠብ (me tte atxeb)	ተ አጥጠብ	te atxxeb	ተ አጥጠብ ኧ	te atxxeb e
	2	አጥበ	atxibe		ተ አጥበ	te atxibe	ተ አጥበ አ አል	te atxibe o al
	3	አጥብ	atxib		ተ አጠብ	te atxeb	ዩ ተ አጠብ አለ ኧ	yee te atxeb ale e
	4	እጠብ	atxeb		ተ አጠብ	te atxeb	ዩ ተ አጠብ	yee te atxeb

However, there are going to be exceptions to the application of the proposed de-synthesization. For example, proper names, such as ኣንዳርጋቸው, which is made up of the words ኣንድ-ኣድርግ-ኣችቸው are exceptions. Proper names of the type ተወልደ-መድህን or ሃይለ-ስልላሴ could be made single-word, two-word, or hyphenated names depending on the choice of individuals. Moreover, certain words that are grammatically easier to keep as single words, such as the Amharic word ይሆን (as in "ት መጣ ይሆን?"), which is made up of the two words ዩ and ሆን shall be considered indivisible. Similarly, the words ብምኳኑ <bimikhuanu> and በመሆኑ <bemehonu>, which mean "as a result" or "therefore," in Tigirinya and Amharic, respectively, shall remain indivisible.

The Ethiopic Divisions

The Ethiopic divisions are one of the most important features of Ethiopic grammar.

As mentioned above, almost all base verbs have four verb inflections in each grammatical voice. These inflections have certain characteristics that separate them from each other—such as the type of pronouns that they can be paired with—and will be categorized into what we shall refer to as DIVISIONS. Understanding the divisions is the key to Ethiopic grammar. In fact, the divisions are one of the most important features of Ethiopic grammar introduced by this book. The discovery and use of the Ethiopic divisions is a direct result of the concept of de-synthesization or reverse derivation introduced in this chapter. Since very little can be known about Ethiopic grammar without the concept of the divisions, a large portion of Volume II (Chapters 1 to 8) is dedicated to the divisions.

CHAPTER 5

OVERVIEW OF LANGUAGE CRISIS AND MISCOMMUNICATION IN ETHIOPIA

Politics and government are public activities, and so politicians and public servants should use language that people find clear, accurate and understandable… [T]oo often official language distorts or confuses meaning. This is damaging because it can prevent public understanding of policies and their consequences, and can also deter people from getting access to public services and benefits. We conclude that bad official language which results in tangible harm—such as preventing someone from receiving the benefits or services to which they are entitled—should be regarded as "maladministration"… Bad official language deserves to be mocked, but it also needs to be taken seriously.

—UNITED KINGDOM PARLIAMENTARIANS' REPORT
Bad Language: The Use and Abuse of Official Language, 2009

IN THIS CHAPTER

Currently, Ethiopia is in the midst of a language crisis despite its great civilization and anthropological history. The state of human language and communication in today's Ethiopia has never been at a more critical stage and will have profound implications for generations to come. Bad language and the resulting miscommunication are the most visible manifestations of the Ethiopian language crisis. The unprecedented socio-economic progress in Ethiopia requires ever more accurate and efficient communication. On the contrary, the nation's language assets are being neglected to the extent that, ironically, Ethiopian urbanites are today a lot less able to communicate accurately using their first language than their counterparts in the countryside. Embarrassing as it may be for a proud nation like Ethiopia, most grown up urbanite speakers of South Central Amharic, regardless of social position or educational status, are unable to complete most verbal and written communications using correct grammar, such as correct grammatical tenses, and accurate vocabulary. For the purpose of this book, BAD LANGUAGE shall be defined as the use of a particular language as a means of communication without properly following the conventional rules of the language thereby creating miscommunication. Bad language, which is different from the grammatical and orthographic challenges inherent in Ethiopic (Chapter 4: Overview of Ethiopic Morphology and the Concept of De-Synthesization) but compounded by it, is a growing chronic problem in Ethiopia. Since the use of language as a means of communication presupposes that both the speaker and the listener have the same understanding of the rules of the language or grammar, the immediate consequence of substandard or bad language use is miscommunication. Merriam-Webster.com defines miscommunication as 'failure to communicate clearly.' The definition provided by Dictionay.com is 'to communicate mistakenly, unclearly, or inadequately.'

Bad language use seems to be growing in Ethiopia at a time when the need for accurate communication has become most urgent.

Depending on the situation, the consequences of mistaken, unclear, or inadequate communications could be simple annoyances; or they could endanger individual persons' lives or the prosperity and security of a nation. During emergency evacuations, complicated medical procedures, handling of hazardous materials, conducting security searches, or at a time of war, accurate communication or lack thereof could mean the difference between life and death. However, most miscommunications happen during daily routines under less dramatic circumstances making the consequences often unnoticed or seem trivial and, therefore, continue to affect relational, professional, economic, political, and social progress of society for generations—unless a comprehensive language reform is implemented. It is not my intention to champion for a prescriptive type of grammar for Ethiosemitic languages. However, it is clear that in a nation where the use of language as effective means of communication has not been properly developed, setting the groundwork for proper language use is long overdue.

Background to the Ethiopian Language Crisis

Amharic and other Ethiopian languages are not supported by an extensive body of literary works and scientific studies that characterize other major languages of the world due to various historical reasons. Lack of proper language policy by successive governments, decades of sociopolitical turmoil, and extreme poverty are among the problems that hampered quality education and implementation of innovative ideas for language development. Moreover, dependence on English as the medium of instruction in the country meant that there was very little need to develop Ethiopian languages.

While bad language use affects both Tigirinya and Amharic, the problem is more prevalent in urban Ethiopia where Amharic is more popular. Interestingly, the Amharic spoken in rural Amhara, the birthplace of Amharic, shows fewer signs of bad language use than what we shall refer to as SOUTH CENTRAL AMHARIC—the Amharic spoken outside of rural Amhara, particularly in the major urban areas such as Addis Ababa. It is important to make the distinction between Amharic proper and South Central Amharic (SCA). SCA is distinct not only because of a slightly different accent but also more importantly by the extremely bad use of grammar and poor vocabulary combined with informal expressions and slang.

Owing to its size and socio-economic and political status, the influence of Addis Ababa over the rest of Ethiopia is monumental.

I propose that one of the most important reasons for the prevalence of bad language use in South Central Amharic is the change of the Ethiopian centre of politics to areas south of what is today Amhara Region. Unlike Tigirinya, South Central Amharic lost its original homeland long time ago, which brought about adverse consequences to the quality of the language as much as it helped expand it. When the seat of government moved to central Ethiopia at the end of the 19th century and rulers continued using Amharic as the official language, the language suddenly lost its stronghold—the Amhara hinterland where it was born. Suddenly, Amharic was exposed to too many second language speakers who did not yet master its grammar, vocabulary, and writing system, resulting in the deterioration of Amharic's power to convey accurate information, while at the same time helping rapidly increase the number of new speakers. Further, I propose that the lack of a very strong literary culture meant that the 'broken' Amharic of the multitudes of new speakers could not be counteracted by the availability of printed materials in Amharic that could serve as a bulwark against the erroneous use of the language. There is no doubt that non-native Amharic speakers have enriched and still continue to enrich South Central Amharic, and that its status as the language of the central government has somewhat helped it grow in vocabulary (though very little of it has trickled down to the general public). However, because it is affected by the widespread use of bad language, it can also be argued that South Central Amharic is a victim of its own success.

Unfortunately, what most people consider to be standard Amharic is only that spoken in Addis Ababa and a few other major towns in the country. As a result, today, poor language use is widespread in almost all cities including the nation's capital Addis Ababa, where Amharic is the working language, and many other Ethiopian languages are also spoken. In addition to being the seat of government and where most of the Ethiopian news media organizations and broadcasters are stationed, what goes in Addis Ababa affects the rest of the country as far as bad language use is concerned. Effective communication requires the provision of information relevant to the circumstances. In other words, the type and quality of information exchanged in a given communication determine the effectiveness of the communication or the desired outcome of the communication. Language is a powerful tool for communication but its power for communication relies on intricate grammatical rules that must be observed for the speaker and listener to understand each other correctly.

Most journalists, university professors, politicians and government officials in Ethiopia, who may otherwise be highly sophisticated, are not immune to bad language use. Most of these people were born into and raised in a society that was too busy coping with socio-economic and political ills that lingered for generations and therefore did not have the will or the need to study and develop language as an effective means of communication. Compounding the problem has been the use of English as the medium of instruction throughout Ethiopia from beyond grade six to higher education. Unfortunately, this has now resulted in what can be described as the Ethiopian language crisis, in which, Ethiopia is using a borrowed language, English, and using it extremely badly at the same time systematically, if unwittingly, destroying its domestic languages.

Bad Styles or Habits

It has been said that bad habits die hard, but all efforts must be done to unlearn bad habits that have menaced proper language use in Ethiopia. The major bad habits related to the use of Tigirinya and Amharic are discussed below.

Use of *Bado* Words

One of the poorest language uses in contemporary Ethiopic is the use of what we shall call *bado words* in conversations. The word "bado" in Tigirinya and Amharic means, "empty," "non-existent," or "zero." Therefore, *bado* words are words that have no meaning on their own but are used as placeholders for a word, phrase or concept that a speaker could not supply during a conversation for various reasons. *Bado* words are extremely common, especially in Amharic conversations, that any given conversation between any group of people, even at formal gatherings (though less frequently), contain multiple occurrences of them. The reasons for the use of *bado* words can be a temporary loss of memory, cultural tolerance for inaccurate communication, and the failure of the education system in general. Often, *bado* words are not replaced by the intended words before or after the speaker finishes uttering his or her thoughts, in part because the speaker may not want to pause to think and supply the missing words. Sometimes the listener offers the missing words, if he or she knows them, by interjecting into the speech. However, since the average conversation contains too many *bado* words, the listener often politely ignores them. On the other hand, sometimes the speaker may not want to be too clear or too straightforward, such as when discussing things considered taboo, prompting him or her use *bado* words.

Often, the average person is unable to articulate an idea or event very well in a concise manner and therefore resorts to the use of too many *bado* words in a socially tolerated culture that somehow the listener would know the missing word, phrase or concept. Or if the listener is so interested, he or she would ask questions followed by answers by the speaker and then with more questions and answers until the desired level of clarity is achieved. Unfortunately, this style of conversation is 'normal' in urban areas and compounds the problem of ineffective communication. Ineffective communication is not only limited to the general population, but it also affects professionals, intellectuals, and politicians with severe consequences to the development of the country.

Tigirinya and Amharic have single-word *bado* words and phrasal *bado* words that undermine effective communication. The single-word *bado* words used in Tigirinya and Amharic are ክሲታይ <kisitay> and እንትን <initin>, respectively, which do not have a direct equivalent in English. However, phrasal equivalents in English would be "what's his name," "what's his face," etc. Amharic also uses additional, if less frequently used, *bado* words, such as ምኑም <minum> as in ሰዊም ምኑም አንድ ላይ ዩ ኖር አለለ ኡ. The use of *bado* words, especially in Amharic, does not seem to be new. More than a century ago, Armbruster (1908) included at least one reference to the Amharic *bado* word እንትን in his book *Initia Amharica: An Introduction to spoken Amharic*. However, it appears that the frequency of the use of *bado* words in Ethiopic has increased over time because of increased urbanization, the influence of slang, the declining quality of language education in the country, and

The use of *bado* words in Ethiopic conversations, which is an extremely bad habit, should be discouraged.

the continued use of English as the medium of instruction in the nation. While I have no scientific data, personal observations I made regarding language use in less urbanized areas of Tigiray and Amhara regions show that there is very little use of *bado* words in those areas.

The prevalence of the practice of using *bado* words is such that it is destroying the capacity of the languages, especially that of South Central Amharic, to convey accurate information. To illustrate this, consider the following transcript from a town hall meeting in 2014 in which, His Excellency Foreign Minister Tedros Adhanom Ghebreyesus was being asked a question in Amharic from a particular audience member who won the laughter of the audience by their use of too many *bado* words that totally obscured their question. Of the two questions the person attempted to present to the minister, the second more interesting one is presented below. In total the person used six *bado* words, including using three of them in the same sentence, which ended up making no sense. The person also used several English words, even though each of the English word used has a simple Amharic equivalent. Although, the speaker seemed fluent in Amharic, the most interesting thing may even be that they ended up providing no question at all. My translation of the words below follows the Amharic transcript, which shows the English words originally used by the person in Latin letters.

> ሁለተኛው ጥያቄዬ ደግሞ international የሆነ question ነው። ይሄ በአሁኑ ሰዓት በዓለም ላይ ያለው እንትን ነው-- climate change፤ እና ደኖች እየተጨፈጨፉ ነው። ደኖች እያለቁ ነው። ግን ደኖቹ የሚያልቁት በምን ምክንያት ነው? ከችግር አንጻር ነው። ችግሩ ምንድን ነው? ሰዎች ሌላ አይነት ምንም አይነት አማራጭ ስለሌላቸው፣ ያንን እንጭት ለቀን እንትን-ኣቸው ለልጆቻቸው ማሳደጊያም ሆነ ለጉሮሯቸው ሲሉ ያንን እንጨት እንትን እያሉ ይሸጣሉ። ያ ደን እንትን በሚልበት ሰዓት ያው ረሃቡም ምኑም አብሮ ነው እንትን የሚለው እና፣ anyway፤ thank you።[1]
>
> And my second question is a question that is international. It is this *bodo word* that is in the world at this hour [sic]—climate change; so forests are being destroyed. But, what is the cause of the destruction of the forests? It is in respect [sic.] of destitution. What is the problem? Since people do not have any other another [sic.] kind of option, that wood [sic.], for their daily *bado word* whether for raising their children or for their feeding, they sell that wood by doing *bado word.* At the hour [sic.] that forest becomes *bado word,* obviously famine and *bado word* together become *bado word* so, anyway, thank you.

Use of *Anitata* or *Aniteta* instead of *Anitumita* or *Anituta*

Always use *anitumita* or *anituta* in formal settings, when not sure, or when refering to persons who would otherwise be referred to in their last name, for example, in a Western context.

The use of the informal *ATTATA* or *ANICETA*, in Tigirinya and Amharic respectively, instead of the formal *ATTUMITA* or *ANITUTA* refers to the wrong way of addressing a person in the informal/non-polite style where the formal/polite style is more appropriate. The Amharic term *anituta*—from 'anitu,' another word for the polite form of the 2PS pronoun, and 'ta,' an Ethiopic noun making morpheme—is an existing term that refers to the use of formal or polite pronouns in referring to or addressing someone in the second person or the third person. The equivalent Tigirinya word is what I propose to be *anitumita* from the Tigirinya words 'anitum' and 'ta,' similar to the manner the Amharic term is constructed. On the other hand, I am proposing the words *anitata* and *aniteta* for Tigirinya and Amharic respectively from the words *anita* and *anite* and the common noun maker *ta* to represent the practice of referring to or addressing a person in an informal, friendly, or sometimes even disrespectful manner. The closest comparison to the use of *anitumita* or *anituta* in the Western culture is the manner of addressing a person by his or her last name, while *anitata* or *aniteta* is equivalent to addressing a person by his or her first name.

The informal/non-polite forms are often wrongly used in situations where the formal/polite forms should be used such as in national news articles. Indicative of racial and gender bias, the less polite terms are often used when the reference is made to a non-Ethiopian person, regardless of skin colour, and especially when that person is female. For example, a 2014 Amharic article on a national newspaper about the life and achievements of the American author, poet, dancer, and singer Ms. Maya Angelou, who died at age 86, referred to her in the informal/diminutive *aniteta* style, while the President of the United States was referred to in the formal/polite *anituta* style in the same article.[2] Such inappropriate addressing of a person is especially wrong since, in the Ethiopian cultural norm, the formal/polite style is considered even more fitting to older people.

Discussing the visit to Ethiopia by United States President Barack Obama in 2015, the title and subtitle of an Amharic article by another national newspaper referred to the president in the informal/non-polite style before it switched to the formal/polite style typical of the inconsistencies in Amharic literature as follows:

> ኦባማ ስለዴሞክራሲ አልተናገረምን [non-polite]?
> ኦባማ ኬንያንና ኢትዮጵያን ጎብኝቶ [non-polite] ወደ አገሩ ተመልሷል [non-polite]። ጉብኝቱ ታሪካዊ ነበር። በሥልጣን ላይ እያሉ [polite] ኢትዮጵያን የጎበኙ [polite] የመጀመሪያው የአሜሪካ ፕሬዚዳንት ናቸው [polite]። [3]

The first of the following two sentences from another news article also indicates gender bias within the Ethiopian context by referring to the two people in the article (who happen to be male and female siblings), using the polite or formal form *anituta* to the male and the informal form *aniteta* to the female. The second sentence, typical of the inconsistencies in Amharic literature, reverts to the formal form to refer to the same female.

> የ72 ዓመቱ አዛውንት ... ታምማ [non-polite – the female] ዘውዲቱ ሆስፒታል የተኛች [non-polite – the female] እህታቸውን [polite – the male] ለመጠየቅ ሄዱ [polite – the male]:: ሆስፒታል ደርሰው [polite – the male] እህታቸው [polite – the male] ወደተኙበት [polite – the female] ክፍል ለመሄድ የሊፍቱን መጥሪያ ሲጫኑት [polite – the male] ተከፈተ::[4]

Confusing Presumption for Politeness

When requesting someone to do something, speakers of Amharic often unknowingly use expressions that are problematic at best and rude at worst. Consider the following sentence, which may be considered offensive if it is not an innocent mistake:

> እድምተኞች ኣችችን ጥሪ ኣችችን ን ኣክብር ኣችቹህ ይህ ን ስብሰባ ለ መ ክካፈል በ መ ገኝኘት ኣችቹህ እን ኣመሰግን ኣልለ ን። ኣሁን ት ቅቀመጥ ኣልለ ኣችቹህ።
>
> Dear invitees, thank you for responding to our invitation and for being here to attend this meeting. Now, you will sit down.

Obviously, the problem is in the second sentence. Whereas the sentence is grammatically correct, it lacks politeness and formality. Often, such grammatical formation is used when people are upset and want to show their authority ordering their subordinates or when they want to threaten someone. For example,

> የ በልላ ህ በ ት ን ሰሃን ት አጥብ ኣልለ ህ! ትንፍሽ እንድ ኣል ት እል!
> You will wash your dish! And you will not answer me back!

Whereas the use of this expression to tell a future course of action ahead of time or to order someone with rudeness is old, anecdotal evidence suggests that confusing such terms for politeness is a more recent development and is currently considered fashionable even during formal events. It is also interesting to note that some Ethiopians who speak English as their second language carry the problem of confusing presumption for politeness into their English. The following transcription from an actual event posted on social media illustrates the problem. While inviting the Ethiopian ambassador to Canada to make a speech at an Ethiopian community event in Toronto, the Ethiopian coordinator of the event, who spoke English as a second language, said the following words:

> "[Your] Excellency Birtukan Ayano, who is ambassador of Ethiopia, you're going to give us a short speech..."[5]

Confusion of Concept or Message

A 2012 article on the website of one of the prominent Amharic-language newspapers in Ethiopia had a title that contradicted the message in the article. The title erroneously read, "የህገወጥ ፊልሞች ኪሳራ በዝቷል." When translated, this would mean: "Illegal films' loss of money has increased." However, from the article one was able to determine that a better title would read: በሕገወጥ የፊልም ቅጂዎች ጠንቅ ኪሳራ በዝቷል (The loss of revenue due to pirated films has increased). The error in the original title was less typographical than a reflection of the current poor language use in the country and society's tolerance of it.

Failure to Apply Correct Yes-No Question Structure

In Tigirinya and Amharic, questions are constructed following certain grammatical rules, although the rules in Amharic are often ignored for yes-no type questions. Every Tigirinya interrogative sentence in the form of a yes-no type question is constructed by adding the Tigirinya question making participle ዶ<do> and a question mark at the end of an otherwise affirmative or declarative sentence. Similarly, every Amharic interrogative sentence in the form of a yes-no type question is constructed by adding one of several Amharic question making elements, such as ነዐ <ni> and ወየ <wey>, and a question mark at the end of an otherwise affirmative or declarative sentence. Amharic speakers often use only intonation instead of a proper sentence structure when making a yes-no question. Such questions are written with just a question mark at the end of an otherwise affirmative sentence. The following are examples of questions asked by a reporter in an interview which was published in a national newspaper.

> በቀለም ትምህርት ላይ ሥነ ጥበብ እንዲታከልበት በመደረጉ በእጅ ሥራ ወይም በዕደ ጥበብ ዙርያ የተገኘ ወይም የታየ አዲስ ነገርና ለውጥ አለ? (Literally: By adding art into academic lessons, there is a new thing and change in handicraft or artwork?)
>
> ኢሕአዴግ በአሁኑ ወቅት በመላ አገሪቱ ዩኒቨርሲቲዎችን የማስፋፋት ሥራ የሚያኪያሂደው ምናልባት ከቀድሞው ሥርዓት በተወረሰ ዕቅድ ነው ማለት ይቻላል?
>
> ይህ ዓይነቱን አካሄድ ተከትለው ውጤታማ የሆኑ አገሮች አሉ?
>
> በዘውድ፣ በደርግና አሁን ባለው ጭምር ካለው የመማርና የማስተማር ሒደትና አገሪቱ ነፃነቷን ጠብቃ ለረጅም ዘመናት ከመኖሯ አኳያ ሲታይ በትምህርት ዘርፍ ከፍተኛ የሆነ መሻሻል ታይቷል ለማለት ይቻላል?

Failure to Use Quotation Marks Where Appropriate and Other Poor Writing Styles

Often written documents show no quotation marks for direct quotes, or when quotation marks are shown, they are applied inconsistently. Moreover, the grammatical tenses used often fail to represent the sequence of action properly; and sometimes several full stops are included in what is supposed to be a single sentence. In the following example from a news article in a national newspaper, the first sentence uses quotation marks for a direct quote, while the second sentence uses none for two direct quotes included in the sentence. Also, notice the absurd use of two Ethiopic full stops between the quotation marks in the first sentence. Moreover, the first sentence uses the Ethiopic present perfect tense, which is wrong because the second sentence, which documented action that took place after the first one, uses the Ethiopic simple past tense.

> እሳቸው የወከሏቸው ሜዲካል ዳይሬክተር “አሁን ስብሰባ ላይ ነኝ፡፡ ስለጉዳዩ ድንገተኛ ክፍል ጠይቁ። ለእኔም የነገሩኝ እነሱ ናቸው” ብለውናል። ድንገተኛ ክፍል ስንጠይቅ በዕለቱ ተረኛ የነበሩትን ዶክተሮች አነጋግሩ የተባልን ሲሆን ተረኛ ዶክተሮቹ በበኩላቸው፤ ኦፐሬሽን እያደረግን ስለሆነ እስከንጨርስ ጠብቁ አሉን።[6]

Redundancy Due to Repeated Words, Such as Pronouns and Verbs

Redundancy is very common in Ethiopic literature, and this happens mostly because of the representation of the subject or object more than once. Consider the following sentence:

> አስተዳዳሪውን ልናናግራቸው እንፈልጋለን። (ኣስተዳዳሪ ኡ ን ል እን ኣንናግር ኣችቸው እን ፈልልግ ኣልለ ን።)
>
> We would like to speak with the administrator. (More literally: The administrator [future indicator] we talk him we want [present indicator] us.)

The subject in the sentence above has been represented three times (**እን**, **እን**, and **ን** / *we*, *we*, and *us*) and the object twice (**ኣስተዳዳሪው** and **ኣችቸው** / *the administrator* and *him*). These repetitions are easy to be overlooked because the old orthography fuses several words into one. Now, let's eliminate as many pronouns as the grammar allows to simplify the sentence. We can eliminate one subject pronoun and one object pronoun by using the infinitive form of the verb and get the same message as follows:

> **ኣስተዳዳሪ ኡ ን መ ኣንናገር እን ፈልልግ ኣልለ ን።** We want to talk to the administrator. (Literally: Administrator the [accusative] to talk we want [present indicator] us.)

The above sentence is concise in that it makes use of words more efficiently than the first sentence. Therefore, the rule of thumb in avoiding redundancy in Ethiopic literature is to apply as few pronouns in a phrase, clause or sentence as possible.

Consider the following sentence, where the words that created redundancy are underlined.

> የ መጀመሪያ ኡ ልጅ ስም ፋሲል ዩ ብባል ነበበር። (Literally: The name of the first child was called Faseel.)

A better sentence would be “የ መጀመሪያ ኡ ልጅ ፋሲል ዩ ብባል ነበበር” by deleting the first underlined word or “የ መጀመሪያ ኡ ልጅ ስም ፋሲል ነበበር,” by deleting the second set of underlined words.

Redundancy in Using the Conjunctions እንና and ም

The Amharic words **እንና** <inna> and **ም** <mi> are conjunctions that are used to connect words much like the English word 'and.' However, using both of them at the same time as in the following sentence creates redundancy.

የ ሸቀጦች ን ዋጋ መ ቀንነስ እንና ኣይነት ኣቾቸው ን ም መ ኣብዛት ለ ገበያ ጥሩ ነው።

The following examples use only one occurrence of the conjunction in each sentence:

የ ሸቀጦች ን ዋጋ መ ቀንነስ እንና ኣይነት ኣቾቸው ን መ ኣብዛት ለ ገበያ ጥሩ ነው።
የ ሸቀጦች ን ዋጋ መ ቀንነስ፣ ኣይነት ኣቾቸው ን ም መ ኣብዛት ለ ገበያ ጥሩ ነው።

Use of Wrong Adjectives When Referring to Nationality

In Tigirinya and Amharic, almost all adjectives for nationality or citizenship end in **ኣዊ** <awee> for the singular form and **ኣዊያን** <aweean> for the plural form. An example is the Ethiopic adjective **ኢትዮጵያዊ** (**ኢትዮጵያ-ኣዊ**) <Etiyopxiyawee (Etiyopxiya-awee)> (in this case the two **ኣ** <a>'s are assimilated into one). However, Tigirinya and Amharic are different in the way they form their adjectives for residents of regions or towns and those for members of a party, group, or association. For example, residents of the regions of Tigiray and Amhara, Tigirayans and Amharas, respectively, are referred to in Tigirinya as **ተጋሩ** <Tegaru> and **ኣምሓሩ** <Amihharu>, while they are referred to in Amharic as **ትግራዮች** <Tigirayoc> and **ኣማሮች** <Amaroc>.

The Tigirinya adjectives for such applications vary, while Amharic almost always uses the name of the party, group, or association as the singular form of the adjective, while it adds the morpheme **ኦች** <oc> at the end of the name for the plural form. Speakers of South Central Amharic, however, wrongly replace the adjective maker **ኣዊ** <awee> with the other adjective maker **ኦች** <oc> to refer to nationals of countries. An example is ***ኣሜሪካኖች** <*Ameireecanoc> from the English adjective 'American.' The correct adjective in Ethiopic is **ኣሜሪካዊያን** <Ameireecaweean> (Americans).

Use of Slang and Informal Expressions in Formal Settings

In addition to the widespread grammatical and syntactic errors, it is common to hear speakers of South Central Amharic routinely use informal expressions and slang even in formal situations. Examples are the use of the word **መኣት** <meat> (disaster, calamity) to mean 'many,' and the phrase **በ ኣሁን ሰዓት** <be ahun seat> (at this hour) to mean 'now,' 'nowadays,' or 'at this time' (**Appendix D**).

Grammar and Vocabulary

The fusional nature of the GTA languages and their phonetic writing system have made it very difficult for speakers of the languages to detect and eliminate grammatically erroneous expressions in the written word, particularly in South Central Amharic where the grammatical rules are ignored more often. These problems are made even more severe due to the negative effects of the use of English as the medium of education in the country.

Guramayilei: Excessive use of Foreign Words in Ethiosemitic languages

English loanwords, phrases, and even idioms have increasingly been creeping into Ethiosemitic languages for several decades now, and the result is what some refer to as *GURAMAYILEI*—a mix of English and Ethiopic that is increasingly decimating Ethiopic grammar. Whereas it is natural for languages to grow by borrowing words from other languages (and this is not new for Ethiosemitic languages), the rate at which English is allowed to infiltrate into these languages and the negative way it is affecting their grammar is staggering. In addition to the healthy interactions with and borrowing of words from Ethiocushitic languages, Ethiosemitic languages had for generations borrowed words from other languages, such as Arabic and Italian, slowly and without creating structural damage to the receiving languages. However, the fact that English has been the mandatory medium of instruction in Ethiopian schools since the 1950's means that it has been relentlessly damaging Ethiopian languages unbeknownst to most speakers. In the first decades of the 21st century, this phenomenon has become even acuter probably due to Ethiopia's massive education drive and the effect of technology and globalization, although the insertion of European words into Ethiopic dates back many decades (Desita, 1970).

Nevertheless, anecdotal evidence suggests that a generation ago, it was relatively rare to hear English words in conversations outside of the media and the elite. Today, it is almost impossible not to hear several English words in any conversation no matter how rudimentary the conversation may be. Often speakers of Tigirinya and Amharic insert English words in their conversations when equivalent Tigirinya or Amharic words are already available and should suffice. While this problem is widespread in written materials, it is even more acute in the spoken language. It should be noted that despite their world-class excellence, Ethiopian professionals and politicians are often poor communicators, which is, without a doubt, a sign of the influence of the failing Ethiopian educational system. Ethiopian professionals and politicians are often ill-equipped to provide accurate information during interviews and presentations or when making public speeches, in addition to using too many English words and phrases.

Ghelawdewos Araia (2013) argued that the unnecessary and often inexcusable borrowing of too many English words by the elite—including by journalists and high-level politicians—into Ethiopian languages is detrimental to the Ethiopian society. Araia further argued that,

> The majority of educated Ethiopians ... either speak in ... Amharic or other Ethiopian languages bombarded with English [words], even when they address illiterate peasants who don't understand English at all. It has become increasingly fashionable for urbanite "educated" Ethiopians to use *Guramayle* (English and Ethiopian languages) to exhibit that they are civilized and modern....They speak without due consideration of their audience... I watch Ethiopian TV nightly news almost every day and I am dumbfounded to witness that almost all journalists, member[s] of parliament, ministers, government bureaucrats, regional state [presidents] etc speak in *Guramayle*.... The transparency of the PM [Haile Mariam Desalegn] is to be admired, but I am afraid it could be compromised by lack of effective communication... I have no doubt in my mind that the Ethiopian journalists and the PM are honest people and they had no intention of deliberately confusing Ethiopians, but since commu-

> nication proposes answering questions as well as explaining and clarifying what the intended audience does not already know, both the journalists and the PM have an obligation to communicate with untainted Amharic.... Admittedly, sometimes, we all are tongue-tied when we express ourselves and we tend to employ English words in order to overcome the problem, but we must always bear in mind that we must strive to instantly recover from our incoherence and use the language that the people understand.[7]

Perhaps the most disturbing effects of the uncontrolled use of English words, phrases and terminologies in Ethiopian languages is the way Ethiopic grammar and syntax are damaged to the extent that many messages intended to be communicated essentially fail or become extremely mangled and difficult to understand. Consider, for example, the following transcript from an online video showing a tour of one of the largest hydroelectric dams under construction in Ethiopia in which a project engineer was giving government officials details of the project. My transcription of the engineer's words is provided below in the traditional Ethiopic script with the originally used English words shown with Latin letters. In my translation that follows, I have tried to preserve the original flaws in the message that badly affected the Amharic grammar resulting in *guramayilei.*

> ምናልባት ቅድም እዛጋ ሲባል የሰማችሁትን ነገር አሁን ሰፋ አድርገን ምናይበት ቦታ ላይ ነው ያለነው። ቅድም እንደ ሰማችሁት፣ የተከዜ civil structureኡ ወይም ደሞ dam catchment area ወይም ደሞ stored የሆነውን ውሃ stored የተደረገበት area ላይ ነው አሁን ያለነው። እዚጋ የምታዩት የdam structureኡን ነው። ቅድም ሲባል እንደ ሰማችሁት፣ የdam structureኡ double curvature arch dam አልያም ደግሞ culvert dam ከሚባሉት የdam typeኦች የሚመደብ ነው። Horizontally ስታዩት ወደ 460 ሜትር ይረዝማል፤ vertically ቁመቱ 188 ሜትር ያክል ነው ማለት ነው። እና ይህ dam አሁን ባለበት capacityው 9 ቢሊዮን cubic ሜትር ውሃ የመያዝ አቅም አለው—full rate በሚሞላበት ሰዓት ማለት ነው። በዛ ውሃ ደግሞ የዓመት energyኦችን 981 megawatt-hour ያመነጫል ተብሎ ነው ጣቢያው ሲገነባ የተገነባው።

> We are probably at a place where we can look at what you heard over there earlier more broadly. As you heard it earlier, it is at the Tekezei's civil structure or dam catchment area or the stored water [sic.], the area where it is made stored [sic.], that we are now. What you are seeing here is the dam's structure. As you heard it earlier being said [sic], the dam's structure is categorized as one of those dam types called double curvature arch dam or else [sic.] culvert dam. When you see it horizontally [sic.], it stretches for 460 meters; vertically it means [sic.] that it is as much as 188 meters. So this dam, at the capacity it has now, it has the capacity [sic.] to hold 9 billion cubic meters water [sic.]—that means at the hour [sic.] it is filled full rate [sic]. And with that water, it is in the thought that our yearly energy [sic.] will produce 981 megawatt-hour that the plant was built when it was being built [sic].

In the following additional examples, which were accessed from social media, although no translation has been provided, the English words are shown using Latin letters to clarify the problem. Notice the shockingly poor grammar use which is unfitting to professionals and which is the direct result of the use of foreign words without appropriate sentence structure in mind. Ethiopic grammar is almost always obliterated when a foreign verb is used in a sentence carelessly, although foreign nouns and adjectives can also damage sentence structure to a lesser extent. (Note that the Ethiopic orthography used in the examples below shows the proposed de-synthesization with traditional Ethiopic.)

Speaker 1 – operations manager of a factory:

[Company name] ሙሉ-ለ-ሙሉ የ ማስፋፊያ ሥራ ዉ ን ጨርሶ አሁን በ ኣዲስ ማሽን ዘመናዊ በ ሆነ ማሽን ወደ ማምረቻ ውስጥ ገብተን ኣል። አሁን የ ምርት ሂደት ላይ ነው የ አለ ን። Fabrica-ኣችን ምን ይ መሰል ኣል የ ም ዪ ይለ ው ን ነገር እየ ኣንድ-ኣንድ ኡ ን ነገር ገለፃ ል ኣድርግ ል ኣችሁ። ይህ እዚህ ጋር ፊት ለ ፊት የ ም ት መለከት ኡ ት pulling tower ይባል ኣል። ይህ pulling tower ምድን ነው የ ም ዪ አደርገ ው፣ compressor machine-ኦች ኃይለኛ ሙቀት ስለ የ ም ዪ ፈጥሩ፣ ማሽኖቹን ለማቀዝቀዝ የ ም እን ጠቀምበት cooling tower ነው። እዚ ጋ የ ም እን መለከተ ው utility የ ም እን እል ኣቸው compressor machine-ኦች ናቸው የ ኣሉት። High pressure ነው compress የ ም ዪ ኣደርግ ኡ ት። Pre-form የ ም ዪ ባለው ን material ሙቀት ከ ኣገኘ በ ኋላ ለ blow mold machine፣ blow ለማደርግ የ ም እን ጠቀም በ ት፣ ኣየር የ ም ዪ ታመቅ በ ት ማሽኖች ናቸው፤ ከፍሎች ናቸው። እነኝህ compressor machine-ኦች ይ ባል ኣሉ። እዛ ጋ የ እ ም ት መለከት ኡ ት reservoir tanker ነው። ሁለት የ [ው ሃ] ጉድጓድ[ኦች] ኣሉ ን። 150 ሜትር ላይ እና 120 መትር ላይ የ ም ይ ገኝ ኡ በስልመትሰብር? pumb ኣማካኝ ነት ቀጥታ ወደ reservoir tanker ዪ ሄድ ኣል፣ ውሃ ዉ። 50፣000 ሊትር የ መ ያዝ አቅም ኣለው። reservoir tanker ኡ ቀጥታ ወደ treatment plant ዪ ሄድ ኣል። Treatment plant እንዴት ዪ ሰራ ኣል? እላይ ወጥተ ን የ ኣለ ው ን ነገር ኣንድ-በ-ኣንድ እን እየ ው። ይህ treatment plant ኣችን ነው። ማንኛው ም የ ውሃ ፋብሪካ ላይ፣ በ ማንኛ ው ም የ አገር ደረጃ ላይ ያለ የ ውሃ ማጣሪያ ማሽኖች እነዚህ ናቸው። መጀመሪያ ከ reservoir tanker የ መጣ ዉ ውሃ ቀጥታ sand filter ውስጥ ይ ገባ ኣል። ይሄ sand filter እንለው ኣለ ን። ሶስት ኣይነት grade የ ኣለ ኣቸው sand-ኦች ውስጥ ኡ ኣሉ ት። ውሃ by nature ይዝ ኦ ት የ ም ዪ መጣ ዉ suspended particle-ኦች ኣለ ኡ ት። እነዚያ ን suspended particle-ኦች የ ም ዪ ኣስ ወግድ ል ን ይህ sand filter ነው። Activated carbon ውስጥ ዪ ገባ ኣል። Activated carbon ውሃ በ ተፈጥሮ ዉ bad smell-ኦች ል ዪ ኖር ኡ ት ዪ ችል ኣል ኡ። እነዚያ bad smell-ኦች ሙሉ ለ ሙሉ ዪ ኣስቀር ል ን ኣል። Chlorine-ን ሙሉ-ለ-ሙሉ እዚህ activated carbon ውስጥ ዪ ኣስቀር ል ን ኣል። እዚ ጋ micro filter-ኦች ኣል ኡ። እነዚህ micro filter-ኦች size ኣቸው five micro ነው። ከ five micro size በላይ የ ኣል ኡ particle-ኦች ከ ኣል ኡ ሙሉ-ለ-ሙሉ እነዚህ filter-ኦች ውስጥ ይ ቀር ኣል ኡ መ ኣለት ነው።

Speaker 2 – laboratory technician in the same factory:

እዚህ የ ም እን ሰራ ው ያው የ ውሃ ው ን ጥራት ከ source-ኡ ጀምር ኦ የ ም ን ጠቀመ ው ያው ground water ነው። Ground water መ ጠቀም ኣችን ኣንደኛ beneficiery ነው፣ ምክንያት ኡ ም፣ ከ patogenic bacteria-ኦች nill ነው። ስለዚህ፣ ምንም እንኳን የ ተለየ ማጣሪያ ብ ኣል እን ጠቀም እራሱ ground water መሆን ኡ ለ እዚያ ነገር safe ነው። እና micro test እን ሰራ ኣለን። Microbiology test ማለት ያቹኛ ዋ form ነ ኣት። Microbiology ውሃ ውስጥ ምን ኣይነት bacteria ኣለ ው ወይም የለ ው ም የ ም ዪ እለ ው ን ነገር check እን ኣደርግ ኣለ ን። እዚህ ጋር የ ም እን ኣየ ዉ physio-chemical analysis ነው። Physically የ ውሃ ዉ ን parameter እን ኣይ ኣለ ን። Or chemical check፣ chemical ስ እን እል chemical add ኣድርገ ን check የ ም እን ኣደርገ ኣቸው ነው። እና በ ውሃ ው ውስጥ ምን ያህል ion-ኦች፣ እነዚህ lable ኡ ላይ የ ተ ጻፍ ኡ ion-ኦች ኣል ኡ። የ እነዚህን ion concentration measure እን ኣደርግ ኣለ ን። የ ተለያይ ኡ instrument-ኦች ኣል ኡ ን። እነዚህ instrument-ኦች የ ውሃ ው ን እየ ኣንድ-ኣንድ ኡ ን በ ውሃ ውስጥ የ ም ዪ ገኝ ኡ ion-ኦች ምን ያህል መመጣጠን ኣቸው ን መ ኣለት ነው። Positive ion-ኦች ኣል ኡ፣ negative ion-ኦች ኣል ኡ፣ እነዚያ ለ ጤና ምቹ በ ሆነ መልክ ኡ መመጣጠን ኣቸው ን check እን ኣደርግ ኣለ ን። እሱ ነው ዋናው ነገር የ ም ዪ ሰራ ዉ ነገር የ ውሃ ው ን clearness ወይም turbidity ው ን check እን ኣደርግ ኣለ ን። PH ኡ ን፣ እነዚህ የ ም ት ኣይ ኡ ኣቸው ኣጠቃላይ የ laboratory መሳሪያኦች ውሃ ውስጥ የ ም ይ ገኝ አ ው ን chemical test check የ ም እን ኣደርግ በ ት ነው፤ እዚህኛ ው room ውስጥ በ ኣጠቃላይ መ ኣለት ነው።

Such use of language will obliterate Ethiopian languages to the extent that they will resemble creole languages and the current Ethiopian languages may not be recognized after a few generations. However, these problems do not necessarily show the irresponsibility of people who use foreign words (although some people do so with irresponsibility), but the general lack of government language policy and the near-complete failure of the education system in Ethiopia because of the singular reason of using English as the medium of instruction.[8] Such use of foreign words should not be tolerated in a nation of 100 million strong where the total number of English speakers may be a few thousand and most taxpayers would not be able to understand what is being said and therefore could constitute maladministration. Government must play a strong role in reversing this trend, such as by sponsoring the production of technical dictionaries and the eventual introduction of Amharic into higher educational institutions as the medium of instruction (Chapter 13: More on the Ethiopian Language Crisis and Proposed Solutions.)

Confusion of Grammatical Tenses: Conflict in the Sequence of Events and Grammatical Tenses Employed to Describe Them

Perhaps one of the most striking evidence for the deterioration of the capacity of South Central Amharic to convey accurate information is the fact that few speakers of Amharic outside of rural Ethiopia can correctly describe action or events that took place before the moment of speech using the appropriate grammatical tenses. Whereas this problem is almost inexistent in rural areas, anecdotal evidence suggests that the problem is worsening in urban areas where the school system produces generation after generation of graduates who are linguistically stunted. For example, while a few decades ago past events were never described in the present tense or the present perfect tense, nowadays it appears that such use of grammar is widespread making conversations confusing at best and incomprehensible at worst.

In the following example from an article on an Amharic newspaper, the first sentence uses the present perfect tense; while the second sentence, which documents action that apparently occurred later, uses the simple past tense (note that the text contains other grammatical errors). My approximate translation of the text follows the actual text below from the newspaper.

> እሳቸው የወከሏቸው ሜዲካል ዳይሬክተር "አሁን ስብሰባ ላይ ነኝ፡፡ ስለጉዳዩ ድንገተኛ ክፍል ጠይቁ። ለእኔም የነገሩኝ እነሱ ናቸው" ብለውናል። ድንገተኛ ክፍል ስንጠይቅ በዕለቱ ተረኛ የነበሩትን ዶክተሮች አነጋግሩ የተባልን ሲሆን ተረኛ ዶክተሮቹ በበኩላቸው፤ ኦፕሬሽን እያደረግን ስለሆነ እስክንጨርስ ጠብቁ አሉን።[9]
>
> The medical director that he assigned in his place *has* told us … to check with the Emergency Room …. When we checked with the Emergency Room ….the doctors on duty *told* us to wait…

In grammar, the present perfect tense cannot be used for an action that had taken place before another action that took place in the past and is reported in the past tense. The reason is that grammatical tenses are predicated on the sequence or timing of actions in the real world and are understood as such by speakers and listeners. Therefore, tenses are not arbitrary or artificial constructs that can be ignored in a sophisticated 21st-century society. Such erroneous use of tenses can have unintended devastating consequences depending on the situation such as during administration of healthcare that depends on intricate medical procedures.

The following is another example of the use of a wrong tense in an Amharic sentence broadcasted on a state television, with my translation following.

> የታላቁ የኢትዮጵያ ህዳሴ ግድብ ከሶስት ዓመት በኋላ ተሰርቶ ሲጠናቀቅ፣ 74 ቢሊዮን ሜትር ኩብ ውሃ የመያዝ አቅም አለው።
>
> When the construction of the Great Ethiopian Renaissance Dam is completed after three year [sic.], it has [sic.] the capacity to hold 74 billion cubic meters water [sic.].

A correct form of the above sentence is given below.

> ታላቅ ኡ የ ኢትዮጵያ ህድዳሴ ግድድብ ግንባታ ከ ሶስት ዓመታት በኋላ ሲ ጥጠናቅቀቅ፣ 74 ቢሊዮን
> ሜትር ኩብ ያህል ውሃ የ መያዝ አቅም ይ ኖር አ ኡ አል።

Traditional proverbs, songs, and lullabies are also affected by this problem. Consider the following lines from a popular Amharic lullaby with my translation following.

> አንዲት ልጅ ነበረች ከራር የሚሏት፣
> ድንጋይ ላይ ቁጭ ብላ ነፋስ ወሰዳት።
>
> There was a girl who is [sic.] called *Kirar*,
> The wind took her away, she seating [sic.] on a boulder.

A more correct form of the phrases is given below.

> አንዲት ልጅ ነብበረች ከራር የ አል ኡ አት፣
> ድንጋይ ላይ እንደ ተ ቀምመጥ አ ች ነፋስ ወስሰድ አ አት።
>
> There was a girl who was called Kirar,
> The wind took her away while seated on a boulder.

Interestingly, such problems are carried over into English by Ethiopians who speak English as a second language. The following text, from the official website of the Entoto Observatory and Space Centre, the first-ever Ethiopian space initiative, exemplifies the language crisis in Ethiopia where even highly educated individuals are unable to prepare good technical literature in any language—foreign or domestic (Chapter 13).

> The idea of establishing Entoto Observatory and Space Science Research Center (EORC) has been [sic.] initiated during the establishment of ESSS in 2004. The first initiative has set out [sic.] by ESSS Board members and decided the establishment of Astronomy and Space Science research centers at Entoto and other Highlands of Ethiopia. The construction of the center has been [sic.] started in 2008/2009. In January 2013 the center has [sic.] established an independent research center with name [sic.] Entoto Observatory and Research Center by 32 public universities, ESSS and Unity University to utilize and administer [sic.].[10]

Confusion of Grammatical Voices: Problems in Using Passive-Intransitive Verbs and Active-Intransitive Verbs

Tigirinya and Amharic grammars employ transitive and intransitive verbs, which are further divided into ACTIVE-INTRANSITIVE VERBS and PASSIVE-INTRANSITIVE VERBS. The difference between active-intransitive verbs and passive-intransitive verbs is in the way they are inflected within the Ethiopic divisions (Volume II: Chapter 11: Types of Verbs in Tigirinya and Amharic). Although, neither one of the intransitive verb types can take direct objects, many speakers of both Tigirinya and Amharic tend to use intransitive verbs in the active voice form with a direct object. The direct object employed in such errors is always what is otherwise the subject of the sentence when the correct rules of grammar are applied. Such a wrong sentence construction makes a false subject which is almost always a non-existent third person singular male (3PSM) pronoun—understood as an inanimate grammatical person like the English pronoun 'it.' Note that such wrong use of a non-existent pronoun is different from the use of what is referred to in linguistics as a 'dummy pronoun.'

Intransitive verbs are some of the most misused grammatical elements in Tigirinya and Amharic.

Consider the Tigirinya single-word sentence *ጠምዩኒ'ሎ and its Amharic equivalent *ርቦኛል, which are grammatically wrong but very common expressions nowadays. When de-synthesized, they become *ጠሚ-ኡ-ኒ-ኣል-ኦ and *ርብ-ኦ-ኝ-ኣል-(ኦ) respectively. When translated into English, both provide the grammatically wrong expression: "*It has hungered me." The *it* in the Tigirinya word is represented by the pronouns ኡ and ኦ, while in Amharic it is represented by the pronouns ኦ and the optional ኦ. On the other hand, the object *me* is represented by the Tigirinya object pronoun ኒ and its Amharic equivalent ኝ. The problem with those Ethiopic single-word sentences is that they are derivatives of passive-intransitive verbs that have been applied in an active voice setting with the subject *it* being the doer of the action and the object *me* being the receiver of the action. If anything, the grammatical structure of the words tend to lean towards providing the meaning that *something* is hungry and needs to eat *me*, rather than *I* am hungry and need to eat *something*. The correct expressions for the above examples are ተ ጠሚ ኤ ኢ ኤ and ተ ርብ ኤ ኣልለ ኦ ሁ, in Tigirinya and Amharic respectively, which consist of passive-intransitive verbs with no direct object and mean, "I am hungry" (syntactically, similar to "I have starved").

Other examples of difficult to decipher sentences include the Tigirinya single-word sentence *ሒሹኒ'ሎ and its Amharic equivalent *ተሸሎኛል, which are supposed to mean "I have recovered [from a sickness]." When de-synthesized, it becomes clear to see that the words are confused collections of passive-intransitive verbs wrongly applied in the active voice form with direct objects. The de-synthesized forms are as follows: *ሒሽ-ኡ-ኒ-ኣለ-ኦ and *ተሸል-ኦ-ኝ-ኣል respectively. The direct objects in the Tigirinya example are ኡ and ኦ, while the direct objects in the Amharic example is ኦ. The correct expressions for the above examples are ሒሽ ኤ ኢ ኤ and ተ ሸል ኤ ኣልለ ኦ ሁ, respectively for Tigirinya and Amharic.

Tigirinya and Amharic are replete with the wrong use of active-intransitive verbs and passive-intransitive verbs in the active voice form (**Appendices E, F, and G**), although passive-intransitive verb forms are rare in Tigirinya. In both languages, the easiest way to determine whether or not the application of a certain verb in an active voice form is correct is by substituting the object pronoun in the sentence with a pronoun from another grammatical person. If the sentence fails to make sense semantically with the new pronoun, it is a good indication that the verb cannot be used in the active voice form. The erroneous expressions are glorified slang and probably originated as jokes a few generations ago. Nonetheless, they have gained acceptance by almost all speakers of Ethiopic to the extent that they have all but dislodged their grammatically correct counterparts. As such, the correct grammatical forms are considered archaic or are used by rural communities who are generally considered backward by many urbanites. As a result, this problem will probably prove to be the most entrenched and thus most difficult to correct. An example of a classical work containing such errors is the following piece by Qeny Geita Yofitahei Nigusei, one of Ethiopia's influential poets of the early 20th century:

የሰማይ አሞራ ልጠይቅሽ ወሬ፣
ተቃጥሏል መሰለኝ ሸተተኝ አገሬ።

There are three grammatical errors in the poem which are both found in the second line—it refers to 'my country' in the male form rather than the grammatically correct female form and uses the non-existent verb derivatives *መሰለኝ and *ሸተተኝ, which are active-intransitive verbs wrongly used as transitive verbs. The following is probably the best way to correct the errors in the poem:

የ ሰማይ አሞራ ል እ ጠይቅ ሽ ወሬ፣
ስ ላል ት ቃጥጠል ላል ቀርረች ም፣ ት ሸት አልለ ች ላገር ኤ።

Subject-Person-Voice Disagreement

Mistakes with applying the wrong personal pronoun for the object or applying the verb in the wrong voice are extremely common in Tigirinya and Amharic. Consider the Tigirinya sentence *ጸጉረይ ተሓጸብኩ and its Amharic equivalent *ፀጉሬን ታጠብኩ each of which is a two-word sentence in the old orthography and literally means "I got washed, my hair." There is a grammatical problem in each sentence. The first word ጸጉረይ / ፀጉሬን (my hair) is a word derivative in the first person possessive form, whereas the second word ተሓጸብኩ / ታጠብኩ (I got washed) is a complete sentence with its own subject in the first person and a transitive verb in the passive voice. There is a mismatch of either the pronouns or the voice or both. Before trying to resolve the issues in each sentence, the questions to ask are: Who did the washing? Is the emphasis needed at the fact that *the* hair has been washed or *who* washed the hair? To show emphasis on the fact that the hair has been washed, the sentence ጸጉሪ ኤ ተ ሓጸብ አ / ጸጉር ኤ ተ ኣጥጠብ አ meaning "My hair got washed" (literally: My hair, it got washed) will show no subject-person-voice conflict and therefore suffice. If the emphasis is on who washed the hair, there can be various options to indicate that. Therefore, the sentence could be ን ጸጉሪ ኤ ሓጸብ ኩ / ጸጉር ኤ ን ኣጥጠብ ሁ (I washed my hair) or ን ጸጉሪ ኤ ኣሕጸብ ኩ / ጸጉር ኤ ን ኣስ ኣጥጠብ ሁ (I had my hair washed [by someone]) or something similar depending on who did the actual washing. Similarly, ኣእዳወይ ተሓጸብኩ / እጆቼን ታጠብኩ should be corrected to ኣእዳው ኣኤ ሓጸብ ኩ / እጆች ኤ ን ኣጥጠብ ሁ (I washed my hands).

Wrong Application of Phrasal Intransitive Verbs

In Ethiosemitic, a phrasal verb is made up of a morpheme and an engine (a phrasal-verb-making) verb (for more on phrasal verbs, refer to Volume II: Chapter 25: Types of Verbs in Tigirinya and Amharic). A feature of substandard language use in Ethiopic is the use of intransitive phrasal verbs as transitive verbs with a direct object. For example, consider the sentences *ደስ ኢሉኒ and *ደስ አለኝ in Tigirinya and Amharic, respectively, each of which is a sentence made up of a phrasal verb and two pronouns. The first sentence *ደስ ኢሉኒ, which is supposed to be a Tigirinya sentence should not even be used in Tigirinya because ደስ is not a Tigirinya morpheme. Similarly, the Tigirinya congratulatory term *እንኳዕ ደስ በለኩም is wrong twice—because it uses the same non-Tigirinya morpheme (or one that is not naturalized into Tigirinya) to create an intransitive verb and then uses the intransitive verb as if it was a transitive verb with a direct object. The correct Tigirinya congratulatory term is እንኳዕ ተ ሓጎስ ኩም! (Congratulations!). The second sentence, which is the Amharic sentence *ደስ ኣለኝ, has two problems. Firstly, the phrasal verb wrongly engages a direct object, although it is an intransitive verb.

Secondly, it is made up of the wrong phrasal-verb-making (engine) verb. The correct engine verb for the morpheme ደስ in Amharic is መ ሰኘኘት. Similarly, the Amharic congratulatory term *እንኳን ደስ አላችሁ is incorrect. The correct term is: እንኳን ደስ ተ ሰኘኘ አችችሁ! (Congratulations!) In formal settings, an even more correct congratulatory term in Amharic is እንኳን ተ ደሰት አችችሁ, which doesn't use a phrasal verb (phrasal verbs are less formal in Amharic). Other wrong applications of phrasal verbs and their correct forms are shown below:

*ቅር አለኝ → ቅርር ተ ሰኘኘ አ ሁ

*ትዝ አለኝ → አስ ተ አወስ ሁ

*ግራ ገባኝ → ግራ ተ ጋብባ ሁ

Ghost Subjects and Unwarranted Direct Objects

One of the problems associated with the traditional Ethiopic orthography is the inability to prevent unwarranted pronouns from lurking into Ethiopic grammar. For example, with the following Tigirinya and Amharic words mentioned previously *ጠምዩኒ'ሎ and *ርበኛል, there is a ghost subject *it* that *hungers the direct object *me*. The words are not saying, "It makes me hungry." They are instead saying, "*It has hungered me (It is hungry of me)," while what is wanted to be communicated is simply, "I am hungry." The *it* is the ghost subject that is not required at all, while the *me* is the subject that is wrongly assigned the role of a direct object. The fusional languages of Ethiopic and the alphasyllabic and phonemic nature of their writing systems explain why incorrect applications of intransitive verbs is so endemic in Ethiopic.

Interestingly, even transitive verbs can take unwarranted direct objects as can be explained by the Tigirinya and Amharic words ሰልቹይኒ and ሰለቸኝ. These are single word sentences each of which are utilizing a transitive verb with the meaning 'to be tired of something.' Used in the right context, ሰልቹይኒ (ሰልቹ-ኡ-ኒ) and ሰለቸኝ (ሰለቸ-አ-ኝ) mean, "He got tired of me." However, often people use this word to mean that they got tired of something. The correct expression is ሰልቹ ኤ ኦ and ሰለቸ ሁ ት.

Similarly, active-intransitive verbs are also wrongly used as in the following Tigirinya and Amharic single-word sentences *ጸይቡኒ and *ጠበበኝ. Both words literally mean, "It tightened me," although what is meant is, "It is too tight for me." The correct expressions are ን ኣይ ጸብቢብ ኢ ኡ and ለ እኔ ጠብባብ ነው respectively.

Wrong Use of Causative Verbs, the Accusative Particle and Nouns as Verbs

In Ethiopic grammar, especially in Amharic grammar, there is widespread use of certain grammatical elements and constructions in the wrong way.

Wrong Application of Causative Verbs:

A causative verb is a form of a verb that indicates who or what causes an action or change of state. In Ethiopic grammar, certain verbs can be transformed into a causative form by simply adding the causative particle አ <a> or the causative morpheme አስ <as> depending on whether the language is Giiz, Tigirinya or Amharic and on the specific verb in question. In order to evoke the use of the causative, a subject must cause an action or a change of state to something or someone else. However, because of bad language use in Ethiopic (especially in

Amharic), the causative verb is used even if the cause of the action and the doer or receiver of the action are one and the same. For example, consider the following wrong single-word Amharic sentence *አስነጠስኩ. Most people routinely use this expression to mean, "I sneezed," but a more literal translation of it is: "I caused [someone] to sneeze." The correct construction for the intended meaning is "አነፕጠስ ሁ," from the infinitive verb form መ አነፕጠስ (to sneez). Similarly, the following list shows the wrong expressions with their corrections:

- Pseudo-causative verb: *አሳዘነችኝ።

  → Correct construction: በ እርሷ አዘን ሁ።

- Pseudo-causative verb: *አሳልኩኝ።

  → Correct construction: ሳል ሁ።

Consider the following sentence, which is another example of wrong application of a causative verb.

የታላቁ የኢትዮጵያ ህዳሴ ግድብ ግንባታ ለሰከንድም ቢሆን አያቆምም!

Notice the wrong use of the causative verb in the verb derivative አያቆምም (አል-ይ-አቆም-ም), which provides the following more literal (but not exact) translation for the previous sentence: "The construction of the Great Ethiopian Renaissance Dam it will not make it stop [sic.] for a second!" The problem with the use of the causative verb is that it has created two subjects: *the dam* and *it*. Causative verbs indicate who or what causes an action. The dam cannot at the same time be the one whose construction is interrupted and the cause of the interruption, which means that the primary personal pronoun ይ <iee> (it) attached to the causative verb is a second grammatical subject, which is forbidden by Ethiopic grammar. Since what was meant was, "The construction of the Great Ethiopian Renaissance Dam will not stop for a second" the solution is to use a non-causative form of the verb as follows:

የ ታላቁ የ ኢትዮጵያ ህዳሴ ግድድብ ግንባታ ለ ሰከንድ ም ብ ይሆን አል ይ ቆም ም!

Wrong Application of the Accusative Case:

The Amharic accusative case, which uses the particle ን to mark a direct object, is often misused. (Such a problem does not exist in Tigirinya since it does not have an accusative case.) The following are example of wrong applications of the Amharic accusative particle.

- ያንን እቃ (double use of accusative case)

  → Correct phrase is ያ ን እቃ

- በዚያን ወቅት (unnecessary use of accusative case)

  → Correct phrase is በዚያ ወቅት

Wrong Application of Nouns as Verbs:

An example of a wrong use of a noun as a verb with the corresponding wrong application of a subject and an object is *ቀፈፈኝ. The noun so used is ቀፋፊ, which means 'disgusting.' The correct expression is ለ እኔ ቀፋፊ ነው (It is disgusting to me).

Confusion and Inconsistency in Grammatical Gender Assignment

Absurd as it is, it is common to find written materials that are inconsistent in their grammatical gender use—which is a particularly common problem in Amharic. There are four grammatical genders in Tigirinya—the singular male, singular female, plural/polite male, and plural/polite female; while there are three grammatical genders in Amharic—the singular male, singular female, and plural/polite. Often, articles, paragraphs and even single sentences inconsistently use grammatical gender, such as by assigning the female and male genders to the same thing. In Ethiopic grammar, gender (as with quantity) is expressed by the verb derivative and not by subject, although both are required to agree. The inconsistency in the grammatical gender assignment often happens when the subject is inanimate, such as the city of Addis Ababa in the example below, although it also occurs when humans are involved. Gender assignment in spoken South Central Amharic is extremely inconsistent and this seems to have spilled into the written word. Consider the following text, which is condensed from a 3-page, 1550-word article on a national newspaper discussing the city of Addis Ababa, which first assigns the female gender to the city, then the male gender, and then back to the female gender followed by the male gender, and so on.

> አዲስ አበባ ያለ ፕላን በዘፈቀደ የተቆረቆረች ከተማ ነች [female]።..... አዲስ አበባም ከእነዚህ ከተሞችና የገጠር አካባቢዎች ጋር በአግባቡ ተሳስሮ [male] መጠቀም ይችል ነበር። .... አዲስ አበባ የኦሮምያ ልዩ ዞን ከተሞችን ትጠቀልላለች [female] የሚል ስጋት በስፋት እየተንፀባረቀ ነው ... አዲስ አበባ ተስፋፍቶ [male] የኦሮሚያ ልዩ ዞን ከተሞችና አካባቢዎችን ይጠቀልላል የሚለው የተሳሳተ ግንዛቤ ነው። .... አዲስ አበባስ ከእያንዳንዳቸው ጋር ተናቧል [male] ወይ ሲባል አሁንም አልተናበበም። ..... አዲስ አበባ የኢትዮጵያ ህዝቦች ዋና ከተማ ናት [female]፡..............አዲስ አበባ ከተማ ለማደግ የሚያስፈልገው መሬት የለውም [male] ማለት አይደለም። ... አዲስ አበባ ከ25-30 ዓመት ድረስ እስከ 8 ሚሊዮን ህዝብ ሳትቸገር [female] መያዝ ትችላለች።............አዲስ አበባ የራሱን [male] በራሱ ክልል፣ በምክር ቤት ደረጃ በአዋጅ ማፀደቅ አለበት።............አዲስ አበባ አስር ክፍለ ከተሞች አላት [female]።[11]

(For more on the Tigirinya and Amharic grammatical genders, refer to *Grammatical Gender in Tigirinya and Amharic* section in Chapter 14 of Volume II)

Nonuse or Improper Use of Plural Forms of Words

The benefit of using appropriate plural words to indicate things that are two or more is the added level of clarity to the information being conveyed. Such clarity is particularly useful considering the fact that the importance of many things encountered in our daily lives as social beings is in their singularity or plurality. Most of the time, the emphasis on quantity is on whether the unit of something is one (singular) or more than one (non-singular). The importance of the non-singular is its contrast to the singular. In other words, how many things there are in a particular set of non-singular things as long as they are more than one is often (but not always) less important than the fact that they are not singular. For example, the contrast between the information in the phrases 'my wife' and 'my wives' is much greater than that in the phrases 'my two wives' and 'my three wives.' Similarly, consider the contrast in the message conveyed in the sentences 'Our *people* live in harmony' and 'Our *peoples* live in harmony.' It can be deduced from the first sentence that *people* is made up of individuals, while in the second sentence, *peoples* is made up of two or more people groups. Therefore, while the first sentence seems to indicate that the individuals who make up the people live harmoniously, in the second sentence, different people groups, such as nations or ethnic groups, live harmoniously. Yet, another example is the contrast between the sentences 'Our *country* benefits' and 'Our *countries* benefit.'

While speakers of Tigirinya sometimes fail to use proper plural forms of words as required, speakers of South Central Amharic routinely fail to make use of any pluralization where necessary. Even though the Amharic grammar provides plural forms of almost all countable nouns and adjectives, illiteracy and the dismal level of Amharic literature means that plural forms of nouns are very often applied improperly or are omitted altogether. An example is ኣይን ኤ ተ ኣምምመ ኦ ኣል <Ayin ei te amimme o al> which means, "My eye is sick." Most speakers of Central Amharic use such a sentence regardless of whether only one eye or both eyes are affected.

Another improper way of pluralization in Ethiopic grammar involves redundancy due to what may be referred to as over pluralization (or double pluralization). Over pluralization occurs when a noun is pluralized by applying two of Ethiopic's pluralization methods to the same word. Almost all pluralization methods in Tigirinya and Amharic are inherited from Giiz, which employed different pluralization methods for different set of words. Amharic, which has developed its own pluralization method on top of those inherited from Giiz, has disproportionately more occurrences of errors of over pluralizations than Tigirinya. This happens when Amharic speakers first apply one of the Giiz pluralization methods to a given word and then top it off with another Giiz pluralization method or Amharic's unique pluralization method, which uses the morpheme ኦች <oc>, as if to ensure that if one fails the other sticks. An example is the over pluralized word *ሕፃናቶች (*ሕፃን-ኣት-ኦች) <*hitxan-at-oc> (dashes added for clarity) from the noun ሕፃን <hitxan> (baby), whose correct plural form is either ሕፃናት or ሕፃኖች, but not a mix of both. Other examples of over pluralized words are *ዓመታቶች (*ዓመት-ኣት-ኦች) <*amet-at-oc>, *ኣዕዋፋት <aiiwafat> and *ኣዕዋፎች (*ኣዕ-ዋፍ-ኦች) <ai-waf-oc>. *ኣዕዋፋት <aiiwafat> is classical pluralization applied twice for ዒፍ <eeef> (bird) in Tigirinya or ወፍ <wef> in Amharic. The correct plural form is ኣዕዋፍ. Over pluralization, which is bad language, is like adding an 's' to children (*childrens), bacteria (*bacterias), and feet (*feets), for example.

With the arguable exception of the Amharic plural making morpheme ኦች, which theoretically can be used in the plural form of any countable noun or adjective in Amharic, the Ethiopic grammar requires that every countable noun and adjective conform to the particular pluralization method prescribed to it by grammatical rules and tradition. For example, Ethiopic grammar dictates that certain words be pluralized by the addition of the suffix ኣት <at>, which cannot be used on words that are required to be pluralized by the addition of the suffix ኣን <an>, etc. The classical pluralization methods inherited from Giiz can be subdivided into regular and irregular ones and are the more formal methods of pluralization even for Amharic (for more on the Tigirinya and Amharic pluralization methods, refer to Volume II: Chapter 12: Ethiopic Pluralization and Naturalization of Foreign Words).

Redundancy Due to Ghost Pronouns

In Tigirinya and Amharic, certain unnecessary morphemes, such as pronouns and particles, get moulded into word derivatives creating what may be referred to as ballooned words. An unnecessary morphemes in such a word could be referred to as a ghost pronoun or a ghost particle. The reason why ballooned words exist in Ethiopic may be due to effects of the combination of a phonetic syllabic alphabet and synthetic languages, which makes it difficult to identify 'ghost' elements in the grammar.

The following are examples of ghost pronouns, which are underlined:

Incorrect: ከወዲያ ላለኸው — Correct: ከ ወዲያ ለ አልለ ህ

Incorrect: ከወዲህ ላለሁት — Correct: ከ ወዲህ ለ አልለ ሁ

Incorrect: ተኛሁኝ — Correct: ተኝኛ ሁ

Incorrect: አየሁኝ — Correct: አይየ ሁ

Incorrect: ነገ ነው የምሄደው። — Correct: ነገ ነው የ ም እ ሄድ።

Incorrect: እሰጥሃለሁኝ። — Correct: እ ሰጥ ህ አልለ ሁ።

Incorrect: የተባበሩት መንግስታት (ተመድ) — Correct: የ ተ ባብበር ኡ መንግስታት (ተባመድ)

PART III

PROPOSED ORTHOGRAPHIC REFORMS

Chapter 6

Hiddasei Giiz: Proposed Alphabetic Reform

Revolution is ... a never-ending process for us. We never had a final blue-print as to how to do things. We only had general directions and the details had to be worked out in practice through experimentations, through making mistakes and learning from them.

—Prime Minister Meles Zenawi (1955—2012)

[S]cript reform calls not only for a competent professional assessment of the technical aspects of the script but also for a careful weighing of these against the psychological and socio-political factors that have a bearing on the written word and all that it stands for.

—Abraham Demoz (1935-1994)

IN THIS CHAPTER

Part of the proposed language reform consists of the reform of the Ethiopic script and can be referred to as HIDDASEI GIIZ. Hiddasei is a Giiz word which means "reform," "renewal," "revival," or "renaissance." Three of the most important reforms that the Ethiopic script urgently needs are what shall be referred to as ALPHABETIZATION, CHARACTER REDUCTION, and BICAMERALIZATION. The aim is to dramatically transform the Ethiopic writing system to respond to the needs of 21st-century communication by extracting all of the required elements for the reform from the existing script itself.

The Ethiopic script is an alphasyllabary with each character being a fusion of a consonant and one or two vowels. The original Ethiopic script was expanded after it was inherited by Tigirinya and Amharic, which modified it by adding characters to represent sounds that did not exist in Giiz, the language that originally used the traditional Ethiopic script. Each alphabet has a MAIN SET of characters and an EXTENSION SET of characters. The main set of characters, which is traditionally shown in a table chart, is composed of alphasyllabic characters each of which represents a consonant and a vowel and is found at the intersection of a consonantal row and a vowelic column. The main set of characters in the Tigirinya alphabet consists of 22 consonantal rows and seven vowelic columns (knowns as orders) that make up 224 (32 x 7) characters. The main set of characters in the Amharic alphabet consists of 24 consonantal rows with seven vowelic columns that make up 238 (34 x 7) characters. In a typical Ethiopic alphabetic chart that combines the GTA alphabets (**Table 6.1**), each row represents a consonantal value and each column represents a vowelic value, and the combination creates a unique character in each cell.

Ethiopic consists of a modified version of the original consonant-only letters from its predecessor proto-Ethiopic and diacritically modified versions of the consonantal letters in the vowel orders. Each consonantal letter is copied and modified six times so that, in total, there are seven syllables produced by the letter indicating the effects of the seven vowels in Ethiopic that were, hitherto, never separately shown. The alphabet uses diacritics that represent the vowels to modify the consonantal letters in their prescribed order. The diacritics are not always the same in a given order, though there are many instances where an order can have many characters using the same diacritic. Consider the character ሁ from the 2nd order and compare it to its base character ሀ in the 1st order (**Table 6.1**). The only difference between the two characters is the horizontal stroke, or diacritic, on the right side of the 2nd order letter. Almost all characters in the 2nd order use this diacritic to modify the base character or glyph as follows:

ሀ/ሁ, ለ/ሉ, ሐ/ሑ, መ/ሙ, ሠ/ሡ, ረ/ሩ, ሰ/ሱ, ሸ/ሹ, ቀ/ቁ,
ቐ/ቑ, በ/ቡ, ቨ/ቩ, ተ/ቱ, ቸ/ቹ, ኀ/ኁ, ነ/ኑ, ኘ/ኙ, አ/ኡ,
ከ/ኩ, ኸ/ኹ, ወ/ዉ, ዐ/ዑ, ዘ/ዙ, ዠ/ዡ, የ/ዩ, ደ/ዱ, ጀ/ጁ,
ገ/ጉ, ጠ/ጡ, ጨ/ጩ, ጰ/ጱ, ጸ/ጹ, ፀ/ፁ, ፈ/ፉ, ፐ/ፑ.

The only exceptions are ረ/ሩ, and ፈ/ፉ , which modify their 2nd order characters by adding a stroke at the bottom. On the other hand, the 6th order has the least consistency. The following list compares each of the 1st order characters with its 6th order equivalent:

ሀ/ህ, ለ/ል, ሐ/ሕ, መ/ም, ሠ/ሥ, ረ/ር, ሰ/ስ, ሸ/ሽ, ቀ/ቅ,
ቐ/ቕ, በ/ብ, ቨ/ቭ, ተ/ት, ቸ/ች, ኀ/ኅ, ነ/ን, ኘ/ኝ, አ/እ,
ከ/ክ, ኸ/ኽ, ወ/ው, ዐ/ዕ, ዘ/ዝ, ዠ/ዥ, የ/ይ, ደ/ድ, ጀ/ጅ,
ገ/ግ, ጠ/ጥ, ጨ/ጭ, ጰ/ጵ, ጸ/ጽ, ፀ/ፅ, ፈ/ፍ, ፐ/ፕ.

Proposed Alphabetization of Ethiopic

For the purposes of the Ethiopic script reform, ALPHABETIZATION shall be defined as the transformation of the traditional Ethiopic script into a truly alphabetic script with separate consonants and vowels. Alphabetization of Ethiopic will involve the extraction and separation of the abstract consonants and vowels inherent in the Ethiopic alphasyllables and, therefore, is a two-stage process consisting of CONSONANTIZATION and VOWELIZATION. The idea for a comprehensive reform of the Ethiopic script that would create separate consonants and vowels has been floated by many scholars and students of Ethiopic for more than the past hundred years (Chapter 14: The Politics of Reform: Previous Efforts for and Opposition to Language Reform). The benefits of alphabetization of Ethiopic include the reduction and manageability of characters, better readability through easier character recognition (both for humans and machines), seamless integration with technology, the possibility of introducing a bicameral letter case system, ease of stemming, keyboard integration and standardization, spelling standardization, ease of alphabetizing and proper collation, and accurate romanization (Chapter 9) and GIIZIZATION (Chapter 10).

Alphabetization and bicameralism are concepts that Ethiopic never employed throughout its 3000-year history.

Table 6.1: The combined Giiz, Tigirinya, and Amharic (GTA) alphabets or *feedels*

		MAIN SET							EXTENSION SET					
	ORDER	1ST	2ND	3RD	4TH	5TH	6TH	7TH	EXT. 1ST	EXT. 3RD	EXT. 4TH	EXT. 5TH	EXT. 6TH	3RD + 1ST
1	h	ሀ	ሁ	ሂ	ሃ	ሄ	ህ	ሆ						
2	l	ለ	ሉ	ሊ	ላ	ሌ	ል	ሎ			ሏ			
3	hh	ሐ	ሑ	ሒ	ሓ	ሔ	ሕ	ሖ			ሗ			
4	m	መ	ሙ	ሚ	ማ	ሜ	ም	ሞ			ሟ			ፙ
5	sx	ሠ	ሡ	ሢ	ሣ	ሤ	ሥ	ሦ			ሧ			
6	r	ረ	ሩ	ሪ	ራ	ሬ	ር	ሮ			ሯ			ፘ
7	s	ሰ	ሱ	ሲ	ሳ	ሴ	ስ	ሶ			ሷ			
8	sh	ሸ	ሹ	ሺ	ሻ	ሼ	ሽ	ሾ			ሿ			
9	q	ቀ	ቁ	ቂ	ቃ	ቄ	ቅ	ቆ	ቈ	ቊ	ቋ	ቌ	ቍ	
10	qh	ቐ	ቑ	ቒ	ቓ	ቔ	ቕ	ቖ	ቘ	ቚ	ቛ	ቜ	ቝ	
11	b	በ	ቡ	ቢ	ባ	ቤ	ብ	ቦ			ቧ			
12	v	ቨ	ቩ	ቪ	ቫ	ቬ	ቭ	ቮ						
13	t	ተ	ቱ	ቲ	ታ	ቴ	ት	ቶ			ቷ			
14	c	ቸ	ቹ	ቺ	ቻ	ቼ	ች	ቾ			ቿ			
15	hx	ኀ	ኁ	ኂ	ኃ	ኄ	ኅ	ኆ	ኈ	ኊ	ኋ	ኌ	ኍ	
16	n	ነ	ኑ	ኒ	ና	ኔ	ን	ኖ			ኗ			
17	ny	ኘ	ኙ	ኚ	ኛ	ኜ	ኝ	ኞ			ኟ			
18	-	አ	ኡ	ኢ	ኣ	ኤ	እ	ኦ			ኧ			
19	k	ከ	ኩ	ኪ	ካ	ኬ	ክ	ኮ	ኰ	ኲ	ኳ	ኴ	ኵ	
20	kh	ኸ	ኹ	ኺ	ኻ	ኼ	ኽ	ኾ	ዀ	ዂ	ዃ	ዄ	ዅ	
21	w	ወ	ዉ	ዊ	ዋ	ዌ	ው	ዎ						
22	-	ዐ	ዑ	ዒ	ዓ	ዔ	ዕ	ዖ						
23	z	ዘ	ዙ	ዚ	ዛ	ዜ	ዝ	ዞ			ዟ			
24	jz	ዠ	ዡ	ዢ	ዣ	ዤ	ዥ	ዦ			ዧ			
25	y	የ	ዩ	ዪ	ያ	ዬ	ይ	ዮ						
26	d	ደ	ዱ	ዲ	ዳ	ዴ	ድ	ዶ			ዷ			
27	j	ጀ	ጁ	ጂ	ጃ	ጄ	ጅ	ጆ			ጇ			
28	g	ገ	ጉ	ጊ	ጋ	ጌ	ግ	ጎ	ጐ	ጒ	ጓ	ጔ	ጕ	
29	tx	ጠ	ጡ	ጢ	ጣ	ጤ	ጥ	ጦ			ጧ			
30	cx	ጨ	ጩ	ጪ	ጫ	ጬ	ጭ	ጮ						
31	px	ጰ	ጱ	ጲ	ጳ	ጴ	ጵ	ጶ			ጷ			
32	x	ጸ	ጹ	ጺ	ጻ	ጼ	ጽ	ጾ			ጿ			
33	xs	ፀ	ፁ	ፂ	ፃ	ፄ	ፅ	ፆ						
34	f	ፈ	ፉ	ፊ	ፋ	ፌ	ፍ	ፎ			ፏ			ፚ
35	p	ፐ	ፑ	ፒ	ፓ	ፔ	ፕ	ፖ			ፗ			

Consonantization

In the context of Ethiopic, consonantization shall refer to the permanent reassignment of certain characters from the Ethiopic script to represent only consonantal sounds as the first stage of the alphabetization process. Since Ethiopic was a consonantal writing system before acquiring its seven orders representing the seven vowels in the fourth century, the task of consonantization of Ethiopic will not be difficult. *Giiz*, the first of the seven orders, did not have its characters modified when the seven orders were devised and has the simplest typeface of all orders. Therefore, the first order characters of the Giiz, Tigirinya, and Amharic alphabets (**Table 6.2**), most of which were originally part of the consonant only Proto-Ethiopic script, are the best candidates for consonants of the reformed alphabet.

Table 6.2: The 1st order (also called *giiz*) characters in the Giiz, Tigirinya, and Amharic (GTA) alphabets or *feedels*

1	2	3	4	5	6	7	8	9	10	11	12	13	14	15	16	17	18	19	20	21	22	23	24	25	26	27	28	29	30	31	32	33	34	35
ሀ	ለ	ሐ	መ	ሠ	ረ	ሰ	ሸ	ቀ	ቐ	በ	ቨ	ተ	ቸ	ኀ	ነ	ኘ	አ	ከ	ኸ	ወ	ዐ	ዘ	ዠ	የ	ደ	ጀ	ገ	ጠ	ጨ	ጰ	ጸ	ፀ	ፈ	ፐ
h	l	hh	m	sx	r	s	sh	q	qh	b	v	t	c	hx	n	ny	e	k	kh	w	ee	z	jz	y	d	j	g	tx	cx	px	x	xs	f	p

Vowelization

In the context of Ethiopic, vowelization shall refer to the permanent assignment of certain characters from the Ethiopic script to represent the seven Ethiopic vowels as the second and last stage of the alphabetization process. Thanks to the fourth-century invention of the Ethiopic seven orders, the task of assigning characters to represent the Ethiopic vowels is not difficult. The seven orders are vowel based, however fused the vowels may be in the characters. The vowels the diacritics represent in the seven orders can be shown as follows: e, u, ee, a, ei, i, o as per their proposed romanization values (Chapter 9: Proposed Standard System for the Romanization of Ethiopic). These vowels already exist in the *elif* (አ) family of characters that represent Ethiopic glottal sounds. These characters can be used to represent the hitherto hidden vowels primarily because the አ characters are vowels more so than consonants. In fact, it can be argued that they are true vowels due to the way they affect and assimilate other vowels and consonants—an idea shared by some scholars who do not consider glottalic characters as consonants at all. For example, consider the de-synthesized Amharic sentence መጥት ኦ ኣለ, which means, "He has come." In the old writing system, this is a single-word sentence written as መጥቷል።. Note that ት <t>, the glottalic characters ኦ <o>, and ኣ <a> have been assimilated into the character ቷ <toa>, showing that ኦ and ኣ are vowels. Both Tigirinya and Amharic are awash with this phenomenon, which makes the introduction of characters dedicated for vowels all the more vital for preserving the root word. Therefore, I propose to use the entire orders of the glottalic character *elif* – አ, ኡ, ኢ, ኣ, ኤ, እ, and ኦ – as the Ethiopic vowels (for similar reform ideas by scholars of a previous generation, refer to Chapter 14).

How Alphabetization of Ethiopic Works

Alphabetization of Ethiopic is a very simple concept given the alphasyllabic nature of the Ethiopic script, which fuses a consonant and a vowel in each character.

Since the traditional Ethiopic script is a set of characters each of which is a fusion of a consonantal sound and one or two vowelic sounds, each character can be separated into its consonantal and vowelic values. Some scholars of Ethiopic wrongly consider the first order as having no vowel fused in them. While this may be true of their visual appearance because the letterforms did not change since they were adopted from the ancient consonant-only script, the same cannot be said of the sounds they represent today. Whereas they were originally only consonants and had no diacritics, they have nonetheless been made to represent phonemes with an implied Ethiopic 'e' vowel for generations since the development of the vocalized alphasyllabary.

There is no evidence to suggest that the 1st order characters were originally vocalized the way they are vocalized today, i.e., with the implied use of the Ethiopic abstract vowel 'e'. In fact, since the ancient Ethiopic script, which gave rise to the traditional Ethiopic script, did not have vowel indication, the reader was expected to supply the vowels depending on context. That being the case, the consonant-only script represented all possibilities for vowel indication. The Ethiopic 1st order characters, except the *elf* and *eyin* characters, will, therefore, become the consonants of the proposed alphabet. The *elf* and *eyin* characters, with their seven orders, will become the vowels. When Ethiopic is broken down into consonants and vowels, it becomes easy to show the combinations necessary to represent the phonemes created by the corresponding characters in the traditional script (**Tables 6.3** and **6.4**).

However, even when broken down into its consonantal and vowelic equivalents, the combined Ethiopic alphabet has a total of 41 letters (34 core characters from the 1st order and the vowels of the seven orders, i.e. አ, ኡ, ኢ, ኣ, ኤ, እ, and ኦ), which undoubtedly are still too many for a robust world-class alphabet envisioned by the proposed reform. Forty-one letters are too many considering the keys available on the average computer keyboard, smartphones, and other electronic devices—which have increasingly become necessities in a modern world. In addition to alphabetic keys, keyboards also must contain keys for numbers, punctuation, space bar and other elements, which necessitate the efficient use of keyboard real estate (Chapter 12).

More importantly, too many letters in the Ethiopic alphabet will continue to hinder progress in other areas, while fewer letters will be easier to memorize with little effort. The ability to learn and memorize the alphabetical order can play a crucial role in determining the accuracy and reliability of communication. For example, a quick memorization of the alphabetical order will facilitate accurate cataloguing, collating, and retrieving of information including in dictionaries and for listing of medical terms, pharmaceutical products, and other highly sensitive information. For this reasons, reducing the alphabet to a more manageable size is one of the reforms I propose in this book and will require the elimination of some characters based on scientific analysis.

Table 6.3: How the Ethiopic Main Set characters break down into their consonantal and vowelic values

	GIIZ (1st Order)	KAIIB (2nd Order)	SALIS (3rd Order)	RABII (4th Order)	HAMIS (5th Order)	SADIS (6th Order)	SABII (7th Order)
1	ሀ = ሀዐ	ሁ = ሀዑ	ሂ = ሀዒ	ሃ = ሀዓ	ሄ = ሀዔ	ህ = ሀዕ	ሆ = ሀዖ
2	ለ = ለዐ	ሉ = ለዑ	ሊ = ለዒ	ላ = ለዓ	ሌ = ለዔ	ል = ለዕ	ሎ = ለዖ
3	ሐ = ሐዐ	ሑ = ሐዑ	ሒ = ሐዒ	ሓ = ሐዓ	ሔ = ሐዔ	ሕ = ሐዕ	ሖ = ሐዖ
4	መ = መዐ	ሙ = መዑ	ሚ = መዒ	ማ = መዓ	ሜ = መዔ	ም = መዕ	ሞ = መዖ
5	ሠ = ሠዐ	ሡ = ሠዑ	ሢ = ሠዒ	ሣ = ሠዓ	ሤ = ሠዔ	ሥ = ሠዕ	ሦ = ሠዖ
6	ረ = ረዐ	ሩ = ረዑ	ሪ = ረዒ	ራ = ረዓ	ሬ = ረዔ	ር = ረዕ	ሮ = ረዖ
7	ሰ = ሰዐ	ሱ = ሰዑ	ሲ = ሰዒ	ሳ = ሰዓ	ሴ = ሰዔ	ስ = ሰዕ	ሶ = ሰዖ
8	ሸ = ሸዐ	ሹ = ሸዑ	ሺ = ሸዒ	ሻ = ሸዓ	ሼ = ሸዔ	ሽ = ሸዕ	ሾ = ሸዖ
9	ቀ = ቀዐ	ቁ = ቀዑ	ቂ = ቀዒ	ቃ = ቀዓ	ቄ = ቀዔ	ቅ = ቀዕ	ቆ = ቀዖ
10	ቐ = ቐዐ	ቑ = ቐዑ	ቒ = ቐዒ	ቓ = ቐዓ	ቔ = ቐዔ	ቕ = ቐዕ	ቖ = ቐዖ
11	በ = በዐ	ቡ = በዑ	ቢ = በዒ	ባ = በዓ	ቤ = በዔ	ብ = በዕ	ቦ = በዖ
12	ቨ = ቨዐ	ቩ = ቨዑ	ቪ = ቨዒ	ቫ = ቨዓ	ቬ = ቨዔ	ቭ = ቨዕ	ቮ = ቨዖ
13	ተ = ተዐ	ቱ = ተዑ	ቲ = ተዒ	ታ = ተዓ	ቴ = ተዔ	ት = ተዕ	ቶ = ተዖ
14	ቸ = ቸዐ	ቹ = ቸዑ	ቺ = ቸዒ	ቻ = ቸዓ	ቼ = ቸዔ	ች = ቸዕ	ቾ = ቸዖ
15	ኀ = ኀዐ	ኁ = ኀዑ	ኂ = ኀዒ	ኃ = ኀዓ	ኄ = ኀዔ	ኅ = ኀዕ	ኆ = ኀዖ
16	ነ = ነዐ	ኑ = ነዑ	ኒ = ነዒ	ና = ነዓ	ኔ = ነዔ	ን = ነዕ	ኖ = ነዖ
17	ኘ = ኘዐ	ኙ = ኘዑ	ኚ = ኘዒ	ኛ = ኘዓ	ኜ = ኘዔ	ኝ = ኘዕ	ኞ = ኘዖ
18	አ (ኧ) = አ / ዐ	ኡ = ኡ / ዑ	ኢ = ኢ / ዒ	ኣ = ኣ / ዓ	ኤ = ኤ / ዔ	እ = እ / ዕ	ኦ = ኦ / ዖ
19	ከ = ከዐ	ኩ = ከዑ	ኪ = ከዒ	ካ = ከዓ	ኬ = ከዔ	ክ = ከዕ	ኮ = ከዖ
20	ኸ = ኸዐ	ኹ = ኸዑ	ኺ = ኸዒ	ኻ = ኸዓ	ኼ = ኸዔ	ኽ = ኸዕ	ኾ = ኸዖ
21	ወ = ወዐ	ዉ = ወዑ	ዊ = ወዒ	ዋ = ወዓ	ዌ = ወዔ	ው = ወዕ	ዎ = ወዖ
22	ዐ = ዐዐ / አአ (ኧ) = ዐ / አ	ዑ = ዑዑ / ኡኡ = ዑ / ኡ	ዒ = ዒዒ / ኢኢ = ዒ / ኢ	ዓ = ዓዓ / ኣኣ = ዓ / ኣ	ዔ = ዔዔ / ኤኤ = ዔ / ኤ	ዕ = ዕዕ / እእ = ዕ / እ	ዖ = ዖዖ / ኦኦ = ዖ / ኦ
23	ዘ = ዘዐ	ዙ = ዘዑ	ዚ = ዘዒ	ዛ = ዘዓ	ዜ = ዘዔ	ዝ = ዘዕ	ዞ = ዘዖ
24	ዠ = ዠዐ	ዡ = ዠዑ	ዢ = ዠዒ	ዣ = ዠዓ	ዤ = ዠዔ	ዥ = ዠዕ	ዦ = ዠዖ
25	የ = የዐ	ዩ = የዑ	ዪ = የዒ	ያ = የዓ	ዬ = የዔ	ይ = የዕ	ዮ = የዖ
26	ደ = ደዐ	ዱ = ደዑ	ዲ = ደዒ	ዳ = ደዓ	ዴ = ደዔ	ድ = ደዕ	ዶ = ደዖ
27	ጀ = ጀዐ	ጁ = ጀዑ	ጂ = ጀዒ	ጃ = ጀዓ	ጄ = ጀዔ	ጅ = ጀዕ	ጆ = ጀዖ
28	ገ = ገዐ	ጉ = ገዑ	ጊ = ገዒ	ጋ = ገዓ	ጌ = ገዔ	ግ = ገዕ	ጎ = ገዖ
29	ጠ = ጠዐ	ጡ = ጠዑ	ጢ = ጠዒ	ጣ = ጠዓ	ጤ = ጠዔ	ጥ = ጠዕ	ጦ = ጠዖ
30	ጨ = ጨዐ	ጩ = ጨዑ	ጪ = ጨዒ	ጫ = ጨዓ	ጬ = ጨዔ	ጭ = ጨዕ	ጮ = ጨዖ
31	ጰ = ጰዐ	ጱ = ጰዑ	ጲ = ጰዒ	ጳ = ጰዓ	ጴ = ጰዔ	ጵ = ጰዕ	ጶ = ጰዖ
32	ጸ = ጸዐ	ጹ = ጸዑ	ጺ = ጸዒ	ጻ = ጸዓ	ጼ = ጸዔ	ጽ = ጸዕ	ጾ = ጸዖ
33	ፀ = ፀዐ	ፁ = ፀዑ	ፂ = ፀዒ	ፃ = ፀዓ	ፄ = ፀዔ	ፅ = ፀዕ	ፆ = ፀዖ
34	ፈ = ፈዐ	ፉ = ፈዑ	ፊ = ፈዒ	ፋ = ፈዓ	ፌ = ፈዔ	ፍ = ፈዕ	ፎ = ፈዖ
35	ፐ = ፐዐ	ፑ = ፐዑ	ፒ = ፐዒ	ፓ = ፐዓ	ፔ = ፐዔ	ፕ = ፐዕ	ፖ = ፐዖ

Table 6.4: How the Ethiopic Extension Set characters break down into their consonantal and vowelic values

	GIIZ (EXTENSION 1st Order)	KAIIB (EXTENSION 2nd Order)	SALIS (EXTENSION 3rd Order)	RABII (EXTENSION 4th Order)	HAMIS (EXTENSION 5th Order)	SADIS (EXTENSION 6th Order)	SABII (EXTENSION 7th Order)
1		–		ሏ = ለዑዓ			
2		–		ሗ = ሐዑዓ			
3		–		ሟ = መዑዓ			
4		–		ሧ = ሠዑዓ			
5		–		ሯ = ረዑዓ			
6		–		ሷ = ሰዑዓ			
7				ሿ = ሸዑዓ			
8	ቈ = ቀዑዐ	–	ቊ = ቀዑዒ	ቋ = ቀዑዓ	ቌ = ቀዑዔ	ቍ = ቀዑዕ	? = ቀዑዖ
9	ቘ = ቐዑዐ	–	ቚ = ቐዑዒ	ቛ = ቐዑዓ	ቜ = ቐዑዔ	ቝ = ቐዑዕ	? = ቐዑዖ
10				ቧ = በዑዓ			
11				ቷ = ተዑዓ			
12				ቿ = ቸዑዓ			
13	ኈ = ኀዑዐ	–	ኊ = ኀዑዒ	ኋ = ኀዑዓ	ኌ = ኀዑዔ	ኍ = ኀዑዕ	? = ኀዑዖ
14				ኗ = ነዑዓ			
15				ኟ = ኘዑዓ			
16				(ኧ)* = ዑዓ			
17	ኰ = ከዑዐ	–	ኲ = ከዑዒ	ኳ = ከዑዓ	ኴ = ከዑዔ	ኵ = ከዑዕ	? = ከዑዖ
18	ዀ = ኸዑዐ	–	ዂ = ኸዑዒ	ዃ = ኸዑዓ	ዄ = ኸዑዔ	ዅ = ኸዑዕ	? = ኸዑዖ
19				ዟ = ዘዑዓ			
20				ዧ = ዠዑዓ			
21				ዷ = ደዑዓ			
22				ጇ = ጀዑዓ			
23	ጐ = ገዑዐ	–	ጒ = ገዑዒ	ጓ = ገዑዓ	ጔ = ገዑዔ	ጕ = ገዑዕ	? = ገዑዖ
24				ጧ = ጠዑዓ			
25				ጿ = ጸዑዓ			
26				ፇ = ፀዑዓ			
27				ፏ = ፈዑዓ			
28				ፗ = ፐዑዓ			

*Proposed value

Proposed Script Streamlining

As part of the reform of the Ethiopic script, which needs to be streamlined, I propose the elimination or obsoletion of certain characters from the consonantal rows and the dissolution of the Ethiopic vowelic orders (2nd to 7th orders). Script streamlining shall involve the elimination of redundant characters and the substitution of rarely used characters by digraphs.

Proposed Elimination of Redundant Characters

Redundant and rarely used characters add to the complexity of the Ethiopic writing system without adding much value to it.

I propose the elimination of redundant characters to help make the Ethiopic script more efficient by purging all but only one of the characters in a MULTIPLICATE CHARACTER SET. A multiplicate character set consists of characters that share the same phonemic value. Although multiplicate character sets are present only in Amharic among the GTA alphabets, character purging due to Amharic's multiplicate characters will affect the Giiz and Tigirinya alphabets because of the proposed BICAMERIZATION discussed later in this chapter and the need for alphabetic harmonization (Chapter 13: The Ethiopian Language Crisis and Recommended Solutions). Amharic has several characters inherited from Giiz that originally had unique sounds but lost their uniqueness in Amharic. These characters can be categorized into the following four groups according to their Amharic phonemic values:

- H group (quadruplicate): ሀ, ሐ, ኀ, and ኸ
    Keep ሀ and eliminate ሐ, ኀ, and ኸ
- S group (duplicate): ሠ and ሰ
    Keep ሰ and eliminate ሠ
- X group (duplicate): ጸ and ፀ
    Keep ጸ and eliminate ፀ
- Vowel group (duplicate): አ, ኡ, ኢ, ኣ, ኤ, እ, and ኦ; and ዐ, ዑ, ዒ, ዓ, ዔ, ዕ, and ዖ
    Keep አ, ኡ, ኢ, ኣ, ኤ, እ, and ኦ and eliminate ዐ, ዑ, ዒ, ዓ, ዔ, ዕ, and ዖ

Proposed Ethiopic Letter Digraphs

As part of script streamlining, I propose the creation of digraphs, each of which will substitute a rarely used character and help streamline the script. I believe that rarely used characters impede communication by unnecessarily enlarging the alphabet, inhibiting easy memorization of the alphabet, crowding out valuable real estate on computer keyboards, and complicating typesetting and calligraphy, among other things. Substitution of a rarely used character by a digraph will preserve the phoneme hitherto represented by a unique character or glyph and still help reduce the size of the alphabet. A digraph is a pair of letters used to represent a single phoneme regardless of the sound values of the individual letters constituting the digraph. In other words, a digraph is a combination of two letters—which can be consonants, vowels, or a consonant and a vowel—which may or may not always fully correspond to the sum of the individual phonemic values of the characters but is assigned to represent a new sound. 'Sh' and 'ch' are examples of digraphs in English, which are used for words like 'she' and 'church.'

Digraphs are useful for representing sounds that would not otherwise be represented by individual letters of a given alphabet. English uses several digraphs to represent many of its 44 or so speech sounds, some of which would not otherwise be represented with an individual letter. Similarly, digraphs can be used for the purpose of replacing some characters of the traditional Ethiopic script to reduce the size of the alphabet and avoid the challenges of managing an excessive number of characters. English and other European languages, for example, replaced characters like the thorn (Þ), wynn (Ƿ), and eth (Đ) with other letters and digraphs a few centuries ago helping reduce the size of their alphabets. In that regard, it is imperative to set the parameters for determining which letters to substitute. The following points will be considered to identify characters for substitution:

1. Characters representing the least NATURALIZED phonemes from foreign words in Giiz, Tigirinya or Amharic:

    Throughout its history, Ethiopic has acquired several newer phonemes through the acquisition of loanwords. Over time, many of such phonemes have become naturalized through morphological derivation or VERBIFICATION as is the case with phonemes borrowed from Ethiocushitic languages. I propose that NATURALIZATION is achieved when a loanword (and its foreign phonemes, if it has any), such as a noun, becomes nativized into Ethiopic as evidenced by the malleability of the word in Ethiopic grammar (e.g. inflection) and widespread adoption of any of its foreign phonemes in the construction of new indigenous words. Also, I propose that VERBIFICATION of a word (or its phonemes) is achieved when it (or its phonemes) passes the grammatical threshold of entering use as a verb in all the Ethiopic DIVISIONS. An example of a fully naturalized English word is the noun በዕረውሽ <birush> (brush) and its Amharic verb form መዐ በየረረዐሽ <me borresh> 'to brush.' However, it can be said that none of the phonemes borrowed from Europe (originally from Greek) have been fully nativized or verbized in Ethiopic grammar. (For more on nativization and verbization in Ethiopic grammar, refer to Volume II: Chapter 12: Pluralization and Management of Loanwords in Ethiopic.) Merely being used in loanwords does not imply nativization of a particular phoneme and, therefore, a character representing such a phoneme should not be allowed to crowd the Ethiopic script. The characters representing the least nativized European sounds are:

    ቨ <v>, ጰ <px>, and ፐ <p>

    ጰ and ፐ are characters that were used at least as far back as the fourth century A.D. but have not been fully nativized to this day. The failure to nativize may be a reflection of the lack of continuous contact between Giiz and Greek, which is in contrast to the continuous contact between Ethiosemitic and Ethiocushitic languages, which has resulted in many Cushitic sounds being nativized in Ethiosemitic languages.

2. Characters representing the least nativized regional sounds in Tigirinya:

    While some Ethiocushitic sounds are not present in either Tigirinya or Amharic, the characters ቸ <c> and ዠ <jz>, which represent the sound borrowed from Ethiocushitic, are not yet fully nativized in Tigirinya. Even though these characters are used in loanwords, it is more efficient to replace them with digraphs.

3. Characters representing the least used native sounds in Tigirinya and Amharic:

Tigirinya and Amharic have characters in their alphabets that are rarely used, even though they were originally inherited from Giiz or were borrowed from Ethiocushitic and are fully nativized. These are sounds represented by the following characters:

ኸ <kh>, ዠ <jz>, and ጨ <cx>.

4. Elimination and substitution of the ሐ <hh> character in Giiz and Tigirinya:

The sound represented by the Giiz and Tigirinya character ሐ <hh> is a glottalized h sound. The characters ሐ <hh> and ሀ <h> are unique because they are the only consonants in Ethiopic that are not geminated. Gemination will be shown by doubling the consonant where applicable (Chapter 8: Other Proposed Orthographic Reforms). However, since doubling ሀ will not represent gemination, it provides the opportunity to eliminate ሐ and substitute it with a doubled ሀ as a digraph.

5. Elimination and substitution of the *eyin* character in Giiz and Tigirinya:

The *eyin* family of characters (ዐ, ዑ, ዒ, ዓ, ዔ, ዕ, and ዖ) are also glottalic and can be used as lowercase alternatives to the *elif* family of characters (አ, ኡ, ኢ, ኣ, ኤ, እ, and ኦ). Since, presumably, most Ethiopic writing will be in the proposed lowercase letters, the *eyin* characters shall be assigned to form the lowercase letterforms for their simpler typefaces as compared to the *elif* characters, which will be used for uppercase letterforms. (Later in this chapter, proposed bicameral letter case system will be discussed.) However, in contrast to Amharic, the sounds represented by the *eyin* characters in Giiz and Tigirinya are different from those represented by the *elif* characters, which will pose a challenge if the *eyin* characters assume the same phonemic role as the *elif* characters. However, since Giiz and Tigirinya will benefit from separate glyphs for the uppercase and lowercase letterforms, these languages will have to lose the historical role the *eyin* characters played and find another way to substitute that role.

The most sensible way to do that seems to double the vowels to represent the sounds that were hitherto represented by the *eyin* characters. (While doubling of consonants indicates gemination, doubling of vowels in Giiz and Tigirinya will not imply vowel elongation, which does not affect Ethiosemitic languages.) Consider, for example, the word ዓለም <aalem> (world), which is traditionally spelled the same in all the GTA languages. The first character ዓ <aa> is the *eyin* 4th order form. In Amharic, the word can phonemically be written as አለም <alem> without changing the pronunciation, but not in Giiz and Tigirinya. For Giiz and Tigirinya, the letter needs to be doubled to preserve the pronunciation as follows:

ዓዓለም <aalem> or ኣኣለም <AALEM>

Now that the characters for substitution have been identified, the next step is to assign a pair of characters (called a digraph) for each character to be eliminated. There are two types of proposed digraphs in Ethiopic—consonant digraphs and vowel digraphs. Each consonant digraph is made up of a pair of consonants, while each vowel digraph is made up of a pair of vowels. Each proposed con-

Table 6.5: The proposed Ethiopic consonant digraphs

	OBSOLESCENT CHARACTER		PROPOSED EQUIVALENTS		PROPOSED DIGRAPH		REMARKS
1	ሠ	<sx>	ሠ + በ	<s + b>	ሠበ	<sx>	Giiz only
2	ቸ	<c>	ሸ + በ	<sh + b>	ሸበ	<c>	Tigirinya only
3	ኸ	<kh>	ከ + ሀ	<k + h>	ከሀ	<kh>	Tigirinya and Amharic
4	ዠ	<zh>	ዘ + በ	<z + b>	ዘበ	<zh>	Tigirinya and Amharic
5	ቨ	<v>	በ + ዘ	<b + z>	በዘ	<v>	Tigirinya and Amharic
6	ጨ	<cx>	ጠ + በ	<tx + b>	ጠበ	<cx>	Tigirinya and Amharic
7	ጰ	<px>	በ + ጠ	<b + tx>	በጠ	<px>	Giiz, Tigirinya and Amharic
8	ፀ	<xs>	ፀ + በ	<x + b>	ፀበ	<xs>	Giiz only
9	ፐ	<p>	በ + ሀ	<b + h>	በሀ	<p>	Tigirinya and Amharic

Table 6.6: How the proposed consonant digraphs relate to the traditional orthography

	GIIZ (1st Order)	KAIIB (2nd Order)	SALIS (3rd Order)	RABII (4th Order)	HAMIS (5th Order)	SADIS (6th Order)	SABII (7th Order)
1	ሠ = ሠበዐ	ሡ = ሠበዑ	ሢ = ሠበዒ	ሣ = ሠበዓ	ሤ = ሠበዔ	ሥ = ሠበዕ	ሦ = ሠበዖ
2	ቸ = ተበዐ	ቹ = ተበዑ	ቺ = ተበዒ	ቻ = ተበዓ	ቼ = ተበዔ	ች = ተበዕ	ቾ = ተበዖ
3	ኸ = ከሀዐ	ኹ = ከሀዑ	ኺ = ከሀዒ	ኻ = ከሀዓ	ኼ = ከሀዔ	ኽ = ከሀዕ	ኾ = ከሀዖ
4	ዐ = ዐዐ	ዑ = ዑዑ	ዒ = ዒዒ	ዓ = ዓዓ	ዔ = --	ዕ = ዕዕ	ዖ = --
5	ዠ = ዘበዐ	ዡ = ዘበዑ	ዢ = ዘበዒ	ዣ = ዘበዓ	ዤ = ዘበዔ	ዥ = ዘበዕ	ዦ = ዘበዖ
6	ቨ = በዘዐ	ቩ = በዘዑ	ቪ = በዘዒ	ቫ = በዘዓ	ቬ = በዘዔ	ቭ = በዘዕ	ቮ = በዘዖ
7	ጨ = ጠበዐ	ጩ = ጠበዑ	ጪ = ጠበዒ	ጫ = ጠበዓ	ጬ = ጠበዔ	ጭ = ጠበዕ	ጮ = ጠበዖ
8	ጰ = በጠዐ	ጱ = በጠዑ	ጲ = በጠዒ	ጳ = በጠዓ	ጴ = በጠዔ	ጵ = በጠዕ	ጶ = በጠዖ
9	ፀ = ፀሀዐ	ፁ = ፀሀዑ	ፂ = ፀሀዒ	ፃ = ፀሀዓ	ፄ = ፀሀዔ	ፅ = ፀሀዕ	ፆ = ፀሀዖ
10	ፐ = በሀዐ	ፑ = በሀዑ	ፒ = በሀዒ	ፓ = በሀዓ	ፔ = በሀዔ	ፕ = በሀዕ	ፖ = በሀዖ

Table 6.7: Proposed unique digraphs for replacing the *eyin* family of characters in Giiz and Tigirinya

	NAME	ORIGINAL CHARACTER		COMBINATION	EXAMPLES		
1	[Reserved]						
2	eyin kaiib	ዑዑ	<uu>	kaiib + kaiib	ዑዑነዓ	<uuna>	(wreckage, ruin)
3	eyin salis	ዒዒ	<uee>	salis + salis	ዒዒለዓ	<eeela>	(water well)
4	eyin rabii	ዓዓ	<ua>	rabii + rabii	ዓዓዕዕየዕነዕተዒ	<aaiiyinitee>	(eyes)
5	[Reserved]						
6	eyin sadis	ዕዕ	<ui>	sadis + sadis	ዕዕየየዖ	<iiyyo>	(job, occupation)
7	[Reserved]						

Note: The traditional *eyin* characters ዐ, ዔ and ዖ have no use in Giiz and Tigirinya and, therefore, will not have digraphs. Strictly speaking, the *eyin* characters do not function as vowels, but rather as consonants or semi-vowels. Therefore, in essence, the first letter in each digraph is a consonant or semi-vowel, while the second letter is a true vowel.

Table 6.8: The proposed Ethiopic vowel digraphs

	NAME	ORIGINAL CHARACTER		COMBINATION	EXAMPLES
1	2nd giiz	ዑዐ	<ue>	kaiib + giiz	ቀዑዐ from the traditional character ቈ
2	[Reserved]				
3	2nd salis	ዑዒ	<uee>	kaiib + salis	ቀዑዒ from the traditional character ቊ
4	2nd rabii	ዑዓ	<ua>	kaiib + rabii	ቀዑዓ from the traditional character ቋ
5	2nd hamis	ዑዔ	<uei>	kaiib + hamis	ቀዑዔ from the traditional character ቌ
6	2nd sadis	ዑዕ	<ui>	kaiib + sadis	ቀዑዕ from the traditional character ቍ
7	2nd sabii	ዑዖ	<uo>	kaiib + sabii	ቀዑዖ (no equivalency in the traditional alphabet)

sonant digraph (**Table 6.5**) can be paired with each proposed vowel to create the phoneme represented by the character it replaces (**Table 6.6**). The proposed special vowelic digraphs for replacing the *eyin* family of characters (**Table 6.7**) are different from the vowelic digraphs proposed to represent the vowelic sounds of the EXTENDED SET of the traditional Ethiopic script (**Table 6.8**).

The character subset in the traditional Ethiopic script is made up of, without exception, a consonantal sound and two vowelic sounds. The proposed free standing vowels make it possible to create all characters of the subset by making use of a consonant and two vowels. The possibility of creating more digraphs to represent more sounds is almost endless for both consonants and vowels, and this is particularly useful for the adoption of the alphabet by non-Ethiosemitic languages inside or outside Ethiopian borders (for more on this, refer to Chapter 13).

THE DRAFT REFORMED ETHIOPIC ALPHABETS

The basic letters of the proposed draft Giiz, Tigirinya, and Amharic alphabets (**Tables 6.9, 6.10,** and **6.11**) show that Tigirinya and Amharic will have an identical set of letters except for the Tigirinya letter ቐ and the Amharic letter ቸ, each of which does not exist in the other alphabet. The Tigirinya and Amharic alphabets will shed or reassign twelve core characters, while the Giiz alphabet will shed or reassign the six core characters ሐ, ሠ, ዐ, ጸ, ፀ, and ፐ, each of which is replaced by a digraph (**Table 6.5**). One of the reasons for the rearrangement of characters in the reformed Giiz alphabet is to allow for uniformity between the three alphabets, which need BICAMERALIZATION.

For example, while there is no doubt that the phonemic distinction between the characters ሠ (sx) and ሰ (s) as well as between ጸ (x) and ፀ (xs) were known for speakers of Giiz, neither Tigirinya nor Amharic recognize these distinctions. Therefore, each duplicate character has been assigned to the lowercase form in all the three alphabets. In addition, their romanization values will be made the same so that ሠ and ሰ have the value of 's', while ጸ and ፀ have the value of 'x.' ኀ <hx> is the only originally Giiz core character that will not be retained in the reformed Tigirinya and Amharic alphabets, but will be retained in the reformed Giiz alphabet because of its presumed, although now lost, unique phonemic value for the language.

Table 6.9: The basic letters of the draft reformed Giiz alphabet

1	2	3	4	5	6	7	8	9	10	11	12	13	14	15	16	17	18	19	20	21	22	23	24	25	26
ሀ	ለ	መ	ረ	ሰ	ቀ	በ	ተ	ኀ	ነ	ከ	ወ	ዘ	የ	ደ	ገ	ጠ	ጸ	ፈ	አ	ኡ	ኢ	ኣ	ኤ	እ	ኦ
h	l	m	r	s	q	b	t	hx	n	k	w	z	y	d	g	tx	x	f	e	u	ee	a	ei	i	o

Table 6.10: The basic letters of the draft reformed Tigirinya alphabet

1	2	3	4	5	6	7	8	9	10	11	12	13	14	15	16	17	18	19	20	21	22	23	24	25	26	27	28	29
ሀ	ለ	መ	ረ	ሰ	ሸ	ቀ	ቐ	በ	ተ	ነ	ኘ	ከ	ወ	ዘ	የ	ደ	ጀ	ገ	ጠ	ጸ	ፈ	አ	ኡ	ኢ	ኣ	ኤ	እ	ኦ
h	l	m	r	s	sh	q	qh	b	t	n	ny	k	w	z	y	d	j	g	tx	x	f	e	u	ee	a	ei	i	o

Table 6.11: The basic letters of the draft reformed Amharic alphabet

1	2	3	4	5	6	7	8	9	10	11	12	13	14	15	16	17	18	19	20	21	22	23	24	25	26	27	28	29
ሀ	ለ	መ	ረ	ሰ	ሸ	ቀ	በ	ተ	ቸ	ነ	ኘ	ከ	ወ	ዘ	የ	ደ	ጀ	ገ	ጠ	ጸ	ፈ	አ	ኡ	ኢ	ኣ	ኤ	እ	ኦ
h	l	m	r	s	sh	q	b	t	c	n	ny	k	w	z	y	d	j	g	tx	x	f	e	u	ee	a	ei	i	o

The proposed reformed alphabets are based on the ሀ-ለ-መ (*hoy-lewee-may*) alphabetic order and not the alternative አ-በ-ገ (*elif-beit-gemil*) order. Although some have aruged that the later alphabetic order is older, I propose the former more popular one be retained. The reform of the Giiz alphabet as used by the Giiz language—as opposed to the Tigirinya or Amharic alphabets—may appear to be irrelevant because the language no longer has native speakers. However, it continues to serve vital roles among Ethiopians and Ethiopianists today such as for liturgy and the study of grammar. Reforming the Giiz alphabet, just like the Tigirinya and Amharic alphabets, will help unlock the keys for understanding Giiz grammar and make Giiz more accessible to future generations. In fact, it may well usher in a golden age for Giiz grammar since its decline several centuries ago.

Proposed Bicameralization of Ethiopic

As part of the reform of the Ethiopic script, I propose the BICAMERALIZATION of the Ethiopic writing system. Bicameralization of Ethiopic shall be defined as the introduction of a bicameral script, which is a script with two sets of letters—one set of letters variously referred to as capital, uppercase or majuscule letters and another set of letters referred to as lowercase or minuscule letters—such as the Latin alphabet. In a given bicameral script, the two letter cases correspond to each other and are equal in value. In its three-thousand-year history, Ethiopic has always been a unicameral or unicase alphabet without distinctive upper and lower cases. However, as modern communication becomes ever so sophisticated, the need for a bicameral Ethiopic alphabet cannot be overemphasized. Capitalization options will greatly improve clarity where a unicase script cannot achieve such as in identifying proper nouns that would otherwise be similar to other nouns or words.

Consider the following sentence from a video documentary reflecting on Mohamed Amin's historic footages of the great Ethiopian famine of 1984 and Tigiray's recent achievement in the restoration of its environmentally degraded lands:

> When his images were broadcast globally in 1984, they helped to inspire both Live Aid and We Are The World.[1]

'Live Aid' and 'We Are The World' are names of two different music bands and therefore are proper nouns. If they were not proper nouns, the sentence would have looked as follows: *When his images were broadcast globally in 1984, they helped to inspire both live aid and we are the world.* Though not grammatically perfect, the second sentence may provide a different message than original one since it may appear that it is not discussing any music bands or not containing any proper nouns. Avoiding such an ambiguity may be one of the greatest benefits of using a bicameral letter case system. Even automated translation systems may take advantage of the ease of identifying proper nouns (which may or may not need to be directly translated) in contrast to ordinary words.

The traditional Ethiopic alphabet is completely unable to make distinctions between ordinary words and proper nouns. However, the proposed Ethiopic alphabet shall be able to provide clarity with words and phrases that benefit from a bicameral letter case system. Until now, only the romanization of Ethiopic words could reliably provide such clarity, which illustrates the benefits of introducing uppercase and lowercase letters for Ethiopic (**Table 6.12**). (In the next section and in Chapter 7, we will look at the proposed bicameral script, which will help add clarity to written text. It is my hope that if the nation adopts the proposed reform, Ethiopic font developers will follow the examples provided in this book to design fonts suitable for a bicameral letter case system.)

In addition to providing stylistic preferences in choosing between the uppercase and lowercase letters for writing, a bicameral script is helpful for text in all block letters which is often used to call attention to something or to provide a warning regarding certain situations. Other benefits of a bicameral script include arguably the increased readability of text,[2] and the opportunity bicameral script provides to use an uppercase letter for a specific symbol and a lowercase letter for another. For example, in the International System of Units (SI), which uses the Latin letters for its symbols, all multiple prefix symbols—exception for da (deca), h (hecto), and k (kilo)—are uppercase letters; while all submultiple prefix symbols are lowercase letters.[3] The letters and their letter cases can readily be transliterated to the proposed bicameral Ethiopic alphabet (for more on this, refer to Chapter 11: Proposed Giizization of Numerical Terms).

Proposed Ethiopic Uppercase and Lowercase Letterforms

As with the introduction of consonants and vowels, the introduction of uppercase and lowercase letterforms for Ethiopic does not require major alteration of existing characters or forging of new ones. The reform will, therefore, honour the Ethiopic heritage by adopting all of the uppercase consonantal letterforms entirely from the 1st Ethiopic order, while taking most of the proposed lowercase letters from one of the rest of the seven orders, most prevalent being the 2nd order (**Table 6.13**).

Table 6.12: Examples of the benefits of capitalizing the first letters of words in the context of Ethiopic

PROPER NOUN		NOUN	
ETHIOPIC WORD	**TRANSLATION**	**ETHIOPIC WORD**	**TRANSLATION**
Hibiret Afireeqa / Ye Afireeqa Hibiret	African Union	hibiret Afirieeqa / ye Afire-eqa hibiret	African cooperation/union
Selamawee Wiqeeanos	Pacific Ocean	selamawee wiqeeanos	a peaceful ocean
Qeyyih Bahiree/Qey Bahir	Red Sea	qeyyih bahiree/qey bahir	a red sea
Idaga Aaribee	[a town in Tigiray]	idaga-aaribee	a Friday market
Addees Abeba	Addis Ababa	addees abeba	a new flower
Qeyyih/Qey Shibbir	[a campaign of terror carried out by the Derig regime in the 1970s]	shibbir	terror
Lewitxee/Lewitx	[the abolition of the monarchy and the usurpation of power by the Derig regime]	lewitxee/lewitx	change
Agere Selam	[a town in Amhara]	agere-selam	a peaceful region
Amilak	God	amilak	a god
Sebat Beit	[an Ethiopian people group]	sebat beitoc	seven houses
Miirabawee	Western	miirabawee	western
Wib Migibbeit	[name of a restaurant]	wib migibbeit	a beautiful restaurant
Hhawilitee	[an archaeological site in Axum]	hhawilitee	a monument
Arat Keelo	[a location in Addis Ababa]	arat keelo[oc]	four kilos
Hibiretesebawee	Socialist	hibiretesebawee	social
Beitekirisiteean	the Church	beitekirisiteean	a church
Birihan	[a proper noun]	birihan	light
Selam	[a proper noun]	selam	peace
Birikhitee	[a proper noun]	birikhitee	a blessed person [female]
Debub Afireeqa	South Africa	debub(awee) Afireeqa	south(ern) Africa
Debub Sudan	South Sudan	debub Sudan	south Sudan
Derig	The Provisional Military Government of Socialist Ethiopia (1974 – 1991)	derig	committee
Ye Etiyopxiya Hiziboc Abiyotawee Deimokira-seeawee Ginibar (EHADG)	Ethiopian Peoples' Revolutionary Democratic Front (an Ethiopian coalition of political parties)	Ye Etiyopxiya hiziboc abiy-otawee, deimokiraseeawee ginibar [fellig e u nebber].	Ethiopian peoples [had needed a] revolutionary, democratic front.

Table 6.13: The proposed uppercase and lowercase letterforms and their application in the GTA languages

	PROPOSED ROMANIZATION	PROPOSED UPPERCASE LETTERFORM	PROPOSED LOWERCASE LETTERFORM	PROPOSED USE FOR GIIZ	PROPOSED USE FOR TIGIRINYA	PROPOSED USE FOR AMHARIC
1	h	ሐ	ሀ (previously 1st order)	√	√	√
2	l	ለ	ላ	√	√	√
3	m	መ	ማ	√	√	√
4	r	ረ	ር (previously 6th order)	√	√	√
5	s	ሰ	ሠ (previously 1st order)	√	√	√
6	sh	ሸ	ሻ	none	√	√
7	q	ቀ	ቂ (previously 3rd order)	√	√	√
8	qh	ቐ	ቒ (previously 3rd order)	none	√	none
9	b	በ	በ	√	√	√
10	t	ተ	ቲ (previously 3rd order)	√	√	√
11	c	ቸ	ቺ (previously 3rd order)	none	none	√
12	n	ነ	ን (previously 6th order)	√	√	√
13	ny	ኘ	ኝ (previously 6th order)	none	√	√
14	k	ከ	ኮ (previously 7th order)	√	√	√
15	w	ወ	ወ (previously 1st order)	√	√	√
16	z	ዘ	ዛ	√	√	√
17	y	የ	ይ (previously 6th order)	√	√	√
18	d	ደ	ዳ	√	√	√
19	j	ጀ	ጃ	none	√	√
20	g	ገ	ጋ	√	√	√
21	tx	ጠ	ጣ	√	√	√
22	x	ጸ	ፀ (previously 1st order)	√	√	√
23	f	ፈ	ፊ (previously 3rd order)	√	√	√
24	e	አ	ዐ (previously 1st order)	√	√	√
25	u	ኡ	ዑ (previously 2nd order)	√	√	√
26	ee	ኢ	ዒ (previously 3rd order)	√	√	√
27	a	ኣ	ዓ (previously 4th order)	√	√	√
28	ei	ኤ	ዔ (previously 5th order)	√	√	√
29	i	እ	ዕ (previously 6th order)	√	√	√
30	o	ኦ	ዖ (previously 7th order)	√	√	√

Note: Where not indicated otherwise, the proposed lowercase letterforms are from the traditional 4th (rabii) order. The √ sign indicates that the letter is proposed for use in the corresponding language.

Table 6.14: The final letters of the proposed reformed Giiz alphabet

	1	2	3	4	5	6	7	8	9	10	11	12	13	14	15	16	17	18	19	20	21	22	23	24	25
UPPER CASE	ሐ	ለ	መ	ረ	ሰ	ቀ	በ	ተ	ነ	ከ	ወ	ዘ	የ	ደ	ገ	ጠ	ጸ	ፈ	አ	ኡ	ኢ	ኣ	ኤ	እ	ኦ
LOWER CASE	ሀ	ለ	ማ	ር	ሠ	ቃ	በ	ቲ	ን	ኮ	ወ	ዘ	ይ	ዲ	ጋ	ጣ	ፀ	ፊ	ዐ	ዑ	ዒ	ዓ	ዔ	ዕ	ዖ
	h	l	m	r	s	q	b	t	n	k	w	z	y	d	g	tx	x	f	e	u	ee	a	ei	i	o

Table 6.15: The final letters of the proposed reformed Tigirinya alphabet

	1	2	3	4	5	6	7	8	9	10	11	12	13	14	15	16	17	18	19	20	21	22	23	24	25	26	27	28	29
UPPER CASE	ሐ	ለ	መ	ረ	ሰ	ሸ	ቀ	ቐ	በ	ተ	ነ	ኘ	ከ	ወ	ዘ	የ	ደ	ጀ	ገ	ጠ	ጸ	ፈ	አ	ኡ	ኢ	ኣ	ኤ	እ	ኦ
LOWER CASE	ሀ	ለ	ማ	ር	ሠ	ሻ	ቃ	ቓ	በ	ቲ	ን	ኝ	ኮ	ወ	ዘ	ይ	ዲ	ጃ	ጋ	ጣ	ፀ	ፊ	ዐ	ዑ	ዒ	ዓ	ዔ	ዕ	ዖ
	h	l	m	r	s	sh	q	qh	b	t	n	ny	k	w	z	y	d	j	g	tx	x	f	e	u	ee	a	ei	i	o

Note: ኀ may be used as an alternative glyph for the proposed Ethiopic uppercase letter ሐ, in much the same way as the Roman glyphs g and g are representations of the same letter.

Table 6.16: The final letters of the proposed reformed Amharic alphabet

	1	2	3	4	5	6	7	8	9	10	11	12	13	14	15	16	17	18	19	20	21	22	23	24	25	26	27	28	29
UPPER CASE	ሐ	ለ	መ	ረ	ሰ	ሸ	ቀ	በ	ተ	ቸ	ነ	ኘ	ከ	ወ	ዘ	የ	ደ	ጀ	ገ	ጠ	ጸ	ፈ	አ	ኡ	ኢ	ኣ	ኤ	እ	ኦ
LOWER CASE	ሀ	ለ	ማ	ር	ሠ	ሻ	ቃ	በ	ቲ	ቺ	ን	ኝ	ኮ	ወ	ዘ	ይ	ዲ	ጃ	ጋ	ጣ	ፀ	ፊ	ዐ	ዑ	ዒ	ዓ	ዔ	ዕ	ዖ
	h	l	m	r	s	sh	q	b	t	c	n	ny	k	w	z	y	d	j	g	tx	x	f	e	u	ee	a	ei	i	o

Note: ኀ may be used as an alternative glyph for the proposed Ethiopic upper case letter ሐ, in much the same way as the Roman glyphs g and g are representations of the same letter.

The final letters of the Giiz, Tigirinya, and Amharic alphabets (**Tables 6.14, 6.15,** and **6.16**) consist of separate uppercase and lowercase letterforms. It is important to note that some of the glyphs need to be slightly modified to create a clear distinction between the two cases (Chapter 7) to enhance readability, visual appeal, and character recognition, among other things. While the proposed uppercase letterforms have few if any ascenders and descenders, the lowercase letterforms vary with regards to their ascenders and descenders—some having ascenders and descenders while others having none. Although the details of font development and design will be left for Ethiopic font developers, I propose the overall proportions of the uppercase and lowercase letters in the next chapter. The aim is to establish the most important elements in a letterform that distinguish it from its counterpart in the other letter case set, as well as establishing the parameters for the creation of glyphs that are not just beautiful on their own but are beautiful collection of glyphs that relate to each other.

Chapter 7

Hiddasei Giiz: Proposed Typographic Reform

Typography is the craft of endowing human language with a durable visual form, and thus with an independent existence. Its heartwood is calligraphy—the dance, on a tiny stage, of the living, speaking hand—and its roots reach into living soil, though its branches may be hung each year with new machines.

—Robert Bringhurst,
Renowned Canadian typographer and poet

Greater than the tread of mighty armies is an idea whose time has come.

—Victor Hugo (1802 – 1885),
One of the greatest French writers

IN THIS CHAPTER

Typography refers to the arrangement of type to enhance written communication through well-defined, unambiguous, readable, and appealing text form. As part of the proposed language reform introducing an Ethiopic alphabet with a bicameral letter case system, typographic modifications are required to create basic parameters for the uppercase and lowercase forms for each letter. Known as bicameral scripts, many writing systems in the Western world have two distinct cases. Examples of bicameral scripts are the Greek, Cyrillic, and Latin alphabets. In ancient times, Roman inscriptions and writing on papyrus did not allow for cursive handwriting and, therefore, the Latin alphabet was originally a unicase alphabet, i.e. an alphabet with only one case. However, the development of parchment and vellum made it possible to write quicker with cursive letters, which eventually led to the creation of the Latin lowercase letterforms near the end of the first millennium A.D. Today, users of the Latin alphabet enjoy the benefits of an alphabet with two letter cases, which include the added power for accuracy, emphasis, and style.

The development of Ethiopic letterforms suitable for the upper and lower cases requires modification and management of the existing characters, which will help establish a clear distinction between the two lettercases without necessarily creating new letterforms. The introduction of a bicameral letter case system for Ethiopic will have many benefits including:

- For preserving extra characters that otherwise would have to be made obsolete because they are redundant characters. With respect to Amharic's redundant characters where two characters represent the same phoneme, one of them has been assigned as the uppercase form of the letter for that phoneme, while the other has been assigned as the lowercase form of the letter. Examples are ሐ and ሀ (H / h), ሰ and ሠ (S / s), ጸ and ፀ (X / x), አ and ዐ (E / e) and ኡ and ዑ (U / u). (The fact that the letters in each pair have very little similarity is useful for differentiating the two lettercases more clearly.)

- More clarity by capitalizing the first letter of every proper noun so that it is not mistaken for an ordinary word.
- The opportunity to use the uppercase form of a letter for a specific symbol and the lowercase form for another. For example, with the International System of Units (SI), most multiple prefix symbols are uppercase letters, while all submultiple prefix symbols are lowercase letters. (See Chapter 11 for giizization of the SI prefix symbols.)
- More stylistic preferences in having the option of uppercase or lowercase letterforms for writing.
- The opportunity to slightly simplify at least the lowercase letterforms without overtly changing anything.
- Arguably increased readability of text.

Historically, the power of typography for efficient written communication has not been fully exploited for the Ethiopic writing system for various reasons. Although illiteracy and poverty may be some of the reasons, there should be no doubt that the orthographic and grammatical challenges discussed in this book which hindered the growth of a strong literary culture have also contributed to the minimal level of typographic development. As a result, typesetting and development of fonts as instruments for presenting well-organized, orderly, and visually appealing writing system have been virtually unknown to Ethiopia for centuries. With fewer characters to deal with in the proposed reformed alphabet, Ethiopic typographers can usher in a golden age for Ethiopic typesetting starting with the design of appropriate typeface for the uppercase and lowercase letterforms.

Anatomy of the Ethiopic Characters

The Ethiopic letterforms are rich with features that include curves, projecting strokes, (ascenders and descenders), horizontal crowning bars, legs, and feet. Many of the Ethiopic characters, which number in the hundreds, are double-legged while some are single-legged or even triple-legged (**Table 7.1** and **Figure 7.1**). In the third to the seventh Ethiopic orders (most of which will now be obsolete), many of the characters have even more features that include rings, horizontal strokes, and crooked stems (**Table 7.2**). Moreover, almost every character has a different height that makes text in Ethiopic look disorganized and thus lack the predictable, rhythmical, and calligraphic orderliness evident in other scripts of the world. Although each glyph is a masterpiece in its own right, the most significant problem associated with the anatomy of the Ethiopic characters is that every glyph does not seem to relate to every other glyph. In other words, there appears to be a very little visual correlation between any two glyphs when it comes to height and form, which can be corroborated by analyzing any printed Ethiopic text.

The anatomy of the Ethiopic characters has grown more and more complicated over time.

Table 7.1: Anatomy of the Ethiopic letterforms (core or 1st order characters only)

SPECIAL FEATURE		CHARACTER	COUNT
Legged	Single legged	ቀ ቐ ተ ቸ ነ ኀ ኘ የ ገ ፐ	10
	Double legged	ለ ሰ ሸ በ ቨ አ ከ ኸ ዘ ዠ ጰ ጸ	12
	Triple legged	ሐ ጠ ጨ	3
Horizontal bar	Upper bar (crown)	ሸ ቐ ቨ ቸ ኘ ኸ ጀ ገ ፐ	9
	Middle bar (crossbar)	ተ ቸ ዘ ዠ	4
	Bottom bar (footing)	ረ ደ ጀ ፈ	4
Other	Looped	መ ወ ዐ ፀ	4
	With a head	የ ደ ጀ ጰ ጸ	5
	Cup type	ሀ ሠ	2
	With rings	ጨ	1

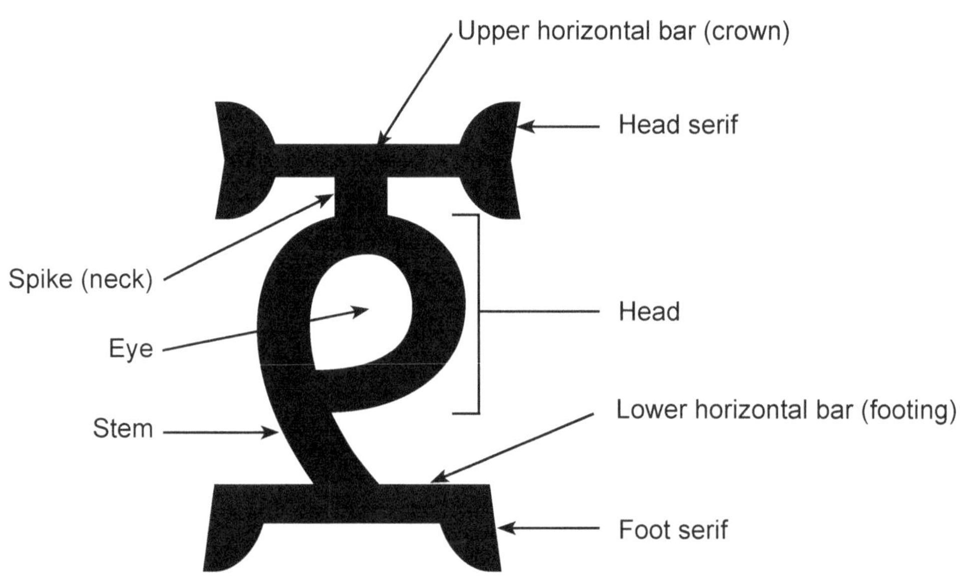

Figure 7.1: Anatomy of the Ethiopic character ጀ

Table 7.2: Ethiopic diacritical marks and the anatomy of the Ethiopic letterforms

SPECIAL FEATURES	CHARACTERS
Horizontal strokes	
Upper right	ር ና ኛ ፍ
Upper left	ሕ ቅ ት ን ኝ ዝ
Middle right	ሁ ሉ ሑ ሙ ሱ ሹ ቡ ቩ ኁ ኑ ኙ ኡ ኩ ኹ ዑ ዙ ዡ ዩ ጉ ጡ ጩ ፁ ፑ
Middle left	ብ ቭ
Lower right	ቁ ቑ ቱ ቹ ዉ ዩ ዱ ጁ ጹ ጱ
Bottom right	ሊ ሒ ሲ ሺ ቂ ቒ ቢ ቪ ኂ ቲ ቺ ኂ ኒ ኚ ኢ ኪ ኺ ዚ ዢ ጊ ጢ ጪ ጺ ጲ ፒ
Bottom left	ቃ ቓ ኃ ታ ቻ ያ ጋ ፓ
Virtical strokes (descenders)	
Right descenders	ሃ ላ ሓ ማ ሩ ሳ ሻ ባ ቫ ኣ ካ ኻ ዋ ዓ ዛ ዣ ዳ ጃ ጣ ጻ ጳ ፃ ፋ
Left descenders	ሖ ሞ ሶ ሾ ቦ ቮ ኦ ኮ ኾ ዎ ዖ ዞ ዦ ዶ ጆ ጦ ጾ ጶ ፆ ፖ
Descenders with horizontal srokes	ሂ ሚ ዊ ዒ ዲ ጂ ፂ
Descenders with rings	ሄ ሜ ዌ ዔ ጬ ጮ ፄ
Rings	
Top	ቶ ቾ ቆ ቖ
Upper right	ሆ ሮ ኆ ኖ ኞ ፎ
Bottom right	ሌ ሔ ሬ ሴ ሼ ቄ ቔ ቤ ቬ ቴ ቼ ኄ ኔ ኜ ኤ ኬ ኼ ዜ ዤ ዴ ጄ ጌ ጤ ጼ ጴ ፌ ፔ
Left side	ል ግ
Rings on horizontal strokes	ሎ ቈ ቘ ኰ ዀ ዬ ጐ ጬ
Horizontal bars	
Top bar	ሯ ኧ ዂ
Bottom bar	ሏ ሗ ሟ ሷ ሿ ቋ ቛ ቧ ቯ ቷ ቿ ኋ ኗ ኟ ኳ ዃ ዟ ዧ ዷ ጇ ጓ ጧ ጯ ጿ ጷ ፏ ፗ
Bottom bar with a ring	ቌ ቜ ኌ ኴ ዄ ጔ
Miscellaneous	
Crooked stem	ህ ች ቕ እ ክ ኽ ጥ ጭ ፕ
Spikes (slant or strait)	ስ ሽ ዕ ፅ ኅ
Leafy (type 1)	ቍ ቝ ኍ ኵ ዅ ዱ ጕ
Leafy (type 2)	ቍ ቝ ኍ ኵ ዅ ጕ
Miscellaneous	ሪ ራ ኅ ይ ፉ ፊ

The 15th century Ethiopic Octateuch, which constituted part of the collections of Emperor Teiwodiros (Tewodros) II and was looted by the British during the Anglo-Abyssinian War of 1867, is an example of such text (**Figure 7.2**). Although a trained scribe most likely wrote it, there is no evidence that the calligrapher used guidelines to give form and consistency of height to the characters.[1] Another example is a text from a 1513 Ethiopic Psalter, which is the first Ethiopic book issued from a printing press[2] (**Figure 7.3**). Although there is some measure of orderliness in the text, it is clear that the typography still presents the look of being a little disorganized and lacking relationship between most glyphs occurring next to each other. Another example is a text of the Ethiopian national anthem typed using an Ethiopic typewriter with obvious modifications by hand (**Figure 7.4**). Even within the same character family, discrepancies in height and form are typical (**Figure 7.5**). Similarly, even within the 1st order Ethiopic, which is the original consonantal Ethiopic script, characters do not adhere to a straight line at the top, at the bottom, or anywhere in between (**Figures 7.6** to **7.14**).

Figure 7.2: "A portion of the Octateuch in Ethiopian, British Library Oriental MS. 480, containing Genesis 29:11-16": Wikipedia. Original source: Plate XVIII. The S.S. Teacher's Edition: The Holy Bible. New York: Henry Frowde, Publisher to the University of Oxford, 1896.

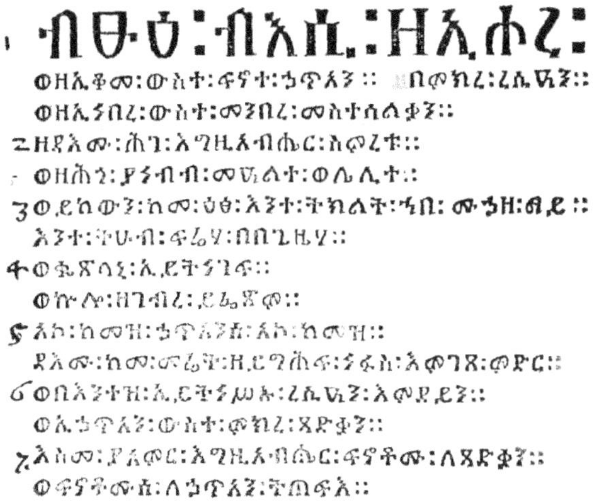

Figure 7.3: Psalm 1 in the 1513 Ethiopic Psalter *Psalterium David et cantica aliqua in lingua Chaldea [Giiz].* Image courtesy of King's College London. Reproduced with permission. Desaturated from the original.

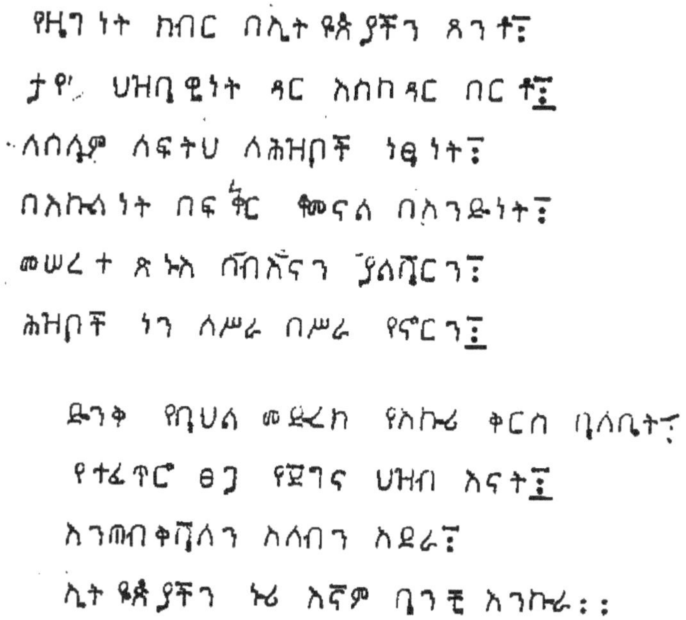

Figure 7.4: "Ethiopian anthem (since 1992) in Amharic": Wikipedia. Licensed under CC BY-SA 3.0. Desaturated from original.

These examples illustrate how Ethiopic typography failed to create visually appealing and easily readable text despite being able to produce beautiful individual glyphs. According to FontForge, developer of one of the leading font making software, a typeface must be born out of a system. FontForge further stated that,

> The single biggest issue that makes type design different is the need for every glyph in the typeface to work with every other glyph. This often means that the design and spacing of each part of the typeface ends up being a series of careful compromises. These compromises mean that we can best think about typeface design as the creation of a wonderful collection of letters but not as a collection of wonderful letters. In other words we must think about the group and how it will perform together and prioritize this over any question of what is wonderful in a single letter.[3]

One of the ways to describe the problem with traditional Ethiopic typography is that Ethiopic text almost never has flowline—baseline and capline or any horizontal lines that the text adheres to in order to help guide the eye across a page and create the look of orderliness. This becomes more obvious with large letters, such as with newspapers headlines, where it is easy to see and compare the texts of several headlines on the same page (**Figure 7.6**). The lack of orderliness is almost always independent of the particular font used (**Figures 7.7** to **7.14**). Some font developers have tried to align the glyphs between a lower baseline and an upper capline (**Figure 7.14**) with very little success because of two reasons. First, the sheer number of characters in the traditional Ethiopic writing system means that there are too many shapes and sizes to consider in designing Ethiopic typefaces possibly frustrating even the most ardent designer and software developer.[4] The second, perhaps more important, reason is that the anatomy of the Ethiopic characters requires more than an upper and lower horizontal guidelines to frame the characters and create a clear horizontal alignment that gives them orderliness and readability when they are put together in text form.

The Three Horizontal Bands of Ethiopic

Analysis of the anatomy of the Ethiopic characters provides that three horizontal 'bands' are required to create a sense of alignment and orderliness. Four guidelines create three bands, which frame the 'mass' of a glyph at the middle, ascenders and crowns at the top, and descenders at the bottom. The most significant part of an Ethiopic glyph from a graphical alignment point of view is what we shall refer to as 'MASS', which is the part of a character between the ascender and descender bands. The mass is where the glyph has the widest form or where it bulges to give the glyph the visual weight (**Figure 7.15**). The configuration of randomly selected letters shows that some of them have parts that extend into the ascender or descender bands, while others fall only within the centre band because they have no projecting elements outside of the mass. However, the exercise required that the characters be scaled to fit within the bands since virtually none of the traditional Ethiopic typefaces were designed with the three bands in mind. Thus minor modification of the glyphs is required as proposed in the following sections.

Flowlines are horizontal lines that break the space into horizontal bands. They can be used to help guide the eye across the page and can be used to impose starting and stopping points for text and images to be aligned.

ሀሁሂሃሄህሆ መሚምሞሟ ሠሢሥሦ ተታቴትቶ ወዊዌውዎ

ዐዒዔዕዖ ቸቻቼቿችቾ ጠጣጤጥጦ ፀፂፄፅፆ ፈፉፊፋፌፍፎ

Figure 7.5: Randomly selected character families in the Nyala font showing considerable variations in height and form

ጅግራ ያዝ፤ ሩጫ ከፈለግክ
ልቀቃት፣ ሥጋ ከፈለግክ እረዳት

Figure 7.6: Editorial title of the Amharic weekly *Addis Admass* in its issue of *Hiddar* 11, 2008 (E.C.). Notice the lack of horizontal alignment in the text, which is typical in Ethiopic.

Modification of the Ethiopic Letterforms

Modification of the Ethiopic letterforms or glyphs is concurrent with the overall reform proposed in this book and will consist of aligning each of the Ethiopic glyphs within the three Ethiopic horizontal typographic bands discussed above, as well as selecting the uppercase and lowercase letterforms that will suit the desired look of orderliness and readability. The letterforms of the traditional script will not help make a proper typographic differentiation between the proposed uppercase and lowercase forms because they were not originally designed for a bicameral letter case system (**Figures 7.7** to **7.14**). However, with the minor modifications discussed in the following sections, they can easily be used for such purpose.

Considering the benefits of a bicameral letter case system and the availability of more than enough characters, Ethiopic can easily be modified to show separate glyphs for the lowercase and uppercase letterforms. It must be noted, however, that some Ethiopians wrongly associate the traditional Ethiopic letterforms, particularly those that we shall refer to as the King Ezana family of fonts[5] (**Figures 7.5** to **7.10**)—which have similar shapes and forms to the text in Ethiopia's handwritten historic manuscripts—as being the sole representations of the Ethiopic script that cannot be modified. However, anyone of those letterforms is simply one of the many ways of expressing an abstract grapheme or character in a written form. In other words, although many people may be more familiar with any particular glyph, the grapheme is greater than the glyph, and as such, there can be many ways of representing the grapheme which should be considered as the more important element of the Ethiopic writing system.

Form refers to the most basic shape of a grapheme, irrespective of typeface, such as that which distinguishes the glyph for the uppercase from the glyph for the lowercase of the same letter.

ሐለመረሰሸቀቐበተቸነኘከወዘየደጀገጠጸፈ

ሀላማርሠሻቃቓበቲቺንኛኮወዛይዳጃጋጣፀፊ

Figure 7.7: The proposed uppercase (top) and lowercase (bottom) consonants in the Nyala font

ሐ ለ መ ረ ሰ ሸ ቀ ቐ በ ተ ቸ ነ ኘ ከ ወ ዘ የ ደ ጀ ገ ጠ ጸ ፈ

ሀ ላ ማ ር ሠ ሻ ቃ ቓ በ ቲ ቺ ን ኛ ኮ ወ ዛ ይ ዳ ጃ ጋ ጣ ፀ ፊ

Figure 7.8: The proposed uppercase (top) and lowercase (bottom) consonants in the Ethiopia Jiret font

ሐለመረሰሸቀቐበተቸነኘከወዘየደጀገጠጸፈ

ሀላማርሠሻቃቓበቲቺንኛኮወዛይዳጃጋጣፀፊ

Figure 7.9: The proposed uppercase (top) and lowercase (bottom) consonants in the Ethiopic Hiwua font

ሐለመረሰሸቀቐበተቸነኘከወዘየደጀገጠጸፈ

ሀላማርሠሻቃቓበቲቺንኛኮወዛይዳጃጋጣፀፊ

Figure 7.10: The proposed uppercase (top) and lowercase (bottom) consonants in the Ethiopic WashRa Bold font

ሐ ለ መ ረ ሰ ሸ ቀ ቐ በ ተ ቸ ነ ኘ ከ ወ ዘ የ ደ ጀ ገ ጠ ጸ ፈ

ሀ ላ ማ ር ሠ ሻ ቃ ቓ በ ቲ ቺ ን ኛ ኮ ወ ዛ ይ ዳ ጃ ጋ ጣ ፀ ፊ

Figure 7.11: The proposed uppercase (top) and lowercase (bottom) consonants in the Gothic-inspired Ethiopic Yigezu Bisrat font

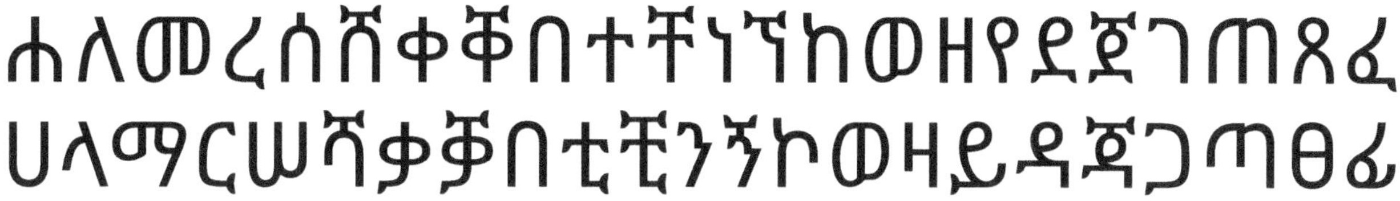

ሐለመረሰሸቀቐበተቸነኘከወዘየደጀገጠጸፈ
ሀላማርሠሻቃቓበቲቺንኝኮወዛይዳጃጋጣፀፊ

Figure 7.12: The proposed uppercase (top) and lowercase (bottom) consonants in the Noto Sans Ethiopic font

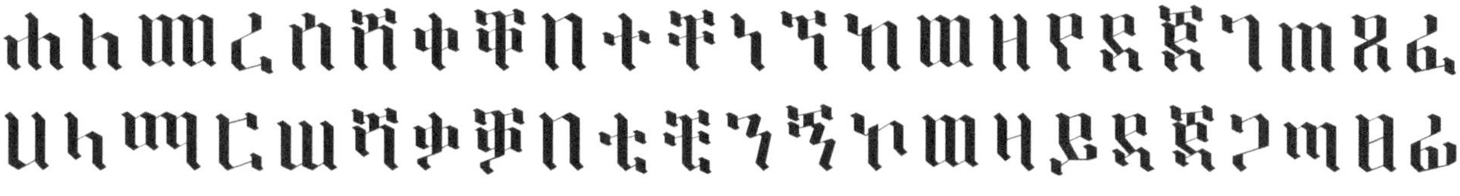

ሐለመረሰሸቀቐበተቸነኘከወዘየደጀገጠጸፈ
ሀላማርሠሻቃቓበቲቺንኝኮወዛይዳጃጋጣፀፊ

Figure 7.13: The proposed uppercase (top) and lowercase (bottom) consonants in the Ethiopic Tint font

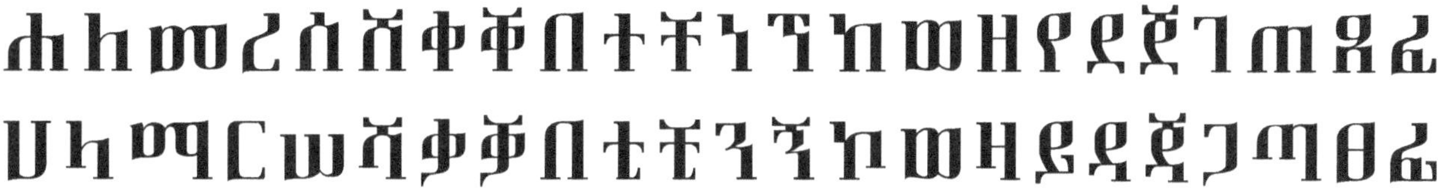

ሐለመረሰሸቀቐበተቸነኘከወዘየደጀገጠጸፈ
ሀላማርሠሻቃቓበቲቺንኝኮወዛይዳጃጋጣፀፊ

Figure 7.14: The proposed uppercase (top) and lowercase (bottom) consonants in the Ethiopic Fantuwua font

Defining the Uppercase Letterforms

An uppercase letterform, like its lowercase counterpart, is one of the written versions of the abstract grapheme that represents a particular phoneme. The uppercase letterforms are intended to be used for certain purposes which include:

- Headings for letters, articles, newspapers, and other written communications;
- To provide emphasis on warning texts, place names, notice boards, placards, posters, billboards, etc.;
- To conform with capitalization rules such as the use of a capital letter at the beginning of a sentence and for the first letter of a proper noun;
- Used with acronyms and initialisms;
- Commercial use such as in trademarks, brand names, etc.

The uppercase letterforms shall be selected with the following criteria:

1. All uppercase letterforms shall be from the ancient consonantal Ethiopic script, which later became the 1st vowelic order of the traditional Ethiopic writing system in use today. Since the uppercase forms are considered the original representative forms of the alphabet (lower case forms in the Latin alphabet were developed following informal more cursive handwriting), the proposed Ethiopic uppercase forms shall only contain characters from the ancient consonantal Ethiopic script. The characters made obsolete in the proposed reform and those that were added to the Tigirinya and Amharic alphabets in the last few centuries and form part of the reform are exceptions.
2. Where a phoneme is represented by two or more graphemes, the more complicated form shall be selected for the uppercase version of the letter to provide a more aggressive shape. A glyph with an aggressive shape fits the requirement for an uppercase letter, while at the same time it frees the simpler glyph for the lowercase letterform, which will be used in most writing.
3. The shape of the letters in the uppercase will be dependent on a particular font, but there shall be three height variations in the uppercase letterforms, which simulate three horizontal bands when written as text. The mass or substantial part of all glyphs shall fall within the centre band. Ascenders and descenders shall stretch to the top of the top band and the bottom of the bottom band, respectively.

Figure 7.15: The three horizontal bands of Ethiopic shown for randomly selected letters in the Ethiopia Jiret font.

Defining the Lowercase Letterforms

A lowercase letter or a small letter is another version of its uppercase or capital letterform. As can be observed on other bicameral scripts, lowercase letters are easier to write because of their simpler and cursive forms and are easier for reading because they create differently shaped chunks of letters as opposed to text in all capital letters. They also serve as an additional set of letterforms duplicating their application in various forms of writing and style without increasing the number of letters in the alphabet. The possibility of an additional set of letterforms contrasts with the traditional Ethiopic script, whose large number is a cause of many of the problems associated with the Ethiopic writing system. The lowercase letterforms shall be selected with the following criteria:

1. Shall be visually as distinct from their uppercase equivalents as possible. The more difference there is in looks or form between the uppercase and lowercase forms of a particular letter, the better it is for easier recognition of the lettercases.
2. Shall be those that can make handwriting, especially cursive handwriting, particularly easy. For example, the *eyin* characters, such as ዐ, shall become the lowercase vowel forms since they have simpler forms than the *elf* characters, such as አ, which shall become the uppercase vowel forms.
3. Shall contain more ascenders and descenders to create contrast with the uppercase letterforms and provide ‘movement,’ especially with free handwriting.
4. Shall take into consideration the most logical way to connect any two letters during handwriting. Analysis of Ethiopic shows that descenders are useful in such exercises, although there is an optimum number of characters with descenders beyond which there will be too many similar glyphs within the lowercase forms.
4. Shall have the ‘mass’ of each letterform be contained within the center horizontal band, while ascenders and descenders shall fall within the upper and lower bands, respectively.

The selection of the proposed lowercase letterforms are based on the results of extensive handwriting exercises I conducted to satisfy the above criteria. The letterforms were selected from the various Ethiopic vowelic orders (1st to 7th orders) in contrast to the selection of the uppercase letterforms, which were all taken from the Ethiopic 1st order (BASE CHARACTERS). Moreover, the proposed letterforms have been further modified to perfect them for their purpose. I felt a little more freedom in making slight modifications to the lowercase letterforms as they were themselves modifications to letterforms from an earlier consonantal script.

The Proposed Letterforms

The proposed letterforms (**Figures 7.16, 7.17,** and **7.19**), which make use of hypothetical horizontal bands to create an orderly set of letters are presented in this section. While the more detailed features of typography, such as tracking and kerning, need to be worked out by font developers for their respective fonts, the proposed letterforms are intended to lay the general principles of proportion, height, and horizontal alignment for both the uppercase and lowercase letterforms. A sample text in the Kahssay Eliana font with the proposed typographic reform shows the beauty of a 'wonderful collection of letters' rather than a 'collection of wonderful letters' with each glyph working well with every other glyph (**Figure 7.18**).

Figure 7.20 shows a more stylized version of the Kahssay Birikhitee font, while **Figure 7.21** shows the Ethiopic numerals in the Kahssay Birikhitee font. Note that the Ethiopic numerals are not affected by the proposed typographic modification with the basic forms remaining unaltered. However, the numeral ፼ (10,000) is proposed to be dropped along with other proposals affecting the numerical rules (for more on the Ethiopic numerals, refer to Chapter 11: Proposed Giizization of Numerical Terms). New Unicode standard code values will be required to distinguish the proposed uppercase and lowercase letterforms from the traditional script for computer applications. Although Unicode standard code values currently exist for all the Ethiopic characters in the proposed revised alphabet (since no new characters have been created), a new Unicode standard code chart for the proposed orthography will ensure that the traditional orthography is still accessible using computer application and that it is not erased from technology.

Figure 7.16: The proposed letterforms in the Kahssay Eliana font showing the anatomy of some of the uppercase (top) and lowercase (middle) letterforms and a complete set of the uppercase and lowercase letterforms (bottom) of the alphabet.

Figure 7.17: Selected proposed letterforms in the sans-serif Kahssay Misiraq font (designed for this book) showing the anatomy of the uppercase (a) and lowercase (b) letterforms; rows of the uppercase (c) and lowercase (d) letterforms; and a combination of the uppercase and lowercase letterforms (e) in the bold typeface; and a sample text (f).

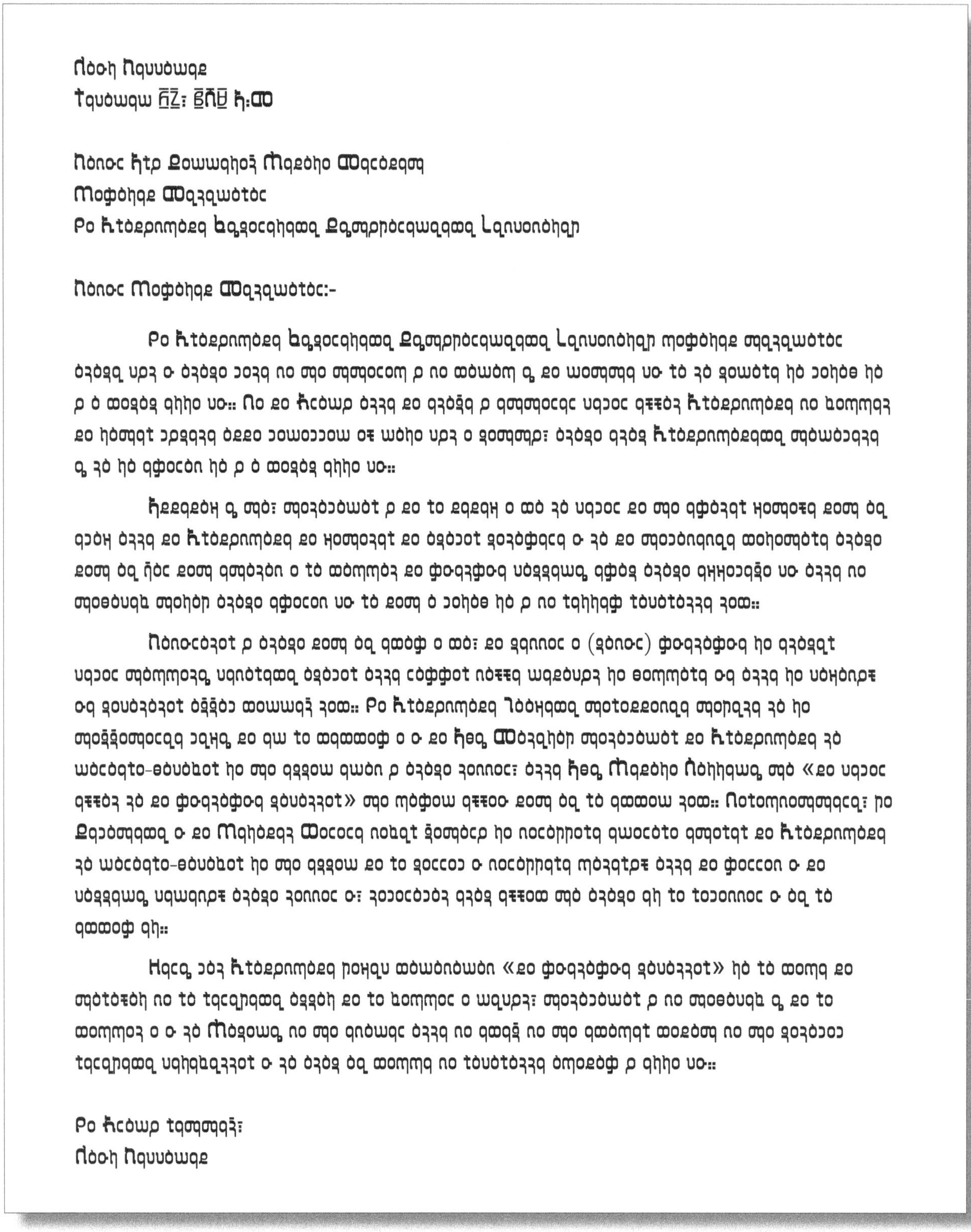

Figure 7.18: An open letter to the Ethiopian premier using the proposed alphabet and typography in the Kahssay Eliana font.

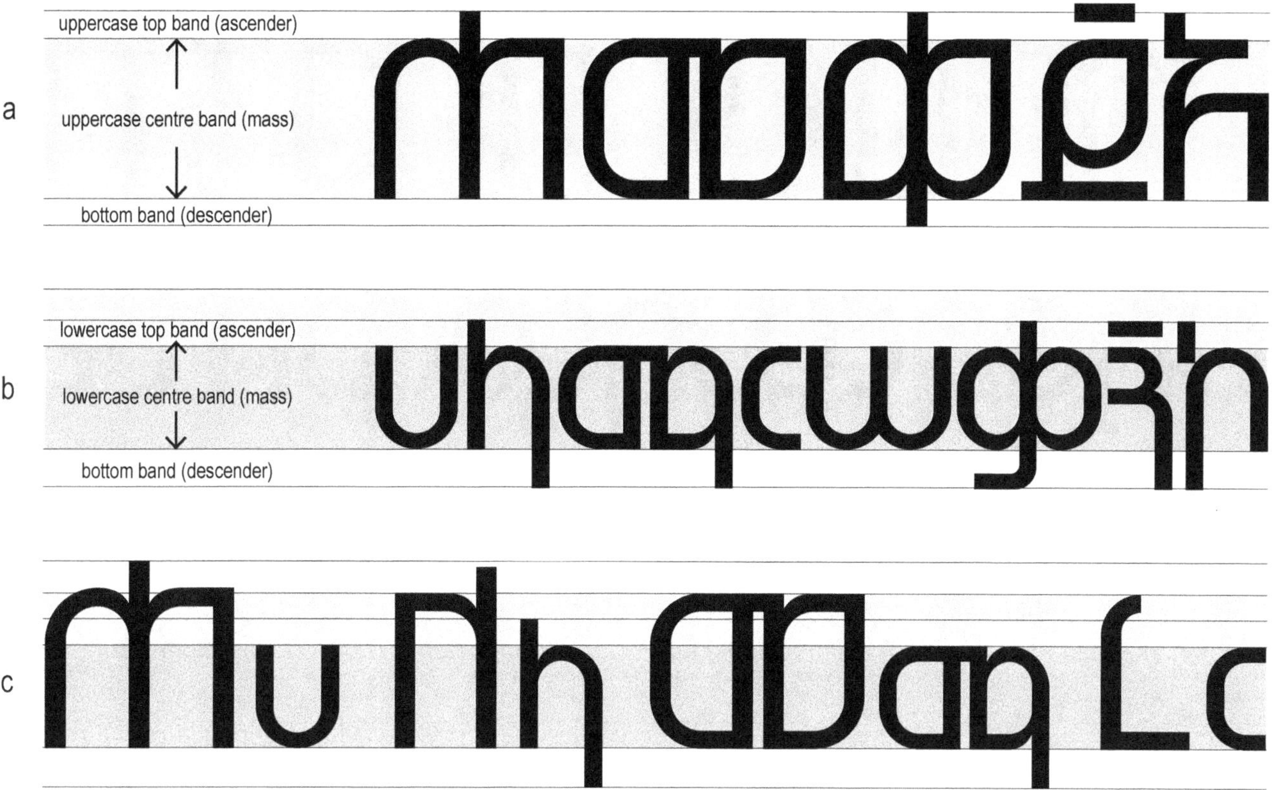

d

e

f

Figure 7.19: The proposed letterforms in the sans-serif Kahssay Birikhitee font (designed for this book) showing the anatomy of the uppercase and lowercase letterforms (a, b, and c); a complete set of the uppercase and lowercase letterforms (d and e); and a sample text ('Federal Democratic Republic of Ethiopia') in Tigirinya (f).

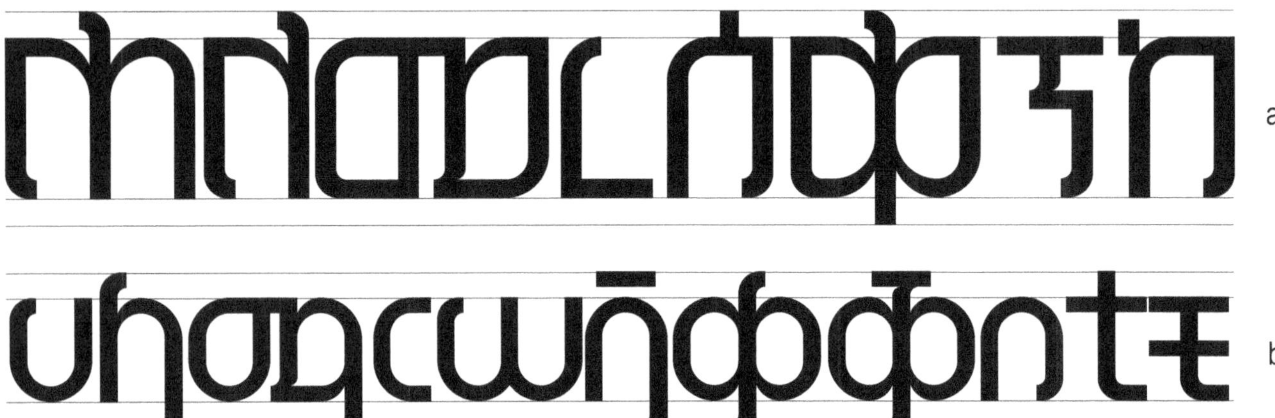

Figure 7.20: The proposed letterforms in the stylized Kahssay Birikhitee font (designed for this book) showing the anatomy of the uppercase and lowercase letterforms (a and b) and a complete set of the uppercase and lowercase letterforms (c and d).

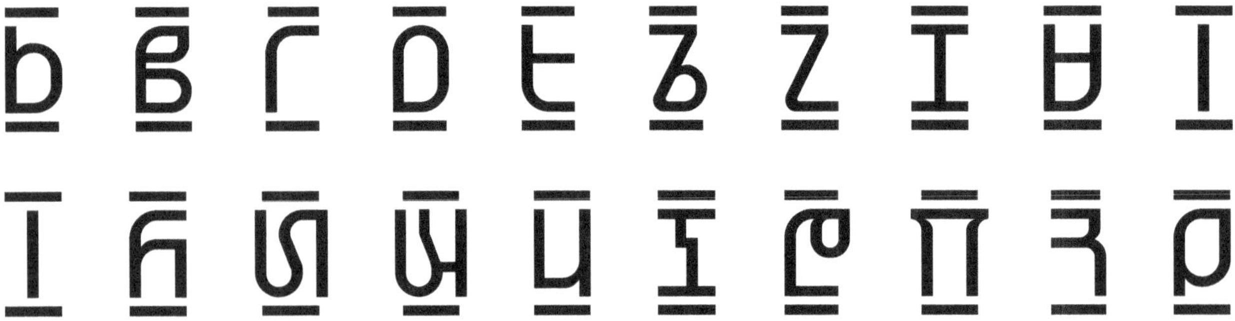

Figure 7.21: The Ethiopic numerals (1,2,3...10 (top) and 10,20,30...100 (bottom)) in the Kahssay Birikhitee font.

CHAPTER 8

HIDDASEI GIIZ: OTHER PROPOSED ORTHOGRAPHIC REFORMS

˥o ȯʒʒq noh o ḣq ஒp tȯɔɔqɔ o ⁝

—ANONYMOUS,
A Tigirinya proverb pointing out the challenges with naming the characters of the vocalized Ethiopic script

Ṅoꝏ qʒȯஒ ꝏqȯ ḣo bqஒoh mȯnon⁞ qhqq ꝏqȯ ḣo ꝏqoḣocq ꝏqoӉȯɔon ȯq ꝏqꝏqc qh—qʒȯஒ ꝏqȯ no qɯqc 'ᴜq' nȯḣo ρ⁞ qhqq ꝏqȯ no qɯqc 'ꝏq' nȯḣo ρ።

A person will either learn from the wisdom of literature, or he or she will learn from the troubles of life—either effortfully uttering the sounds of the alphabet, or unwittingly uttering the sounds of disappointment.

—POET LAUREATE TSEGAYE GABRE-MEDHIN (1936 – 2006)

In this chapter

In order for the reform of the Ethiopic writing system to be effective in addressing the communication needs of a modern Ethiopian society, it needs to be comprehensive enough to cover all features of the orthography in addition to the introduction in Chapter 6 of a truly alphabetic script with distinct consonants and vowels. In this chapter, I expand on and propose codifying of the Ethiopic orthographic rules to work in concert with the reformed alphabet.

Proposed Orthographic Rules

There are very few recognized orthographic rules in the GTA languages, and this has negatively affected communication for generations. In this section, I try to address this problem by concentrating only on some of the most important orthographic rules for Ethiopic. They are proposed rules for vowel application, gemination, capitalization, alphabetizing, acronyms, syllabification, and punctuation.

General Vowel Rule

The traditional Ethiopic orthography follows very few rules, which makes written communication in Ethiopia ineffective.

All words, including nouns and verbs, must show at least one vowel after every consonant or consonantal digraph unless otherwise prescribed by the *sadis* or 6th order vowel rule (next section). The GENERAL VOWEL RULE shall apply for all words when using the Ethiopic writing system and when transliterating using the proposed romanization of Ethiopic exclusive of personal names, proper names, trade names, names for private use, or words that otherwise will not need to be included in Ethiopic lexicography. Recommended rules for such words is to limit the number of consonants without a vowel between them to a maximum of two, except when using a digraph; and to limit the number of consonants in a digraph to a maximum of three.

The semivowel ϱ <y> corresponds to the vowels ɋ <ee> and ɋ̧ <ei>. As a result, the vowels ɋ and ɋ̧ are often pronounced with the sound of the semivowel ϱ. Similarly, the semivowel ꝏ <w> corresponds to the vowels ơ <u> and ρ <o>, which means that the vowels are often pronounced with the ꝏ sound.

Sadis (6th Order) Vowel Rules

The *sadis* vowel, represented by the Ethiopic letter ɵ <i>, is often a weak vowel. In many languages, a weak vowel is not always indicated in texts. This is also true of traditional romanization of Ethiopic, which is notoriously inconsistent with regard to the transliteration of the *sadis* vowelic order. Consider the Amharic word tɵcɵɑqɑqɵɯ <tirimmis> (chaos, disarray), which consists of four different consonants (ignoring the doubling of the consonant ɑq) and the vowel ɵ used three times. Since ɵ is a weak vowel, all of its occurrences within the word would not be marked if we use the SERA* transliteration method. However, this method does not fully appreciate the fact that Ethiosemitic languages, as a rule, require at least one vowel between any two consonants in a single word. This is best demonstrated by the consistency in the consonant-vowel order of almost all verbs in all the Ethiopic DIVISIONS (Volume II: Part I: The Ethiopic Grammatical Divisions).

The reformed Ethiopic, however, shall have consistent spelling by following the following rules with regards to the sixth vowel:

- The *sadis* vowel shall always be marked when it occurs within a word except the following special rules
- The *sadis* vowel shall not be marked when it happens to be present or is assumed to be present at the end of a word with at least one other vowel present elsewhere in the word (eg. tɵɧ[ɵ] = tɵɧ <til> (worm)). However, with a single-letter consonantal word or a single-digraph word, the *sadis* vowel shall be present even though it ends the word (e.g., ʇɵ <ni> (us) and ɧ̄ɵ <shi> (you [2PSF])).
- The *sadis* vowel shall not be marked when it would otherwise be followed by a morpheme that begins with a vowel (e.g., ɑqomɵcɔ[ɵ]ɋɋ = ɑqomɵcɔɋɋ <metxiregeea> (broom)).

*Note: SERA (System for Ethiopic Representation in ASCII) is one of the systems available for transliterating Ethiopic words using computer keyboards.

Traditional Ethiopic orthography has been extremely resistant to gemination rules among other rules.

- In a compound word, the *sadis* vowel shall not be marked when it ends the first word if the next word begins with the same consonant as the last word (eg. ɵqɑq + ɑqoɦqmnqq = ɵqɑqɑqoɦqmnqq <*xeem*melacxeea>) because of the effect of gemination, which is marked by doubling a consonant. However, the vowel is marked in other situations (e.g., nócóɋóɦónów <biridilibis>, ωommóɦonomm <setxxilebetxx>).

Gemination Rules

In linguistics, gemination refers to the elongation of consonantal sounds. Ethiosemitic languages are highly affected by consonant elongation, although they are not affected by vowel elongation. Gemination in Ethiosemitic languages is most visible with verb inflections, particularly verb inflections involving the passive voice. However, the traditional Ethiopic orthography does not have a method to mark gemination despite previous efforts by some scholars to that effect.[1] With the proposed reformed alphabet, gemination shall be marked by doubling a consonantal letter except the consonant u <h>, which is not affected by gemination. Since gemination, which is often understood as the elongation of a consonantal sound, can also be understood as being the doubling of a consonant with a weak *sadis* vowel wedged in between. Therefore, doubling of a consonant to mark gemination in written documents makes the most sense, which was almost impossible to achieve with the traditional orthography.

The rule for marking gemination of Ethiopic digraphs shall be to double the second letter of the digraph rather than doubling both letters or doubling the first letter. Doubling both letters is not only wasteful, but it also can create the wrong impression that there are two phonemes represented side by side. On the other hand, doubling the first letter, which is the basic component of an Ethiopic digraph, will create the false impression that gemination is shown for a single letter consonant rather than for a digraph. This problem will not happen when the second letter is doubled because the reader will first notice the digraph before noticing that the second letter is doubled. Moreover, since the second letter in each of the proposed Ethiopic digraphs is less important and often is used in more than one digraph, it will be easy to identify it as part of a digraph even if doubled.[2] Ethiosemitic languages do not have appreciable variations in vowel length and, therefore, vowel length shall not be marked in the writing systems for Ethiosemitic languages. However, vowel length is an important feature in Ethiocushitic languages, such as Oromiffa, and the adoption of the Ethiopic alphabet for Ethiocushitic languages will require the representation of vowel length such as by means of doubling the vowels (Chapter 13: More on the Ethiopian Language Crisis and Proposed Solutions).

Capitalization Rules

As a result of their widespread use and ease of access for reference, this book proposes the adoption of the English capitalization rules as they are or with minor modifications to suit Ethiopic's unique needs. The major rules include:

- Capitalization of the first letter of a sentence
- Capitalization of the first letter of every proper name, including capitalization of the first letter of each of the words in a proper noun phrase

- Capitalization of the first letter of each of the days of the week
- Capitalization of the first letter of the name of a month
- However, none of the first person pronouns or any other pronouns need to be capitalized except when they:
  - Appear at the beginning of a sentence,
  - Are included in a title,
  - Are part of a proper name, or
  - Are used to refer to God.

Alphabetizing Rules

Alphabetizing or alphabetical order of Ethiopic text shall be based on the sequence of the letters shown in the proposed reformed Ethiopic alphabet (the h-l-m order) and the following rules:

- Each geminated consonant shall be considered as a single letter for the purpose of alphabetizing. Therefore, the Tigirinya word uqꝏot <heewet> (life), for example, will appear before uuqɦoꝏq <hhalewa> (vigilance) in an alphabetically ordered list. Note that the first vowel in the first word is a 3rd order vowel while the first vowel in the second word is a 4th order vowel.
- Every consonantal digraph, except uu, consists of two different consonants and shall be considered as being made up of two separate letters for the purpose of alphabetizing. Therefore, the Amharic words moɑɱoʒq <txemenei> (chalk) and mnocóȹ <cxeriq> (cloth), for example, would be separated by several other words in an alphabetical listing of words.[3]
- The space between elements of a verb (such as in the passive voice form) and those in phrasal verbs and causative verbs shall be ignored for the purpose of alphabetizing. Examples are the Tigirinya verb to uuqɔρɯ as in to uuqɔρɯ ɦo (I was delighted) and the Amharic causative verb qɯ tqcoȹ as in ɑɱo qɯ tqcoȹ (to help reconcile or mediate). Therefore, for example, the causative verb qɯ tqcoȹ will appear before the noun qɯótqcqȹq (mediator) in an alphabetical listing.

The Rules for Acronyms, Initialisms, and Abbreviations

For the purpose of describing this rule, the terms acronym and intialism shall be understood as interchangeable. For formal writing, the following rules are proposed:

- Letters in an acronym shall end with the Ethiopic two-dot punctuation (፡). However, if the acronym ends a sentence, the last letter shall be followed by the Ethiopic four-dot punctuation (።) or another mark, such as an exclamation mark, as applicable (e.g.: ኤ፡ፌ፡ዲ፡ሪ፡ (E.F.D.R.))
- Acronyms shall be in capital letters.
- Acronyms shall ignore the second letter of geminated or doubled consonants (e.g. Ꭿoʠqh Ӻóʠqɔq Ϻuóɑɱónqη̄η̄q shall be Ꭿ፡Ӻ፡Ϻ፡)
- Acronyms shall ignore the second letter of digraphs (e.g. Ꚙóʠʠoɯ Πmqꝏóhρɯ Ϻρɯónuqtqh shall be Ꚙ፡Π፡Ϻ፡)
- Except for the passive voice marker particle to <te>, acronyms do not need

to include definite articles, particles, and most prepositions. For example, in the following examples, the Tigirinya and Amharic particles ʒqϱ <nay> and ϱo <ye> are not included in the Ethiopic acronyms for the Federal Democratic Republic of Ethiopia (F.D.R.E.).

ʒqϱ ፌtóϱρnmóϱq ቧqϱocqhqɷq ዴqመρhócqwqqɷq Lqnuonóhqh (ፌ:ቧ:ዴ:L:)

ρo ፌtóϱρnmóϱq ቧqϱocqhqɷq ዴqመρhócqwqqɷq Lqnuonóhqh (ፌ:ቧ:ዴ:L:)

The acronym for the Ethiopian Peoples' Revolutionary Democratic Front would be as follows:

ρo ፌtóϱρnmóϱq ጠóнónnρ፰ ኸnóϱρtqɷq ዴqመρhócqwqqɷq ገóʒónqc (ፌ:ጠ:ኸ:ዴ:ገ:)

- When present in a proper noun phrase, the passive voice maker to <te> must be included in the acronym for such a phrase because it affects meaning.

ρo †o ∩qnnoc o መoʒóɔówótqt (†:∩:መ:)	(United Nations)
ρo †o ∩qnnoc o ጠqɔocqto ኸመqcqhq (†:∩:ጠ:ኸ:)	(United States of America)
∩óbóhq ኸφuouot †o መohhowótq (∩:ኸ:†:መ:)	(Returned Goods Room)
ρo †o መohhqn̄ ቾφqρ፰ ∩óbóh (†:መ:ቾ:∩:)	(Returned Goods Room)

Syllabification and the Ethiopic Vowel Rules

With the revised orthography, every consonant or consonantal digraph in a word shall be followed by at least one vowel except that a *sadis* vowel ending a word is not marked. However, the *sadis* vowel shall not be dropped if the word contains a single consonant. As dictated by Ethiopic grammar, one or more vowels are required between any two consecutive consonants within a word except that a vowel is not required within a consonantal digraph; and there shall be no word made up entirely of a consonant or consonants. In Ethiosemitic languages, the Ethiopic vowel rule dictates that every consonant or consonantal digraph unite with one or two vowels to create a syllable. However, this rule shall be waived with transliteration of foreign words, if necessary, such as with the transliteration of English words with one syllable. (A better representation of foreign syllables is another, though minor, benefit of the proposed Ethiopic orthography.) Ethiosemitic languages are phonemically spelled and this makes establishing or identifying the following rules of syllabification relatively easier.

- For the purpose of syllabification, when a single consonant ends a three letter word (such as nqt) the whole word shall be considered as a single syllable.
- When a doubled consonant ends a word (such as in nocc), the resulting syllables shall be as follows: no·cc
- When two vowels end a word (such as mócóɔqq), the last consonant makes up the last syllable with the two vowels as follows: mócó·ɔqq
- When a vowel or vowels follow a doubled consonant, a syllable shall be formed as follows: መom·mq

The following are additional examples:

መo nó·hqt።

መo mom·mqt።

ȟ·tȯ·ƨρ·nmȯƨq፣ ḣ·nq·ɯq·ʒqq፣
qcqη̄፣ ɑqq·co·η̄qq፣
ɑqo η̄ȯ·ħocȯ·ħoc፣ toη̄ȯ·ħocȯ·ħq·cq፣
ɑqo qη̄ȯ·ħocȯ·ħoc፣ qη̄ȯ·ħocȯ·ħq·cq፣
ɑqo ɷȯ·ƍoƍ፣ ɑqo ɷ·ɷo·ƍoƍ፣ to·ɷoƍ·ƍqƍ̄።

Proposed and Existing Ethiopic Punctuation

Tigirinya and Amharic have inherited most of the Giiz punctuation. However, modern writing has necessitated the adoption of European punctuation, especially as used in English. As a result, Ethiopic punctuation combines Ethiopian and European symbols (**Table 8.1**). In addition to the most commonly used punctuation marks, all mathematical symbols shall be adopted as they are as used in English. The now almost archaic two-dot Ethiopic punctuation, which was used as word separator for centuries, is proposed to be used as an abbreviation mark and a decimal mark. Its function as a decimal point is demonstrated in the following example of a monetary value with the proposed birr sign (Chapter 12: Proposed Standardization of the Ethiopic Keyboard).

ብ1፣250፣000፡00

Table 8.1: List of the most prominent Ethiopic punctuation with retained and newly proposed functions

	GLYPH	PROPOSED OR RETAINED FUNCTION	SOURCE	REMARKS
1	፡	abbreviation mark/decimal point	Ancient Ethiopic	previously a word separator, proposed as an abbreviation mark and a decimal mark
2	፣	comma	Ethiopic	
3	፤	semicolon	Ethiopic	
4	።	period (full stop)	Ancient Ethiopic	
5	፡-	preface colon	Ethiopic	
6	፥	colon	Ethiopic	
7	※	section mark	Modern Ethiopic	
8	⁝	question mark	Modern Ethiopic	
9	፨	paragraph separator	Ethiopic	
10	!	exclamation mark	European	
11	()	parenthesis	European	
12	“ ” ‹‹ ››	quotation marks	European	
13	/	slash	European	often used for contraction of words, especially with proper names
14	—	dash	European	
15	...	ellipsis	European	

Additional Proposed Reforms

Additional proposed reforms include restoration of the Ethiopic letter names and the introduction of a spelling alphabet for Ethiopic.

Proposed Restoration of the Ethiopic Letter Names

The Ethiopic script had letter names before it became a vocalized script. Ethiopic became an alphasyllabary by fusing vowel sounds into its core characters in the 4th century. Since then it has been vocalized, which means that the name of each character is the same as its phonemic value, which is comparable to the phonics method used to teach the Latin alphabet. The reasons for restoring the Ethiopic letter names in the proposed reformed alphabet can be summarized as follows:

1. The letter names are indispensable for sounding out the spelling of words independent of the phonics or pronunciation if the spelling is requested to clarify a particular word. For example, during a phone conversation between two people, a word uttered by one may not be clearly intelligible to the other either because of poor telephone network, a different pronunciation of the word, or the existence of one or more words with similar pronunciation that can be confused. In such a case, the confusion can easily be removed by spelling out the word. With the traditional orthography, one cannot tell the spelling of a word without at the same time pronouncing the word itself, thereby not being able to provide an alternative option for clarity.[4]
2. The letter names are indispensable for pronouncing abbreviations consisting of initial letters (initialism) written in the proposed orthography.
3. The proposed alphabets are no longer alphasyllabaries and, therefore, the vocalic names no longer apply.

All of the core characters in the Ethiopic script had letter names different from their vocalized value, while few of the characters created after Giiz ceased to exist as a popular language have letter names. Although the original letter names still survive,[5] several new characters require new names. New names can be created following the most prevalent pattern in the ancient letter names, for example, by using the morpheme ዓየ <ay>, the most common denominator in the Ethiopic letter names, as a suffix after the character to be named (**Table 8.2**). With regards to characters that used to function as separate characters but are now the uppercase and lowercase forms of the same letter, only the simpler of the two former names is retained while the other one is abandoned. The following are the glyphs that have either dropped their previous letter names or did not previously have known letter names:

Consonants:

ጠ ሠ ኀ ቀ ተ ኘ ቧ ፀ

Vowels:

ኸ ኹ ኺ ኻ ኼ ኽ ኾ

ዐ ዑ ዒ ዓ ዔ ዕ ዖ

Table 8.2: Proposed and existing Ethiopic letter names

	NAME		ROMAN.	UPPER CASE	LOWER CASE	REMARKS
1	hoy	(uoջ)	h	ሐ	u	ሐ and u are proposed to be variants of the same letter
2	lawee	(ɧqꝏɋ)	l	ለ	ɧ	
3	may	(ɑɥqջ)	m	መ	ɑɥ	
4	riis	(cȯȯω)	r	ረ	c	
5	sat	(ωqt)	s	ሰ	ω	ሰ and ω are proposed to be variants of the same letter
6	shay*	(η̄qջ)*	sh	ሸ	η̄	
7	qaf	(фqь)	q	ቀ	ф	
8	qhay*	(ф̄qջ)*	qh	ቐ	ф̄	
9	beit	(nꝙt)	b	በ	n	
10	taw	(tqꝏ)	t	ተ	t	
11	cay *	(ŧqջ)*	c	ቸ	ŧ	
12	nehas	(ɿouqω)	n	ነ	ɿ	
13	nyay*	(ɿ̄qջ)*	ny	ኘ	ɿ̄	
14	kaf	(ɦqь)	k	ከ	ɦ	
15	wewee	(ꝏoꝏɋ)	w	ወ	ꝏ	
16	zey	(нoջ)	z	ዘ	н	
17	yeman	(ջoɑɥqɿ)	y	የ	ջ	
18	denit	(ꝗoɿȯt)	d	ደ	ꝗ	
19	jay*	(ꝗ̄qջ)*	j	ጀ	ꝗ̄	
20	gemil	(ɔoɑɥȯɧ)	g	ገ	ɔ	
21	txeyit	(moջȯt)	tx	ጠ	m	
22	xedey	(ɵoꝗoջ)	x	ጸ	ɵ	ጸ and ɵ are proposed to be variants of the same letter
23	ef	(oь)	f	ፈ	ь	
24	giiz*	(ɔȯȯн)*	e	አ	o	አ and o are proposed to be variants of the same letter
25	kaiib*	(ɦqȯn)*	u	ኡ	ơ	ኡ and ơ are proposed to be variants of the same letter
26	salis*	(ωqɧȯω)*	ee	ኢ	ɋ	ኢ and ɋ are proposed to be variants of the same letter
27	rabii*	(cqnȯȯ)*	a	ኣ	q	ኣ and q are proposed to be variants of the same letter
28	hamis*	(uqɑɥȯωȯ)*	ei	ኤ	ꝙ	ኤ and ꝙ are proposed to be variants of the same letter
29	sadis*	(ωqꝗȯω)*	i	እ	ȯ	እ and ȯ are proposed to be variants of the same letter
30	sabii*	(ωqnȯȯ)*	o	ኦ	ρ	ኦ and ρ are proposed to be variants of the same letter

Note that asterisks (*) indicate proposed names. The original names for ሐ, ω, and ɵ have been dropped and are now named the same as u, ሰ, and ጸ respectively, since they are now proposed to be the uppercase or lowercase forms of their respective letters.

Table 8.3: Proposed Ethiopic spelling alphabet and Morse Code

	NAME		UPPERCASE	LOWERCASE	CODE WORD	ETHIOPIC MORSE CODE
1	hoy	(υρჲ)	ጠ	υ	υqɔoc	· · · ·
2	lewee	(ɧoɷq)	ᑎ	ɧ	ɧqɧqnoɧq	· _ · ·
3	may	(ɱqჲ)	ႧD	ɑɥ	ɑɥoȸoɧo	_ _
4	riis	(cȯɯ)	Ꮭ	c	ɯoɑɥocq	· _ ·
5	sat	(ɯqt)	ṅ	ɯ	conoȯȯ/conoȯ	· · ·
6	shay	(ῆqჲ)	ᾱ	ῆ	ῆqῆoɑɥoɿɿq	· · · _
7	qaf	(ȸqƀ)	ȸ	ȸ	ȸqcq	_ _ · _
8	qhay	(ȸqჲ)	ȸ	ȸ	ȸoȝqɑɥ	· · _ _
9	beit	(nqt)	Π	n	nqɿqῆqɿȯɔoɧ	_ · · ·
10	tewee	(toɷq)	†	t	tȯɔȯcqჲ	_
11	cay	(ŧqჲ)	Ŧ	ŧ	ŧqჲȯɿq	_ · _ ·
12	nehas	(ɿoυqɯ)	ነ	ɿ	ɿoȸȸoɑɥȯt	_ ·
13	nyay	(ɿ̄qჲ)	ኘ	ɿ̄	ȝqɿ̄ɿ̄q	· _ _ ·
14	kaf	(ɦqƀ)	Ἡ	ɦ	ɦonocρ	_ · _
15	wewee	(ɷoɷq)	Ꮗ	ɷ	ɷoɧȯȝqq	· _ _
16	zey	(ʜoჲ)	H	ʜ	ʜoɑɥoɿ	_ _ · ·
17	yeman	(ჲoɱqɿ)	ρ	ჲ	ჲoυq	_ · _ _
18	denit	(ȝoɿȯt)	Ք	ȝ	ȝonon	_ · ·
19	jay	(ȝ̄qჲ)	Ք̄	ȝ̄	ȝ̄ȯȝ̄ȝ̄ȯɔq	· _ _ _
20	gemil	(ɔoɱqȯɧ)	ገ	ɔ	ɔqɑɥȯnqɧɧq	_ _ ·
21	txeyit	(ɱoჲȯt)	ጠ	m	moɑɥoɿq	· _ · _
22	xedey	(ȹoȝoჲ)	Ջ	ɵ	ɵoυυqჲ/ɵoυqჲ	_ · · _
23	ef	(oƀ)	Ƀ	ƀ	ƀocoɯ	· · _ ·
24	giiz	(ɔȯȯʜ)	ħ	o	oco	·
25	kaib	(ɦqȯn)	ኩ	o	oɔqɿȯȝq	· · _
26	salis	(ɯqɧȯɯ)	ኪ	q	qʜqɿq/qtqρ...	_ _ _ _
27	rabii	(cqnȯȯ)	ካ	q	qɷqɯq	· _
28	hamis	(υqɱqȯɯȯ)	ኬ	q	qȝoɿ	_ _ _ ·
29	sadis	(ɯqȝȯɯ)	ክ	ȯ	ȯɿȯȝ̄ocq	· ·
30	sabii	(ɯqnȯȯ)	ኮ	ρ	ρcρɑɥqq	_ _ _

Note: Each of the proposed code word is the same for the respective uppercase and lowercase letterforms.

Table 8.4: The NATO phonetic alphabet

LETTER	TELEPHONY	MORSE CODE	LETTER	TELEPHONY	MORSE CODE
A	Alfa (Alpha)	•_	N	November	_•
B	Bravo	_•••	O	Oscar	___
C	Charlie	_•_•	P	Papa	•__•
D	Delta	_••	Q	Quebec	__•_
E	Echo	•	R	Romeo	•_•
F	Foxtrot	••_•	S	Sierra	•••
G	Golf	__•	T	Tango	_
H	Hotel	••••	U	Uniform	••_
I	India	••	V	Victor	•••_
J	Juliett	•___	W	Whiskey	•__
K	Kilo	_•_	X	X-ray	_••_
L	Lima	•_••	Y	Yankee	_•__
M	Mike	__	Z	Zulu	__••

Note: Further work may be needed to establish a type of Morse Code for Ethiopic.

Proposed Spelling Alphabet and Ethiopic Morse Code

A spelling alphabet is a collection of words that are used to represent alphabetic letters in oral communication. Also known as voice procedure alphabet, radio alphabet, or telephone alphabet, a spelling alphabet consists of words that begin with a letter that they are used to represent providing additional clarity when needed. Such clarity is especially useful in situations where the name of a given letter may sound confusingly similar to one or more of the other letters in the alphabet. When pronounced over a radio, a telephone, a public address system, or other voice communication modes where visual clues are absent, or when they are pronounced by a person who speaks Ethiopic as their second language, some letters can be mistaken for others. Various alphabets, including English, French, German, Italian, Turkish, Greek and Russian, have spelling alphabets. Similarly, Ethiopic needs a spelling alphabet, such as the one proposed in this section. The proposed spelling alphabet and Morse Code for Ethiopic (**Table 8.3**) presupposes the restoration of the Ethiopic letter names and most of its code words are names of geographical locations to celebrate the diversity of Ethiopia. Spelling alphabets can help in communicating accurate spelling in various situations. During radio communication, flight and navigation, telemedicine, intelligence gathering, and military actions, for example, accurate spelling can be critical. An example of a spelling alphabet for military purposes is the NATO phonetic alphabet (**Table 8.4**), which is based on the Latin alphabet. The proposed codes for the Ethiopic Morse Code closely correspond to the International Morse Code in so far as the Latin letters phonetically correspond to the Ethiopic letters. I have proposed new codes[6] for the Ethiopic letters with no direct equivalency in the ISO basic Latin alphabet and have allocated the **.__.** code to the Ethiopic letter ፐ/ፕ from the Latin letter P/p.

Benefits of the Proposed Alphabetic Reform

Alphabetization will benefit users of Ethiopic in many ways. Some of the benefits are discussed below.

Correct and Uniform Spelling

Leslau (1973) correctly observed that Amharic spelling lacked consistency. Part of the reason for the widespread lack of consistency in Ethiopic spelling is that the Ethiopic traditional orthography allows words to be written almost exactly as they sound, even when the root words and their pronunciations change for various grammatical and phonemic reasons. As a result, it is difficult to identify the basic morphophonemic elements responsible for many of the Ethiopic word derivatives.

As far as Ethiosemitic languages are concerned, correct spelling can only be achieved with alphabetization. For example, the Amharic de-synthesized sentence መጥት ኦ ኣል (He has come) is often written in the traditional orthography as the single-word sentence መጥቷል. Notice that the characters ኦ <o> and ኣ <a> are assimilated into the character ቷ <toa>, showing that ኦ and ኣ are vowels. It is interesting to note that ኦ represents the third person singular male (3PSM) pronoun in DIVISION 2, while መጥት <metxit> and ኣል <al> are the main and the auxiliary verbs, respectively, in DIVISION 2. Such distinctions are often lost with inflected words in the traditional Ethiopic orthography.

While de-synthesization of Ethiopic without the introduction of alphabetization may at first glance seem to be sufficient in addressing this problem, a more detailed look at the benefits of alphabetization shows why that is not the case. For example, when the Tigirinya verb uuqeon is used in sentences in the three Ethiopic orthographies (**Table 8.5**)—the traditional (synthesizing), the transitional (de-synthesizing only) and the reformed (de-synthesizing and reformed alphabet)—such as with the use of the Ethiopic 2PPM, 2PSF, and 2PPF pronouns as subjects and the 3PSM pronoun as an object, it becomes clear that the proposed orthography is far superior to the other orthographies. Only the proposed or-

Table 8.5: Spelling inconsistencies in Tigirinya with the traditional Ethiopic orthography

	SYNTHESIZED		DE-SYNTHESIZED		REFORMED ORTHOGRAPHY	
1	ሓጸብኩምዎ	<hhaxebikumiwo>	ሓጸብ ኩም ዎ	<hhaxeb kum wo>	uuqeon ɧoɑq ρ	<hhaxeb kum o>
2	ሓጸብኪዮ	<hhaxebikeeyo>	ሓጸብ ኪ ዮ	<hhaxeb kee yo>	uuqeon ɧq ρ	<hhaxeb kee o>
3	ሓጸብክንኦ	<hhaxebikinio>	ሓጸብ ክን ኦ	<hhaxeb kin o>	uuqeon ɧó ʒ ρ	<hhaxeb kin o>

Table 8.6: Spelling inconsistencies in Amharic with the traditional Ethiopic orthography

	SYNTHESIZED		DE-SYNTHESIZED		REFORMED ORTHOGRAPHY	
1	ገበናዬ	<gebebayei>	ገበና ዬ	<gebena ei>	ɔonoʒq ɋ	<gebena ei>
2	መንገዴ	<menigedei>	መንገድ ኤ	<meniged ei>	ɑqoʒóɔoʠ ɋ	<meniged eiv>

thography shows the same spelling for all the occurrences of the object pronoun in the three sentences. The traditional orthography shows it variously in the three sentences due to the effects of nearby vowels or custom of pronunciation. Similar problems also are present with phrases using possessive pronouns as demonstrated with Amharic phrases (**Table 8.6**). In the examples, the traditional orthography variously shows the first person possessive pronoun as ዬ and ኢ. However, the same pronoun is present in both expressions and can only be clearly shown by using the reformed alphabet.

Ability to Represent Gemination

One of the failures of the traditional Ethiopic orthography has been its inability to indicate gemination despite the fact that gemination is an important feature of Ethiosemitic languages. As discussed earlier, some Ethiopian scholars—including Haddees Alemayyehu who is best known for his 1965 Amharic classic novel *Fiqir Isike Meqabir* (Love Till the Grave)—had attempted to create a method to mark gemination. Haddees Alemayyehu correctly avoided doubling the alphasyllabic characters of the traditional Ethiopic script to mark gemination because, unlike a Latin letter, an Ethiopic character written twice is read twice as separate syllables and would not indicate gemination unless the syllable belongs to the 6th order. The method he and other innovators used, instead, is to show two dots over each germinated character. However, this method was never implemented beyond two or so individual literary works. Marking gemination in an alphasyllabic script, which fuses consonants and vowels together, without a comprehensive reform of Ethiopic was probably a futile attempt. Gemination or consonant elongation is best understood as the sound of a double consonant with a weak *sadis* vowel sandwiched in between. The problem with marking the characters of the traditional script for gemination was that each character is named or vocalized the same as it is pronounced, which means that it was probably difficult for the general public to understand what the gemination marks were trying to show since every character has a fixed vocalized value. By contrast, the proposed orthographic reform, which introduces a separate letter for each consonant and vowel, provides the opportunity to correctly mark gemination by doubling consonants for the first time in the history of Ethiopic.

Collation

Collation is the process of organizing written information in a set order. Collation is applicable in the gathering, categorizing, cataloguing, and filing documents, among other document processing. One example of collation is the listing of items in alphabetical order, which was hitherto difficult (although not impossible) to do with the traditional Ethiopic orthography due to the sheer number of characters and the inability of most literate people to quickly remember the Ethiopic alphabetical order. Moreover, the widespread spelling inconsistencies, and the unhealthy dependence on English as a medium of communication, meant that listing items in the traditional Ethiopic alphabetical order was a futile attempt. With only twenty-nine letters for each of their respective proposed reformed alphabet, Tigirinya and Amharic will be well positioned to harvest the benefits of alphabetical ordering like never before.

Better Ability to Represent New Sounds

One of the failures of the traditional Ethiopic script has been that it is unable to cope with new sounds without needing to create brand new glyphs representing each new phoneme making the already large set of characters even larger. This problem was particularly apparent when the script was adopted by non-Ethiosemitic languages a few generations ago. Unlike the traditional Ethiopic script, the reformed Ethiopic script will allow the representation of new sounds by using digraphs without the need to create new glyphs.

The proposed orthography will undoubtedly be a better writing system for Oromiffa and other non-Ethiosemitic languages in the country for two important reasons. First, it has two more vowels than the Latin alphabet, which makes it more suitable to Oromiffa, for example, which needs up to ten vowels. Second, it has more consonants than the Latin alphabet, including ቀ, ጎ, ጐ, ጠ, and ፀ that are needed, by many non-Ethiosemitic languages in Ethiopia (Chapter 13).

Reading Speed and Accuracy

One of the benefits of the proposed orthography will be improved reading skills. The reduced number of letters in the alphabets will help to recognize the difference between letters at a glance, and the modularization of Ethiopic grammar will help produce fewer confusing words.

Recognition of Root Words, Stemming, and Language Technology

One of the benefits of the proposed reformed alphabet is the ease of identifying morphological similarities.

<u>Stemming</u>:

Stemming is the process of reducing an inflected or derived word into its lowest form—its root word. By not being rigidly phonemic, the proposed writing system will help the recognition of root words easily. Consider, for example, the Tigirinya infinitive verb form ምፍታው <mifitaw>, which is written using the traditional orthography and means 'to like.' One of its word derivatives is ፈቲኻዮዶ? <Feteekhayodo?>, which is a single-word sentence and means, "Did you like it?". Another of its word derivatives is ፈትየዮ <fetiyieyo> in the sentence ፈትየዮ ነይሬ, which means, "I had liked it." It is clear that the only Ethiopic character common to the infinitive verb and the two derivatives above is ፈ <f>. When the words are romanized, the Latin letters f and t become common to all the words but are still not enough to establish a clear relationship between the words. For the students of Tigirinya and Amharic, finding the root word of a word derivative is a daunting task because of the inability to make see the relationship between the root word and its derivatives. The solution, I propose, is the use of the reformed alphabetized Ethiopic writing system, which would show the above verb as ɑqȯ ɓȯtqo, which is romanized as *mi fitau* and not *miftaw*, which is the traditional romanization of the verb. Note that the last letter is u and not w. The important thing here is that the last sound is created by a vowel and not by a consonant. As we shall see, in Amharic and Tigirinya, the vowels in a verb change to reflect grammatical tense, among other things, but consonants almost never change, and the verb structure remains intact for the most part. The last vowel changes between o and ȯ. The following are additional examples:

Ꮭotqȯ ɦq ρ ąρ?	<Feteei ka o do?>
Ꮭotqȯ ą ρ ʒoϱȯc ą	<Feteei ei o neyir ei>
Ꮭotqȯ o ρ	<Feteei u o>

Argaw and Asker (undated paper) stated that stemming is used in natural language processing (NLP), information retrieval (IR), machine translation (MT) and text classification. Moreover, it will be easily applied to language technologies, such as in machine reading and speech synthesis.

CHARACTER RECOGNITION:

One of the most significant benefits of the proposed orthography is the ease with which character recognition can be achieved because it will not only help reduce the total number of characters in the writing system but also reduce too many similar and confusing characters that have hitherto been the hallmark of the traditional Ethiopic script. The problem of a large number of characters in some scripts has been cited as a reason for the lack of progress in successful character recognition methods. Referring to African indigenous scripts, Meshesha and Jawahar (undated paper) argued that,

> Research in the recognition of African indigenous scripts faces major challenges due to (i) the use of large number [of] characters in the writing and (ii) existence of large set of visually similar characters.[7]

With only twenty-nine letters for each of their respective proposed reformed alphabet, Tigirinya and Amharic will be well positioned to harvest the benefits of character recognition methods, which will have many technological applications.

CLARITY & AVOIDANCE OF THE PHONETIC TRAP

As an alphasyllabary, the traditional writing system often hides true vowels, showing instead what are referred to as semivowels. The following are examples:

ው instead of o and ዋ instead of q

ይኸዉን'ዩ instead of ȯq ɦooʒ q o

When a noun or pronoun which ends with a vowel other than the *sadis* vowel is followed by the Amharic definite article ዑ, (see the section *Articles in Tigirinya and Amharic* in Chapter 14 of Volume II) it produces the sound shown by the traditional orthography as ዉ <wu>. Similarly, when a noun or pronoun which ends with a vowel other than the *sadis* vowel is followed by the other definite article in Amharic, ዑኣ, it produced the sound represented by the traditional orthography as ዋ <wa> (**Table 8.7**). Another example that demonstrates the problems associated with the traditional Ethiopic orthography is the pronoun ዕኢ <iee>, which is present in various grammatical persons in both Tigirinya and Amharic, but hitherto was completely hidden. The proposed reformed orthography makes it easier to show this pronoun (**Table 8.8**) and other hidden pronouns and articles.

CURSIVE HANDWRITING

Among other benefits, the proposed Ethiopic orthography will be easier for handwriting, especially by allowing cursive handwriting for speed as well as style. The fact that there are so few letters to write again and again means that it would be easier to master speedy writing with the proposed reformed alphabet.

Table 8.7: How the traditional orthography fails to clearly show definite articles especially for Amharic

	OLD	TRANSITION	SEMIVOWEL VALUE	NEW ORTHOGRAPHY		ENGLISH
1	ጠረጴዛዉ	ጠረጴዛ ዉ	ዉ = ዓ + ዑ	ጠዐረዐበጠዔዘዓ ዑ	<txerepxeiza u>	the [MDA] table
2	ብዕሩ	ብዕር ኡ	-	በዕዕረ ዑ	<biir u>	the [MDA] pen
3	በሬዉ	በሬ ዉ	ዉ = ዔ + ዑ	በዐረዔ ዑ	<berei u>	the [MDA] ox
4	ገበናዬ	ገበና ኤ	ዬ = ዓ + ዔ	ገዐበዐነዓ ዔ	<gebena ei>	my privacy
5	ላሟ	ላም ዋ	ዋ = ዑዓ	ለዓመ ዑዓ	<lam ua>	the [FDA] cow
6	ላሞ	ላም ዎ	ዎ = ዖ	ለዓመ ዖ	<lam o>	your cow
7	በጓ	በግ ዋ	ዋ = ዑዓ	በዐገ ዑዓ	<beg ua>	the [FDA] sheep
8	በጉ	በግ ኡ	-	በዐገ ዑ	<beg u>	the [MDA] sheep

Note: MDA stands for male definite article and FDA stands for feminine definite article

Table 8.8: The hitherto hidden Tigirinya and Amharic pronoun ዕዒ <iee>

	OLD	TRANSITION	SEMIVOWEL VALUE	NEW ORTHOGRAPHY		ENGLISH
	ሲመጣ	ስ ዪ መጣ	ዪ = ዕዒ	ሰዕ ዕዒ መዐጠዓ	<si iee metxa>	when he comes
	እንዲመጣ	እንድ ዪ መጣ	ዪ = ዕዒ	ዕነዕደ ዕዒ መዐጠዓ	<inid iee metxa>	that he may come
	ይምጣ	ዪ ምጣ	ዪ = ዕዒ	ዕዒ መዕጠዓ	<iee mitxa>	let him come

Note: ይ = ዕዒ

PART IV

OTHER PROPOSED STANDARDS FOR ETHIOPIC

Chapter 9

Proposed Standard System for the Romanization of Ethiopic

It is charged with three inscriptions, in different languages and characters, commemorating a gift of corn from Ptolemy Philadelphus to the inhabitants of that part of the country [Egypt]; particularly mentioning Memphis, and the month *Mecbir*, the sixth month in the Egyptian year. The first inscription is in hieroglyphicks, the second in the old Coptick, or vulgar character of the ancient Egyptians, and the last in Greek capitals.

—The Gentleman's Magazine, 1802

It is arguable that no one system of transliteration [of Ethiopic] can ever satisfy the needs both of the linguist or specialist and of the "man in the street."

—Stephen Wright, 1964

IN THIS CHAPTER

In a globalized 21st-century world, frequent communications between various entities around the world have increasingly become critical for success, which intern is dependent on the ability to use mutually intelligible writing systems. Businesses and government agencies often encounter words from foreign languages in their international communications either in a familiar script or in a different script that requires rendering text into one's script. Often such communications involve the exchange of information through documents, among others, bank drafts, import-export permits, investment licenses, customs documents, property deeds, memorandums of understanding, and product descriptions. Such exchange of information between different languages and writing systems necessarily involves the translation, transcription, transliteration, or combinations thereof, of various words and phrases that can have critical legal, commercial, or security implications. Examples of such words are personal names, proper names, product names, technical terms, trademarks, and geographical names.

While I believe that comprehensive and highly sophisticated language materials must be developed to help facilitate the translation of words, especially technical terms, from major world languages to Ethiopian languages and vice versa; the scope of this chapter is limited to proposing a standard method for the romanization of Ethiopic. In an increasingly sophisticated world, where accuracy is critical, a standard system of romanization—involving transliteration, transcription, or both—is necessary to make Ethiopian materials available to the rest of the world in a consistent and accurate manner.

In today's globalized world, the need for the translation, transcription, and transliteration of documents between Ethiopian and foreign languages has become unprecedented.

Many languages in the world that use a non-Latin alphabet have a standardized system of romanization. Examples are Chinese, Japanese, Korean, and Slavic languages including Russian. Similarly, both Tigirinya and Amharic need a transliteration system developed through a scientific approach, such as the one I propose in this chapter. The fact that English, the de facto global language, uses a Latin-based alphabet means that most transliterations will involve the Latin alphabet. Moreover, since the Latin script is adopted by more languages in the world than any other script, a standard romanization will facilitate communication between Ethiopians and speakers of many other languages in the world. Although based on English phonology for the most part, in preparing the proposed system, I have followed what Wright (1964) referred to as the long-standing tradition of transliterating Ethiopic "consonants as in English, vowels as in Italian" because of the unpredictable role of vowels in English.[1]

Definition of Terms

Romanization

Romanization is the systematic rendering of text from a non-Latin alphabet, such as Ethiopic, into the Latin alphabet (also known as the Roman alphabet). While translation is the process of translating words or text from a source language to a target language—with the emphasis being the replacement of words from a source language with words of equivalent meaning in the target language—romanization is the rendering of words or text from a source script into the Latin script—with the emphasis being the transplantation of words or text from one script into another. Transliteration and transcription are different forms of rendering text from one script into another that can be employed by romanization.

Transliteration and Transcription

Transliteration is the conversion of text from one script to another by representing each letter or character in the target script, while transcription is the conversion of text from one script to another based on the phonemic values of the text. Transliteration helps mirror the letters between two scripts, while transcription helps mirror the pronunciation represented by the letters. In other words, with transliteration, there is a one-to-one correspondence between the letters of the text in the original and target languages; while with transcription, there is a one-to-one correspondence in the phonemes of the texts in the original and target languages.

ግእዝ	ካዕብ	ሣልስ	ራብዕ	ኃምስ	ሳድስ	ሳብዕ
ሀ ha	ሁ hu	ሂ hi	ሃ ha	ሄ he	ህ ho	ሆ hω
ለ la	ሉ lu	ሊ li	ላ la	ሌ le	ል lo	ሎ lω
ሐ ha	ሑ hu	ሒ hi	ሓ ha	ሔ he	ሕ ho	ሖ hω
መ ma	ሙ mu	ሚ mi	ማ ma	ሜ me	ም mo	ሞ mω
ሰ ſa	ሱ ſu	ሲ ſi	ሳ ſa	ሴ ſe	ስ ſo	ሶ ſω
ረ ra	ሩ ru	ሪ ri	ራ ra	ሬ re	ር ro	ሮ rω
ሠ sa	ሡ su	ሢ si	ሣ sa	ሤ se	ሥ so	ሦ sω
ቀ ka	ቁ ku	ቂ ki	ቃ ka	ቄ ke	ቅ ko	ቆ kω
በ ba	ቡ bu	ቢ bi	ባ ba	ቤ be	ብ bo	ቦ bω
ተ ta	ቱ tu	ቲ ti	ታ ta	ቴ te	ት to	ቶ tω
ኀ ha	ኁ hu	ኂ hi	ኃ ha	ኄ he	ኅ ho	ኆ hω
ነ na	ኑ nu	ኒ ni	ና na	ኔ ne	ን no	ኖ nω
አ a	ኡ v	ኢ i	ኣ a	ኤ e	እ o	ኦ ω
ከ cha	ኩ chu	ኪ chi	ካ cha	ኬ che	ክ cho	ኮ chω
ወ wa	ዉ wu	ዊ wi	ዋ wa	ዌ we	ው wo	ዎ wω
ዐ a	ዑ v	ዒ i	ዓ a	ዔ e	ዕ o	ዖ ω
ዘ za	ዙ zu	ዚ zi	ዛ za	ዜ ze	ዝ zo	ዞ zω
የ ia	ዩ iu	ዪ ii	ያ ia	ዬ ie	ይ io	ዮ iω
ደ da	ዱ du	ዲ di	ዳ da	ዴ de	ድ do	ዶ dω
ገ ga	ጉ gu	ጊ gi	ጋ ga	ጌ ge	ግ go	ጎ gω
ጠ tha	ጡ thu	ጢ thi	ጣ tha	ጤ the	ጥ tho	ጦ thω
ጰ pa	ጱ pu	ጲ pi	ጳ pa	ጴ pe	ጵ po	ጶ pω
ጸ za	ጹ zu	ጺ zi	ጻ za	ጼ ze	ጽ zo	ጾ zω
ፀ za	ፁ zu	ፂ zi	ፃ za	ፄ ze	ፅ zo	ፆ zω
ፈ fa	ፉ fu	ፊ fi	ፋ fa	ፌ fe	ፍ fo	ፎ fω
ፐ pa	ፑ pu	ፒ pi	ፓ pa	ፔ pe	ፕ po	ፖ pω
a paruũ.	v longũ.	i longũ.	a longũ.	e longũ.	e paruũ.	o lõgũ.

Figure 9.1: Romanization of the main set of the Ethiopic characters in the Ethiopic Psalter of 1513 *(Psalterium David et cantica aliqua in lingua Chaldea)*. Image courtesy of King's College London. Reproduced with permission. Desaturated from the original.

Drawbacks of Traditional Romanization Systems of Ethiopic

To date Ethiopia does not have an officially sanctioned method for the romanization of Ethiopic.

Various systems for the romanization of Ethiopic have been in use for generations, although no one system has been able to satisfy all the modern needs of Ethiopic. The system of romanization shown in the *Psalterium David et cantica aliqua in lingua Chaldea* (David's Psalter and Song of Songs in the [Giiz][2] Language) (**Figure 9.1**), which was published by Marcellus Silber in 1513, was probably the earliest attempt ever made to create a system of romanization for Ethiopic since the decline of Axum—which had relations with Rome and ancient Greece and even minted its own coins with Greek inscriptions. Among the problems with this outdated system are the use of the glyphs 'ɑ' (Latin alpha) and 'a' as different vowels, the use of the vowel o for the Ethiopic 6th order, in addition to using a peculiar vowel sign (ꝏ) to represent the Ethiopic 7th order.

Owing to various foreign contacts exposing Ethiopians to different European orthographies, romanization of Ethiopic around the middle of the 20th century was influenced by a "strong (but not always refined) flavour of French, Italian, English or (occasionally) German ingredients" so that Menigesha was variously spelled as "Menguecha, Mengascia, Mangasha or Mangascha," and Siyyum as "Seyoum and Sium," for example (Wright, 1964). Wright further argued that such inconsistencies posed a great challenge for librarians for filing based on alphabetical order as well as for foreign firms with standing mailing lists in the country.[3] Similarly, Young (1997) observed that there was no standard means of transcribing Ethiopian names of people and other words into English. Even government agencies do not have a standard system of romanization with the only possible exception being the Ethiopian cartographic spelling system—which is almost exclusively used for cartography.

The problems associated with other traditional methods for the romanization of Ethiopic include the use of letters with diacritics, which are difficult to reproduce using regular computer keyboards; the use of a single Latin letter to render more than one Ethiopic consonant or vowel sound, or the application of more than one Latin letter to the same Ethiopic consonant or vowel sound; the application of Latin letter cases to differentiate between consonants of different sounds; and inconsistent application of Latin vowel letters to render the Ethiopic sixth order vowel sound. The problem associated with the application of more than one Latin letter to the same Ethiopic consonant or vowel sound could happen within the same Ethiopic language or between two or more Ethiopic languages. For example, as of November 2016, the BGN/PCGN 2007 System for the Romanization of Tigirinya (**Table 9.1**) and the BGN/PCGN 1967 System for the Romanization of Amharic (**Table 9.2**)—which are documents jointly prepared by the United States Board on Geographic Names and United Kingdom's Permanent Committee on Geographical Names—show significant discrepancies especially with the rendering of the Ethiopic vowel sounds, which are otherwise identical in both languages. As a result, the inconsistencies in the romanization of individual Ethiopic consonantal sounds (**Table 9.3**) and individual Ethiopic vowel sounds (**Table 9.4**) are compounded when any one of the Ethiopic characters or alphasyllables (each of which is made up of a consonant and one or more vowel) is rendered in the Latin script. For example, the sixth order Ethiopic

Table 9.1: The BGN/PCGN 2007 System for the Romanization of Tigirinya.[4]

	1ST ORDER	2ND ORDER	3RD ORDER	4TH ORDER	5TH ORDER	6TH ORDER	7TH ORDER	EXTENSION 4TH ORDER
1	ሀ he	ሁ hu	ሂ hi	ሃ ha	ሄ hie	ህ h / hĭ	ሆ ho	
2	ለ le	ሉ lu	ሊ li	ላ la	ሌ lie	ል l / lĭ	ሎ lo	ሏ lwa
3	ሐ ḥe	ሑ ḥu	ሒ ḥi	ሓ ha	ሔ hie	ሕ h / hĭ	ሖ ho	
4	መ me	ሙ mu	ሚ mi	ማ ma	ሜ mie	ም m / mĭ	ሞ mo	ሟ mwa
5	ረ re	ሩ ru	ሪ ri	ራ ra	ሬ rie	ር r / rĭ	ሮ ro	ሯ rwa
6	ሰ se	ሱ su	ሲ si	ሳ sa	ሴ sie	ስ s / sĭ	ሶ so	ሷ swa
7	ሸ she	ሹ shu	ሺ shi	ሻ sha	ሼ shie	ሽ sh / shĭ	ሾ sho	ሿ shwa
8	ቀ k’e	ቁ k’u	ቂ k’i	ቃ k’a	ቄ k’ie	ቅ k’ / k’ĭ	ቆ k’o	ቋ k’wa
9	ቐ kh’e	ቑ kh’e	ቒ kh’i	ቓ kh’a	ቔ kh’ie	ቕ kh’ / kh’ĭ	ቖ kh’o	ቛ kh’wa
10	በ be	ቡ bu	ቢ bi	ባ ba	ቤ bie	ብ b / bĭ	ቦ bo	ቧ bwa
11	ቨ ve	ቩ vu	ቪ vi	ቫ va	ቬ vie	ቭ v / vĭ	ቮ vo	
12	ተ te	ቱ tu	ቲ ti	ታ ta	ቴ tie	ት t / tĭ	ቶ to	ቷ twa
13	ቸ che	ቹ chu	ቺ chi	ቻ cha	ቼ chie	ች ch / chĭ	ቾ cho	ቿ chwa
14	ነ ne	ኑ nu	ኒ ni	ና na	ኔ nie	ን n / nĭ	ኖ no	ኗ nwa
15	ኘ nye	ኙ nyu	ኚ nyi	ኛ nya	ኜ nyie	ኝ ny / nyĭ	ኞ nyo	ኟ nywa
16	አ e / ’e	ኡ u / ’u	ኢ i / ’i	ኣ a / ’a	ኤ ie / ’ie	እ ĭ / ’ĭ	ኦ o / ’o	
17	ከ ke	ኩ ku	ኪ ki	ካ ka	ኬ kie	ክ k / kĭ	ኮ ko	ኳ kwa
18	ኸ khe	ኹ khu	ኺ khi	ኻ kha	ኼ khie	ኽ kh / khĭ	ኾ kho	ዃ khwa
19	ወ we	ዉ wu	ዊ wi	ዋ wa	ዌ wie	ው w / wĭ	ዎ wo	
20	ዐ ‘e	ዑ ‘u	ዒ ‘i	ዓ ‘a	ዔ ‘ie	ዕ ‘ / ‘ĭ	ዖ ‘o	
21	ዘ ze	ዙ zu	ዚ zi	ዛ za	ዜ zie	ዝ z / zĭ	ዞ zo	ዟ zwa
22	ዠ zhe	ዡ zhu	ዢ zhi	ዣ zha	ዤ zhie	ዥ zh / zhĭ	ዦ zho	ዧ zhwa
23	የ ye	ዩ yu	ዪ yi	ያ ya	ዬ yie	ይ y / yĭ	ዮ yo	
24	ደ de	ዱ du	ዲ di	ዳ da	ዴ die	ድ d / dĭ	ዶ do	ዷ dwa
25	ጀ je	ጁ ju	ጂ ji	ጃ ja	ጄ jie	ጅ j / jĭ	ጆ jo	ጇ jwa
26	ገ ge	ጉ gu	ጊ gi	ጋ ga	ጌ gie	ግ g / gĭ	ጎ go	ጓ gwa
27	ጠ t’e	ጡ t’u	ጢ t’i	ጣ t’a	ጤ t’ie	ጥ t’ / t’ĭ	ጦ t’o	ጧ t’wa
28	ጨ ch’e	ጩ ch’u	ጪ ch’i	ጫ ch’a	ጬ ch’ie	ጭ ch’ / ch’ĭ	ጮ ch’o	ጯ ch’wa
29	ጰ p’e	ጱ p’u	ጲ p’i	ጳ p’a	ጴ p’ie	ጵ p’ / p’ĭ	ጶ p’o	
30	ጸ ts’e	ጹ ts’u	ጺ ts’i	ጻ ts’a	ጼ ts’ie	ጽ ts’ / ts’ĭ	ጾ ts’o	ጿ ts’wa
31	ፈ fe	ፉ fu	ፊ fi	ፋ fa	ፌ fie	ፍ f / fĭ	ፎ fo	ፏ fwa
32	ፐ pe	ፑ pu	ፒ pi	ፓ pa	ፔ pie	ፕ p / pĭ	ፖ po	

Note: The romanization of the Tigirinya vowels closely matches most informal systems in use today in that it employs no diacritics except for the diacritical mark (breve) over i in the 6th order showing a short vowel, where alternately no vowel may be shown depending on whether or not a vowel is heard when the syllable is pronounced. Interestingly, although the Ethiopic vowels are virtually identical between Tigirinya and Amharic, the 1967 BGN/PCGN system for the romanization of Amharic (**Table 9.2**) shows significant differences in the romanization of vowels of the 3rd, 5th, and 6th orders between the two languages.

Table 9.2: The BGN/PCGN 1967 System for the Romanization of Amharic.[5]

	1ST ORDER	2ND ORDER	3RD ORDER	4TH ORDER	5TH ORDER	6TH ORDER	7TH ORDER	EXTENSION 4TH ORDER
1	ሀ hā	ሁ hu	ሂ hī	ሃ ha	ሄ hē	ህ h / hi	ሆ ho	
2	ለ le	ሉ lu	ሊ lī	ላ la	ሌ lē	ል l / li	ሎ lo	ሏ lwa
3	ሐ hā	ሑ hu	ሒ hī	ሓ ha	ሔ hē	ሕ h / hi	ሖ ho	
4	መ me	ሙ mu	ሚ mī	ማ ma	ሜ mē	ም m / mi	ሞ mo	ሟ mwa
5	ሠ se	ሡ su	ሢ sī	ሣ sa	ሤ sē	ሥ s / si	ሦ so	
6	ረ re	ሩ ru	ሪ rī	ራ ra	ሬ rē	ር r / ri	ሮ ro	ሯ rwa
7	ሰ se	ሱ su	ሲ sī	ሳ sa	ሴ sē	ስ s / si	ሶ so	ሷ swa
8	ሸ she	ሹ shu	ሺ shī	ሻ sha	ሼ shē	ሽ sh / shi	ሾ sho	ሿ shwa
9	ቀ k’e	ቁ k’u	ቂ k’ī	ቃ k’a	ቄ k’ē	ቅ k’ / k’i	ቆ k’o	ቋ k’wa
10	በ be	ቡ bu	ቢ bī	ባ ba	ቤ bē	ብ b / bi	ቦ bo	ቧ bwa
11	ቨ ve	ቩ vu	ቪ vī	ቫ va	ቬ vē	ቭ v / vi	ቮ vo	
12	ተ te	ቱ tu	ቲ tī	ታ ta	ቴ tē	ት t / ti	ቶ to	ቷ twa
13	ቸ che	ቹ chu	ቺ chī	ቻ cha	ቼ chē	ች ch / chi	ቾ cho	ቿ chwa
14	ኀ hā	ኁ hu	ኂ hī	ኃ ha	ኄ hē	ኅ h / hi	ኆ ho	ኋ hwa
15	ነ ne	ኑ nu	ኒ nī	ና na	ኔ nē	ን n / ni	ኖ no	ኗ nwa
16	ኘ nye	ኙ nyu	ኚ nyī	ኛ nya	ኜ nyē	ኝ ny / nyi	ኞ nyo	ኟ nywa
17	አ ā / ’ā	ኡ u / ’u	ኢ ī / ’ī	ኣ a / ’a	ኤ ē / ’ē	እ i / ’i *	ኦ o / ’o	
18	ከ ke	ኩ ku	ኪ kī	ካ ka	ኬ kē	ክ k / ki	ኮ ko	ኳ kwa
19	ኸ he	ኹ hu	ኺ hī	ኻ ha	ኼ hē	ኽ h / hi	ኾ ho	
20	ወ we	ዉ wu	ዊ wī	ዋ wa	ዌ wē	ው w / wi	ዎ wo	
21	ዐ ‘ā	ዑ ‘u	ዒ ‘ī	ዓ ‘a	ዔ ‘ē	ዕ ‘ / ‘i	ዖ ‘o	
22	ዘ ze	ዙ zu	ዚ zī	ዛ za	ዜ zē	ዝ z / zi	ዞ zo	ዟ zwa
23	ዠ zhe	ዡ zhu	ዢ zhī	ዣ zha	ዤ zhē	ዥ zh / zhi	ዦ zho	ዧ zhwa
24	የ ye	ዩ yu	ዪ yī	ያ ya	ዬ yē	ይ y / yi	ዮ yo	
25	ደ de	ዱ du	ዲ dī	ዳ da	ዴ dē	ድ d / di	ዶ do	ዷ dwa
26	ጀ je	ጁ ju	ጂ jī	ጃ ja	ጄ jē	ጅ j / ji	ጆ jo	ጇ jwa
27	ገ ge	ጉ gu	ጊ gī	ጋ ga	ጌ gē	ግ g / gi	ጎ go	ጓ gwa
28	ጠ t’e	ጡ t’u	ጢ t’ī	ጣ t’a	ጤ t’ē	ጥ t’ / t’i	ጦ t’o	ጧ t’wa
29	ጨ ch’e	ጩ ch’u	ጪ ch’ī	ጫ ch’a	ጬ ch’ē	ጭ ch’ / ch’i	ጮ ch’o	ጯ ch’wa
30	ጰ p’e	ጱ p’u	ጲ p’ī	ጳ p’a	ጴ p’ē	ጵ p’ / p’i	ጶ p’o	
31	ጸ ts’e	ጹ ts’u	ጺ ts’ī	ጻ ts’a	ጼ ts’ē	ጽ ts’ / ts’i	ጾ ts’o	ጿ ts’wa
32	ፀ ts’e	ፁ ts’u	ፂ ts’ī	ፃ ts’a	ፄ ts’ē	ፅ ts’ / ts’i	ፆ ts’o	
33	ፈ fe	ፉ fu	ፊ fī	ፋ fa	ፌ fē	ፍ f / fi	ፎ fo	ፏ fwa
34	ፐ pe	ፑ pu	ፒ pī	ፓ pa	ፔ pē	ፕ p / pi	ፖ po	

Note that the system does not show romanization values for characters in the Amharic Extension Set other than the 4th order characters; and the use of Roman letters with macrons: ā for certain characters in the 1st order, ī for the 3rd order, and ē for the 5th order.

Table 9.3: Examples of some traditional systems of romanization for selected Ethiopic consonantal sounds

ETHIOPIC CHARACTER	ሐ	ሸ	ቀ	ቐ	ቸ	ኀ	ኘ	ኸ	ዐ	ዠ	ጀ	ጠ	ጨ	ጰ	ጸ	ፀ
IPA	ħ	ʃ	k'	ʁ'	ʧ	h	ɲ	h	ʕ	ʒ	ʤ	t'	ʧ'	p'	ts'	ts'
Marcellus Silber	h	-	k	-	-	h	-	-	a	-	-	th	-	p	z	z
Scholars[6]	ḥ	š	q	q	č	h̲	ñ	k̲	ʿ	ž	ǧ	ṭ	ċ	p̣	ṣ	ṡ
Informal	h	sh	k	k	ch	h	gn	-	-	-	j	t	ch	p	ts	ts
Informal	H	sh	q	-	ch	h	ny	-	-	-	j	T	CH	P	S/zs	S
SERA[7]	H	x	q	Q	c	'h	N	K	ʿ	Z	j	T	C	P	S	'S
BGN/PCGN 2007 Tigrinya	ḥ	sh	k'	kh'	ch	ḥ	ny	kh	ʿ	zh	j	t'	ch'	p'	ts'	ts'
BGN/PCGN 1967 Amharic	h	sh	k'	-	ch	h	ny	h	ʿ	zh	j	t'	ch'	p'	ts'	ts'
US Library of Congress	ḥ	š	q	q̄	č	h̲	ñ	x	ʿ	ž	ǧ	ṭ	ċ	p̣	ṣ	ṡ

Table 9.4: Examples of some traditional systems of romanization for Ethiopic vowel sounds

ETHIOPIC ORDER	1st	2nd	3rd	4th	5th	6th	7th Order
IPA	ə	u	i	a	e	ɨ	o
Marcellus Silber	ɑ	u	i	a	e	o	ꝏ
Scholars[6]	ä	u	i	a	e	ə	o
Informal	e	u	i	a	e / ee	i / -	o
Informal	a	oo	i / ee	a	ie	e / -	o
SERA[7]	e	u	i	a	E	-	o
BGN/PCGN 2007 Tigrinya	e	u	i	a	ie	- / ĭ	o
BGN/PCGN 1967 Amharic	e	u	ī	a	ē	- / i	o
US Library of Congress	a	u	i	ā	é	e / -	o

character ጺ <xi> can have as many as 36 different renderings in the Latin script from the values in **Table 9.3** and **9.4** as the following examples show (which is simply unacceptable for a nation that desperately needs to develop a culture of efficient communication):

ṣə, ṣi, ṣ, tsi, tse, ts, Se, Si, S, zo, zsi, zse, zs, ts'i, ts'

The System for Ethiopic Representation in ASCII (SERA), is probably the closest thing Ethiopic has to a convention for transliteration into the Latin script without the use of diacritical marks (although it uses the apostrophe as one). Although primarily devised for inputting text using Latin-based computer keyboards to be able to write in the Ethiopic script, it has also been used as a system for romanization of Ethiopic. Developed in the 1990's by various professionals, some of the

A standard system of romanization of Ethiopic is indispensable for socio-economic progress of the nation.

basic weakness of the system as a means for the romanization of Ethiopic are its inability to represent the Ethiopic sadis vowel as dictated by Ethiopic grammar, its use of letter cases to differentiate between different phonemes (eg. e and E, and q and Q), and the use of the semivowel W in the Ethiopic extension set. Naturally syllabic, the *SADIS* VOWEL RULE of the Ethiopic grammar dictates that every consonant, especially within a verb, be followed by at least one vowel (Chapter 8: Other Proposed Orthographic Reforms). Word inflection in Ethiopic occurs primarily through changes in the vowels within a word, often without affecting the consonants, and the *sadis* vowel is one of the most affected ones in word inflections. The use of letter cases for transliteration is problematic because it forces all text always to have mixed lettercases and never only the lowercase or only the uppercase letterforms, which may be required for emphasis, caution, or style. Moreover, note only does such a system not allow for capitalization of the first letter of a sentence or the first letter of a proper noun, depending on a particular word, but also shows capital letters in the middle of words making the entire text look unnatural (e.g., *ityoPya* for ኢትዮጵያ). The use of the labiovelar 'w' to represent a vowel in the Ethiopic extension system is inaccurate. The more accurate use is the vowel 'u' (Chapter 8).

Pervasive spelling inconsistency in Ethiopic literature from the use of the traditional Ethiopic script, even when romanization is not involved, is a problem that is compounded during romanization. The traditional Ethiopic spelling is highly vulnerable to spelling inconsistencies (Chapter 3: Overview of Ethiopic Grammatical and Orthographic Problems), which include inconsistent omission of vowels and consonants during word derivation due to variations in pronunciation between different geographical areas or even between individuals. Other problems, such as the inability to show gemination and the absence of capitalization in the traditional Ethiopic writing system create ambiguity for transliteration and, therefore, add to the inconsistencies associated with the various currently used methods for the romanization of Ethiopic. Moreover, multiplicate characters representing the same phoneme, at least in the case of Amharic, create additional challenges for consistency in the romanization of Ethiopic. Allen [et al.] (2014) stated that the "Ethiopic script often has multiple syllables corresponding to the same Latin letter, making it difficult to assign unique Latin names"[8] for many characters. Regarding the dilemma associated with the challenges of transliterating Ethiopic, Wright (1964) lamented that "whatever the basic framework we adopt, we shall always be liable to face the alternatives of being inconsistent or of tacitly "correcting" the Amharic spelling (which may involve scientific impropriety)," and that "there can be few people, Ethiopians as well as foreigners, who have regular contact with transliterations of Ethiopian words, for whom the present chaotic situation is not a source of inconvenience and dismay."[9]

The problems associated with the romanization of Ethiopic is an obstacle to accurate communication and thus an obstacle to the socio-economic progress of the nation. In order to permanently resolve this problem, I propose a standard system of romanization based on a scientific analysis of the Ethiopic writing system and grammar.

The Proposed System of Romanization

The benefits from a standard system of romanization of Ethiopic will literally extend beyond Ethiopia's boarders.

Tested over five years on thousands of Tigirinya and Amharic words, the proposed system for the romanization of Ethiopic (**Table 9.5**) is intended to closely replicate Ethiopic sounds or phonemes as much as possible using letters of the Latin alphabet at the same time providing a one-to-one transliteration of letters as unique as the Ethiopic script. The system has been developed to such accuracy and efficiency that it can be used to transliterate virtually any word or text of any length and kind in Tigirinya and Amharic by paralleling every consonant, vowel, or combination thereof, virtually without creating ambiguities typical of most methods of romanization of Ethiopic. Similarly, the system can be informally used to write text in Giiz, Tigirinya or Amharic (and probably most other Ethiopian languages) in circumstances where the Ethiopic letters are not immediately available, such as where computer systems and keyboards do not support Ethiopic. Such text can even be converted back to the Ethiopic script, if necessary, with a simple computer application given the adoption of a universally applicable standard method for the transliteration of Ethiopic.

The proposed system, which is primarily a system of transliteration rather than transcription, aims to address two main problems—the lack of enough consonants in the Latin alphabet to represent many 'non-European' Ethiopic phonemes and the fact that the Latin alphabet does not have enough vowel letters to represent all seven Ethiopic vowels. Therefore, although the proposed romanization is an adaptation of the Latin alphabet as used in English, several non-European sounds have been represented by proposed digraphs uniquely developed for Ethiopic (**Tables 9.6** and **9.7**). The transliteration method I propose is born out of the need to render letters of the Ethiopic script into the Latin script without the dreaded diacritical marks. The method includes letters that do not have direct equivalency in the Latin script, which necessitated the re-engineering of the phonemic values of the Latin letters while still avoiding diacritical marks.

The benefits of transliteration of Ethiopic into the Latin script far exceed any perceived need for absolute accuracy in rendering phonemes, which is impossible to achieve even between European languages. The most important aim of transliteration of Ethiopic, therefore, is accuracy in written communication to guarantee that every Ethiopic word can be spelled in the Latin script with the exact and predictable correlation between the two scripts regardless of some minor discrepancy in pronunciation. There is no guarantee, for example, that 'a' and 'aa' will be pronounced any differently by non-Ethiopians, who mostly make very little distinction between a single consonant and a double consonant for gemination. Therefore, the main purpose of accurate transliteration of Ethiopic is primarily for accuracy of written communication. Ethiopians will be the final arbiters for how transliterated documents should be pronounced as long as there is a standard system for the romanization of the Ethiopic script. Romanization is intended to benefit Ethiopians to avoid confusion and must be designed by Ethiopians to satisfy their needs. Official romanization of Chinese and Korean, for example, are designed by their respective nations for their own benefit.

Romanization of the Proposed Ethiopic Consonants and Vowels

For the proposed system, I have followed the traditionally accepted convention of assigning romanization values based on, where possible, phonemic equivalencies between the Ethiopic and Latin letters (**Table 9.5**). In doing so, I was able to utilize 24 of the 26 Latin letters—with the two anomalies being the Latin letters p and v, whose phonemes are not native to Ethiopic. Given the 30 Ethiopic letters between the GTA alphabets, the deficit is addressed by making use of Latin digraphs, most of which closely match the phonemic values of the respective Ethiopic letters. Examples are sh, ny, and ee. The letter x is proposed to represent the Ethiopic letter Ꭺ (lowercase: ɵ). It is also proposed to form the proposed digraphs tx, cx, and px (**Tables 9.5** and **9.6**). Other proposed digraphs consist of pairs of other letters. (Note that, when and if the bare minimum representation of phonemes or sounds is desired for reasons of simplicity, methods for standard transcription, as opposed to transliteration, of Tigirinya and Amharic can be considered by simply dropping the second letter of each digraph.) Nevertheless, comparisons to other traditional methods for the romanization of Ethiopic (**Table 9.5**) shows that the proposed system is still the simplest most consistent and easy-to-use method.

Compared to the Ethiopic consonants, transliteration of the Ethiopic vowels using Latin letters is more difficult primarily because there is very little direct equivalency between the Ethiopic and Latin vowels despite the fact that a handful of vowels affect all the syllables in Ethiopic (and all language, for that matter). Traditionally, the discrepancies between the vowels of the two scripts is resolved either by applying diacritical marks to one or more Latin vowel letters to get the extra two vowel signs. Informally, one or two of the Latin vowel letters are used often inconsistently to represent more than one Ethiopic vowel sound.

Traditionally, the method used to romanize the Ethiopic sixth order (the weakest) vowel is probably the most inconsistent of all the Ethiopic orders. Not including letters with diacritics or the inverted e symbol (ə), the most common way of representing the sixth order consists of one of three options—using the vowel 'i,' or the vowel 'e,' or skipping it altogether—which are often applied inconsistently even within the same text. On the other hand, the most common method of representing the Ethiopic third order vowel, which is one of the most consistent, uses the vowel 'i.' However, this method often creates ambiguity between the third and sixth order vowels. The sixth order is the most occurring vowel in Ethiopic grammar, while the third order is the least occurring vowel. The third order vowel can easily be romanized by using double e (ee). Therefore, I propose the use of a double e (ee) for the third order in favour of using the simple single letter vowel 'i' for the most occurring sixth order. With respect to the proposed romanization of Ethiopic vowels, note the following:

- 'E' is equivalent to the Ethiopic vowel ħ (lowercase: o). However, virtually no word begins with this vowel sound in Ethiopic grammar. Therefore, 'e' can be assigned for transliterating the vowel ɋ when the Ethiopic vowel appears at the begging of a word, which otherwise is transliterated as 'ee'.

- The choice of the digraph 'ei' for q̥ compares to the traditionally used di-

Table 9.5: The proposed system of romanization and comparisons to other systems in use

	REFORMED GIIZ		PROPOSED ROMANIZATION		TRADITIONALLY USED PHONETIC SYMBOLS			PRE-REFORM UNICODE ID		REMARKS AND EXAMPLES
	UPPER CASE	LOWER CASE	UPPER CASE	LOWER CASE	IPA	OTHER	INFORMAL	UPPER CASE	LOWER CASE	
1	[illegible]	[illegible]	H	h	h	h	h	1200	1203	
2	[illegible]	[illegible]	L	l	l	l	l	1208	120B	
3	[illegible]	[illegible]	M	m	m	m	m	1218	121B	
4	[illegible]	[illegible]	S	s	s	s	s	1230	1223	
5	[illegible]	[illegible]	R	r	r	r	r	1228	122D	
6	[illegible]	[illegible]	Sh	sh	ʃ	š	sh	1238	123B	sh as in shoe
7	[illegible]	[illegible]	Q	q	k’	ḳ	k	1240	1242	q as in *Qedam*
8	[illegible]	[illegible]	Qh	qh	ʁ’	ḳʰ	k	1250	1252	qh as in *Meqhele*
9	[illegible]	[illegible]	B	b	b	b	b	1260	1263	
10	[illegible]	[illegible]	T	t	t	t	t	1270	1272	
11	[illegible]	[illegible]	C	c	ʧ	č	ch	1278	127A	ch as in church
12	[illegible]	[illegible]	N	n	n	n	n	1290	1295	
13	[illegible]	[illegible]	Ny	ny	ɲ	ñ	gn	1298	129D	gn as in lasagna
14	[illegible]	[illegible]	K	k	k	k	k	12A8	12AB	
15	[illegible]	[illegible]	W	w	w	w	w	12C8	12CB	
16	[illegible]	[illegible]	Z	z	z	z	z	12D8	12DB	
17	[illegible]	[illegible]	Y	y	j	y	y	12E8	12ED	
18	[illegible]	[illegible]	D	d	d	d	d	12F0	12F3	
19	[illegible]	[illegible]	J	j	ʤ	ǧ	j	1300	1303	j as in joke
20	[illegible]	[illegible]	G	g	g	g	g/gh	1308	130B	
21	[illegible]	[illegible]	Tx	tx	t’	ṭ	t	1320	1323	
22	[illegible]	[illegible]	X	x	ts’	ṣ	ts	1338	1340	
23	[illegible]	[illegible]	F	f	f	f	f	1348	134A	
24	[illegible]	[illegible]	E	e	ʔə	ʾä	a	12D0	(12D0)	e as in berth
25	[illegible]	[illegible]	U	u	ʔu	ʾu	u	12D1	(12D1)	o as in who
26	[illegible]	[illegible]	Ee	ee	ʔi	ʾi	i	12D2	(12D2)	ee as in beet
27	[illegible]	[illegible]	A	a	ʔa	ʾa	a	12D3	(12D3)	a as in father
28	[illegible]	[illegible]	Ei	ei	ʔe	ʾe	e	12D4	(12D4)	as last é in résumé
29	[illegible]	[illegible]	I	i	ʔɨ	ʾə	i/[-]*	12D5	(12D5)	i as in quality
30	[illegible]	[illegible]	O	o	ʔo	ʾo	o	12D6	(12D6)	o as in hotel

Table 9.6: Proposed system of romanization for the proposed Tigirinya and/or Amharic consonant digraphs

	PROPOSED CONSONANT COMBINATIONS			REPLACED CHARACTER	PROPOSED ROMANIZATION			TRADITIONALLY USED PHONETIC SYMBOLS			REMARKS / EXAMPLES
	UPPER CASE	SENTENCE CASE	LOWER CASE		UPPER CASE	SENTENCE CASE	LOWER CASE	IPA	OTHER	INFORMAL	
1	ሰሰ	ሰu	uu	ሐ	HH	Hh	hh	ħ	ḥ	h	ሰuqꝏóнq̧ȝ <Hhawizein>
2	n̄n	n̄n	n̄n	ቸ'	C	C	c	ʧ	č	ch	Ŧnqɛóȝq <Cayina> (China)
3	hሰ	hu	ɦu	ኸ	KH	Kh	kh	x	x		
4	Hn	Hn	ʜn	ዠ	ZH	Zh	zh	ʒ	ž	-	
5	mn	mn	ɱn	ጨ	CX	Cx	cx	tʃ'	č̣	ch	mnomnnonówq <cxecxxebisa>
6	nm	nɱ	nɱ	ጰ	PX	Px	px	p'	p̣	p	
7	nሰ	nu	nu	ፐ	P	P	p	p	p	p	nuɸɦqɯ <polees> (police)
8	nH	nʜ	nʜ	ቨ	V	V	v	v	v	v	nʜqɛócoɯ <vayires> (virus)

Table 9.7: Proposed system of romanization for the proposed Giiz and Tigirinya special vowel digraphs

	PROPOSED VOWEL COMBINATIONS			REPLACED CHARACTER	PROPOSED ROMANIZATION			TRADITIONALLY USED PHONETIC SYMBOLS			REMARKS / EXAMPLES
	UPPER CASE	SENTENCE CASE	LOWER CASE		UPPER CASE	SENTENCE CASE	LOWER CASE	IPA	OTHER	INFORMAL	
1	-	-	-	ዐ	-	-	-	-	-	-	[Reserved]
2	ƕƕ	ƕo	oo	ዑ	UU	Uu	uu	ʕu	ʿu	'u	uudet (revolution)
3	ħħ	ħq	qq	ዒ	EEE	Eee	eee	ʕi	ʿi	'i	eeewal (kitten)
4	ɧɧ	ɧq	qq	ዓ	AA	Aa	aa	ʕa	ʿa	'a	aalem, aayinee (world, eye)
5	-	-	-	ዔ	-	-	-	-	-	-	[Reserved]
6	ɦɦ	ɦó	óó	ዕ	II	Ii	ii	ʕɨ	ʿə	'i	xaiiree (effort)
7	-	-	-	ዖ	-	-	-	-	-	-	[Reserved]

graph 'ie,' which is an inferior option. I propose rearranging the digraph to *ei* to represent the Ethiopic vowel better in all its occurrences. Although, when q̧ occurs inside a word or at the end of a word, such as in ሰóɦɦqɯq̧, the contrast between *Sillasei* and *Sillasie* is not stark (traditionally, the word is romanized as *Selassie*). However, when the vowel begins a word as in ɧq̧qoȝ (Eden), it becomes apparent that the better romanization is *Eiden* and not *Ieden*.

Romanization of the Proposed Ethiopic Digraphs

As discussed in Chapter 6, Ethiopic digraphs are proposed for Tigirinya and Amharic to eliminate redundant characters from the Ethiopic script. Among the phonemes that can be represented by digraphs are those that are either foreign and exist only within loanwords, or are used so seldom that it is more efficient to replace each of them with a digraph. An example is the digraph nн which is proposed to replace the traditional Ethiopic character ቨ which, in turn, was introduced to Ethiopic relatively recently to represent the same phoneme that the Latin letter 'v' represents. There are no indigenous Ethiopic words that use the phoneme represented by ቨ. In fact, all words that use the character ቨ or one of its seven orders are loanwords, such as ቫይረስ <vayires> (virus). These digraphs will not be counted as additional members of the alphabet, just as digraphs in English are not added to the count of the twenty-six letters of the English alphabet. The proposed digraph n̄n represents ቸ in the Tigirinya alphabet since the phoneme represented by ቸ is rarely used in Tigirinya, while the Amharic alphabet has kept it because of its more frequent use in the language.

There are two types of proposed digraphs in Ethiopic—consonant digraphs and vowel digraphs. Each consonant digraph consists of a pair of consonants, and each vowel digraph consists of a pair of vowels. The proposed system for the romanization of consonant digraphs makes use of Latin digraphs and single letters (**Table 9.6**), while the romanization for the proposed special vowel digraphs, which are proposed to replace the *eyin* character family in Tigirinya and Giiz, makes use of three-letter and two-letter Latin digraphs (**Table 9.7**). The *eyin* character have still retained their distinctive phonemic values in Tigirinya, while in Amharic, they have merely become the same as the *elif* character family. The proposed consonant digraphs are created using n as one of the pair of letters that form a digraph except for the digraphs uu and ɦu. The choice of n is often phonemic, but not always. As such, the phonemes represented by the pairs may not always fully correspond to the normal values of the two characters combined. The proposed orthography allows for creating any desired combination of vowels and consonants to achieve specific results, with the transliteration of such combinations following the proposed romanization rules (**Tables 9.5** and **9.6**). For example, the Tigirinya word mόooɑq ('delicious'), would be transliterated as *txiuum* with the special vowel digraph 'uu,' and the Amharic word ɑqoqŧ ('mortal' or 'a dead person'), would be transliterated as *muac* with the vowel digraph 'ua.'

The phonemes represented by the Ethiopic digraphs are not necessarily equal to the sum of the values of each letter in each pair (**Table 9.6**). Consequently, there are Latin digraphs that do not necessarily correspond to the proposed basic romanization values for individual letters (**Table 9.5**). For example, the Ethiopic digraph mn has been assigned the proposed Latin digraph cx, whereas the corresponding individual values for m and n are 'tx' and 'b,' respectively. Although the Ethiopic digraph mn is a reasonable choice for replacing the traditional Ethiopic affricate character ጨ, the corresponding romanization is not based on a direct transliteration of mn. Instead of the direct transliteration value of 'txb,' the digraph 'cx,' which is partly based on the affricate's phonemic value, is proposed to avoid complication of the system. There will, as a result, be a small discrepancy between the Ethiopic digraphs and the Latin digraphs during alphabetical ordering, but this is unavoidable given the efficiency of the proposed system of romanization.

Proposed Latin digraphs for the romanization of Ethiopic digraphs, such as cx for mn, shall be referred to as INDIRECT ROMANIZATION to distinguish them from the proposed Latin digraphs for Ethiopic letters, such as tx for m, which shall be referred to as DIRECT ROMANIZATION. Ethiopic digraphs shall not be transliterated using direct romanization except for the purpose of transliterating Ethiopic acronyms as discussed later in this chapter.

ROMANIZATION OF GEMINATED ETHIOPIC LETTERS AND DIGRAPHS

GEMINATION, which is the stressing or lengthening of consonantal sounds, is one of the most important features of Ethiosemitic languages.[10] Unlike the traditional orthography, the proposed orthography is intended to show gemination by doubling the consonant. This method is directly applicable to the romanization of Ethiopic. (Gemination does not affect υ — the first consonant in the Ethiopic alphabets—and, as such, υυ is a proposed Tigirinya digraph and is not intended to show gemination.) Consider the Tigirinya word tonnqóó, which means 'brave' or 'courageous,' and the Amharic word qqqqw, which means 'new.' The second consonant in the Tigirinya word and the first consonant in the Amharic word are doubled to indicate gemination, and the words are transliterated with the corresponding Latin letters doubled as *tebbaii* and *addees*, respectively. For consonant digraphs, the proposed way of showing germination is by doubling the second letter of the pair, which is applicable for both Ethiopic and Latin digraphs (**Tables 9.5** and **9.6**). Consider the word mnomnnonówq, which is the staple food in Guragei and other communities in southern Ethiopia. The word has the proposed Ethiopic digraph mn <cx> used twice. In the second occurrence of the digraph, the second consonant of the digraph is doubled to show gemination, which is transliterated as *cxecxxebisa*.

ROMANIZATION OF ETHIOPIC INITIALISMS

If necessary, direct romanization shall be utilized for Ethiopic initialisms to preserve some features of the original text. An Ethiopic initialism may have a cultural, commercial, literary, or other significance that might otherwise be lost during transliteration. For example, consider the following initialisms:

> ħ:ጠ:ወ = ρo ħtóepnmóeq ጠqʒq ወqʒqwótqc
> *Ye Etiyopxiya Txena Meenisiteir* (E.Tx.M) (Ethiopian Ministry of Health)
>
> ወ:t:ጠ:ቀ = ወoɔocówq tóħħqh ጠnomnnonówq ʒó ቀóaqoaqqቀóaqoaq
> *Megerisa Tikkal Cxecxxebisa ni Qimemaqimem* (M.T.Tx.Q)

The initialism in the first example would be romanized as E.Tx.M (although alternatively the initialism E.M.H can be used for the English text), while the initialism in the second example would be romanized as M.T.Tx.Q. Notice that it is the initials of the Ethiopic long text that was romanized rather than the initials of the transliterated long text. For this reason, each of the proposed Latin digraphs for direct romanization of individual Ethiopic letters (**Table 9.5**) shall be considered as a single letter for the purpose of transliterating Ethiopic initialisms, while each of the Latin digraphs for indirect romanization of an Ethiopic digraph (**Table 9.6** and **9.7**) shall be considered as two letters.

Romanization of the Ethiopic Punctuation

In modern times, more and more punctuation marks have been introduced from European orthographies into the Ethiopic orthography, which previously only used the ancient Ethiopic punctuation marks. Sentence structure and the rules for the use of punctuation marks in Tigirinya and Amharic are almost always identical, but often different from the punctuation rules of European languages, such as English. Therefore, the romanization of Ethiopic punctuation (**Table 9.8**) is approximate and must be used based on context. All other punctuation marks adopted from European orthographies, such as the question mark and the quotation mark and all mathematical symbols shall be romanized directly. The Ethiopic two-dot punctuation mark has all but disappeared from modern Ethiopic literature. For centuries it was used as a word separator but it has now become redundant due to the modern use of white space between words. Since it has lost its original purpose and there is no need to reinstate that purpose, I propose in Chapter 8 that the Ethiopic two-dot punctuation mark now take a new role as an abbreviation mark (or a letter separator for Ethiopic initialisms) and a decimal mark. The two-dot mark shall therefore be romanized as a dot.

Table 9.8: Proposed system of romanization for Ethiopic punctuation

	ETHIOPIC PUNCTUATION	DESCRIPTION	ROMANIZATION	EXAMPLE
1	፡	proposed letter separator in acronyms	. (dot)	ፌ፡ዴ፡ሪ፡ኢ (F.D.R.E)
2	፣	comma	, (comma)	
3	፤	semicolon	; (semicolon)	
4	፦	preface colon	: (colon)	
5	፥	colon	: (colon)	
6	።	full stop	. (period)	
8	፧	question mark	? (question mark)	
9	※	section mark	§ (section mark)	
10	፨	paragraph mark	¶ (pilcrow)	

Note: The modern Ethiopic punctuation includes more punctuation marks adopted from European orthography, which include parenthesis and the question mark. These punctuation marks can for the most part be directly used for romanization.

Romanization of the Ethiopic Numerals

Ethiopic has its own numerals (**Table 9.9**) that are easily romanized, but in what may be compared to the Roman numerals, the Hindu-Arabic numerals have almost completely supplanted them in modern times. Like the Roman numerals, the Ethiopic numerals lack the concept of zero, are unable to represent large numbers, and are not based on digital-positional notation, and therefore are unfit for advanced mathematical operations. Nevertheless, the Ethiopic numerals are still in use especially with publications involving traditional themes. Romanization of Ethiopic numerals is relevant to access the aforementioned documents in addition to other historic and liturgical documents requiring knowledge of the Ethiopic numerical system.

Romanization of the Traditional Ethiopic Script

All written documents in Ethiosemitic languages prior to the reform will effectively belong to the traditional Ethiopic (TE) orthography. Romanization of documents in the TE will, therefore, need to choose one of two options, depending on the purpose intended. Firstly, the romanization can be done by first converting the text into the reformed Ethiopic (RE) orthography, then following the rules of romanization for the reformed Ethiopic writing system as discussed earlier in this chapter. The second, more practical, option would be to directly transliterate text written in the TE orthography as is, letter by letter (or more correctly, syllabus by syllabus) without changing the inherent grammatical and orthographic features of the text. Direct romanization of traditional Ethiopic is a language-dependent exercise and, therefore, the romanization value for a given Ethiopic character may differ from one Ethiopian language to the other (**Tables 2.1, 2.2, 2.3, 2.4, 2.5, 2.6** and **2.7**). The options for the romanization of traditional Ethiopic require consideration of the following issues:

1. The traditional Ethiopic orthography does not show gemination: Since TE does not show gemination, there seems to be no reason why its romanization should. If the aim is to preserve the integrity of the original document as is, gemination need not be marked during romanization unless there is a specific need for it.
2. The traditional orthography is highly fusional with the inconsistent omission of vowels and consonants during word derivation, which can cause challenges.
3. Characters that have now been dropped in the RE alphabet may have to be romanized using the values for the Ethiopic digraphs that replaced the deleted characters of the TE alphabet
4. Amharic's use of first order (giiz) characters for sounds that should be in the fourth order (*rabii*), such as አ <e> for ኣ <a>, and ሀ <h> for ሃ <ha>, should be ignored and assumed as if the fourth order was employed. This vowel shift does not affect text in Tigirinya since Tigirinya consistently distinguishes between the first and fourth orders on all of its characters.
5. The traditional Tigirinya character ዒ, which is only found in the alphabetic chart, would be transliterated as 'eei'. (There is no need for the sound represented by this character in the reformed alphabet, since the sound it represents is never used in words.)

Table 9.9: Comparison of some Ethiopic numerals to the Roman and Hindu-Arabic numerals

ETHIOPIC NUMERALS	ROMAN NUMERALS	HINDU-ARABIC NUMERALS	ETHIOPIC NUMERALS	ROMAN NUMERALS	HINDU-ARABIC NUMERALS	ETHIOPIC NUMERALS	ROMAN NUMERALS	HINDU-ARABIC NUMERALS	ETHIOPIC NUMERALS	ROMAN NUMERALS	HINDU-ARABIC NUMERALS
፩	I	1	፲	X	10	፻፲	CX	110	፩፻	C	100
፪	II	2	፳	XX	20	፻፳	CXX	120	፪፻	CC	200
፫	III	3	፴	XXX	30	፻፴	CXXX	130	፫፻	CCC	300
፬	IV	4	፵	XL	40	፻፵	CXL	140	፬፻	CD	400
፭	V	5	፶	L	50	፻፶	CL	150	፭፻	D	500
፮	VI	6	፷	LX	60	፻፷	CLX	160	፮፻	DC	600
፯	VII	7	፸	LXX	70	፻፸	CLXX	170	፯፻	DCC	700
፰	VIII	8	፹	LXXX	80	፻፹	CLXXX	180	፰፻	DCCC	800
፱	IX	9	፺	XC	90	፻፺	CXC	190	፱፻	CM	900
፲	X	10	፩፻	C	100	፪፻	CC	200	፩ሺ	M	1000
፲፩	XI	11	፻፩	CI	101	፪፻፩	CCI	201	፩ሺ ፩፻	MC	1100
፲፪	XII	12	፻፪	CII	102	፪፻፪	CCII	202	፩ሺ ፪፻	MCC	1200
፲፫	XIII	13	፻፫	CIII	103	፪፻፫	CCIII	203	፩ሺ ፫፻	MCCC	1300
፲፬	XIV	14	፻፬	CIV	104	፪፻፬	CCIV	204	፩ሺ ፬፻	MCD	1400
፲፭	XV	15	፻፭	CV	105	፪፻፭	CCV	205	፩ሺ ፭፻	MD	1500
፲፮	XVI	16	፻፮	CVI	106	፪፻፮	CCVI	206	፩ሺ ፮፻	MDC	1600
፲፯	XVII	17	፻፯	CVII	107	፪፻፯	CCVII	207	፩ሺ ፯፻	MDCC	1700
፲፰	XVIII	18	፻፰	CVII	108	፪፻፰	CCVIII	208	፩ሺ ፰፻	MDCCC	1800
፲፱	XIX	19	፻፱	CIX	109	፪፻፱	CCIX	209	፩ሺ ፱፻	MCM	1900
፳	XX	20	፻፲	CX	110	፪፻፲	CCX	210	፪ሺ	MM	2000
፳፩	XXI	21	፻፲፩	CXI	111	፪፻፲፩	CCXI	211	፩ሺ	M	1000
፳፪	XXII	22	፻፲፪	CXII	112	፪፻፲፪	CCXII	212	፪ሺ	MM	2000
፳፫	XXIII	23	፻፲፫	CXIII	113	፪፻፲፫	CCXIII	213	፫ሺ	MMM	3000
፳፬	XXIV	24	፻፲፬	CXIV	114	፪፻፲፬	CCXIV	214	፬ሺ		4000
፳፭	XXV	25	፻፲፭	CXV	115	፪፻፲፭	CCXV	215	፭ሺ		5000
፳፮	XXVI	26	፻፲፮	CXVI	116	፪፻፲፮	CCXVI	216	፮ሺ		6000
፳፯	XXVII	27	፻፲፯	CXVII	117	፪፻፲፯	CCXVII	217	፯ሺ		7000
፳፰	XXVIII	28	፻፲፰	CXVIII	118	፪፻፲፰	CCXVIII	218	፰ሺ		8000
፳፱	XXIX	29	፻፲፱	CXIX	119	፪፻፲፱	CCXIX	219	፱ሺ		9000
፴	XXX	30	፻፳	CXX	120	፪፻፳	CCXX	220	፲ሺ		10000

Other Proposed Systems of Conversions (Grammar)

Anglicization of the Ethiopic Personal Pronouns

Tigirinya and Amharic have ten grammatical persons each (**Tables 9.10** and **9.11**) and, as is the case with most grammatical features of both languages, most of the Tigirinya grammatical persons correspond to the respective Amharic grammatical persons and vice versa. As part of being DIVISION dependent, each grammatical person can have as many as three personal pronouns in Tigirinya and as many as five personal pronouns in Amharic. Anglicization of the Tigirinya and Amharic grammatical persons (**Tables 9.12** and **9.13**) shows the complexity of converting personal pronouns from Ethiosemitic languages into English—a Germanic language with only seven grammatical persons.

Table 9.10: The Tigirinya grammatical persons

	PERSON	ACRONYM
1	First person singular	1PS
2	First person plural	1PP
3	Second person singular male	2PSM
4	Second person plural male / polite singular male	2PPM
5	Second person singular female	2PSF
6	Second person plural female / polite singular female	2PPF
7	Third person singular male	3PSM
8	Third person plural male / polite singular male	3PPM
9	Third person singular female	3PSF
10	Third person plural female / polite singular female	3PPF

Note: The polite singular is the formal form of the singular for the 2nd and 3rd persons

Table 9.11: The Amharic grammatical persons

	PERSON	ACRONYM
1	First person singular	1PS
2	First person plural	1PP
3	Second person singular male	2PSM
4	Second person singular female	2PSF
5	Second person plural	2PP
6	Second person singular polite	2PS – R
7	Third person singular male	3PSM
8	Third person singular female	3PSF
9	Third person plural	3PP
10	Third person singular polite	3PS – R

Note: The polite singular is the formal form of the singular for the 2nd and 3rd persons

Table 9.12: The Tigirinya personal pronouns and their English equivalents

	PERSON	DIVISION	PRIMARY PRONOUNS			UNIVERSAL PRONOUNS (DIV. 2 PRIMARY PRON.)			SECONDARY PRONOUNS		
			TGR.	ROM.	ENG.	TGR.	ROM.	ENG.	TGR.	ROM.	ENG.
1	1PS	DIV. 1	ɧơ	ku	I	ɋ	ei	I/me/my/ mine*	ɋɿɋ	anei	I
		DIV. 2	ɋ	ei							
		DIV. 3	[ɧ]ȯ	[k]i							
		DIV. 4									
2	1PP	DIV. 1	ɿq	na	we	ɿq	na	we/us/ our/ ours*	ɿȯυυȯɿq	nihhina	we
		DIV. 2									
		DIV. 3	ɿȯ	ni							
		DIV. 4									
3	2PSM	DIV. 1	ɧq	ka	you	ɧq	ka	you/ your/ yours*	ɿȯɯȯɧq (qttq)	nisika (atta)	you
		DIV. 2									
		DIV. 3	tȯ	ti							
		DIV. 4	-	-							
4	2PPM	DIV. 1	ɧơɑq	kum	you	ɧơɑq	kum	you/ your/ yours*	ɿȯɯȯɧơɑq (qttơɑq)	nisikum (attum)	you
		DIV. 2									
		DIV. 3	tȯ -ơ	ti – u							
		DIV. 4	ơ	u							
5	2PSF	DIV. 1	ɧq̧	kee	you	ɧq̧	kee	you/ your/ yours*	ɿȯɯȯɧq̧ (qttq̧)*	nisikee (attee)	you
		DIV. 2									
		DIV. 3	tȯ - q̧	ti-ee							
		DIV. 4	q̧	ee							
6	2PPF	DIV. 1	ɧȯɿ	kin	you	ɧȯɿ	kin	you/ your/ yours*	ɿȯɯȯɧȯɿ (qttȯɿ)*	nisikin (attin)	you
		DIV. 2									
		DIV. 3	tȯ - q	ti-ee							
		DIV. 4	q	a							
7	3PSM	DIV. 1	o	e	he/it	ơ	u	he/him/ his/it/its*	ɿȯɯȯơ	nisiu	he
		DIV. 2	ơ	u							
		DIV. 3	ȯq̧	iee							
		DIV. 4									
8	3PPM	DIV. 1	ơ	u	they	ρɑq	om	they/ them/ their/ theirs	ɿȯɯȯρɑq	nisiom	they/ he*
		DIV. 2	ρɑq	om							
		DIV. 3	ȯq̧- o	iee-u							
		DIV. 4									
9	3PSF	DIV. 1	ot	et	she/it	q	a	she/her/ hers	ɿȯɯȯq	nisia	she
		DIV. 2	q	a							
		DIV. 3	tȯ	ti							
		DIV. 4									
10	3PPF	DIV. 1	q	a	they	oɿ	en	they/ them/ their/ theirs*	ɿȯɯȯoɿ	nisien	they/ she*
		DIV. 2	oɿ	en							
		DIV. 3	ȯq̧ - q	iee-a							
		DIV. 4									

Table 9.13: The Amharic personal pronouns and their English equivalents

	PERSON	DIVISION	PRIMARY SUBJECT PRONOUNS			OBJECT PRONOUNS		POSSESSIVE PRONOUNS		SECONDARY PRONOUNS	
			AMH.	ROM.	ENG.	AMH.	ENG.	AMH.	ENG.	AMH.	ENG.
1	1PS	1 2 3–4	uo ꝗ [ŋ]ó	hu ei [l]i	I	ɿ̄ó <nyi>	me	ꝗ <ei>	my	óɿꝗ <inei>	I / mine*
2	1PP	1–2 3–4	ɿó óɿɿ	ni inn	we	ɿó <ni>	us	qŧŧóɿ <accin>	our	óɿ̄ɿ̄q <inyya>	we/ ours*
3	2PSM	1–2 3 4	uó tó -	hi ti -	you	uó <hi>	you	uó <hi>	your	qɿóto <anite>	you/ yours*
4	2PSF	1–2 3 4	n̄ó tó - q q	shi ti - ee ee	you	n̄ó <shi>	you	n̄ó <shi>	your	qɿóŧq <anicee>	you/ yours*
5	2PP	1–2 3 4	qŧŧóuo tó - o o	accihu ti – u u	you	qŧŧóuo <accihu>	you	qŧŧóuo <accihu>	your	óɿɿoqɿóto (óɿɿqɿóto) <inneanite> <(innanite)>	you/ yours*
6	2PS - R	1–2 3–4	o óq - o	u iee – u	you	ρ <o>	you*	ρ <o>	your	ócówoρ <iriseo>	you/ yours*
7	3PSM	1 2 3–4	o ρ óq	e o iee	he/it	ωó / tó <wi / ti>	him/ it	o <u>	his/its*	ócówo (ówwo) <irisu> <(issu)>	he/ it/ his*/ its*
8	3PSF	1 2 3–4	oŧ q tó	ec a ti	she	qt <at>	her	oq <ua>	her	ócówoq (ówwoq) <irisua> <(issua)>	she/ her*
9	3PP	1–2 3–4	o óq - o	u iee – u	they	qŧŧoω <accew>	them	qŧŧoω <accew>	their	óɿɿoócówo (óɿɿowo) <inneirisu> <(innesu)>	they
10	3PS - R	1–2 3–4	o óq - o	u iee – u	he/ she	qŧŧoω <accew>	him/ her	qŧŧoω <accew>	his/ her	ócówqŧŧoω (ówwqŧŧoω) <irisaccew> <(issaccew)>	his/ hers

Anglicization of the Ethiopic Grammatical Tenses (Subdivisions)

Anglicization of an Ethiopic grammatical tense is the conversion of an Ethiopic tense into an equivalent English tense. Not all tenses have direct equivalencies between Ethiopic and English. Even within a single language, an action can be expressed in more than one tense. Therefore, I have made an effort to show the closest possible equivalencies for the Ethiopic and English tenses (**Table 9.14**). Even then, there are exceptions for context. For example, the historical present tense in English, especially as used for news headlines, cannot be directly transliterated into Ethiopic without first being changed to the past tense. Similarly, Anglicization of the past tense in an Ethiopic headline will require converting it into the present tense.

Table 9.14: The Ethiopic subdivisions and their equivalent English grammatical tenses

ETHIOPIC SUBDIVISION (TENSE)	ENGLISH GRAMMATICAL TENSE
SUBDIVISION 1.1	Simple past
SUBDIVISION 1.2	Conditional simple
SUBDIVISION 1.3	Conditional perfect
SUBDIVISION 1.4	Past continuous
SUBDIVISION 1.5	Present continuous
SUBDIVISION 1.6	Present perfect continuous
SUBDIVISION 1.7	Future continuous
SUBDIVISION 1.8	Conditional continuous
SUBDIVISION 1.9	Conditional perfect continuous
SUBDIVISION 2.1	Past perfect
SUBDIVISION 2.2	Present perfect
SUBDIVISION 2.3	Future perfect
SUBDIVISION 3.1	Past habitual
SUBDIVISION 3.2	Present simple
SUBDIVISION 3.3	Future simple – (will)
SUBDIVISION 3.4	Future simple – (going to)
SUBDIVISION 3.5	Future in the past
SUBDIVISION 4.1	Command or imperative

Note: Each subdivision is a product of one of the four Ethiopic divisions. The divisions and their subdivisions are discussed in detail in Volume II.

CHAPTER 10

PROPOSED STANDARD SYSTEM OF GIIZIZATION

Not studying his own language to be skilled in reading and writing,
Belittling Amharic grammar and scorning Giiz,
If anyone becomes learned and sophisticated in foreign script,
Foreigners' heritage cannot be our heritage,
Foreigners' heritage cannot be our heritage.

—DESTA TEKILE WELID, 1970
A translation of the Amharic piece

IN THIS CHAPTER

In Chapter 9, we discussed the proposed standard system for the romanization of Ethiopic, which is the rendering of Ethiopic in the Latin script. In this chapter, we will discuss what can essentially be considered as the reverse process—the rendering of Latin script texts in the Ethiopic script—which we shall refer to as GIIZIZATION. The case for a robust standard system of transliteration and transcription presented in Chapter 9 is also applicable for conversion of text from the Latin script to the Ethiopic script. The need for a standard giizization system has never been more urgent in Ethiopia due to increasing contacts between Ethiopian and foreign entities owing to the unprecedented socio-economic progress currently unfolding in Ethiopia and the need for ensuring accurate communication. Globalized 21st-century communication and exchange of information between nations that use different languages and writing systems involve the translation, transcription, and transliteration of text, the accuracy of which affects the intended outcome of each communication.

A standard system of giizization can help facilitate, among other things:

- Efficient communication between domestic and foreign entities, such as between government agencies, non-governmental agencies, business organizations, educational institutions, financial institutions, manufacturers, suppliers, tour operators, and individuals.

- Access to information on legal documents, memorandums of understanding, import-export permits, bank drafts, licenses, customs documents, property deeds, product descriptions, etc.
- Economic and social activities through accurate transliteration and transcription of various words and phrases (such as proper names, trademarks, product names, technical terms, and geographical names) into the Ethiopic script.

The need for a standard method of giizization, i.e. the accurate translation, transcription, and transliteration of foreign texts, can not be overemphasized.

While I believe that comprehensive, highly sophisticated language materials must be developed to help facilitate the translation of words from major world languages to Ethiopian languages and vice versa, the scope of this chapter is limited to proposing a standard method for the conversion of text from the Latin script into the Ethiopic script. In an increasingly sophisticated world, where accuracy is critical, a standard system of giizization—involving transliteration, transcription, or both—is necessary to make foreign materials accessible to Ethiopians for the reasons discussed above.

Definition of Terms

Giizization

The proposed term GIIZIZATION shall be defined as the system of rendering foreign text in the Ethiopic script. The term can be applied for the rendering of any text in the Ethiopic script regardless of the type of foreign script used by the source text. However, the giizization methods proposed in this book only covers the transliteration and transcription of text from a form of the Latin alphabet into the proposed reformed Ethiopic script based, mostly, on English phonology. TRANSLITERATION and TRANSCRIPTION (see Chapter 9 for definition) are forms of rendering text from one script into another that can be employed by giizization at different times or within the same text depending on the desired outcome.

Consider, for example, the English word ‘through.’ When transliterated into the reformed Ethiopic, it becomes tuϲϼo·ɔu based on a letter-by-letter rendering of the word, but the transliteration does not nearly provide the correct pronunciation. (English spelling is unpredictable because it is highly nonphonemic.) In this case, transcription will provide a better pronunciation as follows tuὸco·. Notice the use of the digraph tu which would have been impossible to create using the traditional Ethiopic script without creating a brand new character or glyph. Giizization can employ transliteration and transcription depending on the need for a particular purpose.

Tigirinyaization and Amharicization

Tigirinyaization and Amharicization (Amarinyaization) are proposed terms for use within the context of Giizization. Tigirinyaization shall be defined as the process of converting grammatical persons, personal pronouns, and other grammatical elements from a source language into Tigirinya. Similarly, Amharicization shall be defined as the process of converting grammatical persons, personal pronouns, and other grammatical elements from a source language into Amharic.

Tigirinyaization and Amharicization, which are specific applications of giizization, can serve as blueprints for the development of other applications of giizization within Ethiopia.

Giization involving transliteration is a more challenging exercise than romanization of Ethiopic mainly because of the disconnect between English pronunciation and spelling.

GIIZIZATION OF TEXT WRITTEN IN THE LATIN ALPHABET

For a long time now, Ethiopians have been rendering foreign words in the traditional Ethiopic script for various reasons, but a systematized method of doing so has not been developed until now. In ancient times, these foreign texts were almost always in the Greek alphabet, but in modern times they have for the most part been from European languages involving the Latin alphabet. Because of the widespread use of the Latin alphabet, the giization proposed in this book is a system of rendering text from the Latin script into the Ethiopic script. Today, English is at the forefront of giization involving foreign languages. However, English orthography presents a formidable challenge for giization because it does not follow regular spelling and can be highly unpredictable with its grapheme-phoneme relationships. Often one cannot correctly predict how a certain word is spelled based on its pronunciation unless one had prior knowledge of the same word. Although it only has five vowel letters, English can have as many as 22 vowel sounds, which contrasts to the Ethiopic orthography, which is spelled almost exactly as pronounced with each of its consonants and vowels representing virtually only one phoneme. As a result, giization of English is more complicated than romanization of Ethiopic. To simplify and standardize giization of English, I propose the use of both transliteration and transcription of English text into Ethiopic as needed.

TRANSLITERATION OF TEXT FROM THE LATIN SCRIP

Actual transliteration of text from the Latin alphabet into the Ethiopic was not possible until now due to compatibility issues between the Latin script, which is a true alphabet, and the traditional Ethiopic script, which is an alphasyllabary. By contrast, the proposed Ethiopic writing system provides an opportunity to transliterate any alphabetic script as well as alphasyllabaries. The proposed method for the transliteration of text from Latin to Ethiopic assigns a unique Ethiopic letter or digraph for each of the twenty-six letters of the Latin alphabet (**Table 10.1**). The proposed giization values are to the most part phonetically equivalent to their Latin counterparts, with the possible exceptions being q <ቀ> and x <ፀ>. The root of the Latin letter 'q' dates back to the Phoenician character 𐤒 (qoph), which is also the root of the Ethiopic letter ቀ. The use of the letter x, especially in English, represents different sounds some of which are somewhat closer to ፀ. A unique Ethiopic equivalent must be provided to each of the Latin letters and I have taken into consideration the fact that the romanization values for the Ethiopic letters must be able to be used in reverse for the giization of text in the Latin script.

TRANSCRIPTION OF ENGLISH TEXT INTO ETHIOPIC

A standard system of transcription of English text into Ethiopic is required because of the need to streamline giization of English text. Standard transcription of English can often be used instead of transliteration of English text because it provides more sensible phonemic relationship due to the unpredictability of English spelling. Unlike English spelling, the rules of spelling in the proposed Ethiopic orthography will be simple and predictable. Every consonant almost always represents the same phoneme and every vowel almost always has the same value. To reconcile these differences between the two orthographies, I propose the use

Table 10.1: System for letter conversion from the Latin script to the Ethiopic script

	LATIN LETTERS	ETHIOPIC LETTERS		COMMENTS
		TIGIRINYA	AMHARIC	
1	a	ዓ	ዓ	
2	b	በ	በ	
3	c	ኸበ	ቸ	
4	d	ደ	ደ	
5	e	ዐ	ዐ	
6	f	ፈ	ፈ	
7	g	ገ	ገ	
8	h	ሀ	ሀ	
9	i	ዒ	ዒ	
10	j	ጀ	ጀ	
11	k	ከ	ከ	
12	l	ለ	ለ	
13	m	መ	መ	
14	n	ነ	ነ	
15	o	ዖ	ዖ	
16	p	በሀ	በሀ	
17	q	ቀ	ቀ	
18	r	ረ	ረ	
19	s	ሠ	ሠ	
20	t	ተ	ተ	
21	u	ዑ	ዑ	
22	v	በዘ	በዘ	
23	w	ወ	ወ	
24	x	ፀ	ፀ	
25	y	የ	የ	
26	z	ዘ	ዘ	

of a standard phoneme conversation (**Table 10.2**) that may require further refinement and may need to be updated once every few decades. The capacity of the proposed orthography in supporting a more accurate pronunciation of foreign words, particularly English words, is unprecedented. In fact, it will not only allow for various combinations of vowels to closely represent the original vowel sounds otherwise impossible to represent using the traditional orthography, but it will also allow for the formation of unique digraphs to represent certain foreign phonemes, such as *th* in *this* (ተዑቀሠ). Most English-Ethiopic dictionaries do not provide viable pronunciation keys. Even with those that provide pronunciation keys, the information is often skewed because of the nature of the Ethiopic al-

Table 10.2: System for English to Ethiopic phoneme conversion

	ENGLISH PHONEMES	SOUND (IPA)	EQUIVALENT ETHIOPIC PHONEMES	TEXT	PRONUNCIATION	TRANSLITERATION
1	a	[ɑ:]	q	park	[pɑ:k]	nuqcȯɧ
2		[ei]	ɋq	state	[steit]	ɯtɋqt
3		[æ]	ɋq	stand	[stænd]	ɯtɋqʒȯʠ
4		[ɛə]	ɋoc	care	[kɛə]	ɧɋoc
5		[ə]	o	aroma	[ə'roumə]	ocρoɑq
6	b	[b]	n	boots	[bu:ts]	notȯɯ
7	c	[s]	ɯ	central	['sentrəl]	ɯɋʒȯtȯcoɧ
8		[k]	ɧ	cannery	['kænəri]	ɧɋqʒocɋ
9	ch	[ʧ]	ῆn / ŧ	check	[ʧek]	ῆnɋɧ / ŧɋɧ
10	ck	[k]	ɧ	deck	[dek]	ʠɋɧ
11	d	[d]	ʠ	door	[do:]	ʠρoc
12	e	[i:]	ɋ	veto	['vi:tou]	nʜɋtρo
13		[e]	ɋ	pen	[pen]	nuɋʒ
14		[ə:]	o	university	[ju:ni'və:siti]	ϱoʒonʜocȯɯotɋ
15		[i]	ȯ	electric	[i'lektrik]	ȯɧɋɧȯtȯcɋɧ
16	ea	[i:]	ɋ	near	[ni:]	ʒɋc
17		[e]	ɋ	head	[hed]	uɋʠ
18		[iə]	ɋo	area	[ə:iə]	ocɋo
19	ee	[i:]	ɋ	meet	[mi:t]	ɑqɋt
20	ew	[ju:]	ϱo	new	[nju:]	ʒȯϱo
21	f	[f]	ɓ	formation	[fɔ:'meiʃən]	ɓρcȯɑqɋῆȯʒ
22	g	[dʒ]	ʠ̄	gem	[dʒem]	ʠ̄ɋɑq
23		[g]	ɔ	group	[gru:p]	ɔȯconu
24	h	[h]	u	herbicide	[hə:bisaid]	uocȯnoɯqϱȯʠ
25	i	[i] / [ɪ]	ɋ	filter	['fɪltə]	ɓɋɧȯtoc
26		[aiə]	qϱo	fire	['faiə]	ɓqϱo
27		[ə:]	o	birth	[bə:θ]	nocȯʜu
28		[ai]	qϱ	idea	[aidiə]	qϱȯʠqq
29	j	[dʒ]	ʠ̄	job	[dʒob]	ʠ̄ρqn
30	k	[k]	ɧ	king	[kiŋ]	ɧɋʒɔ
31	l	[l]	ɧ	lime	[laim]	ɧqϱȯɑq
32	m	[m]	ɑq	machine	[mə'ʃi:n]	ɑqoῆɋʒ
33	n	[n]	ʒ	new	[nj:u]	ʒȯϱo

	ENGLISH PHONEMES *(...continued)*	SOUND (IPA)	EQUIVALENT ETHIOPIC PHONEMES	TEXT	PRONUNCIATION	TRANSLITERATION
34	o	[ou]	ρo	stone	[stoun]	ωótρo٦
35		[ɔ]	ρq	fox	[fɔks]	ɓρqɧów
36		[ɔ:]	ρoc	more	[mɔ:]	ɑρoc
37		[ə:]	oc	work	[wə:k]	ɷocóɧ
38		[ə]	o	technology	[tek'nɔlədʒi]	tɋɧó٦ρqɧoᶊq
39	oi	[oi]	ρ℘	noise	[noiz]	٦ρ℘óн
40	oy	[oi]	ρ℘	boy	[boi]	nρ℘
41	p	[p]	nυ	plotter	[plotə]	nυóɧρqtoc
42	ph	[f]	ɓ	physics	['fiziks]	ɓqнqɧów
43	qu	[kw]	ɧo	quick	[kwik]	ɧoqɧ
44	r	[r]	c	rock	[rɔk]	cρqɧ
45	s	[z]	н	closed	[klouzd]	ɧóɧρoнóᶊ
46		[s]	ω	service	['sə:vis]	ωocónнqω
47	sh	[ʃ]	ῆ	shell	[ʃel]	ῆɋɧ
48	t	[t]	t	table	[tebəl]	tɋnoɧ
49	tch	[ʧ]	ῆn / ŧ	match	[maʧ]	ɑqῆn / ɑqŧ
50	th	[ð]	н	this	[ðis]	нυqω
51		[θ]	t	thought	[θɔt]	tρqt
52	tion	[ʃən]	ῆo٦	nation	[neʃən]	٦ɋῆo٦
53	u	[ju:]	(℘)o	tube	[tju:b]	tó(℘)on
54		[ə]	o	mud	[məd]	ɑoᶊ
55	v	[v]	nн	service	[sə:vis]	ωocnнqω
56	w	[w]	ɷ	world	[wərld]	ɷocɧᶊ
57	x	[gz]	ɔóн	example	[ig'za:mpəl]	óɔóнqɑónυoɧ
58		[ks]	ɧów	box	[bɔks]	nρqɧów
59	y	[ai]	q℘	shy	[ʃai]	ῆq℘
60		[i]	q	myth	[miθ]	ɑqн
61		[j]	℘	yard	[jɑ:d]	℘qcᶊ
62		[ə:]	oc	myrtle	[mə:tl]	ɑoctóɧ
63	z	[z]	н	zone	[zoun]	нρo٦
64		[ʒ:]	ᶊn	seizure	[sɪʒə:]	ωqᶊnoc

Table adapted for Ethiopic under creative commons license from uk.wikipedia.org/wiki/Кирилізація_англійської_мови. Note that, with some exceptions, double consonants in English words should not be transliterated into corresponding double consonants in Ethiopic, because that would create gemination in Ethiopic, which the English pronunciation would not have.

phasyllabic writing system. The GENERAL VOWEL RULE and the *SADIS* VOWEL RULE for Ethiopic spelling proposed in Chapter 8 shall be waived with transliteration of words from the Latin alphabet to Ethiopic, if necessary, such as with the transliteration of English words with a single syllable. For example, the English word 'world' would be transliterated as ወርልድ <werld>, but the traditional orthography would show it as ወርሊድ <werilid>, by making it have at least three syllables. Similarly, 'screen' would be transliterated as ስክሪን and not *ሰከሪን.

Ethiopic Digraphs for English

As part of a standard giizization system for English, digraphs may need to be created to represent sounds that do not exist in Ethiopic, such as the sound of *th* in *the*, as well as creating digraphs for English vowel and consonant digraphs or clusters. Examples of English consonant digraphs or clusters requiring Ethiopic equivalents are bl, br, ch, ck, cl, cr, dr, fl, fr, gh, gl, gr, ng, nth, ph, pl, pr, qu, sc, sch, scr, sh, shr, sk, sl, sm, sn, sp, spl, spr, squ, st, str, sw, th, tr, tw, wh, wr, and thr.

Giizization of English Grammatical Elements

As part of giizization of English, a standard system for the representation of English grammatical elements, particularly English personal pronouns and tenses, in Ethiopic is extremely important for accurate communication between speakers of English, on the one hand, and speakers of Tigirinya and Amharic, on the other hand.

Table 10.3: Tigirinya and Amharic equivalents for English personal pronouns

ENGLISH PRONOUNS	TIGIRINYA PRONOUNS	AMHARIC PRONOUNS
1 1st p. singular	1 1st p. singular	1 1st p. singular
2 1st p. plural	2 1st p. plural	2 1st p. plural
3 2nd person	3 2nd p. singular male	3 2nd p. singular male
	4 2nd p. singular female	4 2nd p. singular female
	5 2nd p. plural males or 2nd p. singular male polite or 2nd p. plural male(s) & female(s)	5 2nd p. plural
		6 2nd p. singular polite
	6 2nd p. plural females or 2nd p. singular female polite	
4 3rd p. singular inanimate	7 3rd p. singular male	7 3rd p. singular male
5 3rd p. singular male		
6 3rd p. singular female	8 3rd p. singular female	8 3rd p. singular female
7 3rd p. plural	9 3rd p. plural males or 3rd p. plural male(s) & female(s)	9 3rd p. plural
		10 3rd p. singular polite
	10 3rd p. plural females	

Giization of the English Personal Pronouns

Comparison of the English and Ethiopic grammatical persons and personal pronouns (**Table 10.3**) presents that the Ethiopic personal pronouns are more specific than their English equivalents. For example, Tigirinya and Amharic have four grammatical persons each in the second person category compared to only one for English. Tigirinya and Amharic have ten grammatical persons each, which correspond between the languages to a great extent but do not always have identical values (see the section *Giization within Ethiosemitic Languages* in this chapter).

Giization of the English Grammatical Tenses

Giization of English grammatical tenses attempts to provide the Ethiopic equivalent tense for each of the English tenses (**Table 10.4**). However, English has more grammatical tenses and, therefore, it is not possible to provide direct Ethiopic equivalencies for some of the English tenses. In such instances, the closest possible Ethiopic tenses are provided. Even so, there are still some English tenses which cannot have any equivalencies in Ethiopic, in which case, longer sentences would be required to correctly giize the desired message.

Table 10.4: English Grammatical Tenses and their Ethiopic equivalents

ENGLISH TENSE	EXAMPLE	EQUIVALENT ETHIOPIC TENSE	EXAMPLE
PAST SIMPLE	We worked	Div 1: Subdiv. 1.1	Π̇ocquu ʒq / Π̇occq ʒȯ
PAST PROGRESSIVE	We were working	Div 1: Subdiv. 1.4*	
PAST PERFECT (SIMPLE)	We had worked	Div 1: Subdiv. 2.1	
PAST PERFECT PROGRESSIVE	We had been working	Div 1: Subdiv. 1.4*	
PRESENT SIMPLE	We work	Div 3: Subdiv. 3.2	
PRESENT PROGRESSIVE	We are working	Div 1: Subdiv. 1.5	
PRESENT PERFECT (SIMPLE)	We have worked	Div 2: Subdiv. 2.2	
PRESENT PERFECT PROGRESSIVE	We have been working	Div 1: Subdiv. 1.6	
FUTURE SIMPLE (WILL)	We will work	Div 3: Subdiv. 3.3	
FUTURE SIMPLE (GOING TO)	We am going to work	Div 3: Subdiv. 3.4	
FUTURE PROGRESSIVE	We will be working	Div 1: Subdiv. 1.7	
FUTURE PERFECT (SIMPLE)	We will have worked	Div 2: Subdiv. 2.3	
FUTURE PERFECT PROGRESSIVE	We will have been working	-	
PRESENT TENSE FOR FUTURE*			
CONDITIONAL SIMPLE	We would work	Div 1: Subdiv. 1.2	
CONDITIONAL PROGRESSIVE	We would be working	Div 1: Subdiv. 1.8	
CONDITIONAL PERFECT	We would have worked	Div 1: Subdiv. 1.3	
COND. PERFECT PROGRESSIVE	We would have been working	Div 1: Subdiv. 1.9	

Giizization of Latin Letter Acronyms, Initialisms, and Abbreviations

Giizization of Latin letter acronyms, initialisms, and abbreviations is an important part of giizization of foreign script texts because of the seemingly endless flow of acronyms, initialisms, and abbreviations into Ethiopia from around the world with their unintended negative impacts on Ethiopic grammar. Therefore, I propose the following rules for giizization of Latin letter initialisms (which contrast to the proposed rules for the romanization of Ethiopic initialisms in Chapter 9):

1. Giizization shall avoid the direct phonetic transcription of Latin letter initialisms and direct copying of punctuation into Ethiopic (e.g. ዩ.ኤስ.ኤ for U.S.A.) because of the damage such practices cause to the Ethiopic grammar (for more on this refer to Chapter 5: Language Crisis and Miscommunication in Ethiopia). All transliteration employing giizization must presuppose that the reader has no knowledge of any foreign script or language whatsoever including the Latin script.
2. Doubled consonants shall be ignored for the purpose of acronyms and initialisms.
3. One of the following two options shall be used to giizize Latin letter initialisms:
   - A one-to-one transliteration of letters and punctuation into Ethiopic. The following are examples:

     W.W.W = ወ፡ወ፡ወ (WWW = ወወወ);

     U.S.A = ኡ፡ሰ፡አ (USA = ኡሰአ);

     AIDS = አ፡ኢ፡ዶ፡ሰ
   - Use of initialisms for words after translating the expanded forms first. The following are examples:
     - Worldwide Web (WWW)

       = ħqhoaqöhohuqaq ħqhonq (ħПħ) (Tigirinya)

       = ħhoaqqфob ħaötqc (ħħħ) (Amharic)
     - United States of America (U.S.A.)

       = Mönocq3 Mqɔocqto ħaqq̧cq̧hq (ሐ፡ሐ፡አ)
     - Purchasing power parity (PPP)

       = aqqööco qфöaqq ňoaqotq (ወ፡አ፡ሰ) (Tigirinya)

       = aqowwq ꝏo ňoaqotq qфöaq (ወ፡ሰ፡አ) (Amharic)
     - United Nations Children's Fund (UNICEF) = ኡ፡ኔ፡ኢ፡ቸ፡ኤ፡ፈ

       = Wöaqh Möeqaö3ötq Mönocqt Wo3öɔöwötqt (ወ፡ሐ፡ሐ፡ወ)

       = ꝏo Mönocq3 Wo3öɔöwötqt ꝏo Möeq3qt Ꝺöɔɔpaqq (ሐ፡ወ፡ሐ፡ዶ)

Giization Within Ethiosemitic Languages

Giization within Ethiosemitic languages shall be defined as the process of converting grammatical persons, personal pronouns, and other grammatical elements from a source language to a target language. Tigirinyaization and Amharicization (Amarinyaization) shall refer to such conversions from a source Ethiopian language to Tigirinya and Amharic, respectively. Giization between Ethiopian languages, particularly between Ethiosemitic languages, will not involve transliteration because of the proposed harmonization of the writing system for all Ethiopian languages (for more on this refer to the *Orthographic Harmonization* section in Chapter 13). To a large extent, Tigirinya grammatical elements, including grammatical persons, correspond to those in Amharic and vise versa.

Tigirinyaization of the Amharic Grammatical Persons and Amharicization of the Tigirinya Grammatical Persons

Tigirinyaization of Amharic personal pronouns (**Table 10.5**) and Amharicization of Tigirinya personal pronouns (**Table 10.6**) show similarities as well as differences between the personal pronouns of the two languages. While both languages have the same number of personal pronouns, the correspondence between their personal pronouns is not always one-to-one. This is because, while Tigirinya makes gender distinction for the plural forms of its second and third grammatical persons, Amharic does not.

Tigirinyaization of the Amharic Definite Articles and Amharicization of the Tigirinya Definite Articles

As the Tigirinyaization of Amharic definite articles (**Table 10.7**) and Amharicization of Tigirinya definite articles (**Table 10.8**) show, Tigirinya and Amharic differ in the form of their definite articles. Similar to the grammatical persons, Tigirinya

Table 10.5: Tigirinyaization of Amharic grammatical persons

	AMHARIC	FORMULA	TIGIRINYA
1	First person singular	1PS → 1PS	First person singular
2	First person plural	1PP → 1PP	First person plural
3	Second person singular male	2PSM → 2PSM	Second person singular male
4	Second person singular female	2PSF → 2PSF	Second person singular female
5	Second person plural	2PP → 2PPM/ 2PP → 2PPF	Second person plural male/ Second person plural female
6	Second person singular – Polite or formal (R)	2PS - R → 2PPM/ 2PS - R → 2PPF	Second person plural male/ Second person plural female
7	Third person singular male	3PSM → 3PSM	Third person singular male
8	Third person singular female	3PSF → 3PSF	Third person singular female
9	Third person plural	3PP → 3PPM/ 3PP → 3PPF	Third person plural male/ Third person plural female
10	Second person singular – Polite or formal (R)	3PS - R → 3PPM/ 3PS - R → 3PPF	Third person plural male/ Third person plural female

makes gender distinction in its definite articles for plural nouns. Tigirinya has a total of four definite articles for the following noun types: Singular male, plural male (which includes a combination of males and females of any number), singular female, and plural female nouns. By contrast Amharic has two definite articles: A generic definite article and a singular female definite article.

Table 10.6: Amharicization of Tigirinya grammatical persons

	TIGIRINYA	FORMULA	AMHARIC
1	First person singular	1PS → 1PS	First person singular
2	First person plural	1PP → 1PP	First person plural
3	Second person singular male	2PSM → 2PSM	Second person singular male
4	Second person singular female	2PSF → 2PSF	Second person singular female
5	Second person plural male	2PPM → 2PP/ 2PPM → 2PS - R	Second person plural/ Second person singular - polite
6	Second person plural female	2PPF → 2PP/ 2PPF → 2PS - R	Second person plural/ Second person singular - polite
7	Third person singular male	3PSM → 3PSM	Third person singular male
8	Third person singular female	3PSF → 3PSF	Third person singular female
9	Third person plural male	3PPM → 3PP/ 3PPM → 3PS - R	Third person plural/ Third person singular - polite
10	Third person plural female	3PPF → 3PP/ 3PPF → 3PS - R	Third person plural/ Third person singular - polite

Table 10.7: Tigirinyaization of Amharic definite articles

	AMHARIC	FORMULA	TIGIRINYA
1	Generic definite article o	3P → 3PSM	Singular male definite article tȯ
2		3P → 3PP	Plural definite article tρɑq
3		3P → 3PPF	Plural female definite article to٦
4	Singular feminine definite article ȯq	3PSF → 3PSF	Singular female definite article tq

Table 10.8: Amharicization of Tigirinya definite articles

	TIGIRINYA	FORMULA	AMHARIC
1	Singular male definite article tȯ	3PSM → 3P	Generic definite article o
2	Singular female definite article tq	3PSF → 3P	Singular feminine definite article ȯq
3	Plural definite article tρɑq	3PP → 3P	Generic definite article o
4	Plural female definite article to٦	3PPF → 3P	Generic definite article o

Giizization of Gregorian Calendar Dates and Clock Times

Giizization of calendar dates refers to the conversion of Gregorian calendar dates and time to the Ethiopic (Ethiopian) calendar dates and time. The Ethiopic civil calendar, which is influenced by the ancient Egyptian calendar via the Coptic calendar introduced to Ethiopia by missionaries, is a solar calendar consisting of a regular year of 365 days and a leap year of 366 days.

Giizization of Gregorian Calendar Dates

Except for the negligible difference in the average length of year of 0.002% between the Gregorian year and Ethiopic year, both calendars have the same number of dates in a year. However, the calendars do not start the year or the month on the same day (although the days of the week parallel each other) and do not always have the same number of months. Moreover, depending on a particular date in a year, there is a difference of seven to eight years between the Ethiopian and Gregorian calendars due to differing dates for the Annunciation (of the birth of Jesus Christ)—the event the calendars are based. As the Gregorian calendar is the de facto international standard, the discrepancy between it and the Ethiopic calendar is a challenge for Ethiopians in their international communications. Although giizization of Gregorian calendar dates to Ethiopic is not a new concept, there is an urgent need to standardize it. The following is an example of a Gregorian calendar date giizized into Tigirinya and Amharic, respectively:

Tuesday, September 11, 2001

= ΐlohow⫶ ᏇᎠowόɦocoɑɳ ƃ ⫶ ƃƂƂƃ (*Selus, Mesikerem* 1, 1994)

= ᏇᎠqɦόwoɜɜρ⫶ ᏇᎠowόɦocoɑɳ ƃ ⫶ ƃƂƂƃ (*Makisenyyo, Mesikerem* 1, 1994)

Giizization of a non-Ethiopic calendar date shall involve translation of the name of the day and month into Ethiopic and the conversion of the day of the month and the year into the Ethiopic calendar as shown in the above example. If, however, such a process is cumbersome for a particular purpose, the giizization shall be done by translating the name of the Gregorian month (**Table 10.9**) and day to Ethiopic as a minimum (without converting the day of the month and the year into the Ethiopian calendar). In such a case, one of the following initials, which mean *According to the European calendar*, shall be shown in parenthesis after the date:

Tigirinya:

ħ:ħ for ɦoɑɳ qȸρɵqɵόcq ħɷόcρnuqɷqqɜ

Amharic:

ħ:ħ for όɜόჲo ħɷόcρnuqɷqqɜ qȸȸρmqmoc

Although Giizization of Gregorian calendar dates into Ethiopic calendar dates has been practiced in Ethiopia for a long time, often the media directly uses the Gregorian calendar date as is instead of taking the effort to convert the date into the Ethiopic calendar. This practice, which is part of the Ethiopian language crisis (Chapters 5 and 13) must be stopped since the general public has little knowledge of the Gregorian calendar or has any experience with it.

Table 10.9: List of the Gregorian months and their Ethiopic equivalents

	GREGORIAN MONTHS	ETHIOPIC MONTH ORDER	TIGIRINYA ETHIOPIC MONTHS	AMHARIC ETHIOPIC MONTHS
1	January	5	ՌÍóccq	ՌÍócc
2	February	6	Ռoɦqtqt	ϐoɦɦqtqt
3	March	7	ȸoɔɔqnqt	ȸoɔɔqnqt
4	April	8	ȸqqнqq	ȸqqнqq
5	May	9	˥óʒónpt	˥óʒónpt
6	June	10	Ռ́oʒo	Ռ́oʒq
7	July	11	Ռ́ʊqɑqóɦo	Ռ́qɑqóɦq
8	August	12	ɬouuqɯo	ɬouqɯq
9	September	1	ȸowóɦocoɑq	ȸowóɦocoɑq
10	October	2	Ռóɸɸóɑqótq	Ռóɸóɑqót
11	November	3	Ռ́óʂqc	Ռ́óʂqc
12	December	4	†quówqɯ	†quówqɯ

Giization of European Clock Times

The beauty of the Ethiopian clock time system is that, in contrast to the Western clock time, which begins the day at midnight, it begins the day at down making a visible distinction between the old and the new days with a six-hour difference between the Western and Ethiopian clock systems. Therefore, 6:00 AM (0600) is 12:00 (0000) o'clock day time (DT) according to the Ethiopian system, after which a new day begins (**Table 10.10**). Similarly, when the Western date ends just before 12:00 AM (0000) midnight, the Ethiopian clock reads 6:00 (1800) o'clock night time (NT) and will have six more hours before it ends at dawn.

Table 10.10: Comparison of the Ethiopic and Western clock time systems

ETHIOPIAN MILITARY TIME	ETHIOPIAN TRADITIONAL TIME	WESTERN MILITARY TIME	WESTERN TRADITIONAL TIME
0000 Ethiopian hours	12:00 DT (Sunrise)	0600 hours	6:00 AM
0100 Ethiopian hours	1:00 DT	0700 hours	7:00 AM
0200 Ethiopian hours	2:00 DT	0800 hours	8:00 AM
0300 Ethiopian hours	3:00 DT	0900 hours	9:00 AM
0400 Ethiopian hours	4:00 DT	1000 hours	10:00 AM
0500 Ethiopian hours	5:00 DT	1100 hours	11:00 AM
0600 Ethiopian hours	6:00 DT (Midday)	1200 hours	12:00 PM
0700 Ethiopian hours	7:00 DT	1300 hours	1:00 PM
0800 Ethiopian hours	8:00 DT	1400 hours	2:00 PM
0900 Ethiopian hours	9:00 DT	1500 hours	3:00 PM
1000 Ethiopian hours	10:00 DT	1600 hours	4:00 PM
1100 Ethiopian hours	11:00 DT	1700 hours	5:00 PM
1200 Ethiopian hours	12:00 NT (Sunset)	1800 hours	6:00 PM
1300 Ethiopian hours	1:00 NT	1900 hours	7:00 PM
1400 Ethiopian hours	2:00 NT	2000 hours	8:00 PM
1500 Ethiopian hours	3:00 NT	2100 hours	9:00 PM
1600 Ethiopian hours	4:00 NT	2200 hours	10:00 PM
1700 Ethiopian hours	5:00 NT	2300 hours	11:00 PM
1800 Ethiopian hours	6:00 NT (Midnight)	0000 hours	12:00 AM
1900 Ethiopian hours	7:00 NT	0100 hours	1:00 AM
2000 Ethiopian hours	8:00 NT	0200 hours	2:00 AM
2100 Ethiopian hours	9:00 NT	0300 hours	3:00 AM
2200 Ethiopian hours	10:00 NT	0400 hours	4:00 AM
2300 Ethiopian hours	11:00 NT	0500 hours	5:00 AM

CHAPTER 11

PROPOSED GIIZIZATION OF NUMERICAL TERMS

ȟqhoɑŋ toῆóqqtto፣
    Hoϱ tó ɑŋohhóó quuuocóto፡፡

Falling short as nine,
    Life never achieves the fullness of ten.

—ANONYMOUS
A Tigirinya proverb

ᛖqɑŋóɯq hρɑŋqɑρ፧ ho q3óᶊ ɯoɑ ɔoᶊqt፣
    Πo uqɑŋóɯq ɯoɑρ፧ ɔó3 ɑónot፡፡

Fifty lemons for a man are burden,
    But for fifty men, each is a jewel.

—ANONYMOUS
An Amharic proverb

In this chapter

Although the Giiz, Tigirinya and Amharic (GTA) languages have names for cardinal and ordinal numbers for non-scientific day-to-day use, names of most very large and very small numerals and most mathematical sequences are inexistent and, therefore, foreign words are used without any effort to giizize them. For example, numerical adjectives like million, billion, and trillion; names of sequences like quadruple and quintuple; and names of geometric shapes like pentagon and hexagon have no equivalent names in the GTA languages and are often used as they are. I believe that the development of indigenous terminologies for concepts related to numbers is fundamental for the development of Ethiopian languages fit for a 21st century world. Therefore, this chapter proposes giization of such terms for Tigirinya and Amharic as well as presenting existing terms for reference and for showing the spelling in the proposed reformed Tigirinya and Amharic alphabets.

The Ethiopic Numerals

Ethiopic has its own numerals which have been in use for centuries and are easily recognized by their horizontal strokes at the top and bottom of every numeric symbol. Although they were highly advanced for their times, these numerals are less frequently used today. Compared to the standard Hindu-Arabic numerals (**Table 11.1**) and much like their Roman equivalents, the Ethiopic numerals are less fit for complex mathematical calculations because they lack the concept of zero, are not based on digital-positional notation, and are unable to represent large numeric values. As a result, the Hindu-Arabic numerals are almost exclusively used by professionals and the general public alike instead of the Ethiopic numerals. (For comparison of the Ethiopic and Roman numerals, refer to Chapter 9: Proposed Standard System for the Romanization of Ethiopic.)

Numerals in the Proposed Ethiopic Orthography

The traditional Ethiopic numeral system shall be adopted for the proposed orthography with minimal modification. However, its use will probably continue to be limited to signage, standalone numbers, page numbering and simple math-

Table 11.1: Comparison of the Hindu-Arabic and the Ethiopic numeral systems

A		B		C		D		E		F	
1	፩	21	፳፩	101	፻፩	–	–	211	፪፻፲፩	1100	፩ሺ ፩፻
2	፪	22	፳፪	102	፻፪	–	–	212	፪፻፲፪	1200	፩ሺ ፪፻
3	፫	23	፳፫	103	፻፫	130	፻፴	213	፪፻፲፫	1300	፩ሺ ፫፻
4	፬	24	፳፬	104	፻፬	140	፻፵	214	፪፻፲፬	1400	፩ሺ ፬፻
5	፭	25	፳፭	105	፻፭	150	፻፶	215	፪፻፲፭	1500	፩ሺ ፭፻
6	፮	26	፳፮	106	፻፮	160	፻፷	216	፪፻፲፮	1600	፩ሺ ፮፻
7	፯	27	፳፯	107	፻፯	170	፻፸	217	፪፻፲፯	1700	፩ሺ ፯፻
8	፰	28	፳፰	108	፻፰	180	፻፹	218	፪፻፲፰	1800	፩ሺ ፰፻
9	፱	29	፳፱	109	፻፱	190	፻፺	219	፪፻፲፱	1900	፩ሺ ፱፻
10	፲	30	፴	110	፻፲	200	፪፻	220	፪፻፳	2000	፪ሺ
11	፲፩	–	–	111	፻፲፩	201	፪፻፩	–	–	1000	፩ሺ
12	፲፪	–	–	112	፻፲፪	202	፪፻፪	–	–	2000	፪ሺ
13	፲፫	–	–	113	፻፲፫	203	፪፻፫	300	፫፻	3000	፫ሺ
14	፲፬	40	፵	114	፻፲፬	204	፪፻፬	400	፬፻	4000	፬ሺ
15	፲፭	50	፶	115	፻፲፭	205	፪፻፭	500	፭፻	5000	፭ሺ
16	፲፮	60	፷	116	፻፲፮	206	፪፻፮	600	፮፻	6000	፮ሺ
17	፲፯	70	፸	117	፻፲፯	207	፪፻፯	700	፯፻	7000	፯ሺ
18	፲፰	80	፹	118	፻፲፰	208	፪፻፰	800	፰፻	8000	፰ሺ
19	፲፱	90	፺	119	፻፲፱	209	፪፻፱	900	፱፻	9000	፱ሺ
20	፳	100	፩፻	120	፻፳	210	፪፻፲	1000	፩ሺ	10000	፲ሺ

ematical operations. Unlike the Hindu-Arabic positional numeral system with only ten numeric symbols, the Ethiopic numeric system is additive and contains twenty different numeric symbols, including the archaic symbol ፼, which make it almost impossible to perform highly complex mathematical operations in the standard base 10. The numeral ፼, which is equal to 10000, is historically the Ethiopic numeral with the largest numeric value (**Table 11.2**). In modern use, ፼ is almost entirely abandoned because it groups four consecutive decimal digits as a single unit in contrast to the universally accepted grouping of three decimal digits (as in 1,000) making it incompatible with modern usage. However, since the Ethiopic numeric system does not have a symbol for 1,000, the traditional method to represent a numeric value of four digits is to use the symbol ፻ (equal to 100) preceded by a coefficient ranging from 10 to 99, followed by numerals for tens and ones. (If the value of a digit in the tens or ones is zero, it is omitted from the notation.) For example, 2978 would be written as follows:

2978 = (20 + 9)*100 + (70 + 8)
= 20 then 9 then 100 then 70 then 8
= ፳፱፻፸፰

Table 11.2: The Ethiopic numerals and their values[1]

	1	2	3	4	5	6	7	8	9
× 1	፩	፪	፫	፬	፭	፮	፯	፰	፱
× 10	፲	፳	፴	፵	፶	፷	፸	፹	፺
× 100	፻	፪፻	፫፻	፬፻	፭፻	፮፻	፯፻	፰፻	፱፻
x 10 x 100	፲፻	፳፻	፴፻	፵፻	፭፻	፷፻	፸፻	፹፻	፺፻
× 10,000	፼								

Notwithstanding the absence of an Ethiopic numeric symbol for 1,000, there is an alternative way of representing such a number without using the powers of 100 by simply inserting the Ethiopic word for 'thousand' within the numerals as follows:

2978	=	(2*thousand) + (9*100) + (70 + 8)	
	=	2 then 'thousand' then 9 then 100 then 70 then 8	
	=	፪ ሺሕ ፱፻፸፰	(Tigirinya)
	=	፪ ሺህ ፱፻፸፰	(Amharic)

The use of the words ሺሕ or ሺህ along with Ethiopic numerals for inscribing numeric values in Ethiopic is probably a relatively recent development dating back to the last few centuries and was never employed by Giiz—the ancestral Semitic language in Ethiopia. This modern phenomenon provides an opportunity to create a new numeric symbol and, therefore, I propose that the character ሺ be used as the numeric symbol for 1,000 (**Table 11.1**). ሺ will then be preceded by a coefficient (1 through 999) to represent multiples of 1,000 and followed by numerals for hundreds, tens and ones up to values just below 1,000,000.

The largest number that can be written using the Ethiopic numeral system is debatable, especially due to the ambiguity in the use of the now archaic (or at least rarely used) numeric symbol ፼ (10,000) and the use of the word ሺሕ or ሺህ to account for a missing symbol for 1,000. Some have attempted to represent large numbers using the Ethiopic numerals (**Figure 11.1**), while others have arrived at other fixed numeric values.[2] However, without the ፼ numeric symbol, a simple incremental approach would cap the maximum number at 999,999 (፱፻፺፱ሺ ፱፻፺፱).

For the Ethiopian language reform, I propose dropping the ፼ numeric character altogether. With ፼ out of the way, the largest number that can be written using the Ethiopic numerals is 999,999 (፱፻፺፱ሺ ፱፻፺፱). However, if ሺ is used more than once within a single number, as in ፱፻፺፱ሺ ፱፻፺፱ሺ ፱፻፺፱ (999,999,999; more literally: 999 thousand 999 thousand 999), the maximum number than can be represented using Ethiopic numerals is infinite. An even better alternative may be using Ethiopic initials for million and billion, for example, instead of ሺ as applicable as in the following example:

፱፻፺፱ቢ ፱፻፺፱ሚ ፱፻፺፱ሺ ፱፻፺፱ (999, 999,999,999; more literally: 999 billion 999 million 999 thousand 999)

1)	Start with an arbitrary number.	7,654,321			
2)	From right to left group numbers in sets of two.	[07]	[65]	[43]	[21]
3)	We'll add subscripts for book keeping.	$[07]_3$	$[65]_2$	$[43]_1$	$[21]_0$
4)	Now expand the sets into 10's and 1's and write as separate numbers.	$([07])_3$	$([60][5])_2$	$([40][3])_1$	$([20][1])_0$
5)	Go ahead and convert to Ethiopic numbers.	(፯)$_3$	(፷፭)$_2$	(፵፫)$_1$	(፳፩)$_0$
6)	፻ after odd subscripts, ፼ after even -except 0!	(፯) + (፻)	(፷፭) + (፼)	(፵፫) + (፻)	(፳፩)
7)	Group.	፯፻	፷፭፼	፵፫፻	፳፩
8)	Collect and we're done!	፯፻፷፭፼፵፫፻፳፩			

Figure 11.1: Conversion of a large number into the Ethiopic numeral system.[3]
Source: The Ge'ez Frontier Foundation. Reproduced under Creative Commons license.

Giizization of Terminologies for Numbers, Sequences, and Geometric Shapes

Giizization of Cardinal and Ordinal Numerals

In linguistics, cardinal numerals are words that indicate the number of items in a set, such as the word *two*. On the other hand, ordinal numerals are words that indicate a position in an ordered sequence, such as the word *second*. Regardless of whether the Ethiopic numerals or the Hindu-Arabic numerals are used, the words representing the cardinal numerals and ordinal numerals remain the same in the respective GTA languages and are the basis for giizization (**Tables 11.3, 11.4,** and **11.5**). Traditionally, in Tigirinya, every ordinal numeral above 'tenth' is a phrasal word composed of the word ɑɋonnoḩ <mebbel> and a cardinal numeral. For example, 23rd is written as *mebbel iisiran-selesiten* (literally: *mebbel* twenty-three). This system is cumbersome and difficult to represent using ordinal indicators. Therefore, for the betterment of the language, I propose that Tigirinya extend the use of the ordinal indicator suffix qɐ <ay>, which it traditionally uses for lower ordinal numerals, to all ordinal numerals (**Table 11.5**). Therefore, from the above example, twenty-third shall be written and pronounced as óówócq϶-wqḩówqɐ <ii-siran-salisay>. Alternatively, it can be written as ፳፫qɐ or ፳፫^{qɐ}. For both Tigirinya and Amharic, the Hindu-Arabic numerals can be used as an alternative ordinal indicators as '23qɐ ($23^{\text{qɐ}}$)' for Tigirinya and '23϶q ($23^{\text{϶q}}$)' for Amharic, for example.

Giizization of Mathematical Sequences, Geometric Shapes, and Others

Giizization of names of orders of degree or rank (ranking numerals) (**Table 11.6**); arity (composite numerals) (**Table 11.7**); tuple (**Table 11.8**); fractions (partitive numbers) (**Table 11.9**); polygons (**Table 11.10**); collective numerals of multiple births (**Table 11.11**); residential types (**Table 11.12**); number naming systems for integer powers of ten (**Table 11.13**); and prefixes in the International System of Units (**Table 11.14**) includes existing and newly proposed Ethiopic names.

Examples of proposed verb forms for the giizization of tuples are as follows:

ɑɋó wóḩḩqw | ɑɋo woḩḩow (ɑɋo wwoḩow) – to triple

ɑɋó cónnqóó | ɑɋo connqt - to quadruple

Table 11.3: Names of cardinal numbers in Giiz

HINDU-ARABIC NUMERALS	ETHIOPIC NUMERALS	OLD ETHIOPIC ORTHOGRAPHY	NEW ETHIOPIC ORTHOGRAPHY		TRANSLITERATION
1	፩	ኣሓዱ	quuqʒo	(quuqttq)*	ahhadu
2	፪	ክልኤቱ	ɦóhóq̧to	(ɦóhóq̧tq)	kilieitu
3	፫	ሠለስቱ	wnohowóto	(wnohqw)	sxelesitu
4	፬	ኣርባዕቱ	qcónqóóto	(qcónqó)	aribaiitu
5	፭	ሓምስቱ	uuqɱówóto	(uuqɱów)	hhamisitu
6	፮	ስድስቱ	wóʒówótto	(wówwo)	sidisittu
7	፯	ሰብዓቱ	wonóqqtto	(wonóo)	sebiaattu
8	፰	ሰመንቱ	woɱoʒóto	(woɱoʒq)	semenitu
9	፱	ተስዓቱ	towóqqto	(towo)	tesiaatu
10	፲	ዓሠርቱ	qqwnocóto	(qqwnóco)	aasxeritu
11	፲፩	ዓሠርቱ ወኣሓዱ	qqwnocóto-ɷoquuqʒo		aasxeritu-weahhadu
12	፲፪	ዓሠርቱ ወክልኤቱ	qqwnocóto-ɷoɦóhóq̧to		aasxeritu-wekilieitu
13	፲፫	ዓሠርቱ ወሠለስቱ	qqwnocóto-ɷowuohowóto		aasxeritu-wesxelesitu
14	፲፬	ዓሠርቱ ወኣርባዕቱ	qqwnocóto-ɷoqcónqóóto		aasxeritu-wearibaiitu
15	፲፭	ዓሠርቱ ወሓምስቱ	qqwnocóto-ɷouuqɱówóto		aasxeritu-wehhamisitu
16	፲፮	ዓሠርቱ ወስድስቱ	qqwnocóto-ɷowóʒówóto		aasxeritu-wesidisittu
17	፲፯	ዓሠርቱ ወሰብዓቱ	qqwnocóto-ɷowonóqqto		aasxeritu-wesebiaattu
18	፲፰	ዓሠርቱ ወሰመንቱ	qqwnocóto-ɷowoɱoʒóto		aasxeritu-wesemenitu
19	፲፱	ዓሠርቱ ወተስዓቱ	qqwnocóto-ɷotowóqqto		aasxeritu-weaasxeritu
20	፳	ዕሥራ	óównócq		iisxira
21	፳፩	ዕሥራ ወኣሓዱ	óównócq-ɷoquuqʒo		iisxira-weahhadu
22	፳፪	ዕሥራ ወክልኤቱ	óównócq-ɷoɦóhóq̧to		iisxira-wekilieitu
23	፳፫	ዕሥራ ወሠለስቱ	óównócq-ɷownohowóto		iisxira-wesxelesitu
30	፴	ሠላሳ	wnohqwq		sxelasa
40	፵	ኣርባዓ	qcónqqq		aribaaa
50	፶	ሓምሳ	uuqɱówq		hhamisa
60	፷	ስድሳ	wóʒówq		sidisa
70	፸	ሰብዓ	wonóqq		sebiaa
80	፹	ሰማንያ	woɱqqʒq̧q		semaneea
90	፺	ተስዓ	towóqq		tesiaa
100	፻	ምእት	ɱóót		miit
10,000	፼	እልፍ	óhóɓ		ilif

* Note: Words in parenthesis indicate the female grammatical gender

Table 11.4: Names of cardinal numbers in Tigirinya and Amharic

HINDU-ARABIC NUMERALS	ETHIOPIC NUMERALS*	CARDINAL NUMBERS IN TIGIRINYA		CARDINAL NUMBERS IN AMHARIC	
		TIGIRINYA NAME	TRANSLITERATION	AMHARIC NAME	TRANSLITERATION
0	⁝	nqɋp	bado	nqɋp	bado
1	፩	uuqɋo (uuqʒȯtq)*	hhade (hhanitee)	qʒȯɋ (qʒȯɋqt)	anid (anideet)
2	፪	ɦȯɦȯtto	kilitte	uoɦott	hulett
3	፫	ɯoɦoɯȯto	selesite	ɯpɯȯt	sosit
4	፬	qcȯnqȯȯto	aribaiite	qcqtt	aratt
5	፭	uuqɱoῆȯto	hhamushite	qɱɱȯɯȯt	ammisit
6	፮	ῆȯɋɋȯῆȯto	shiddishite	ɯȯɋɋȯɯȯt	siddisit
7	፯	ῆooqqto	sheuaate	ɯonqtt	sebatt
8	፰	ῆoɱpʒȯto	shemonite	ɯȯɱɱȯʒȯt	simminit
9	፱	tȯῆȯqqto	tishiaate	ɥomoʒ	zetxeny
10	፲	qqɯocȯto	aaserite	qɯɯȯc	assir
11	፲፩	qqɯocȯto- uuqɋo	aaserite- hhade	qɯȯcq-qʒȯɋ	asira- anid
12	፲፪	qqɯocȯto- ɦȯɦȯto	aaserite- kilite	qɯȯcq-uoɦot	asira- hulet
13	፲፫	qqɯocȯto- ɯoɦoɯȯto	aaserite- selesite	qɯȯcq-ɯpɯȯt	asira- sosit
14	፲፬	qqɯocȯto- qcȯnqȯȯto	aaserite- aribaiite	qɯȯcq-qcqtt	asira- aratt
15	፲፭	qqɯocȯto- uuqɱoῆȯto	aaserite- hhamushite	qɯȯcq-qɱɱȯɯȯt	asira- ammisit
16	፲፮	qqɯocȯto- ῆȯɋɋȯῆȯto	aaserite- shiddishite	qɯȯcq-ɯȯɋɋȯɯȯt	asira- siddisit
17	፲፯	qqɯocȯto- ῆooqqto	aaserite- sheuate	qɯȯcq-ɯonqtt	asira- sebatt
18	፲፰	qqɯocȯto- ῆoɱpʒȯto	aaserite- shemonite	qɯȯcq-ɯȯɱɱȯʒȯt	asira- simminit
19	፲፱	qqɯocȯto- tȯῆȯqqto	aaserite- tishiaate	qɯȯcq-ɥomoʒ	asira- zetxeny
20	፳	ȯȯɯȯcq	iisira	uqϱq	haya
21	፳፩	ȯȯɯȯcqʒ- uuqɋo	iisiran- hhade	uqϱq- qʒȯɋ	haya- anid
22	፳፪	ȯȯɯȯcqʒ- ɦȯɦȯto	iisiran- kilite	uqϱq- uoɦott	haya- hulett
23	፳፫	ȯȯɯȯcqʒ- ɯoɦoɯȯto	iisiran- selesite	uqϱq- ɯpɯȯt	haya- sosit
30	፴	ɯoɦqɯq	selasa	ɯoɦqɯq	selasa
40	፵	qqcȯnȯqq	aaribiaa	qcȯnq	ariba
50	፶	uuqɱȯɯq	hhamisa	uqɱȯɯq	hamisa
60	፷	ɯȯɯɯq	sissa	ɯȯɋȯɯq	sidisa
70	፸	ɯonȯqq	sebiaa	ɯonq	seba
80	፹	ɯoɱqʒqq	semaneea	ɯoɱqʒqq	semaneea
90	፺	tqɯȯqq	teisiaa	ɥomoʒq	zetxena
100	፻	ɱqȯtq	meeitee	ɱotp	meto

* Note: The ⁝ sign is proposed Ethiopic numeral for zero (0). Words in parenthesis indicate the female grammatical gender.

Table 11.5: Existing and proposed names of ordinal numbers in Tigirinya and Amharic

ENGLISH ORDINALS	TIGIRINYA ORDINALS			AMHARIC ORDINALS		
	SYM-BOL	TIGIRINYA NAME	TRANSLITERATION	SYM-BOL	TIGIRINYA NAME	TRANSLITERATION
1st	b̄qᶒ	ȹoʂʂqɑɱqᶒ (ȹoʂqɑɱoᶒótq)	qeddamay (qedameyitee)	b̄ʒq	qʒóʂʂoʒʒq	aniddenyya
2nd	B̄qᶒ	ɦqɦóqᶒ (ɦqɦóoᶒótq)	kaliay (kalieyitee)	B̄ʒq	uoɦottoʒʒq	hulettenyya
3rd	C̄qᶒ	ɯqɦóɯqᶒ (ɯqɦóɯoᶒótq)	salisay (saliseyitee)	C̄ʒq	ɯpɯóttoʒʒq	sosittenyya
4th	D̄qᶒ	cqnóqqᶒ	rabiaay	D̄ʒq	qcqttoʒʒq	arattenyya
5th	Ēqᶒ	uuqɑɱóῆqᶒ	hhamishay	Ēʒq	qɑɱɑɱóɯóttoʒʒq	ammisittenyya
6th	Z̄qᶒ	ῆqʂóῆqᶒ	shadishay	Z̄ʒq	ɯóʂʂóɯóttoʒʒq	siddisittenyya
7th	Z̄qᶒ	ῆqoqqᶒ	shauaay	Z̄ʒq	ɯonqttoʒʒq	sebattenyya
8th	Īqᶒ	ῆqɑɱóʒqᶒ	shaminay	Īʒq	ɯóɑɱɑɱóʒóttoʒʒq	simminittenyya
9th	H̄qᶒ	tqῆóqqᶒ	tashiaay	H̄ʒq	ʜomoʒʒoʒʒq	zetxenyyenyya
10th	Īqᶒ	qqɯócqᶒ	aasiray	Īʒq	qɯɯóccoʒʒq	assirrenyya
11th	Īb̄qᶒ	qqɯocóto- ȹoʂqɑɱqᶒ	aaserite- qedamay	Īb̄ʒq	qɯócq- qʒóʂʂoʒʒq	asira- aniddenyya
12th	ĪB̄qᶒ	qqɯocóto- ɦqɦóqᶒ	aaserite- kaliay	ĪB̄ʒq	qɯócq- uoɦottoʒʒq	asira- hulettenyya
13th	ĪC̄qᶒ	qqɯocóto- ɯqɦóɯqᶒ	aaserite- salisay	ĪC̄ʒq	qɯócq- ɯpɯóttoʒʒq	asira- sosittenyya
14th	ĪD̄qᶒ	qqɯocóto- cqnóqqᶒ	aaserite- rabiaay	ĪD̄ʒq	qɯócq- qcqttoʒʒq	asira- arattenyya
15th	ĪĒqᶒ	qqɯocóto- uuqɑɱóῆqᶒ	aaserite- hhamishay	ĪĒʒq	qɯócq- qɑɱɑɱóɯóttoʒʒq	asira- ammisittenyya
16th	ĪZ̄qᶒ	qqɯocóto- ῆqʂóῆqᶒ	aaserite- shadishay	ĪZ̄ʒq	qɯócq- ɯóʂʂóɯóttoʒʒq	asira- siddisittenyya
17th	ĪZ̄qᶒ	qqɯocóto- ῆqoqqᶒ	aaserite- shauaay	ĪZ̄ʒq	qɯócq- ɯonqttoʒʒq	asira- sebattenyya
18th	ĪĪqᶒ	qqɯocóto- ῆqɑɱóʒqᶒ	aaserite- shaminay	ĪĪʒq	qɯócq- ɯóɑɱɑɱóʒóttoʒʒq	asira- simminittenyya
19th	ĪH̄qᶒ	qqɯocóto- tqῆóqqᶒ	aaserite- tashiaay	ĪH̄ʒq	qɯócq- ʜomoʒʒoʒʒq	asira- zetxenyyenyya
20th	ĥqᶒ	óóɯócqᶒ	iisiray	ĥʒq	uqᶒqʒʒq	hayanyya
21st	ĥb̄qᶒ	óóɯócqʒ- ȹoʂqɑɱqᶒ	iisiran- qedamay	ĥb̄ʒq	uqᶒq- qʒóʂʂoʒʒq	haya- aniddenyya
22nd	ĥB̄qᶒ	óóɯócqʒ- ɦqɦóqᶒ	iisiran- kaliay	ĥB̄ʒq	uqᶒq- uoɦottoʒʒq	haya- hulettenyya
23rd	ĥC̄qᶒ	óóɯócqʒ- ɯqɦóɯqᶒ	iisiran- salisay	ĥC̄ʒq	uqᶒq- ɯpɯóttoʒʒq	haya- sosittenyya
30th	Ŵqᶒ	ɯoɦqɯqᶒ	selasay	Ŵʒq	ɯoɦqɯqʒʒq	selasanyya
40th	Ŵqᶒ	qqcónóqqᶒ	aaribiaay	Ŵʒq	qcónqʒʒq	aribanyya
50th	Ūqᶒ	uuqɑɱóɯqᶒ	hhamisay	Ūʒq	uqɑɱóɯqʒʒq	hamisanyya
60th	Īqᶒ	ɯóɯɯqᶒ	sissay	Īʒq	ɯóʂóɯqʒʒq	sidisanyya
70th	P̄qᶒ	ɯonóqqᶒ	sebiaay	P̄ʒq	ɯonqʒʒq	sebanyya
80th	Π̄qᶒ	ɯoɑɱqʒqqᶒ	semaneeay	Π̄ʒq	ɯoɑɱqʒqqʒʒq	semaneeanyya
90th	ʒ̄qᶒ	tqɯóqqᶒ	teisiaay	ʒ̄ʒq	ʜomoʒqʒʒq	zetxenanyya
100th	P̄qᶒ	ɑɱqótqqᶒ	meeiteeay	P̄ʒq	ɑɱotpʒʒq	metonyya

Note: Words in parenthesis indicate the female grammatical gender

Table 11.6: Existing and proposed names of orders of degree or rank (ranking numerals) in Tigirinya and Amharic

ORDER	TIGIRINYA		AMHARIC	
	TIGIRINYA	TRANSLITERATION	AMHARIC	TRANSLITERATION
primary	фoꝗqɑղqꝏɋ	qedamawee	фoꝗqɑղqꝏɋ	qedamawee
secondary	ꝗqɔóɑղqꝏɋ	dagimawee	ꝗqɔóɑղqꝏɋ	dagimawee
tertiary	ɯqɧóɯqꝏɋ	salisawee	ɯqɧóɯqꝏɋ	salisawee
quaternary	cqnóqqꝏɋ	rabiaawee	cqnóqꝏɋ	rabiawee
quinary	υυqɑղóɯqꝏɋ	hhamisawee	υqɑղóɯqꝏɋ	hamisawee
senary	ɯqꝗóɯqꝏɋ	sadisawee	ɯqꝗóɯqꝏɋ	sadisawee
septenary	ɯonóqqꝏɋ	sebiaawee	ɯonóqꝏɋ	sebiawee
octonary	ɯqɑղóɜqꝏɋ	saminawee	ɯqɑղóɜqꝏɋ	saminawee
nonary	toɯóqqꝏɋ	tesiaawee	toɯóqꝏɋ	tesiawee
denary	qqɯócqꝏɋ	aasirawee	qɯócqꝏɋ	asirawee

Table 11.7: Proposed names of arity (composite numerals) in Tigirinya and Amharic

ARITY NAME	TIGIRINYA		AMHARIC	
	TIGIRINYA	TRANSLITERATION	AMHARIC	TRANSLITERATION
nullary	qɧónpqꝏɋ	aliboawee	qɧónpqꝏɋ	aliboawee
unary	noȣóɜqꝏɋ	beyinawee	nóǂǂqꝏɋ	biccawee
binary	ꝗócónqꝏɋ	diribawee	ꝗócónqꝏɋ	diribawee
ternary	ɯoɧoɯótqꝏɋ	selesitawee	ɯpɯótqꝏɋ	sositawee
quaternary	cqnóqqꝏɋ	rabiaawee	cqnóqꝏɋ	rabiawee
quinary	υυqɑղóɯqꝏɋ	hhamisawee	υqɑղóɯqꝏɋ	hamisawee
senary	ɯqꝗóɯqꝏɋ	sadisawee	ɯqꝗóɯqꝏɋ	sadisawee
septenary	ɯonóqqꝏɋ	sebiaawee	ɯonóqꝏɋ	sebiawee
octonary	ɯqɑղóɜqꝏɋ	saminawee	ɯqɑղóɜqꝏɋ	saminawee
nonary	toɯóqqꝏɋ	tesiaawee	toɯóqꝏɋ	tesiawee
denary	qqɯócqꝏɋ	aasirawee	qɯócqꝏɋ	asirawee

The plural forms of the proposed names of multiple births in Tigirinya and Amharic (**Table 11.11**), follows the tradition set by the names for twins, which are existing terms in Tigirinya and Amharic. The female forms of the proposed Tigirinya names shall end with -oȣótɋ <-eyitee> such as ɯoɧoɯótoꝏoȣótɋ <se-lesiteweyitee> for a triplet.

Table 11.8: Existing and proposed names of tuple in Tigirinya and Amharic

TUPLE NAME	TIGIRINYA		AMHARIC	
	TIGIRINYA	TRANSLITERATION	AMHARIC	TRANSLITERATION
empty tuple	nqɋp	bado	nqɋp	bado
single	ʒóɵɵóɦ (uuóɋɋo·óó)	nixxil (ahhadu)	ʒomoɦq (qʒóɋɋqnnq)	netxela (aniddabba)
double	óóɵóɓq (ɋóccón)	iixifee (dirrib)	ómóɓ (ɋóccón)	itxif (dirrib)
triple	ωóɦɦo·ω	sillus	ωóɦɦo·ω	sillus
quadruple	cónno·óó	ribbuii	qcqttómóɓ	arattitxif
quintuple	uuóɑɋɑɋo·ω	hhimmus	qɑɋɑɋóωótómóɓ	ammisititxif
sextuple	ωóɋɋo·ω	siddus	ωóɋɋóωótómóɓ	siddisititxif
septuple	ωónno·óó	sibbuii	ωonqttómóɓ	sebattitxif
octuple	ωóɑɋɑɋo·ʒ	simmun	ωóɑɋɑɋóʒótómóɓ	simminititxif
nonuple	tóωωo·óó	tissuii	ʜomoʒ̃ómóɓ	zetxenyitxif
decuple	óóωωo·c	iissur	qωωócómóɓ	assiritxif

Note: Words in parenthesis indicate alternative forms

Table 11.9: Existing and proposed names of fractions (partitive numbers) in Tigirinya and Amharic

FRACTION		TIGIRINYA		AMHARIC	
		TIGIRINYA	TRANSLITERATION	AMHARIC	TRANSLITERATION
1/2	a half	uuqɋo ɓócóȹq	hhade firiqee	qʒóɋ ɔóɑɋɑɋqɦ̃	anid gimmash
1/3	a third	uuqɋo ωqωp	hhade seeso	qʒóɋ ωqωp	anid seeso
1/4	a quarter	uuqɋo cónóqq	hhade ribieee	qʒóɋ co·n	anid rub
1/5	a fifth	uuqɋo uuqɑɋóɦ̃qɐ	hhade hhamishay	qʒóɋ qɑɋɑɋóωóttoʒ̃ʒ̃q	anid ammisittenyya
1/6	a sixth	uuqɋo ɦ̃qɋóɦ̃qɐ	hhade shadishay	qʒóɋ ωóɋɋóωóttoʒ̃ʒ̃q	anid siddisittenyya
1/7	a seventh	uuqɋo ɦ̃qo·qqɐ	hhade shauaay	qʒóɋ ωonqttoʒ̃ʒ̃q	anid sebattenyya
1/8	an eighth	uuqɋo ɦ̃qɑɋóʒqɐ	hhade shaminay	qʒóɋ ωóɑɋɑɋóʒóttoʒ̃ʒ̃q	anid simminittenyya
1/9	a ninth	uuqɋo tqɦ̃óqqɐ	hhade tashiaay	qʒóɋ ʜomoʒ̃ʒ̃oʒ̃ʒ̃q	anid zetxenyyenyya
1/10	a tenth	uuqɋo qqωócqɐ	hhade aasiray	qʒóɋ qωωóccoʒ̃ʒ̃q	anid assirrenyya
1/100	a hundredth	uuqɋo ɑɋqótqqɐ	hhade meeiteeay	qʒóɋ ɑɋotpʒ̃ʒ̃q	anid metonyya
1/1000	a thousandth	uuqɋo ɦ̃óuuqɐ	hhade shihhawy	qʒóɋ ɦ̃quóʒ̃ʒ̃q	anid sheehinyya

Note: All other fractions, such as 'two-thirds' (2/3) shall be written as ɦóɦóto ωqωptqt in Tigirinya and uo·ɦot ωqωppŧ in Amharic.

Table 11.10: Existing and proposed names of polygons in Tigirinya and Amharic

POLYGON NAME	TIGIRINYA		AMHARIC	
	TIGIRINYA	TRANSLITERATION	AMHARIC	TRANSLITERATION
triangle	ωόḩḩο-ωϽρʖʖρ	sillusgonno	ωρωότ ɑɖqόнοʖ	sosit maizen
quadrilateral	cόnο-όϽρʖʖρ	ribuigonno	qcqtt ɑɖqόнοʖ	aratt maizen
pentagon	υυόɑɖο-ωϽρʖʖρ	hhimusgonno	qɑɖɑɖόωότ ɑɖqόнοʖ	ammisit maizen
hexagon	ωόʂο-ωϽρʖʖρ	sidusgonno	ωόʂʂόωότ ɑɖqόнοʖ	siddisit maizen
heptagon	ωόnnο-όϽρʖʖρ	sibbuigonno	ωοnqtt ɑɖqόнοʖ	sebatt maizen
octagon	ωόɑɖο-ʖϽρʖʖρ	simungonno	ωόɑɖɑɖόʖότ ɑɖqόнοʖ	simminit maizen
nonagon	tόωο-όϽρʖʖρ	tisuigonno	нοmοʖ̃ ɑɖqόнοʖ	zetxeny maizen
decagon	όόωο-cϽρʖʖρ	iisurgonno	qωωόc ɑɖqόнοʖ	assir maizen

Table 11.11: Proposed names for the collective numerals of multiple births in Tigirinya and Amharic

MULTIPLE BIRTH NAME	TIGIRINYA		AMHARIC	
	TIGIRINYA	TRANSLITERATION	AMHARIC	TRANSLITERATION
twin(s)*	ɑɖqʖότq (ɑɖοʖqtο-)*	manita (menatu)*	ɑɖοʖότq(ρŧ)*	menita(oc)*
triplet(s)	ωοḩοωότοωqϱ (-ωρt)	selesiteway (-wot)	ωρωότόɑɖɑɖq(ρŧ)	sositemma(oc)
quadruplet(s)	qcόnqόότοωqϱ (-ωρt)	aribaiiteway (-wot)	qcqttόɑɖɑɖq(ρŧ)	arattimma(oc)
quintuplet(s)	υυqɑɖο-ῆότοωqϱ(-ωρt)	hhamushiteway (-wot)	qɑɖɑɖόωότόɑɖɑɖq(ρŧ)	ammisitimma(oc)
sextuplet(s)	ῆόʂʂόῆότοωqϱ (-ωρt)	shiddishiteway (-wot)	ωόʂʂόωότόɑɖɑɖq(ρŧ)	siddisitimma(oc)
septuplet(s)	ῆοο-qqtοωqϱ (-ωρt)	sheuaateway (-wot)	ωοnqtόɑɖɑɖq(ρŧ)	sebatimma(oc)
octuplet(s)	ῆοɑɖρʖότοωqϱ (-ωρt)	shemoniteway (-wot)	ωόɑɖόʖότόɑɖɑɖq(ρŧ)	siminitimma(oc)
nonuplet(s)	tόῆόqqtοωqϱ (-ωρt)	teshiaateway (-wot)	нοmοʖ̃όɑɖɑɖq(ρŧ)	zetxenyimma(oc)

Note: Words/suffixes in parenthesis indicate plural forms. Both the singular and plura forms for 'twin' are exiting terms in both Tigirinya and Amharic.

Table 11.12: Proposed names of residential types in Tigirinya and Amharic

DWELLING TYPE	TIGIRINYA		AMHARIC	
	TIGIRINYA	TRANSLITERATION	AMHARIC	TRANSLITERATION
simplex	nοϱόʖρ	beyino	nόŧŧρ	bicco
duplex	ʂόcόnρ / ḩqόόnρ	diribo / kaiibo	ʂόcόnρ / ḩqόnρ	diribo / kaibo
triplex	ωqḩόωρ	saliso	ωqḩόωρ	saliso
quadruplex	cqnόρ	rabio	cqnόρ	rabio
quintuplex	υυqɑɖόωρ	hhamiso	υqɑɖόωρ	hamiso
sextuplex	ωqʂόωρ	sadiso	ωqʂόωρ	sadiso

Table 11.13: Proposed Tigirinya and Amharic equivalents to English number naming systems for integer powers of ten

VALUE	ENGLISH NAME	TIGIRINYA NAME	AMHARIC NAME
1 000 000 000 000 000 000 000 000	septillion(s)	ʒȯȯηȯɓɋt(qt)	ʒȯȯηȯɓɋt(qt)
1 000 000 000 000 000 000 000	sextillion(s)	nȯȯηȯɓɋt(qt)	nȯȯηȯɓɋt(qt)
1 000 000 000 000 000 000	quintillion(s)	ɯȯȯηȯɓɋt(qt)	ɯȯȯηȯɓɋt(qt)
1 000 000 000 000 000	quadrillion(s)	uȯȯηȯɓɋt(qt)	uȯȯηȯɓɋt(qt)
1 000 000 000 000	trillion(s)	ɑɋȯȯηȯɓɋt(qt)	ɑɋȯȯηȯɓɋt(qt)
1 000 000 000	billion(s)	tȯȯηȯɓɋt(qt)	tȯȯηȯɓɋt(qt)
1 000 000	million(s)	ȯηȯɓɋ (qȯηqɓ)	ȯηȯɓ (qȯηqɓ)
1 000	thousand(s)	η̄ȯuu (qη̄ȯuuqt)	η̄ɋu (η̄ɋuρŧ)
100	hundred(s)	ɑɋɋȯtɋ (qɑɋɋɋt)	ɑɋotρ (ɑɋotρρŧ)
10	ten(s)	qqɯocȯto (qqɯocȯtqt)	qɯɯȯc (qɯɯȯcρŧ)
1	one(s)	uuqʂo (quuqʂqt)	qʒȯʂ (qʒȯʂρŧ)
0.1	tenth(s)	qqɯȯcȯtqȩ(qt)	qɯɯȯcoʒ̄ʒ̄q(ρŧ)
0.01	hundredth(s)	ɑɋɋȯtqȩ(qt)	ɑɋotρʒ̄ʒ̄q(ρŧ)
0.001	thousandth(s)	η̄ȯuuqȩ(qt)	η̄ɋuȯʒ̄ʒ̄q(ρŧ)
0.000 001	millionth(s)	ȯηȯɓqȩ(qt)	ȯηȯɓoʒ̄ʒ̄q(ρŧ)
0.000 000 001	billionth(s)	tȯȯηȯɓɋtqȩ(qt)	tȯȯηȯɓɋtoʒ̄ʒ̄q(ρŧ)
0.000 000 000 001	trillionth(s)	ɑɋȯȯηȯɓɋtqȩ(qt)	ɑɋȯȯηȯɓɋtoʒ̄ʒ̄q(ρŧ)
0.000 000 000 000 001	quadrillionth(s)	uȯȯηȯɓɋtqȩ(qt)	uȯȯηȯɓɋtoʒ̄ʒ̄q(ρŧ)
0.000 000 000 000 000 001	quintillionth(s)	ɯȯȯηȯɓɋtqȩ(qt)	ɯȯȯηȯɓɋtoʒ̄ʒ̄q(ρŧ)
0.000 000 000 000 000 000 001	sextillionth(s)	nȯȯηȯɓɋtqȩ(qt)	nȯȯηȯɓɋtoʒ̄ʒ̄q(ρŧ)
0.000 000 000 000 000 000 000 001	septillionth(s)	ʒȯȯηȯɓɋtqȩ(qt)	ʒȯȯηȯɓɋtoʒ̄ʒ̄q(ρŧ)

Note: Parenthesis show plural forms. The Ethiopic names for one, ten, hundred, and thousand are existing. The Giiz terms ȯηȯɓ, qȯηqɓ, tȯȯηȯɓɋt and ɑɋȯȯηȯɓɋt are also existing but their values have changed. For example, the value of the Giiz ȯηȯɓ is 10,000, but the new value I proposed for it is 1,000,000. There is no consensus on the values of the Giiz terms tȯȯηȯɓɋt and ɑɋȯȯηȯɓɋt, although they are generally lower than the values I have proposed for them. The table also shows new terms I proposed for values from quadrillion through to septillion, which are similar to tȯȯηȯɓɋt and ɑɋȯȯηȯɓɋt except that they begin with letters found in the Giiz words uuqɑɋȯɯȯto, ɯȯʂȯɯȯtto, ɯonȯqqtto, and ɯoɑɋoʒȯto (five, six, seven, and eight), which are reflective of the order of magnitude in the base 1,000.

Table 11.14: Proposed Tigirinya and Amharic equivalents to the prefixes in the International System of Units

NAME	SYMBOL	FACTOR 10^n	FACTOR 1000^m	PROPOSED ETHIOPIC NAME	PROPOSED ETHIOPIC SYMBOL	DECIMAL
yotta	Y	10^{24}	1000^8	ωqαηό϶ο	ṅΩD	1 000 000 000 000 000 000 000 000
zetta	Z	10^{21}	1000^7	ωqnόο	ṅΠ	1 000 000 000 000 000 000 000
exa	E	10^{18}	1000^6	ωqᶃόωο	ṅṅ	1 000 000 000 000 000 000
peta	P	10^{15}	1000^5	υqαηόωο	ṁ	1 000 000 000 000 000
tera	T	10^{12}	1000^4	cqόnο	L	1 000 000 000 000
giga	G	10^9	1000^3	ωqηόωο	ṅ	1 000 000 000
mega	M	10^6	1000^2	ɦqόnο	ɦ	1 000 000
kilo	k	10^3	1000^1	ɔόόHο	˥	1 000
hecto	h	10^2	$1000^{2/3}$	αηόότο	ΩD	100
deca	da	10^1	$1000^{1/3}$	qωόcο	ħ	10
		10^0	1000^0			1
deci	d	10^{-1}	$1000^{-1/3}$	ɋqωόc	q	0.1
centi	c	10^{-2}	$1000^{-2/3}$	ɋαηόότ	αη	0.01
milli	m	10^{-3}	1000^{-1}	ɋɔόόH	ɔ	0.001
micro	µ	10^{-6}	1000^{-2}	ɋɦqόn	ɦ	0.000 001
nano	n	10^{-9}	1000^{-3}	ɋωqηόω	ω	0.000 000 001
pico	p	10^{-12}	1000^{-4}	ɋcqόn	c	0.000 000 000 001
femto	f	10^{-15}	1000^{-5}	ɋυqαηόω	υ	0.000 000 000 000 001
atto	a	10^{-18}	1000^{-6}	ɋωqᶃόω	ωω	0.000 000 000 000 000 001
zepto	z	10^{-21}	1000^{-7}	ɋωqnό	ωn	0.000 000 000 000 000 000 001
yocto	y	10^{-24}	1000^{-8}	ɋωqαηό϶	ωαη	0.000 000 000 000 000 000 000 001

Note: The proposed Ethiopic prefixes are lowercase letters for the decimal values below 1 and uppercase letters for the decimal values above one in order to correspond to those of the International System of Units.

Chapter 12

Proposed Standardization of the Ethiopic Keyboard

Why can't we have an Amharic typewriter?

—Emperor Minileek (1844 – 1913)

The formal printed address for the guest house we stayed at was "Yeka Sub city around Dinbroa general hospital." That would fit the description of about 1000 other houses, shops, hovels, and apartments. The only access was up an alley with no signs and a latrine ditch on one edge. By the end of the week though, I could have found my way back from quite far away. In Addis—no addresses, just landmarks and memory... What is a detailed address for anyway? The foreigner. Who needs Cartesian coordinates on their GPS? The alien.

—An American visitor, 2011

In this chapter

The first ever Ethiopic book to be printed was published in 1513 in Europe from the press of Marcellus Silber and was entitled *Psalterium David et cantica aliqua in lingua Chaldea* (David's Psalter and Song of Songs in the [Giiz] Language). The book was a result of the collaboration between the Ethiopian community in Rome and Johann Potken (ca. 1470 – ca. 1525), a German clergy who studied Giiz and became proficient enough to publish the Psalms and Song of Solomon in the language. Potken was able to accomplish this through a project he commissioned to cut Ethiopic type fonts—which was the first for the Ethiopic script other than woodcuts—by analyzing, as one of his sources, a manuscript Giiz Psalter still in the possession of the Vatican Library (Vat. etiop. 20), which by then had several other copies.[1]

However, the printing press was not introduced in Ethiopia until around 1900, nearly four centuries since the first publication of the Ethiopic Psalter overseas. Following the introduction of the printing press in Ethiopia, the use of typesetting technology helped reproduce exact replicas of the Ethiopic characters on books, which hitherto were reproduced by handwriting. The first typewriters also arrived in Ethiopia as early as around 1900. Pankhurst (n.d.) stated that in 1903, Emperor Minileek (Menelik) received a typewriter as a present from the American envoy Robert P. Skinner. One of the first modernist Ethiopian leaders, Minileek wondered when he would see an Ethiopic typewriter because the Ethiopic typewriter was not yet made at that time and the few available typewriters were used by expatriates residing in the country (Pankhurst, n.d.).

The Ethiopic Typewriter

Although the typewriter was invented as early as 1714 in England by Henry Mill, it was not until the late 1860s that work on what would eventually become the first commercially successful typewriter began by the American inventor Christopher Latham Sholes and team in Wisconsin, USA. Subsequently, the typewriter was quickly adapted for use in Europe. In Ethiopia, efforts were made to cut Ethiopic characters on the print heads of Latin-letter typewriters in the years following the introduction of the machine in the country. The efforts finally paid off when Ayyana Birru invented the first Ethiopic typewriter in 1923 E.C. (c. 1930).*

Although imperfect, the successful adaptation of the typewriter for Ethiopic was a major breakthrough in the long history of the unique Ethiopian writing system.

Perhaps never in all of the history of the Ethiopic writing system did the problems associated with the sheer number of the Ethiopic characters become more evident than at the introduction of the typewriter. The typewriter exposed the fundamental weakness of the Ethiopic writing system—its massive numbers of characters, which could not practically fit within the typewriter's keyboard. While the movable type of the printing press was able to accommodate virtually any number of characters, that was not possible with the limited number of keys on the typewriter. The frustration with the large number of the Ethiopic characters may be what led Emperor Minileek to try to modify the script, although he was never successful.[2] In the decades before and after the Italian invasion of Ethiopia (1936–41), many scholars called for the reform of the Ethiopic writing system by proposing the reduction of the Ethiopic characters in one way or another. (Chapter 14: The Politics of Reform: Previous Efforts for and Opposition to Language Reform.)

Originally a modification of the English typewriter, the first Ethiopic typewriter was only successfully adapted after the careful selection of the few characters that could be accommodated in the limited number of keys as base glyphs and using other elements, such as a diacritical mark, to create ligated versions of the Ethiopic character set. For example, ሁ, which is a *kaiib* or 2nd order character, is typed by striking one key for the base glyph ሀ and another one for ¬. The key for ¬ was then used for almost all characters in the *kaiib* order, such as ቡ, ሙ, and ሉ. Similarly, ዜ, which is a *hamis* or 5th order character, is typed by striking one key for the base glyph ዘ and another one for ∘. The key for ∘ was then used for almost all characters in the *hamis* order, such as ቤ, ዴ, and ጌ (**Table 12.1**). The keys for the diacritical marks helped reduce the total number of keys required to type Ethiopic characters, but the system was criticized for reducing the quality of the Ethiopic glyphs compared to the traditional Ethiopic glyphs (**Figure 7.4**). Although incredibly innovative for its day, the method of ligating the Ethiopic characters was able to produce characters that were only approximations of the typefaces that the printing press perfected. The spacing between the characters was never consistent, which added to the imperfections of the typewriter compared to the printing press and the traditional handwriting by Ethiopic scribes. For many people, the typefaces that the printing press perfected were never matched by anything until the computerization of Ethiopic a generation ago. However, in spite of its perceived weakness, the Ethiopic typewriter was probably one of the most innovative works ever done for Ethiopic, not least because it also initiated the debate on the reform of the writing system.

*Note: Spencer (1984) incorrectly stated that the Ethiopic typewriter was not yet invented by 1936.

Perhaps a quintessential example of an Ethiopic typewriter, the 1959 Olivetti Diaspron 82 manual typewriter (**Figure 12.1**), consists of the following keys:

- A tab key, a release key, and a advance key (above),
- Writing keys (centre),
- Two sets of shift and caps lock keys (one set on each side), and
- A space bar (below).

The writing keys are 45 and show alphasyllabic, symbolic, and numeric characters in addition to diacritical marks. There are a total of 30 alphasyllabic characters out of which 25 are *giiz* (1st order) characters. Out of the 25 *giiz* characters, 23 are accessed unshifted as are all the Hindu-Arabic numerals. Some non-*giiz* characters are also accessed unshifted, while most of the non-*giiz* characters that found a spot on the keyboard are accessed shifted as well as seven punctuation marks and mathematical symbols. As was common with the typewriter, zero does not have a dedicated key merely sharing the key for the Ethiopic character ዐ. Most of the alphasyllabic characters are basic letterforms from which the rest of the Ethiopic letterforms in all the Ethiopic vowelic orders can be derived with the addition of extra signs or diacritical marks. There are six keys positioned on the right side of the writing keys for typing these diacritical marks in the unshifted and shifted positions. One would overstrike one of the 12 available signs or diacritical marks over a basic letterform to achieve the desired character. Given the hundreds of characters that must be ligated using the basic letterforms and the diacritical marks, Shelemay (2011) observed that "a typist able to produce 15-20 Amharic words a minute was considered to be quite adept," which was still considered an improvement over writing by hand (as cited in Harvard University).[3]

Terrefe Raswork's design of the Ethiopic teleprinter (**Figure 12.2**), which was accepted by the then Imperial Board of Telecommunications in 1965 and was the first Ethiopic teleprinter (Terrefe Raswork, c. 1966), had more keys than the Ethiopic typewriter. Designed with the same concept as the Ethiopic typewriter, it had keys for overstriking diacritical marks over basic letterforms, which together created a ligated version of the Ethiopic characters (**Table 12.1**). The letterforms included on the keyboard were chosen from the Ethiopic MAIN SET based on two criteria: 1) basic letterforms that could be used on their own (mostly from the 1st and 6th orders) and could also be used for constructing other letterforms, and 2) irregular letterforms that were difficult to construct using standard diacritical marks.

Table 12.1: How the typewriter created different variations of the Ethiopic characters from basic letterforms

ORDER	DIACRITICAL KEYS	EXAMPLES OF LIGATED CHARACTERS (BASIC FORMS + DIACRITICS)
1st *giiz*		ሰ→ሸ, ቀ→ቐ, በ→ቨ, ተ→ቸ, ነ→ኘ, ከ→ኸ, ደ→ጀ, ጸ→ጰ,
2nd *kaiib*		ሀ→ሁ, ለ→ሉ, ሐ→ሑ, መ→ሙ, ሰ→ሱ, ሠ→ሡ, ሸ→ሹ
3rd *salis*		ቀ→ቂ, በ→ቢ, ተ→ቲ, ነ→ኒ, ኘ→ኚ, አ→ኢ, ከ→ኪ
4th *rabii*		ቐ→ቓ, ቸ→ቻ, ኸ→ኻ, ዘ→ዛ, ዠ→ዣ, የ→ያ, ደ→ዳ, ገ→ጋ
5th *hamis*		ቀ→ቄ, ዓ→ዔ, የ→ዬ, ጀ→ጄ, ጠ→ጤ, ጨ→ጬ
6th *sadis*		ዐ→ዕ, ፀ→ፅ (most *sadis* characters are typed directly without a diacritical key)
7th *sabii*		ሀ→ሆ, ለ→ሎ, ሐ→ሖ, መ→ሞ, ረ→ሮ, ተ→ቶ, ና→ኖ, ወ→ዎ, የ→ዮ, ገ→ጎ

Figure 12.1 (a) and **(b)**: The Olivetti Diaspron 82 manual Ethiopic typewriter by Olivetti S.p.A., circa 1959. Image courtesy of Collection of Historical Scientific Instruments, Harvard University. Reproduced with permission. Desaturated from the original.

Figure 12.2: The design of the first Ethiopic teleprinter by Terrefe Raswork, circa 1965. Notice that for the most part the unshifted writing keys are dedicated for the 1st order characters (upper signs), while the shifted writing keys are dedicated for characters difficult to ligate (lower signs), which are mostly 6th order characters.

A Summary of the Computerization of Ethiopic

The computerization of Ethiopic was, by and large, an effort by the Ethiopian diaspora dating back to the 1980's and mostly involved individual uncoordinated efforts. Although the then military government had set up the National Computer Center under the auspices of the Ethiopian Science and Technology Commission to computerize Ethiopic, it is believed that more was done by Ethiopians and friends of Ethiopia residing outside of Ethiopia, especially in the United States. The Ethiopian diaspora in the West lived at a time when the IBM Personal Computer dominated the computer market and when access to a personal computer was relatively easier. The development of Ethiopic computer software is a major milestone in the preservation and promotion of Ethiopian languages and culture. The establishment of a link in the late 20th century between information processing technologies and the Ethiopic writing system was a breakthrough for the processing and widespread dissemination of information among Ethiopians like never before in history. Early beneficiaries of Ethiopic word processors included writers, poets, religious institutions, journalists, and government agencies.

It is believed that Ethiopian-born Fesseha Atlaw of San Jose, California, developed the first commercially available Ethiopic word processor in 1985 through Dashen Engineering Company. Atlaw, who was a member of the Unicode Consortium, which assigned codes for the uniform processing of text in various scripts of the world, pushed for the inclusion of the traditional Ethiopic characters in the Unicode code charts. Along with Joseph Becker, co-founders of Unicode and an Officer Emeritus of the Unicode Consortium, Atlaw successfully presented the first Unicode proposal for Ethiopic to the Unicode Technical Committee. Ethiopic was included in the Unicode code charts starting with Version 2.0. Not being a linguist himself and only fluent in Amharic among Ethiopian languages, Atlaw received linguistic assistance from Dr. Tsehaye Teferra, a prominent Ethiopian linguist who lived in Washington, D.C. in the 1980's. While Atlaw is widely considered to be the pioneer in developing and delivering the first usable Ethiopic computer products to customers, many others were also engaged in various activities related to the computerization of Ethiopic. The following summary[4] lists the individuals known by many for their contribution to the development of Ethiopic, which often was not financially rewarding and required enormous investment of personal time and resources.

As a linguist and computer enthusiast, the contribution by Yitna Firdiywok of Middleburg, Virginia, was vital in the development of Ethiopic fonts to be used with existing word processors in 1985, although no product was made commercially available at that time.

Daniel Admassie and others of the then Ethiopian Science and Technology Commission, worked on the development of an Ethiopic word processor. Although it was never commercially available, it is believed that Daniel Admassie eventually developed what is said to be a tiny word processor, Agfari, in 1986.

The computerization of Ethiopic was a major breakthrough for Ethiopia, which is comparable to the successful adaptation of the typewriter for Ethiopic more than half a century ago.

Phillip LeBel of Montclair State University developed Ethiopic fonts for the Apple II computer in 1986, but his product was not commercially available.

Fikade Mesfin of Los Angeles, California, worked on Ethiopic fonts for the Macintosh in 1987.

In 1987, Ethiopian-born scientist and software developer Dr. Aberra Molla of Denver, Colorado, made what may be the first complete set of non-ligated Ethiopic fonts available commercially through the Ethiopian Computers & Software Company.

In 1988, Jeffrey Gillette of Duke University worked on the development of Ethiopic fonts for PC-Write, which was a word processor originally written in 1983. Financed by the US government, the project produced no products that were commercially available.

Abass Yalemeneh of Huston, Texas, owned many Ethiopic fonts, which he made available to customers through Ethio Systems Company in 1987.

Lloyd Anderson of Ecological Linguistics, Washington, D.C., worked on the development of Ethiopic fonts for the Macintosh computers in 1987.

Yemane Russom of Phonetic Systems in Texas was an early researcher of Ethiopic fonts for the Macintosh PC's (c. 1989) and has been offering his product Geez Word through Geez Soft Company.

In 1989, Amha Asfaw of the University of Missouri developed 'Brana,' an Amharic software.

While not a developer of software, Daniel Yacob of Washington, D.C., was instrumental in helping organize a concerted effort for the development of Ethiopic including through several presentations he made at the Unicode Technical Committee on Ethiopic.

Other individuals who contributed to the development of Ethiopic in various capacities, among others, are Mulugeta Kebede, Dr. Kefale G. Giorgis, Michael Tefera, Tewolde Stephanos, Alexander Assefa, Yonas Fisseha, Efrem Habteselassie, Fikre Yibrehu, Yemane Fixum, and Feqade Mesfin.

In the late 1980's Ethiopic word processors became available in the market on disk operating systems (DOS) and by the time the first printers started using them in Ethiopia, the average time for typesetting of a single page had decreased from eight hours to just one.[5]

The Unicode Encoding of Ethiopic

Unicode is a standard maintained by the Unicode Consortium, a not-for-profit organization, for the uniform processing of text in various scripts of the world by assigning a unique number for each character. According to the Consortium, the Unicode encoding standard "provides the basis for processing, storage and interchange of text data in any language in all modern software and information technology protocols." Yacob (2005-2006) stated that Ethiopic was eventually included in the Unicode Standards Version 3.0, which was issued in 2000. Unicode has since provided additional encoding for more Ethiopic characters that are used by other Ethiosemitic and Ethiocushitic languages. According to Julie D. Allen, et al. (2014), the Unicode encoding of Ethiopic takes into consideration glyph variants for some characters similar to the glyph variants of the Latin lowercase letter "a", which do not "coexist in the same font." Therefore, "the particular glyph shown in the code chart for each position in the matrix is merely one representation of that conceptual syllable, and the glyph itself is not the object that is encoded."[16] It took until 2006 for Ethiopic to be supported for the first time by a major computer operating system when the technology giant Microsoft Corporation released the Windows Vista operating system. Three years later, the first Ethiopic keyboard for mobile phones was developed by Nebyou Yirga, one of the first Ethiopian mobile application developers.[6] Apple Inc. products did not support Ethiopic when last checked in 2016. However, the Android operating system by Google Inc. has been supporting Ethiopic for years now.

As of Version 9.0, the Unicode Standards for Ethiopic contains hundreds of alphasyllabic characters, intonation marks, and stress signs used by Giiz, Tigirinya, Amharic, and other Ethiopian languages. The Unicode Version 9.0 for Ethiopic has the following sets:

Ethiopic:	358 characters including syllabes, combining marks, punctuation, and numerals used by the GTA and other languages of Ethiopia (**Table 12.2**);
Ethiopic Supplement:	26 characters specifically for use by the Sebat Beit language and includes Ethiopic tonal marks;
Ethiopic Extended:	79 characters specifically for use by the languages of Mieen, Bileen, and Sebat Beit; and
Ethiopic Extended-A:	32 characters specifically for use by the languages of Gamo-Goffa-Dawiro, Basikeito, and Gumuz.

Of the total 495 Ethiopic characters in Version 9.0, about 332 are traditional characters including Ethiopic numerals and punctuation marks historically used to write the GTA languages. The rest of the alphasyllables are modern modifications devised to suit languages that were never previously written in any script (for my recommendation on reforming and harmonizing the writing systems of the rest of the Ethiopian languages, refer to Chapter 13: More on the Ethiopic Language Crisis and Recommended Solutions.)

'Ethiocode': ES 781:2002

In October 2012, the then Quality and Standards Authority of Ethiopia sanctioned a standard for Ethiopic code named ES 781:2002. An inevitable result of the computerization of Ethiopic and the efforts of several professional individuals and entities, ES 781:2002, Ethiopia's first alphabetic standard, contains 504 characters (**Table 12.3**). According to the Ethiopian Standards Agency, a successor to QSAE and the sole national standards body in the nation, the standard specifies the character set, the order of the characters, number system, punctuation and symbols used by Ethiopic. The standard contains the Hindu-Arabic numerals and mathematical and other symbols adopted from European orthographies in addition to the Ethiopic aslphasyllabary and intonation marks used for liturgy by the Ethiopian Orthodox Church. (For a history of the development of ES 781:2002, refer to Yacob, 2005 – 2006, pp. 121-140.) The sheer size of the alphasyllabic characters shown in the standard, which includes historically newer letterforms for the Ethiopian languages of Awinigee, Mieen, Murisee, Qimanit, Suree, Sebat Beit and Khamitaniga (Yacob, 2005 - 2006) is a testament to the weakness of the Ethiopic script to accommodate new languages without unnecessarily swelling again.

Table 12.2: The Unicode Standard, Version 9.0 code chart for Traditional Ethiopic (including its newer letterforms)

UNICODE VALUE	0	1	2	3	4	5	6	7	8	9	A	B	C	D	E	F
120	ሀ	ሁ	ሂ	ሃ	ሄ	ህ	ሆ	ሇ	ለ	ሉ	ሊ	ላ	ሌ	ል	ሎ	ሏ
121	ሐ	ሑ	ሒ	ሓ	ሔ	ሕ	ሖ	ሗ	መ	ሙ	ሚ	ማ	ሜ	ም	ሞ	ሟ
122	ሠ	ሡ	ሢ	ሣ	ሤ	ሥ	ሦ	ሧ	ረ	ሩ	ሪ	ራ	ሬ	ር	ሮ	ሯ
123	ሰ	ሱ	ሲ	ሳ	ሴ	ስ	ሶ	ሷ	ሸ	ሹ	ሺ	ሻ	ሼ	ሽ	ሾ	ሿ
124	ቀ	ቁ	ቂ	ቃ	ቄ	ቅ	ቆ	ቇ	ቈ		ቊ	ቋ	ቌ	ቍ		
125	ቐ	ቑ	ቒ	ቓ	ቔ	ቕ	ቖ		ቘ		ቚ	ቛ	ቜ	ቝ		
126	በ	ቡ	ቢ	ባ	ቤ	ብ	ቦ	ቧ	ቨ	ቩ	ቪ	ቫ	ቬ	ቭ	ቮ	ቯ
127	ተ	ቱ	ቲ	ታ	ቴ	ት	ቶ	ቷ	ቸ	ቹ	ቺ	ቻ	ቼ	ች	ቾ	ቿ
128	ኀ	ኁ	ኂ	ኃ	ኄ	ኅ	ኆ	ኇ	ኈ		ኊ	ኋ	ኌ	ኍ		
129	ነ	ኑ	ኒ	ና	ኔ	ን	ኖ	ኗ	ኘ	ኙ	ኚ	ኛ	ኜ	ኝ	ኞ	ኟ
12A	አ	ኡ	ኢ	ኣ	ኤ	እ	ኦ	ኧ	ከ	ኩ	ኪ	ካ	ኬ	ክ	ኮ	ኯ
12B	ኰ		ኲ	ኳ	ኴ	ኵ			ኸ	ኹ	ኺ	ኻ	ኼ	ኽ	ኾ	
12C	ዀ		ዂ	ዃ	ዄ	ዅ			ወ	ዉ	ዊ	ዋ	ዌ	ው	ዎ	ዏ
12D	ዐ	ዑ	ዒ	ዓ	ዔ	ዕ	ዖ		ዘ	ዙ	ዚ	ዛ	ዜ	ዝ	ዞ	ዟ
12E	ዠ	ዡ	ዢ	ዣ	ዤ	ዥ	ዦ	ዧ	የ	ዩ	ዪ	ያ	ዬ	ይ	ዮ	ዯ
12F	ደ	ዱ	ዲ	ዳ	ዴ	ድ	ዶ	ዷ	ዸ	ዹ	ዺ	ዻ	ዼ	ዽ	ዾ	ዿ
130	ጀ	ጁ	ጂ	ጃ	ጄ	ጅ	ጆ	ጇ	ገ	ጉ	ጊ	ጋ	ጌ	ግ	ጎ	ጏ
131	ጐ		ጒ	ጓ	ጔ	ጕ			ጘ	ጙ	ጚ	ጛ	ጜ	ጝ	ጞ	ጟ
132	ጠ	ጡ	ጢ	ጣ	ጤ	ጥ	ጦ	ጧ	ጨ	ጩ	ጪ	ጫ	ጬ	ጭ	ጮ	ጯ
133	ጰ	ጱ	ጲ	ጳ	ጴ	ጵ	ጶ	ጷ	ጸ	ጹ	ጺ	ጻ	ጼ	ጽ	ጾ	ጿ
134	ፀ	ፁ	ፂ	ፃ	ፄ	ፅ	ፆ	ፇ	ፈ	ፉ	ፊ	ፋ	ፌ	ፍ	ፎ	ፏ
135	ፐ	ፑ	ፒ	ፓ	ፔ	ፕ	ፖ	ፗ	ፘ	ፙ	ፚ			◌፝	◌፞	◌፟
136	፠	፡	።	፣	፤	፥	፦	፧	፨	፩	፪	፫	፬	፭	፮	፯
137	፰	፱	፲	፳	፴	፵	፶	፷	፸	፹	፺	፻	፼			

Note: The Unicode value for each character is obtained by placing the value at the top of the column behind the value at the beginning of the row. For example, the Unicode value for ሀ at the top left corner of the table is 1200.

Table 12.3: The Ethiopic Standard ES 781:2002

	1	2	3	4	5	6	7	8	9	10
1	ሀ	ሁ	ሂ	ሃ		ሄ	ህ	ሆ	ሇ	
2	ለ	ሉ	ሊ	ላ	ሏ	ሌ	ል	ሎ	ⶀ	
3	ሐ	ሑ	ሒ	ሓ	ሗ	ሔ	ሕ	ሖ		
4	መ	ሙ	ሚ	ማ		ሜ	ም	ሞ	ⶁ	
5	ᎀ		ᎁ	ሟ		ᎂ	ᎃ			ፙ
6	ሠ	ሡ	ሢ	ሣ	ሧ	ሤ	ሥ	ሦ		
7	ረ	ሩ	ሪ	ራ	ሯ	ሬ	ር	ሮ	ⶂ	ፘ
8	ሰ	ሱ	ሲ	ሳ	ሷ	ሴ	ስ	ሶ	ⶃ	
9	ሸ	ሹ	ሺ	ሻ	ሿ	ሼ	ሽ	ሾ	ⶄ	
10	ⶠ	ⶡ	ⶢ	ⶣ		ⶤ	ⶥ	ⶦ		
11	ቀ	ቁ	ቂ	ቃ		ቄ	ቅ	ቆ	ቇ	
12	ቈ		ቊ	ቋ		ቌ	ቍ			
13	ቐ	ቑ	ቒ	ቓ		ቔ	ቕ	ቖ		
14	ቘ		ቚ	ቛ		ቜ	ቝ			
15	ⷀ	ⷁ	ⷂ	ⷃ		ⷄ	ⷅ	ⷆ		
16	በ	ቡ	ቢ	ባ		ቤ	ብ	ቦ	ⶅ	
17	ᎄ		ᎅ	ቧ		ᎆ	ᎇ			
18	ቨ	ቩ	ቪ	ቫ	ቯ	ቬ	ቭ	ቮ		
19	ተ	ቱ	ቲ	ታ	ቷ	ቴ	ት	ቶ	ⶆ	
20	ቸ	ቹ	ቺ	ቻ	ቿ	ቼ	ች	ቾ	ⶇ	
21	ⶨ	ⶩ	ⶪ	ⶫ		ⶬ	ⶭ	ⶮ		
22	ኀ	ኁ	ኂ	ኃ		ኄ	ኅ	ኆ	ኇ	
23	ኈ		ኊ	ኋ		ኌ	ኍ			
24	ነ	ኑ	ኒ	ና	ኗ	ኔ	ን	ኖ	ⶈ	
25	ኘ	ኙ	ኚ	ኛ	ኟ	ኜ	ኝ	ኞ	ⶉ	
26	አ	ኡ	ኢ	ኣ		ኤ	እ	ኦ	ⶊ	ኧ
27	ከ	ኩ	ኪ	ካ		ኬ	ክ	ኮ	ኯ	
28	ኰ		ኲ	ኳ		ኴ	ኵ			
29	ⷈ	ⷉ	ⷊ	ⷋ		ⷌ	ⷍ	ⷎ		
30	ኸ	ኹ	ኺ	ኻ		ኼ	ኽ	ኾ		
31	ዀ		ዂ	ዃ		ዄ	ዅ			
32	ⷐ	ⷑ	ⷒ	ⷓ		ⷔ	ⷕ	ⷖ		
33	ወ	ዉ	ዊ	ዋ		ዌ	ው	ዎ	ዏ	

... continued

	1	2	3	4	5	6	7	8	9	10
34	ዐ	ዑ	ዒ	ዓ		ዔ	ዕ	ዖ		
35	ዘ	ዙ	ዚ	ዛ	ዟ	ዜ	ዝ	ዞ	ⶋ	
36	ዠ	ዡ	ዢ	ዣ	ዧ	ዤ	ዥ	ዦ		
37	ⶰ	ⶱ	ⶲ	ⶳ		ⶴ	ⶵ	ⶶ		
38	የ	ዩ	ዪ	ያ		ዬ	ይ	ዮ	ዯ	
39	ደ	ዱ	ዲ	ዳ	ዷ	ዴ	ድ	ዶ	ⶌ	
40	ዸ	ዹ	ዺ	ዻ	ዿ	ዼ	ዽ	ዾ	ⶍ	
41	ጀ	ጁ	ጂ	ጃ	ጇ	ጄ	ጅ	ጆ	ⶎ	
42	ገ	ጉ	ጊ	ጋ		ጌ	ግ	ጎ	ጏ	
43	ጐ		ጒ	ጓ		ጔ	ጕ			
44	ጘ	ጙ	ጚ	ጛ		ጜ	ጝ	ጞ		
45	ⶓ		ⶔ	ጟ		ⶕ	ⶖ			
46	ⷘ	ⷙ	ⷚ	ⷛ		ⷜ	ⷝ	ⷞ		
47	ጠ	ጡ	ጢ	ጣ	ጧ	ጤ	ጥ	ጦ	ⶏ	
48	ጨ	ጩ	ጪ	ጫ	ጯ	ጬ	ጭ	ጮ	ⶐ	
49	ⶸ	ⶹ	ⶺ	ⶻ		ⶼ	ⶽ	ⶾ		
50	ጰ	ጱ	ጲ	ጳ	ጷ	ጴ	ጵ	ጶ	ⶑ	
51	ጸ	ጹ	ጺ	ጻ	ጿ	ጼ	ጽ	ጾ		
52	ፀ	ፁ	ፂ	ፃ		ፄ	ፅ	ፆ	ፇ	
53	ፈ	ፉ	ፊ	ፋ		ፌ	ፍ	ፎ		
54	ᎈ		ᎉ	ፏ		ᎊ	ᎋ			ፚ
55	ፐ	ፑ	ፒ	ፓ		ፔ	ፕ	ፖ	ⶒ	
56	ᎌ		ᎍ	ፗ		ᎎ	ᎏ			
57	፩	፪	፫	፬	፭	፮	፯	፰	፱	፲
58	፳	፴	፵	፶	፷	፸	፹	፺	፻	፼
59	0	1	2	3	4	5	6	7	8	9
60	።	፡	?	፣	፤	፦	፥	!	¡	.
61	‘	’	«	»	“	”	/	(	)	[
62	]	{	}	<	=	>	\	#	%	&
63	*	−	+	±	×	÷	⁝	፨	※	_
64	᎐	᎑	᎒	᎓	᎔	᎕	᎖	᎗	᎘	᎙
65	፟	‹	›							

THE VARIOUS ETHIOPIC KEYBOARD LAYOUTS AND THEIR DRAWBACKS

With some exceptions, all Ethiopic keyboard layouts are adaptations of the QWERTY keyboard layout, but have no standard sanctioned by any authoritative body. The SERA (System for Ethiopic Representation in ASCII) keyboard input system developed in the 1990's by various concerned Ethiopian professionals was an attempt for such a standard but was never widely adopted. Short of a single standard, most Ethiopic keyboard layout developers match the keys for the Ethiopic characters to the Latin letter keys phonetically so that most systems for typing Ethiopic characters transliterate the letters on the keys (**Figures 12.3, 12.4,** and **12.5**). However, because of the larger number of Ethiopic characters and the fact that the Ethiopic characters are alphasyllables and not letters, typing Ethiopic characters using the QWERTY keyboard layout requires a method of making use of different keystrokes to render most characters. Depending on a specific keyboard layout,* it could take as much as five keystrokes to render a single Ethiopic syllable.

Figure 12.3: Illustration of an Ethiopic keyboard layout (unshifted) by Ge'ez Frontier Foundation/Tavultesoft. Image courtesy of Tavultesoft.

Figure 12.4: Illustration of an Ethiopic keyboard layout (shifted) by Ge'ez Frontier Foundation/Tavultesoft. Image courtesy of Tavultesoft.

Note: The keys show the *sadis* or 6th order characters, which often require only one keystroke. Also note that these are illustrations and, with the exception of keyboards by One Laptop Per Child, most physical keyboards in Ethiopia never show Ethiopic characters engraved or printed on them due to lack of regulations to that effect.

Figure 12.5: Ethiopic keyboard by One Laptop Per Child. Image courtesy of One Laptop Per Child. Notice that the keys show the *giiz* or first order characters, as representative of the characters within individual character family. Also note that the keys for the Latin vowels do not show Ethiopic characters because, although the keys are used as part of a set of keystrokes to produce individual Ethiopic characters, Ethiopic does not have letters for its vowelic sounds.

There have been various computer keyboard layouts devised by various Ethiopic font developers since the first time Ethiopic was computerized. The most common features of these keyboards are the method of combining keys to create the Ethiopic alphasyllables. Most Ethiopic keyboards use one or more of the vowel keys in the English keyboard as the last keystroke in a series of keystrokes required for the rendering of most Ethiopic characters (**Table 12.4**). Of the seven orders of the BASE SET of the Ethiopic script, the *sadis* or sixth order characters are the default typefaces in most Ethiopic keyboards that are rendered with a single keystroke, excluding characters which do not phonetically correspond to the Latin letters (**Figures 12.3** and **12.4**). For example, in most keyboards ህ, which is a 6th order character, is rendered with a single keystroke by pressing the 'H' key; while ሕ, which is also a 6th order character, is rendered by pressing the 'Shift' and 'H' keys simultaneously. On the other hand, some characters require at least five keystrokes in many keyboards. For example, ፄ is often rendered by using the following five keys: 'Shift' + 'S' + 'S' + 'I' + 'E'. Tally of one of the most common key combinations for the BASE SET characters (**Table 12.4**) indicates that it takes a total of 580 keystrokes to render all the 245 characters in the BASE SET. The keystrokes are an average of almost two and a half per character, which is higher than the average of about two keystrokes required to type a consonant and a vowel in the proposed orthography. The characters in the EXTENSION SETS, on average, require even more keystrokes, because they already are a combination of phonemes of other characters from the BASE SET. The 48 characters in the EXTENSION SET require a total of 168 keystrokes, with an average of three and a half keystrokes per character, which compares to the average of

* In this chapter, a physical or virtual keyboard with a panel of keys that operate a computer system and the particular method for entering or typing characters in the system are interchangeably referred to as 'computer keyboard layout' or just 'keyboard layout.'

Table 12.4: Common key combinations for the Ethiopic base set in many Ethiopic keyboards

		KEY COMBINATION	GIIZ	KAIIB	SALIS	RABII	HAMIS	SADIS	SABII	TOTAL KEY-STROKES
			+ E	+ U	+ I	+ A	+ I + E	-	+ O	
1	ሀ	H	he	hu	hi	ha	hie	h	ho	14
2	ለ	L	le	lu	li	la	lie	l	lo	14
3	ሐ	Shift + H	He	Hu	Hi	Ha	Hie	H	Ho	21
4	መ	M	me	mu	mi	ma	mie	m	mo	14
5	ሠ	S + S	sse	ssu	ssi	ssa	ssie	ss	sso	21
6	ረ	R	re	ru	ri	ra	rie	r	ro	14
7	ሰ	S	se	su	si	sa	sie	s	so	14
8	ሸ	X	xe	xu	xi	xa	xie	x	xo	14
9	ቀ	Q	qe	qu	qi	qa	qie	q	qo	14
10	ቐ	Shift + Q	Qe	Qu	Qi	Qa	Qie	Q	Qo	21
11	በ	B	be	bu	bi	ba	bie	b	bo	14
12	ቨ	V	ve	vu	vi	va	vie	v	vo	14
13	ተ	T	te	tu	ti	ta	tie	t	to	14
14	ቸ	C	ce	cu	ci	ca	cie	c	co	14
15	ኀ	H + H	hhe	hhu	hhi	hha	hhie	hh	hho	21
16	ነ	N	ne	nu	ni	na	nie	n	no	14
17	ኘ	Shift + N	Ne	Nu	Ni	Na	Nie	N	No	21
18	አ	-	a	u	i	aaaa	ie	e	o	11
19	ከ	K	ke	ku	ki	ka	kie	k	ko	14
20	ኸ	Shift + K	Ke	Ku	Ki	Ka	Kie	K	Ko	21
21	ወ	W	we	wu	wi	wa	wie	w	wo	14
22	ዐ	-	aaa	uu	ii	aa	iie	ee	oo	16
23	ዘ	Z	ze	zu	zi	za	zie	z	zo	14
24	ዠ	Shift + Z	Ze	Zu	Zi	Za	Zie	Z	Zo	14
25	የ	Y	ye	yu	yi	ya	yie	y	yo	21
26	ደ	D	de	du	di	da	die	d	do	14
27	ጀ	J	je	ju	ji	ja	jie	j	jo	14
28	ገ	G	ge	gu	gi	ga	gie	g	go	14
29	ጠ	Shift + T	Te	Tu	Ti	Ta	Tie	T	To	21
30	ጨ	Shift + C	Ce	Cu	Ci	Ca	Cie	C	Co	21
31	ጰ	Shift + P	Pe	Pu	Pi	Pa	Pie	P	Po	21
32	ጸ	Shift + S	Se	Su	Si	Sa	Sie	S	So	21
33	ፀ	Shift + S + S	SSe	SSu	SSi	SSa	SSie	SS	SSo	28
34	ፈ	F	fe	fu	fi	fa	fie	f	fo	14
35	ፐ	P	pe	pu	pi	pa	pie	p	po	14

Note: The key combinations are based on the Keyman Desktop program for Ethiopic (**Figures 12.3 and 12.4**).

about three keystrokes required to type the equivalent consonant and vowels in the proposed orthography. This shows that the proposed orthography will on average require fewer keystrokes to render a syllable compared to the traditional orthography. Since most written communications will continue to require typing even more than ever before, due to the growing dependency on computers and other electronic devices for communication, I believe that any reduction in the number of keystrokes required to type text will improve the speed and accuracy of communication in Ethiopia.

The complicated character entry methods required for using the Ethiopic keyboard are impediments to computer literacy in Ethiopia.

Unique and Innovative Ethiopic Keyboards

It is worth analyzing two of the most innovative ideas for an Ethiopic keyboard—one by Ethiopass and another by Ethiopian Computers & Software Company—for their unique and innovative approach in trying to tackle the age-old incompatibility issues between the Ethiopic writing system and the computer keyboard.

The by Keyboard Ethiopass: Developed by Guenet Ayele/Ethiopass and made public in early 2016, the characters for this innovative keyboard software are engraved on the physical keys of a Fujitsu Notebook Life-Book A555G laptop keyboard—a rarity for Ethiopic. Among the innovations of the keyboard, according to the information on Ethiopass website, are:[7]

- Its software and architecture originated in the analysis of 11 million occurrences of the Ethiopic characters in the Amharic language in order to select the most frequently used ones.
- As a result, the keyboard allows a single key access to most characters in contrast to the combination of keystrokes necessary to use other Ethiopic keyboards.
- The aim is to ensure typing with minimal keystrokes without having to rely on the Latin letters engraved on the QWERTY keyboard layout; and includes the availability of Ethiopic letter keys in and outside of the keyboard area traditionally reserved for home keys.
- The keyboard, which has 62 Ethiopic characters (60 alphasyllabic characters and two punctuation marks) engraved on it, is organized for direct access to the following characters/keys:
  - 8 vowelic keys: አ ኡ ኢ ኣ ኤ እ ኦ (the seven Ethiopic vowels) and ኧ (the illegitimate Amharic vowel equivalent to the Ethiopic vowel አ)
  - 52 syllabic keys: 15 1st order characters (ለ መ ሰ ረ ቀ በ ተ ቸ ነ ከ ወ የ ደ ገ and ጠ), 8 4th order characters (ላ ማ ራ ባ ታ ና ያ and ጋ), 28 6th order characters (ሀ ል ም ስ ር ቅ ብ ት ች ን ክ ው ይ ድ ግ ጥ ሽኝ ኽ ዝ ዥ ጅ ጭ ጽ ፅ ፍ ፕ and ቭ), and 1 7th order characters (ሆ); and
  - 2 punctuation marks (። and ፤)
- All other characters, including those in the rest of the Ethiopic vowelic orders, are accessed by first striking the respective character from one of the eight vowelic keys and then striking the desired character key. The following is an example:
  - 1st order: አ + ለ = ለ, 2nd order: ኡ + ለ = ሉ, 3rd order: ኢ + ለ = ሊ, 4th order: ኣ + ለ = ላ, 5th order: ኤ + ለ = ሌ, 6th order: እ + ለ = ል, and 7th order: ኦ + ለ = ሎ

Similar to the keyboard by Ethiopian Computers & Software Company, this keyboard is unique among Ethiopian keyboards in its use of keys normally reserved for punctuations and other signs in a standard QWERTY keyboard. By providing more keys for the large number of Ethiopic characters, the keyboard helps reduce the number of keystrokes required to type any specific character to a maximum of two. Unfortunately, this method also crowds the keyboard with alphabetic keys, which take away the keys available for mathematical operations and other symbols; and spreads the alphabetic keys too far apart from the home keys.

The Keyboard by Ethiopian Computers & Software Company: Invented by Ethiopian scientist and software developer Aberra Molla, who previously devised other keyboard layouts and methods of keystrokes for Ethiopic typing, the keyboard is his most refined one with a system for typing every Ethiopic character with a maximum of two keystrokes. By far the most efficient Ethiopic keyboard layout based on the average number of keystrokes required to type Ethiopic text, Molla's U.S. patent application for the keyboard published in 2009 stated,

> The present invention is directed to a system and method for typing Ethiopic characters in a computer system using at most two keystrokes. The rendering of characters is based on the timing between a first and second keystroke and on whether the first and second keystroke[s] are, together, one of a predetermined number of ordered key pairs. Conventional symbol typing may be preserved by a prioritized assignment of the symbols to alternative shift keys. A timing disable key may be defined that allows typing of default characters at a comfortable speed.[8]

An example of the keystrokes using the Aberra Molla's keyboard is as follows:

Shift + G = ገ; G + U = ጉ; G+I = ጊ; G+A = ጋ; G+E = ጌ; G+O = ጎ

Other derivatives of ገ, such as ጓ can be typed by pressing the key for G and then pressing one of the specified sign keys. Giiz numerals are typed by pressing the key for comma (,) and then pressing individual number keys (,+1; ,+2; etc.). Punctuations are typed by pressing 'Shift' and one of the number keys.

Like the Ethiopass keyboard, this keyboard is unique among Ethiopian keyboards in its use of keys normally reserved for punctuations and other signs in a standard QWERTY keyboard. By providing more keys for the large number of Ethiopic characters, the keyboard helps reduce the number of keystrokes required to type any specific character to a maximum of two. Unfortunately, this method also crowds the keyboard with alphabetic keys, which take away the keys available for mathematical operations and other symbols; and spreads the alphabetic keys too far apart from the home keys especially for alphabets of languages other than Amharic. Although its system of timing which determines the character rendered following a combination of keystrokes may be unique, the system's dependency on timing means that it requires greater skill to understand and master the effects of variations in timing. It may especially be challenging for people who formulate their thoughts while typing since the length of their thought process may interfere with the system's timing, which undoubtedly necessitates the use of the backspace key as often as the appearance of a wrong character rendered because of delay in a second input aborting the desired character.

Other Problems Associated with the Various Ethiopic Keyboards

Other problems associated with many Ethiopic keyboards currently in use can be summarized as follows:

- Dependency on the Latin (English) keyboard, which limits the available keys for Ethiopic characters to only 26.
- Lack of a single standard keyboard, which makes it difficult to type on web-based applications, for example, without being forced to study the required key combinations to type all the Ethiopic characters on a particular application.
- Complicated key combinations or strokes required to produce the large number of the Ethiopic characters.
- The inability for manufacturers to produce physical keyboards with Ethiopic characters engraved on them because of two main reasons:
  - Many of the keys are used to create different characters as part of a series of keystrokes undermining the need to engrave many of the characters on them, and
  - The lack of a standard Ethiopic keyboard layout acceptable by everyone even with characters that only require a single keystroke.

Nevertheless, the single most important demise for all Ethiopic keyboards currently in use will probably be that they are keyboards for the problem-ridden traditional Ethiopic orthography, which desperately needs to be reformed as soon as possible.

Proposed Parameters for a Standard Ethiopic Keyboard

The proposed language reform for Ethiopia requires a standard keyboard layout that all Ethiopic software developers and the general public can use. The complexity of using any Ethiopic keyboard is made worse by the availability of different Ethiopic keyboard layouts developed by different software developers. As most users of Ethiopic keyboards could attest, the lack of a standard keyboard since the computerization of Ethiopic has been a great challenge for users. This is especially most evident in the fact that many computer literate Ethiopians who can type in English effortlessly do not know how to do so using Ethiopic. The proposed language reform, which will reduce the Ethiopic characters down to just about 29, will necessitate a new keyboard layout and end the decades-old challenges associated with using Ethiopic on computers.

The most important improvement on the Ethiopic keyboard proposed by this reform may be the assignment of individual keys for individual letters made possible by the dramatic reduction of the characters in the proposed reformed alphabets. With contemporary Ethiopic keyboards where the use of the 'Shift' key or repeated depressing of certain keys is necessary to toggle between two or more characters, it is virtually impossible to dedicate a single key to every character in the traditional Ethiopic script even just for the CORE CHARACTERS.

Core characters are the 1st order consonantal characters and the Ethiopic vowels, which make up a total of 41 characters (Chapter 6).

A truly Ethiopic keyboard layout should, at the minimum, satisfy the following requirements:

1. The keyboard must be based on the QWERTY keyboard layout, the most widespread layout; and the keys assigned to the Ethiopic letter must correspond to the nearest phonemic value of the keys for the English letters, as much as possible. For example, H for ሐ, L for ለ, and M for መ.
2. The vowel keys shall correspond to the romanization values for Ethiopic. For example, E for አ, and U for ኡ.
3. The keyboard must be designed in such a way that the primary goal is to use it for typing Ethiopic characters. Each letter of the reformed Ethiopic alphabet must be engraved or printed on the respective key in such a way that it is prominently positioned on the key.
4. Every letter should have its own key in Ethiopic keyboard. In other words, no two letters should share a single key, except for the upper and lower cases of the same letter and except where a key is shared by different letters of different languages (but not different letters of the same language).
5. The keyboard must be able to be used for typing using Latin letters as a secondary use. The values of the keys must be based on the QWERTY keyboard layout. However, this should only apply to the letters and numerals and not the punctuation marks and other signs, which must follow the proposed layout for the Ethiopic keyboard. The Ethiopic letters must be engraved or permanently printed on the keys with a smaller size engraving for the Latin letters.
6. The 'Shift,' 'Control,' 'Alt,' and 'AltGr' keys should be employed to access additional punctuation, to change the keyboard language mode between the various Ethiopian languages (e.g., Tigirinya, Amharic, and Oromiffa) and English, and to toggle between the Giiz and Hindu-Arabic numerals, etc.
7. The most common Ethiopic punctuation marks, including the Giiz punctuation marks and other commonly used modern punctuation marks adopted from Europe, should be accessed directly or using the 'Shift' key, while additional less frequently used punctuation marks and signs should be able to be accessed using the 'AltGr' key.
8. Must be able to switch to the traditional Ethiopic orthography if so desired.

The Proposed Concept Ethiopic Keyboard

The concept Ethiopic keyboard that I propose (**Figure 12.6**) is based on the requirements I listed in the previous section. The details for a standard Ethiopic keyboard can be refined further to satisfy the communication needs of 21st-century Ethiopia and its various language groups without deviating much from the QWERTY keyboard layout, which is important for a flawless transition between local and international keyboards and computer applications.

The concept keyboard shows the twenty-nine letters of the proposed reformed Ethiopic alphabet and the twenty Ethiopic numerals. If a physical keyboard, such as the one illustrated in **Figure 12.6**, is designed to show names of non-printing keys, the names shall be in the regional working language where it is sold (e.g., Tigirinya for Tigiray and Oromiffa for Oromeea (Oromia)) and in Amharic as per the recommended language policy (Chapter 13). Alternatively, nationally or internationally recognized symbols can be used instead of names for non-printing keys.

There shall be two orthographic modes in the Ethiopic keyboard—the Ethiopic orthographic mode and the European orthographic mode. The default setting shall be the Ethiopic orthographic mode, which contains all the proposed Ethiopic alphabetic letters and punctuation marks, including punctuation marks adopted by Ethiopic from European orthographies, the Hindu-Arabic numerals, and all mathematical and other symbols that are normally included in a computer keyboard (**Figures 12.7** and **12.8**). The European mode shall be accessed through the 'Giiz Lock' key by pressing it once in a manner similar to the 'Caps Lock' key. Development of the proposed concept Ethiopic keyboard may lead to the assignment of additional language modes which can be accessed by clicking the 'Giiz Lock' key for a specified number of times. For example, the Tigirinya letter ቐ <qh> and the Amharic letter ቸ <c>, which share the key for the Latin letter C (ASCII 67) in the proposed concept keyboard, can be manipulated with such a key.

Unshifted keys shall provide the proposed Ethiopic lowercase letters, the Hindu-Arabic numerals, some Ethiopic punctuation marks, some mathematical symbols, and the proposed Ethiopian birr symbol (**Figure 12.9**) in the Ethiopic mode; and the Latin lowercase letters, the Hindu-Arabic numerals, all European punctuation marks (including those that are shared by Ethiopic), some mathematical symbols, and the proposed Ethiopian birr symbol in the European mode (see darker characters on white background in **Figure 12.7**).

Shifted keys shall provide the proposed Ethiopic uppercase letters, additional Ethiopic punctuation marks, additional mathematical symbols, and other symbols in the Ethiopic mode; and the Latin uppercase letters, additional mathematical symbols, and other symbols in the European mode (see darker characters on white background in **Figure 12.8**).

The Ethiopic numerals shall be accessed through the 'Giiz Number Lock' key, with the unshifted keys providing the numerals for ones and one hundred (**Figure 12.7**); and the shifted keys providing the numerals for tens and 1,000 (**Figure 12.8**). The 'Giiz Number Lock' shall be used to toggle between these values regardless of the current orthographic mode.

Notwithstanding the functions described above, the 'Alt' key or the 'AltGr' key can be employed with or without the help of the 'Shift' key, based on further development of the concept keyboard, to temporarily bypass the 'Giiz Lock' key or the 'Giiz Num. Lock' key, which will result in the following three levels of key access:

Level 1: Direct use of a printable key (Unshifted)

Level 2: 'Shift' + a printable key (Shifted)

Level 3: 'Alt' + a printable key

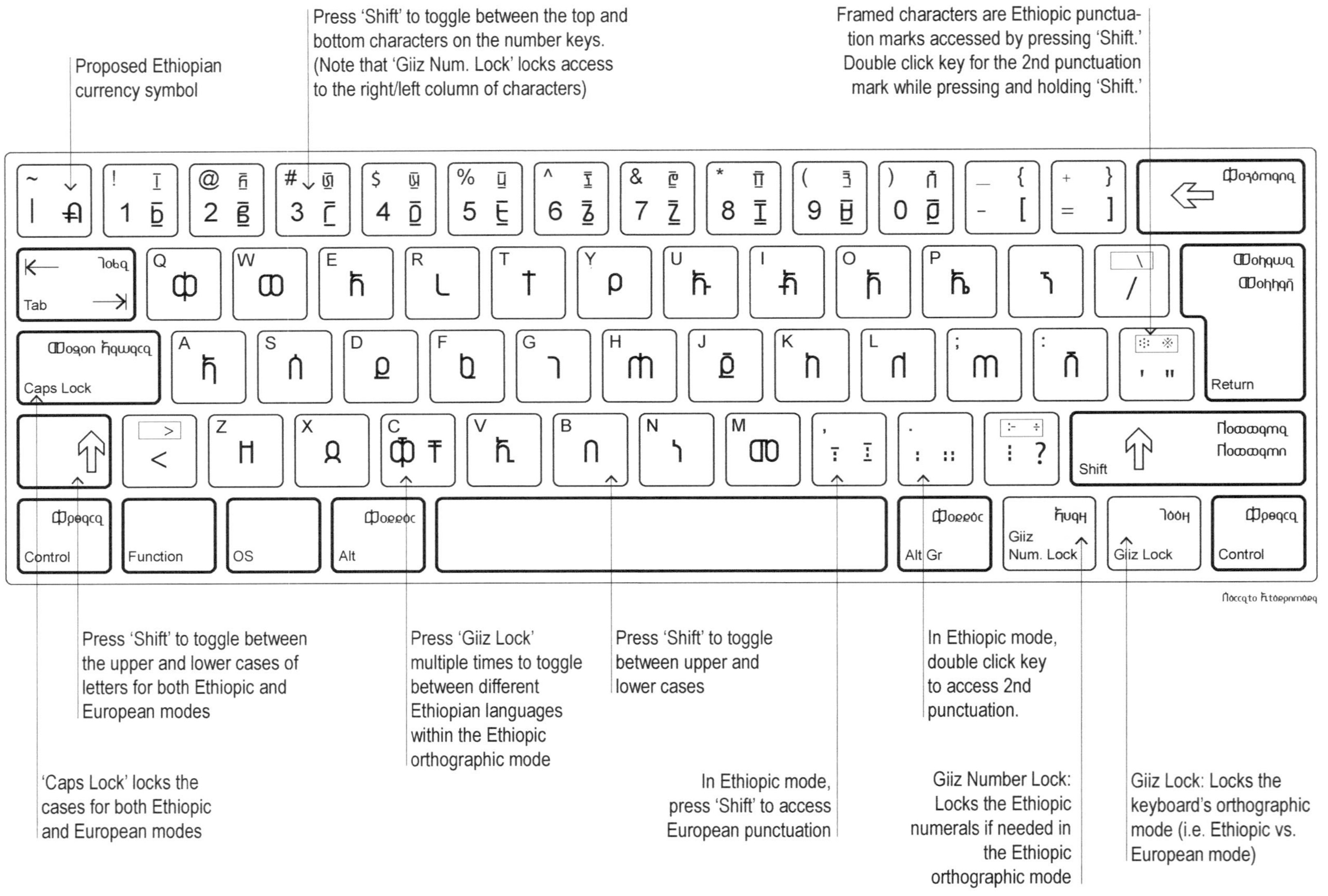

Figure 12.6: The proposed concept Ethiopic keyboard on a modified version of the QWERTY keyboard layout. Note that all the letters of the proposed reformed Ethiopic alphabet are included with every letter shown on an individual key in the respective language. For the most part, the Ethiopic letters phonemically match the Latin letters on the keyboard.

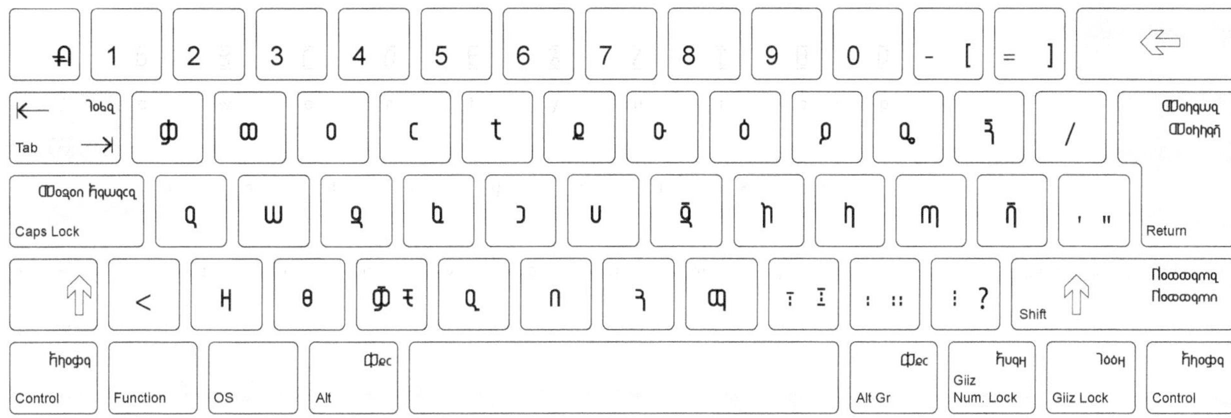

Figure 12.7: Illustration of the characters available in Level 1 (unshifted) mode of the proposed Ethiopic keyboard. In this mode, double clicking the Eth comma key would yield the Eth semicolon. Similarly, double clicking the traditional Eth word separator (:) key would yield the Eth full-stop. To print consecutive commas, press and hold the 'Alt' key and click the Eth comma key as many times as needed. Similarly, to print consecutive word separators, press and hold the 'Alt' key and click the Eth word separator key as many times as needed. To print consecutive semicolons, press and hold the 'Alt' and 'Shift' keys simultaneously and click the Eth comma key as many times as needed. Similarly, to print consecutive full-stops, press and hold the 'Alt' and 'Shift' keys simultaneously and click the Eth word separator key as many times as needed.

Figure 12.8: Illustration of the characters available in Level 2 (shifted) mode of the proposed Ethiopic keyboard. In this mode, to toggle between framed Eth punctuation marks, double click the key. For example, double clicking the Eth preface colon key would yield the Eth colon. Similarly, double clicking the Eth paragraph separator key would yield the Eth section mark. To print consecutive preface colons, press and hold the 'Alt' key and click the Eth preface colon key as many times as needed. Similarly, to print consecutive paragraph separators, press and hold the 'Alt' key and click the Eth paragraph separator key as many times as needed. To print consecutive colons, press and hold the 'Alt' and 'Shift' keys simultaneously and click the Eth preface colon key as many times as needed. Similarly, to print consecutive section marks, press and hold the 'Alt' and 'Shift' keys simultaneously and click the Eth paragraph separator key as many times as needed.

Standard Currency & Other Symbols for Ethiopic

The birr, which is the legal tender in Ethiopia, has never had a currency symbol comparable to other major world currencies other than the ligature *Br.* Setting a truly Ethiopic symbol to represent the Ethiopian currency should not be delayed anymore. I believe it is especially timely to set a currency symbol for the birr now, at a time when Ethiopia urgently needs to reform its languages and set a standard Ethiopic keyboard layout, which will be used extensively for business transactions involving the Ethiopian birr. My proposed Ethiopian currency symbol (**Figure 12.9**), which is presented schematically, is extremely simple, elegant and at the same time remarkably different from the symbols of other world currencies—traits which will make it easily recognizable helping promote Ethiopia and its currency internationally.

The proposed symbol, which can have different looks in different fonts (**Figure 12.10**) has the following characteristics that make it truly Ethiopian.

1. It is based on the Ethiopic script rather than the Latin script (Br).
2. It is reminiscent of the traditional Ethiopic character ብ, which is the first character of the currency's name, ብር <birr>, in the traditional orthography.
3. It is also reminiscent of the letter ∩ <b>, which is the first consonant of the currency's name, ∩ócc <birr>, in the proposed revised orthography.
4. It has a double horizontal line (equal sign) on the left leg characteristic of many notable currency symbols.
5. The equal sign (double horizontal line) symbolizes:
   i. Equal opportunity for citizens in the Ethiopian dream,
   ii. That the birr is equal or aims to be equal among equals in the international currency arena, and
   iii. The sufficiency of paper money to settle depts.
6. The horizontal lines are below the 'centre of gravity' of the main element of the sign, ∩, indicating the stability of the nation and its currency.

Birr 25.00 and twenty-five cents, for example, will respectively look as follows when written in the proposed orthography with the proposed currency symbol:

₳ 25፣00 and ₳ 0፣25

The symbol requires a Unicode standard code value assigned to it, as well as the letters of the proposed reformed alphabet. An example of a currency that recently acquired its own symbol is the Indian rupee. In 2010, India adopted the ₹ sign for its currency with the U+20B9 INDIAN RUPEE SIGN Unicode assignment to join the elite nations which already had their own currency symbols (**Table 12.5**).

In addition to a wide number of mathematical symbols (not including Greek letters) that Ethiopic has already adopted from European orthographies, I propose adoption of the ampersand (&) and the number (#) signs for Ethiopic.

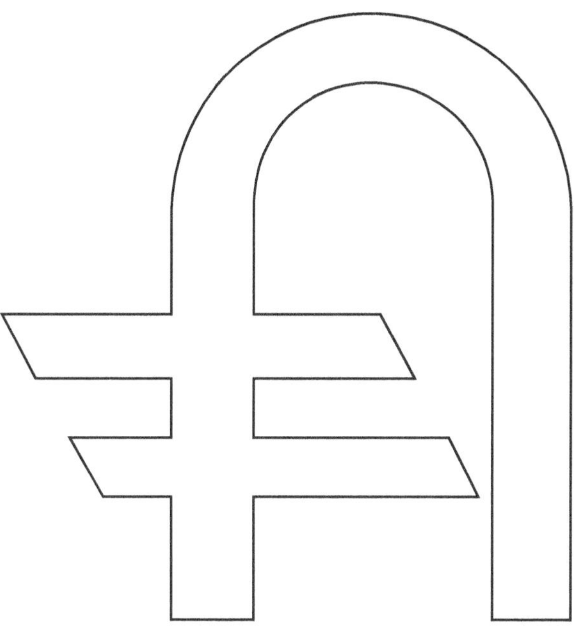

Figure 12.9: A schematic of the proposed currency symbol for the Ethiopian birr.

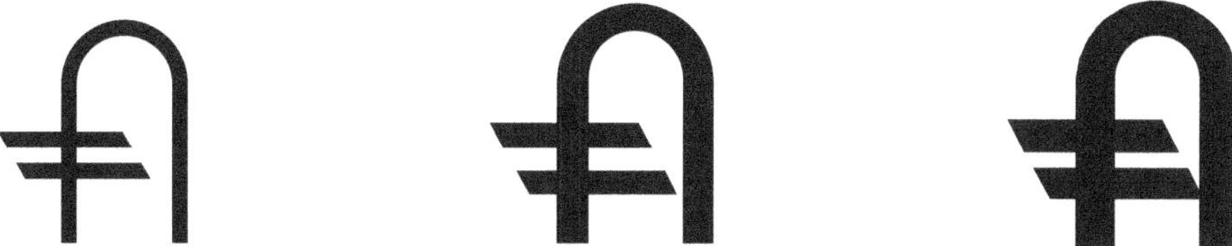

Figure 12.10: The proposed currency symbol for the Ethiopian birr in the Kahssay Misiraq, Kahssay Birikhitee Regular, and Kahssay Birikhitee Bold fonts.

Table 12.5: Standard currency symbols of some major world currencies

CURRENCY	ISO CODE	SYMBOL	REMARKS
Birr	ETB	በ	Proposed symbol for the Ethiopian birr
Dollar	Varies by country	$	Canada, USA, and others
Euro	EUR	€	European Union
Naira	NGN	₦	Nigerian
Pound sterling	GBP	£	United Kingdom
Ruble	RUB	₽	Russian
Rupee	INR	₹	Indian
Won	KRW	₩	South Korean
Yen	JPY	¥	Japanese
Yuan	CNY	¥	Chinese

PART V

THE ROLE OF GOVERNMENT

Chapter 13

More on the Ethiopian Language Crisis and Proposed Solutions

All Ethiopian languages shall enjoy equal state recognition. Amharic shall be the working language of the Federal Democratic Republic of Ethiopia.

—The Ethiopian Constitution

[T]he current education system in Ethiopia is a failed system by many standards. Students go to school and having finished a four-year training, they cannot even [properly] read and write in their own native language... Students complete secondary schools and even [tertiary education] and graduate without gaining sufficient knowledge… In my opinion, the main reason for the failure of the education system in Ethiopia is the government's decision to [keep] the English language as the medium of instruction in the country… the Ethiopian student is obligated to learn in a language he or she does not speak, [which means that] the student has difficulty learning in the English language, and the teacher also has difficulty teaching in the English language.

—Tekeste Negash,
Ethiopian scholar and educationist

IN THIS CHAPTER

Following the liberalization of the sociopolitical space in the early 1990s, Ethiopians wrote a new constitution that reflected the reality of a multilingual nation. The constitution of the Federal Democratic Republic of Ethiopia that came into force in 1995 corrected the historical errors made by previous constitutions and governments with their lopsided language policies, many of which were unwritten. As a solution to this, Article 39 of the Constitution stipulates that "Every nation, nationality and people in Ethiopia has the right to speak, to write and to develop its language; to express and to promote its culture; and to preserve its history." The Constitution provided the legal framework for the establishment of nine federated regions and two special administrative areas that make up the new Ethiopia dreamed by many including those who sacrificed their lives in the struggle against the Derig regime—a military communist dictatorship that ruled Ethiopia from 1974 until it was removed by the coalition forces of the Ethiopian Peoples' Revolutionary Democratic Front in 1991. The regions of the new Ethiopia (**Figure 13.1**) have their own legislative, judiciary, and executive bodies with a working language at the regional level in addition to any other working language they may have for each zone within them (**Table 13.1**).

Figure 13.1: The regions and special administrative areas of Ethiopia

The Constitution also stipulates that "Amharic shall be the working language of the Federal Democratic Republic of Ethiopia." Amharic has been the lingua franca in Ethiopia for the last few centuries. Various Ethiopian leaders in the past 150 years, including the great defender of Ethiopia Emperor Yohannis (Yohannes) IV (1837-1889), who rose from Tigiray, used Amharic to govern. Today, Amharic is spoken as widely as ever before. In fact, anecdotal evidence indicates that more and more people from all corners of the country are learning Amharic as their first language. Amharic is thought in elementary and high schools throughout Ethiopia as a national language in addition to local language instructions in any particular area. In addition to having millions of first language speakers, today Amharic is the most widely spoken second language in Ethiopia according to the 2007 Population and Housing Census. In spite of this Ethiopia does not have a detailed, comprehensive language policy reflecting the complex needs and opportunities that exist for communication in a nation with 80 languages and dialects. The necessity for developing such a policy will be discussed in this chapter.

Ethiopia's language dilemma will have implications for generations to come unless appropriate measures are taken sooner rather than later.

Table 13.1: The official or working languages of the nine regions and two special administrative areas of Ethiopia

NUMBER*	REGION	WORKING LANGUAGE (REGIONAL LEVEL)	WORKING LANGUAGES (ZONAL LEVEL)
R. 1	Tigiray	Tigirinya	Tigirinya
R. 2	Affar	Affarinya	Affarinya
R. 3	Amhara	Amharic (Amarinya)	Amharic, Oromiffa (Oromeea Zone)
R. 4	Oromeea (Oromia)	Oromiffa	Oromiffa, various dialects
R. 5	Somalee	Somaleenya	Somaleenya
R. 6	Beinishanigul & Gumuz	Amharic	Beinishanigul, Gumuz
R. 7 – 11*	Southern*	Amharic	Various
R. 12	Gamibeilla	Amharic	
R. 13	Hareree	Oromiffa, Amharic, Harereenya	
R. 14	Addis Ababa*	Amharic	Amharic
	Direi Dawa (Dire Dawa)*	Amharic, Oromiffa, Somaleenya	
	Eritrea	Tigirinya	Tigirinya

Notes: (1) The region numbers were assigned by the Transitional Government of Ethiopia (1991-95) after the fall of the military government to tentatively identify the newly minted federal regions until these regions gained their official names. Although the general geographic areas where the new regions cover were informally known by the ethnic names of their inhabitants for centuries, despite the arbitrariness of their official boundaries—such as Tigiray, Amhara, Oromo, and Affar—it was necessary to confirm their names through each region's legislature. Today the ethnic distribution and the political boundaries are coterminous. (2) Southern Region is an amalgamation of five regions (Regions 7, 8, 9, 10, and 11), which merged to form a single socio-economic region in 1994. (3) The official name of the Southern Region in English is Southern Nations, Nationalities, and Peoples' Region (SNNPR). (4) Direi Dawa (Dire Dawa) and Addis Ababa are special administrative areas.

THE ROLE OF ENGLISH IN THE ETHIOPIAN LANGUAGE CRISIS

Although additional research may be required, I propose that three fundamental causes have precipitated the current language crisis in Ethiopia (also refer to Chapter 5: Overview of Language Crisis and Miscommunication in Ethiopia). First, South Central Amharic's loss of its stronghold—the Amhara hinterland—combined with illiteracy and lack of a strong literary culture are partly responsible for the deterioration of the language's ability to convey accurate information. Second, Addis Ababa's disproportional role and influence over the rest of the country as the political, cultural, and economic capital city of the country has skewed the development of language in Ethiopia. What Addis does and speaks affects the rest of the country because it is the source of almost all broadcasting services and print media in the country. Addisabans have one of the worst language skills in the nation, which they unfortunately effortlessly export to the rest of the country as residents of the largest urban area in the nation. The third and perhaps the most serious menace that has ravaged Ethiopian languages, particularly Amharic, may be the continued use of English as the medium of instruction past the junior elementary school system of the nation.

Many Addisabans are able to speak languages other than Amharic, Addis' official language, making them conduits for conveying the metropolis' language trends, good or bad, to their ancestral languages and regions.

The Devastating Effect of the Use of English as the Medium of Education

The Ethiopian school system is producing ever increasing number of graduates who are linguistically and professionally stunted.

The dominance of English in Ethiopian schools started sometime after the end of the Italian invasion of Ethiopia in 1941. Before 1941, Emperor Mineelik (Menelik) had established what was the first modern school in Ethiopia in 1908 (Wodajo, 1959) with an emphasis on the study of different languages including Giiz, Amharic, Arabic, Italian, and French. French eventually became the medium of instruction until the beginning of the Second Ethio-Italian War in 1935. By the time the Italians were defeated and schools were reopened, it is said that the war had decimated what was a tiny progress made in modern education in Ethiopia with devastating consequences for generations.[1] Wright (1964) argued, however, that after the restoration of the imperial throne in 1941 "interest in modern printed books [began] to be apparent; the Italian war and occupation had brought many people into contact with new ideas, and shown them the need to adopt new attitudes in a "modernized" world."[2]

In the years following the end of the Second World War, British influence on the government of Emperor Haile Selassie resulted in the installation of a curriculum that mandated the use of English as the medium of instruction from grade seven onwards (i.e. middle, secondary and tertiary educational institutions),[3] making the nation almost entirely dependent on a foreign language for its future. Not only is this a potential area of vulnerability for Ethiopian security, but it is also the main cause of the language crisis currently gripping the nation with devastating socio-economic and political consequences for generations to come.

Ironically, English is choking the development of Ethiopian languages even when very few people finish school with a mastery of the English language. Most students are taught by Ethiopian teachers who studied English as a second language from their teachers who studied English as a second language and so on. Ojo and Umera-Okeke (undated paper) argued that part of the reason for the poor acquisition of English in the Ethiopian school system could be traced back to the flight of foreign teachers, including Britons and Americans, during the 1970's political instability in the country that started with the demise of the Imperial government and the rise to power of the Derig (military junta). The loss of highly educated Ethiopians to the Derig's genocidal campaign *Qey Shibbir* (Red Terror) or self-imposed exile in opposition to the regime resulted in the recruitment of unqualified teachers to higher educational institutions. The result has been generations of graduates who are incapable of articulating almost anything in Amharic, English, or any other language. Many graduates of Ethiopian colleges and universities turn out to be linguistically and professionally stunted after spending much of their school years studying in a language neither they nor their teachers properly understood. According to Baye Yimam (2000 E.C.), employers frequently complain that graduate students at all levels lack the skills to prepare ordinary reports and are unable to formulate their thoughts and express them using correct sentences.

Similarly, Tekeste Negash, who is an educationist and a visiting professor at Addis Ababa University and who was once a student in the Imperial Ethiopia of the 1950's and 60's, argued in an Amharic radio interview (SBS Radio, 2014) that today the Ethiopian education system has failed. According to Negash, even after finishing a four-year training, the majority of students cannot correctly read and

No nation on earth with a sizable population has become developed by using a foreign language as its medium of instruction in its education system.

write in their native language—language that they are taught as one of the subjects in school. Graduates leave secondary schools and even tertiary education without gaining sufficient knowledge due to a poor comprehension of the medium of instruction—the English language. Negash, who was born in the 1940's, further stated that when he was a student, most of his teachers were Americans and Indians. When he finished grade 8 in 1962, the number of grade 8 students in all of Ethiopia was only 8,162, which according to Negash, made it necessary to hire foreign teachers trained in English. However, as the reach of formal education increased in the country such as by the time the Derig came to power in 1974, it became apparent that continuing the English language as the medium of instruction was untenable. Negash further asserted that the great weakness of the education system is that the student is obligated to learn in an environment where he or she struggles to learn in English the same way as the teacher struggles to teach in English.[4] Therefore, it is not difficult to understand the reasons why the majority of students in Ethiopia have very low levels of language skills.

I propose that Ethiopian students are triple burdened.* Firstly, the challenge of having to constantly refer to the dictionary, encyclopedia or other sources to translate foreign words even to work on simple assignments is a great burden that takes crucial time away from the actual goal of learning the subject matter. The burden can eventually wear most students to the point of negatively affecting their performance in school as well as their professional future. In a 2012 Ethiopian Television reportage on a computer interface developed by an Ethiopian computer innovator that used Ethiopic for its input, several computer engineering students at the Addis Ababa University stated that the prospect of using Ethiopian languages directly on a computer application was extremely necessary and beneficial for the nation. Reflecting the sentiment of millions of Ethiopians, the students further stated that most of them had not been able to be connected to the rest of the world because of lack of mastery of English and that many people across the country had been unable to develop their potential due to the language barrier.

Since most resources are provided in English, the students lamented that as soon as they started working on any project, they faced the challenges of dealing with English often involving the necessity of having to spend valuable time looking up the meanings of English words in the dictionary, encyclopedia or other language resources. The fact that a proud people like the Ethiopians should be reduced to learning a foreign language in order to learn their country's history or any other subject is indefensible. A nation that successfully resisted the Scramble for Africa more than a century ago, Ethiopians were never colonized by any nation that could have subjected them to a foreign language or culture. Unfortunately, their own successive governments have been unwittingly imposing a foreign language on them with devastating consequences to generations of students with extremely negative spillover effects on society.

Secondly, learning a foreign language in order to learn another subject is not just a matter of translating words in a dictionary but a great barrier of knowledge to

* As a former student in the Ethiopian school system starting from the primary levels to graduating from Addis Ababa University, I can testify to this with a first hand experience.

students born and raised in a radically different world. Even with a dictionary at hand, the cultural and social context carried in a foreign language, such as some real life examples or idiomatic expressions may not be understood by an Ethiopian student in an Ethiopian context, which could make the learning process excruciatingly painful. Negash (2006) argued that,

> English is not only a language but it is a value system. Attending all classes in English is tantamount to the wholesale adaptation of the culture that the English language represents at the price of one's native language and the values that such language contains.[5]

Lastly, the challenges of having to understand the actual subject (such as calculus or biochemistry) regardless of the medium of instruction is a burden on its own that does not need to be made worse by the addition of other unnecessary burdens. Students from low-income families, which are the majority of Ethiopian students, face even more burden compared to their peers from richer families when it comes to learning foreign languages. Students from wealthier families often go to the choicest schools and get relatively better training in English in addition to being exposed to better learning materials including through video and the Internet, while their poorer peers lack such opportunities.

It is not conceivable that Ethiopia can achieve its full potential without developing and using its own languages at the highest levels, such as in universities and technological and research institutions. Prah (2013) asserted that no country could aim to progress by using a foreign language spoken only by a minority, and Negash (2006) argued that modernization should not mean westernization. Ethiopia cannot be an exception in this regard, and although English should continue to be taught in schools as a subject, it must not be used as the medium of instruction, if the country wants to rescue its education system and bring the language crisis to an end. That the Ethiopic language crisis mainly affects urban areas, where the Ethiopian education system is the strongest, is a testament to the failure of the education system that has for generations relied on English as the medium of instruction as well as a rebuke to the authorities who have continued to ignore the problem.

Negash (2006) argued that the explosive growth of the school system throughout Ethiopia since 1991 coupled with the use of English as the medium of instruction are the fundamental reasons for the current education crisis in the country. In fact, in spite of the unprecedented growth in enrollment, the education system in Ethiopia is actually "on the verge of collapse."[6] In order to eliminate the "curse of English as the medium of instruction," Negash further asserted that in 1980 the Derig's Ministry of Education had entertained the idea of using Amharic as the medium of instruction instead of English, and in 1983 the regime was advised by a committee who reviewed the matter to "study the issue further within the context of a new language policy."[7] Nevertheless, at least officially, the medium of instruction in Ethiopia remains unchanged despite the mounting evidence against using English as the medium of instruction in the nation. It is interesting to note that in some regions, as a sign of desperation, some teachers have stopped teaching in English in grades 7 and 8 according to Negash. Negash (2006) stated that,

> Both teachers and students found themselves in a classic vicious circle. The students could not follow their studies in English because their knowledge of English was poor and the teachers could not help their students since they themselves were not good at it.[8]

Negash attributed the failure rate in grade 10 of 70% to the lack of qualified textbooks in the students' native languages. The situation is not a lot different at higher levels. Ethiopian universities are consistently ranked among the lowest in international metrics even among African universities. The great tragedy of the English language-based Ethiopian school system may be that higher educational institutions produce graduates who, on average, are unable to properly narrate most things verbally, let alone to prepare professional reports and technical literature acceptable by the standards of any language—foreign or domestic (also see Bayei Yimam, 2000 E.C). As Ojo and Umera-Okeke (undated paper) observed, this is the "shock of most expatriate [teachers] in Ethiopia who run into the problem of [not] being understood by these students."[9]

Ethiopian Languages: Use Them or Lose Them

Not being used to their full potential, Ethiopian languages are losing their capacity as efficient communication tools. Just like disuse of muscle necessarily causes muscle wasting, disuse of language can have severe consequences that take root over time as evidenced in Amharic and other Ethiopian languages. Amharic and other domestic languages are being hollowed out quickly because English is eating into their vocabulary and grammar to the extent that the spoken and written communications by the Ethiopian elite today can barely be understood by the vast majority of Ethiopians. Neither are those communications more efficient than they were before the onset of the language crisis a few generations ago. Ethiopian languages are slowly dying since they are not being used in higher levels of communication. In an Amharic radio interview (2014), Negash stated that Amharic had not been made to develop to be used as a language of science and technology and instead of being ushered in properly, informal Amharic was creeping in through the back doors as slang and the slang was being used in schools. Negash criticized the phenomenon and called for the abolition of English language as the medium of instruction because it was hampering the healthy development of native languages. Griefenow-Mewis (2009) lamented the fact that despite having been used as an official language of Ethiopia for a long time, teaching materials for higher grades of education were not developed in Amharic. To make Amharic and other native languages usable in science and technology, Negash recommended that Government make a policy change sooner rather than later since it would take significant time to develop native languages for use in science and technology.

In many ways, the deterioration of Amharic and other Ethiopian languages as vehicles of efficient communication is an unintended result of the use of English as the medium of education in the country. Therefore, Government should put in place a plan to reverse this situation without delay. Government should also ensure that logic, grammar, and rhetoric, among others, are thought in all levels of the education system to create a generation that can communicate to each other more effectively than ever before in the history of Ethiopia. In so doing, not only will Ethiopia be able to give its much deserving students the opportunity to learn better and quicker, but it will also help lay down the foundation for an economically and socially strong society.

Another argument I propose against the use of English as the mandatory medium of education in Ethiopian schools is that it may be unconstitutional. The Ethiopian constitution guarantees the peoples' right to use their languages. Amharic is the working language of the federal government. Regional governments should be given special federal funding so that they can provide special schools (or special classes within regular schools) that use Amharic as the medium of instruction as a choice for students born in other regions or students whose parents are born in other regions and would like to be schooled in Amharic. Such schools or classes will have the local working language of the region as a mandatory subject in their curriculum while Amharic will be used to teach all other subjects.

The federal government may have to work with the regional governments to set up such schools or come up with a nationwide special schools system funded and run by the federal Ministry of Education. Universities and all other higher educational institutions funded by the federal government must use Amharic as their medium of instruction. If regional governments decide to fund their institutions of higher education, they can use their local language as the medium of instruction, especially since this can help them retain the skilled labour they produce. One of the unfortunate consequences of the use of English as the medium of education in Ethiopia has been what is referred to as human capital flight or brain drain. Every year, Africa loses billions of dollars due to brain drain. In effect, Africa subsidizes Western economies by providing them with skilled labour free of charge. Today, many students who were taught by Ethiopian taxpayers' money work in Western nations, particularly in English-speaking countries, at Ethiopia's great expense.

Orthographic Harmonization

The concept of orthographic harmonization, which is part of the solution to the Ethiopian language crisis, shall be defined as the use of alphabets based on a home-grown variety to the exclusion of all foreign varieties so that there is some orthographic harmony among the various writing systems in Ethiopia. Currently, the various alphabets in Ethiopia can be categorized into two major types—Ethiopic-based and Latin-based. Ethiopic-based alphabets include the Giiz, Tigirinya, and Amharic alphabets among others. These are alphabets that are used as the writing systems for Ethiosemitic languages. The Latin-based alphabets, on the other hand, are used by many Ethiocushitic languages, such as Oromiffa and Somaleenya. As the proposed Ethiopic alphabet is home-grown, I propose that all alphabets in Ethiopia be reformed so that each one is Ethiopic-based. The proposed Ethiopic alphabet will not only eliminate the drawbacks of the traditional script—which are often cited as being the reasons Ethiocushitic language groups abandoned the script—but it will surpass the Latin alphabet in its ability to represent the sounds of the various languages in Ethiopia as discussed later in this chapter. The benefits of harmonizing the alphabets of Ethiopia include the social, economic and political issues summarized below:

- Personal names: Avoidance of the errors and confusion for spelling a person's name. A person's name, one of the most important personal identity, is often reflected in the way a particular person chooses to spell his or her name, which is affected by the writing system used. Ethiopian legal documents, such as birth certificates, passports, driver's licenses, professional licenses, social security cards, taxpayer identification cards, property deeds, student transcripts, etc. will require proper legal names and uniform spelling throughout. Unless a person chooses to get his or her name changed following due process of law, the way a person's names are spelled is critical in avoiding identity theft, false convictions, tax evasion, and other legal issues. Such problems are compounded when more than one writing system is involved.
- Brand name and logos: Domestic firms will need only one trade name or logo for ease of brand recognition within the nation irrespective of regional or linguistic differences.
- Transliteration: Transliteration (as opposed to translation) of personal names, trademarks, other words and acronyms will be another hurdle for people-to-people interaction within a single country. Often, transliteration of such words is necessary when there are two different types of alphabets, since such words cannot normally be translated in most cases. Transliteration of words in the international arena from a non-European writing system, such as the Ethiopic writing system, to the Latin alphabet, referred to as romanization, is an unavoidable hurdle in socio-economic and cultural interactions among nations (for more on this, refer to Chapters 9 and 10). However, such complications within a nation arising from the use of two different writing systems must be reconsidered to avoid social and economic costs associated with time and resources spent in transliterating as well as potential errors during transliterating that can have severe consequences depending on the text being transliterated. For example, medical, technological or security terms and acronyms that may be lost during transliteration could be very costly and even lethal.
- Other benefits include seamless integration of systems that use different Ethiopian languages, availability of more vowels and consonants for Cushitic languages (discussed in more detail later in this section), avoidance of the mismatch that can happen due to differences in alphabetical listing of items (such as city names, *woreda* (*wereda*) names, road names, product names, nomenclature of chemicals and drugs, etc.) between two regions or zones that use different writing systems, ability to use the same text to represent the writing system of more than one language on signage (e.g., ħcpαqqq βoʒqnHocóωqtq <Oromeea (Oromia) Yuneeveriseetee> and Ꝕóq̄q̄óɔq ᒥpʈqh <Jijjiga Hoteil>) or for speed limit (e.g., ħαq/ω <km/h>).

In discussing the benefits of Ethiopic-based alphabets for use by all Ethiopians, it must always be assumed that each user has no knowledge of a foreign writing system or language. Therefore, although English is used on some Ethiopian documents alongside Amharic, such as passports, personal names, and other proper names can be transliterated on those documents based on a standard transliteration system such as the standard romanization proposed in Chapter 9.

Proposed Reform of the Oromiffa Alphabet

Oromiffa is the official language of the Oromeea Region of Ethiopia, which is home to 27,158,471 persons including speakers of Amharic and other Ethiopian languages and constitute 36.1% of the national population.[10] Qubei is the name given to Oromiffa's Latin-based alphabet (**Table 13.2**). Following the political liberalization in Ethiopia in the early 1990s, Oromiffa adopted the Latin alphabet as its official writing system, abandoning the traditional Ethiopic writing system it used for generations.

With its diverse cultures, large geographic expanse, immense potential for development, and some of the greatest and kindest people on earth, it can be said that Oromeea is Ethiopia within Ethiopia.

The decision to adopt the Latin alphabet as the writing system for Oromiffa was said to be based on orthographic and phonetic needs of Oromiffa, which are different from those of the Semitic languages. For example, vowel elongation, which is a feature of Cushitic languages, such as Oromiffa, is not a factor in Semitic languages and therefore could not be shown using traditional Ethiopic. Additional disadvantages of the use of the Ethiopic script were said to be its inability to clearly represent gemination and glottal stops as well as the sheer number of characters it has. However, the proposed revised Ethiopic alphabet more than makes up for the shortcomings of the traditional Ethiopic as presented in the next sections.

Table 13.2: The Latin-based Qubei alphabet

A a	B b	C c	CH ch	D d	DH dh	E e	F f
G g	H h	I i	J j	K k	L l	M m	N n
NY ny	O o	P p	PH ph	Q q	R r	S s	SH sh
T t	U u	V v	W w	X x	Y y	Z z	
LONG VOWELS							
AA aa	EE ee	II ii	OO oo	UU uu			

<u>The Drawbacks of the Latin-Based *Qubei* Alphabet:</u>

Although the Latin script was never perfectly suited for Oromiffa, it was undoubtedly a better alternative to the traditional Ethiopic script at the time the Latin letters were adopted. However, with the proposed reformation of the Ethiopic writing system, it is clear to see the shortcomings of the Latin-based *qubei* as summarized below:

- The twenty-six letters of the Latin alphabet do not nearly represent all of the Oromiffa sounds accurately. Oromiffa is an Ethiocushitic language that consists of many non-European sounds, much like its Ethiosemitic neighbours, that cannot be correctly represented using the twenty-six letters. Moreover, Oromiffa has ten vowel sounds, while the Latin letters only have five vowel letters. Although *qubei* uses consonantal and vowel digraphs to represent the additional sounds and long vowels it has (**Table 13.2**), this has made a typical text in Oromiffa heavily crowded with too many digraphs and doubled letters not particularly suitable for efficient communication.

- Vowel letters are the most repeated letters in virtually every text of any significant length and the problem of having to use too many vowel letters in written Oromiffa had not either been considered, or there was no other alternative at the time of adopting the Latin script. Problems associated with too many vowel letters in a text are writing or typing fatigue, eye fatigue, and unnecessary loss of text space. Close to 40 percent of the average Latin-based *qubei* text constitutes doubled consonants and vowels. Although the effect of gemination is unavoidable regardless of the type of alphabet used, Oromiffa can reduce its consonantal and vowel digraphs by adopting an Ethiopic-based *qubei* following the proposed reforms in this book.
- The use of a Latin-based alphabet for Oromiffa negatively affects Oromiffa grammar and spelling due to the common tendency by writers to directly insert foreign words (usually English words) into Oromiffa text without following the appropriate rules of spelling for the language.
- As a result of the many non-European sounds assigned to the Latin-based alphabet, students in Oromeea are obligated to learn effectively three different writing systems—belonging to Oromiffa, Amharic, and English—which is a pedagogical nightmare especially for young people. Students will find it extremely confusing to switch between the different sounds represented by many of the letters of the Oromiffa and English alphabets negatively affecting early learning. By contrast, because of their centuries-old socio-linguistic ties between Ethiocushitic and Ethiosemitic languages, an Ethiopic-based Oromiffa alphabet will effectively reduce the number of alphabets a student in Oromeea has to study down to two, just like his or her counterparts in, for example, Tigiray and Amhara.
- Not adopting the proposed Ethiopic alphabet for Oromiffa will be a disincentive for those who would like to try to learn basic Oromiffa by reading simple printed materials or signage and posters, since very few people outside of Oromiffa would know how to read documents written in the Latin-based Qubei. However, if Oromiffa adopts the proposed alphabet, those who would like to try to learn basic Oromiffa will find it easy to read material written in Oromiffa—such as street names, advertisements, fliers, etc.—thereby creating a conducive environment for people-to-people interaction within the immense nation of Ethiopia. On an Amharic radio interview (2014), noted Ethiopian scholar and educationist Professor Tekeste Negash stated that changing the writing system of Oromiffa to the Latin alphabet was a colossal error since using the Ethiopic script would be very beneficial for speakers of Oromiffa as well as for those who would like to study the language. Negash further argued that the problems associated with the use of the Ethiopic script for Oromiffa could be resolved through research and that the use of the script for Oromiffa would benefit Ethiopia as a whole.

<u>The Proposed Ethiopic-Based *Qubei* Alphabet:</u>

The proposed Ethiopic alphabet is superior to the Latin alphabet due to its accuracy in representing the phonology of Oromiffa, which belongs to the Afro-Asiatic language family like the GTA languages and the rest of the Ethiopian

Table 13.3: The proposed Ethiopic-based Qubei with the Latin-based qubei for comparison

	PROPOSED ETHIOPIC-BASED QUBEI LETTERS					LATIN-BASED QUBEI LETTERS (TO BE REPLACED)	
	NAME		VALUE	UPPER CASE	LOWER CASE	UPPER CASE	LOWER CASE
1	(υρϱ)	hoy	h	ṁ	υ	H	h
2	(ɧoɷq)	lewee	l	ṅ	ɧ	L	l
3	(ɑŋqϱ)	may	m	ɑɒ	ɑŋ	M	m
4	(cόɯ)	riis	r	Ꮭ	c	R	r
5	(ɯqt)	sat	s	ṅ	ɯ	S	s
6	(ŋ̄qϱ)	shay	sh	ñ	ŋ̄	SH	sh
7	(фqɓ)	qaf	q	Ф	ф	Q	q
8	(nq̧t)	beit	b	∩	n	B	b
9	(toɷq)	tewee	t	†	t	T	t
10	(ŧqϱ)	cay	c	Ŧ	ŧ	CH	ch
11	(ʔouqɯ)	nehas	n	ነ	ʔ	N	n
12	(ʔ̄qϱ)	nyay	ny	ኘ	ʔ̄	NY	ny
13	(ɦqɓ)	kaf	k	Ɦ	ɦ	K	k
14	(ꝏoꝏq)	wewee	w	Ꝏ	ꝏ	W	w
15	(ʜoϱ)	zey	z	H	ʜ	Z	z
16	(ϱoɑŋqʔ)	yeman	y	Ρ	ϱ	Y	y
17	(ɋoʔόt)	denit	d	ደ	ɋ	D	d
18	(ɋ̄qϱ)	jay	j	ጀ	ɋ̄	J	j
19	(ɔoɑŋόɧ)	gemil	g	ገ	ɔ	G	g
20	(moϱόt)	txeyit	tx	ጠ	m	X	x
21	(oɓ)	ef	f	Ɓ	ɓ	F	f
22	(ɔόόʜ)	giiz	e	ħ	o	E	e
23	(ɦqόn)	kaiib	u	ኡ	ơ	U	u
24	(ɯqɧόɯ)	salis	ee	ኢ	ɋ	II	ii
25	(cqnόό)	rabii	a	ኣ	q	A	a
26	(υqɑŋόɯό)	hamis	ei	ኤ	q̧	EE	ee
27	(ɯqɋόɯ)	sadis	i	እ	ό	I	i
28	(ɯqnόό)	sabii	o	ኦ	ρ	O	o

languages. In the early 1990's it was successfully argued that the traditional Ethiopic script was not suited to non-Ethiosemitic languages—such as Oromiffa, Somaleenya, and Affarinya—thereby substituting Ethiopic-based alphabets with Latin-based alphabets. It can now be proposed, based on a scientific analysis, that the proposed Ethiopic alphabet will suit Ethiocushitic and many other Ethiopian languages far better than the Latin alphabet ever did. Although this section will only discuss the use of the proposed orthography for Oromiffa, many languages of Ethiopia which use Latin-based alphabets are related, and the arguments can apply to them as well. The proposed Ethiopic-based alphabet for Oromiffa (**Table 13.3**) and juxtaposition of the Latin-based *qubei* letters and the Ethiopic characters (**Table 13.4**) show that Oromiffa will greatly benefit from an Ethiopic-based alphabet.

In every practical sense, the sound represented by the letter 'i' in the Latin-based *qubei* can be replaced by the Ethiopic *sadis* vowel ȯ <i>. The *sadis* vowel is one of the weakest of the seven Ethiopic vowels. Oromiffa also has such a weak vowel; however, it is barely utilized or is synonymous with the sound represented by 'i' in the Latin. The Oromiffa word spelled using the Latin-based *qubei* as *isin* (you), for example, can now be spelled in the proposed Ethiopic-based *qubei* (**Table 13.3**) as ȯɯȯʅ <isin>. In so doing, ȯ keeps its sound value across all Ethiopian languages or will acquire an ever so slightly different value in Ethiocushitic languages, which is far less radical than the changes in sound values between many of the letters of the Latin alphabet and those of the Latin-based *qubei*. Similarly, the short vowel sound represented by the letter 'e' in the Latin-based *qubei* can be replaced by the Ethiopic *giiz* vowel o <e>. An example is the Oromiffa word *eger* (afterwards), which can now be spelled as oɔoc <eger>. The Ethiopic *salis* vowel ɋ <ee> is almost identical to the longer vowel represented by the Latin-based *qubei* as 'ii.' The proposed *qubei* will allow for digraphs (**Table 13.5**) to replace the Latin-based *qubei* digraphs as well as to build new digraphs as needed.

Table 13.4: Juxtaposition of the Latin-based *qubei* and the Ethiopic characters

BASE LETTERS					
a = q	b = ∩	c = ഩ (ɱ∩)	d = ɋ	e = o	f = ƅ
g = ɔ	h = υ	i = ȯ	j = ɋ̄	k = ɧ	l = η
m = ɑq	n = ʅ	o = ρ	p = 𝑇	q = ȹ	r = c
s = ɯ	t = t	u = ơ	v = ∩̆ (∩ʜ)	w = ꝏ	x = m
y = ϱ	z = ʜ				
QUBEI DIGRAPHS					
aa = qq	ch = ŧ	dh = ɋυ	ee = qƅ	ii = ɋ	ny = ʅ̄
oo = ρρ	ph = ጰ	sh = η̄	uu = ơơ		

Table 13.5: Proposed Ethiopic-based qubei digraphs

	OLD QUBEI DIGRAPH/LETTER	OLD GIIZ CHARACTER		INDIVIDUAL ETHIOPIC VALUE		PROPOSED DIGRAPH	
			PROPOSED CONSONANTAL DIGRAPHS				
1	c	ጨ	<cx>	ጠ + በ	<tx + b>	ጠበ	<cx>
2	dh	ዽ	<dh>	ደ + ሀ	<d + h>	ደሀ	<dh>
3	v	ቨ	<v>	በ + ዘ	<b + z>	በዘ	<v>
4	px	ጰ	<px>	በ + ጠ	<b + tx>	በጠ	<px>
5	p	ፐ	<p>	በ + ሀ	<b + h>	በሀ	<p>
			PROPOSED VOWEL DIGRAPHS				
6	aa		-	ዓ + ዓ	<tx + b>	ዓዓ	<aa>
7	oo		-	ዖ + ዖ	<tx + b>	ዖዖ	<oo>
8	uu		-	ዑ + ዑ	<tx + b>	ዑዑ	<uu>

REFORM OF OTHER ETHIOPIC-BASED ALPHABETS

Many Ethiopian languages other than the GTA languages still use a modified form of the Ethiopic script. These languages now need to be reformed as part of the proposed alphabetic harmonization effort by taking the unique requirements of each language into consideration. Unicode Standard, Version 9.0, contains 495 characters for Ethiopic, which includes Ethiopic numeric and punctuation characters as well as characters minted in the last hundred years to meet the needs of languages other than the GTA languages. To reduce such a large number of characters used for many of Ethiopian languages, the following steps should be considered:

- Making use of 'dead' glyphs: For the purpose of Ethiopic orthography, a DEAD GLYPH shall be defined as a glyph or character with no phonemic value in a target language. In another words, if one of the Ethiopian languages does not have the phonetic value represented by a particular Ethiopic character, such as the character **ፀ**, then such a letter is a dead glyph for the language in question. Such a glyph can be reassigned to represent a phoneme unique to that language, such as the phoneme represented by ጸ, which is a glyph not part of traditional Ethiopic and was created within the last few years for the Nilo-Saharan Gumuz language. Oromiffa, for example, has no use for the phoneme represented by the Ethiopic character **ፀ** <x>, which is a dead glyph as far as Oromiffa phonemes are concerned. However, the character can be used to replace the Latin-based *qubei* digraph 'dh', thereby reducing the use of digraphs in Oromiffa and making the most of the Ethiopic alphabet.

- Creating new digraphs: If there will not be enough dead glyphs for any target language to represent its unique phonemes, such phonemes can be represented by new digraphs specific for the language. For example, the digraph በፀ <bx> could be proposed to replace ጸ̌.
- Creating simple diacritic marks: If neither one of the above methods works, simple diacritic marks unique to a target language should be devised and placed over the required letters of the proposed Ethiopic alphabet so as to avoid the creation of unacceptably complicated glyphs, which can hinder the progress of the languages using them. For example, the following glyphs for the languages of Sebat Beit show the debacle of modifying the traditional Ethiopic characters to create new glyphs without making a proper scientific assessment of their merits:

  ጙ ሟ

  The traditional Ethiopic characters already have complicated glyphs in their 2nd to 7th orders, which makes the addition of more elements into the glyphs a terrible exercise. The diacritic mark or marks could be as simple as a dot or a horizontal stroke over the letter, making handwriting of the letter an easier task. And even during typing, a single dead key on a computer keyboard can be used to add diacritic marks to any number of letters.

The benefits of managing the number of Ethiopic letters includes the ability to develop a standard computer keyboard that can fit all the Ethiopic letters without excluding any Ethiopian language.

Legislation for Language Protection and Standardization

Government should strive to put in place laws and regulations to protect and develop Amharic and other domestic languages and to restrict the role of foreign languages, particularly English, in the nation. The first action may be to establish an Ethiopian languages authority or bestow powers to the Academy of Ethiopian Languages and Cultures,[11] for example, with responsibilities to develop language policies and strategies for the protection, development, and promotion of Ethiopian languages. Such an agency would prepare reports on Ethiopian languages and disseminate language materials, such as grammar and orthographic rules, dictionaries, technical terms, and other information as needed for societal use. Owing to the current language crisis in Ethiopia and the large amount of work that needs to be done to reverse the situation, such an agency may have to be granted powers to allow it to quickly implement efficient language standards and rules across many areas of social and business activities ranging from language use on billboards and news media to the preparation of educational materials and product labels. Many nations around the world have language regulatory bodies, such as the Académie française in France and the Arabic Language International Council that to various degrees regulate or influence their nations' language use to ensure accuracy in communication. I believe that accurate communication and a modern, prosperous society are reflections of each other.

LANGUAGE RULES FOR ORGANIZATIONS AND DOMESTICALLY SOLD PRODUCTS

Government should strive to put in place regulations requiring the use of domestic languages for product labeling and detailed product information such as on pharmaceuticals, imported goods, and goods manufactured or produced within Ethiopia. Product labeling may include brand name, product type or name, date of manufacture, expiration date, product contents, ingredients, country of origin, product handling instruction, hazardous materials information, and material safety data sheet (MSDS), among others.

The fact that product labels and product literature should be written in the language of the average person does not need further explanation. However, due to the low level of socio-economic and technological progress as well as the lack of sufficient technical terms and language materials in Ethiopia, Government must devise a strategy to get industry to produce product labels and literature in local languages. It will be even more important to carefully plan a strategy for text on imported goods since foreign manufacturers and suppliers may not have either the financial incentive or available sophisticated Ethiopian language materials that can be used to translate, transcribe, or transliterate technical or scientific terminologies.

The strategy must be designed so that the statutory requirements for the use of local languages are phased in, and everyone gradually adopts the process. For example, in the beginning, only Amharic may be used for labeling with the most basic information, such as product name, expiration date, and country of origin, and the rest of the information may still be provided in English. Over time the requirement may be made more stringent by including all product labeling and information to be written not only in Amharic but also in the regional language where a product is intended to be sold. For example, products destined for Tigiray will use Tigirinya and Amharic in their labeling, while those destined for Oromeea will use Oromiffa and Amharic in their labeling. Amharic, as the working language of the federal government, should be included in all labeling in addition to a regional language where a product is sold. The inclusion of English in any labeling may be left to the discretion of the manufacturer, supplier, or marketing agency as long as the text does not crowd the space required for text in the domestic languages.

On the other hand, text in a label must be sequenced in such a way that the regional language is listed first and then followed by Amharic, the working language of the federal government. Optionally, text in English or any other foreign languages would be written last (**Figure 13.2**). Moreover, the text size and any emphases applied on the two texts must match so that the local language and federal language are made equivalent. If text in a third language, such as English, is used, it must be made to be equivalent in size and emphasis to the texts in the domestic languages or made to be lesser in size and emphasis, but must never be made to appear to dominate or overwhelm the Ethiopic text or to appear to have been given precedence over the domestic languages.

Figure 13.2: An example of a sign with text in Tigirinya, Amharic, and English

Note that the Ethiopic text ⅏oqqнq is shared by both domestic languages.

Government should strive to use domestic languages in all its communication with Ethiopian entities, such as when advertising bids on domestic newspapers. Highly technical documents can provide the opportunity to develop technical words and terminology using domestic languages. However, successive governments in Ethiopia have failed to lead in this area by simply resorting to the use of English because of the ease of accessing document templates and information in English. For example, advertisements posted by several public agencies, including the Ethiopian Trading Enterprise and the National Bank of Ethiopia, on the Amharic version of the Ethiopian Reporter on *Ihhud, Tahxisxasx 5, 2007* showed invitations to tenders in English. Most, if not all, of the advertisements appeared to be addressed to Ethiopian firms, but there was no other version of the advertisements available in Amharic or any other Ethiopian languages elsewhere in the newspaper. Government should also consider legislation that requires every domestic newspaper to post advertisements only in the language of the newspaper (excluding advertisements in any domestic languages) to reverse the worsening trend by foreign agencies and commercial entities which currently routinely advertise on domestic language newspapers in English only.

Government may have to revise the regulations for establishing a business in the country to ensure that business names do not offend Ethiopian language values. Consider, for example, the name **ፔስቲሳይድ አክሽን ኔክሰስ አሶሴሽን** <Peisitee-sayid Akishin Neikisis Asoseishin> (*Pesticide Action Nexus Association*), which is the name of an Ethiopian organization with the noble mission of informing the populace (most of whom do not understand English) about the dangers of uncontrolled pesticide use. However, there seems to be no reason why the organization chose English to base its name. Although, when last checked in 2015, its activities indicated that it had contacts with organizations outside of the country, it was an Ethiopian organization whose main area of work was in Ethiopia. Therefore, it is surprising that there is not even a single word from any of the Ethiopian languages in its four-word name. A possible name for the company in Amharic is **Ꭱoco-Tonqe Lóɑɒóǭǭq Tóɯóɯɯóc ⅏quónoc** <Xere-Tebay Rimijja Tisissir Mahiber>—literally: Pesticide Action Nexus Association. Similarly, although the primary stakeholders of the Ethiopian Commodities Exchange are Ethiopian small-holder farmers, almost all information on the ECX's official website is only presented in English. Few small-holder farmers speak English or any other foreign language. Therefore, presenting the information on the website in Ethiopian languages must be given priority.

Instead of using English words for their name, organizations should strive to respect Ethiopian languages in their domestic activities and use the English language, including for their names, for their activities outside the country if they so choose. Many people seem to think that the use of English provides some appearance of sophistication and therefore lead to popular acceptance. This attitude seems to be taking root in today's society and is a threat to Ethiopian languages, which, as a result, are facing slow but certain death unless government protects them through aggressive language policy and legislation.

Government Initiated and Funded Translation Efforts

For domestic and international companies engaged in business activities in Ethiopia, in addition to the cost of translation of documents to local languages lack of appropriate technical terms and skilled personnel may be daunting. In its issue on December 7, 2015, the English weekly Addis Fortune stated that,

> Language translation being a very sensitive matter, it would have helped if there were translation and interpretation departments at higher education institutions [in Ethiopia]. This concern is shared by Mekonen Lemma, who teaches translation at the Foreign Languages Department of the Addis Abeba University, translating material as well. The field should be well institutionalised and taught to students ... [12]

To tackle the lack of skilled labour and materials in the area of translation services, Government should take the lead in not only preparing its documents in local languages but also in sponsoring language research and development projects. Similar to the efforts by the European Union to facilitate communication by funding the development of machine translation (MT) technologies,[13] the Ethiopian government should support the development of MT technologies to all pairs of Ethiopian languages, as well as to English, the global lingua franca, by starting with the most popular domestic languages. For example, with the top five most popular languages in Ethiopia, MT technologies can be applied to bilingual dictionaries in the following ten pairings:

Tigirinya – Amharic / Amharic – Tigirinya

Tigirinya – Oromiffa / Oromiffa – Tigirinya

Tigirinya – Somaleenya / Somaleenya – Tigirinya

Tigirinya – Seedamanya / Seedamanya – Tigirinya

Amharic – Oromiffa / Oromiffa – Amharic

Amharic – Somaleenya / Somaleenya – Amharic

Amharic – Seedamanya / Seedamanya – Amharic

Oromiffa – Somaleenya / Somaleenya – Oromiffa

Oromiffa – Seedamanya / Seedamanya – Oromiffa

Somaleenya - Seedamanya / Seedamanya – Somaleenya

In the long run, the pairings can be expanded, for example, to the ten most popular languages, which will yield forty-five pairings, and eventually expanded to include all Ethiopian languages.

Government should take the initiative to translate the Constitution and the Ethiopian national anthem into all major Ethiopian languages. School children in their respective regions will benefit singing versions of the Ethiopian national anthem in their mother tongues. The translation of the national anthem, unlike the constitution, may or may not be verbatim, as long as the core message and the general wording and style is closely preserved—a decision that may have to be taken by the legislature.

Government should also pursue the possibility of using the Ethiopic alphabet in the name tags of African Union diplomats if not including Amharic as one of the official languages of the Union. As a founding member and the seat of the Union, as well as having had the proud history of helping Africans win the struggle against colonialism and apartheid, Ethiopia deserves to be honoured by having its national language included among the official languages of the African Union and therefore should work to that end.

Chapter 14

The Politics of Reform: Previous Efforts for and Opposition to Language Reform

It is not what she was that can profit Ethiopia, but what she may become.

—*Ras* Teferee Makonnin,
Who later became Emperor Haile Selassie

It was not for a show that Emperor Minileek tried to reform the *feedel.*

—Kidanewelid Tekilei,
Ethiopian author

Standardization is an act of simplification and aims at the prevention of unnecessary complexity.

—Ethiopian Standards Agency

In this chapter

I believe that the proposed language reform, especially as it applies to the Ethiopic writing system, is long overdue. In an era of great technological advancement in human history, Ethiopia cannot afford to waste its God-given resources—the languages of its industrious people. Like all prized assets in society, languages need to be documented, protected, nurtured, and even modified—yes, modified—to ensure the development and continuity of a highly educated and sophisticated society. To that end it is vital to discuss in this chapter some of the most important studies and recommendations made in history to reform Ethiopic, the challenges faced and criticisms received in the process, and finally my recommendation on how to implement the proposed reform.

The Century-Old Quest for a Better Writing System

The dawn of the 20th century was a potential new era in Ethiopian history due to the arrival of modern technology from Europe, including the arrival of the typewriter. Starting from before 1900, Emperor Minileek (Menelik) tried to modernize his poor, backward nation by utilizing these technological innovations. Unfortunately, the general lack of skilled labour and societal opposition to change denied the country the ability to harness European technological innovations for its benefit. In fact, I would argue that the 20th century was a lost century for the Ethiopic writing system (and for Ethiopia, in general) despite being one of the first scripts in the world to be used in the printing press, the typewriter, and computerized somewhat early. Although there was no lack of scholars with ideas on how to improve Ethiopic throughout most of the century, sadly nothing of relevance has been done to date. Perhaps the most puzzling thing may be that the quest for a better Ethiopic writing system has been in decline in the latter decades of the last hundred years to the extent that there is very little interest on the issue among the current generation of Ethiopian scholars. As a person from this generation, my reform proposal may be considered as an extension (and hopefully a solution) to the century-old quest for a better writing system that began earnestly at the dawn of the 20th century by none other than Emperor Mineelik himself.

In the early decades of 20th century Ethiopia, there was widespread resistance to modern education and technology. For example, Emperor Minileek's first motor vehicle in the country was suspected to be the devil's work of magic since, shocking as it was to the general public, there were no horses drawing it.

The Typewriter's Role in Triggering the Quest for a Better Ethiopic Script

Emperor Mineelik was very enthusiastic about the possibility for the first ever Ethiopic typewriter. The Emperor's enthusiasm, which was remarkable for his time, was reflective of his progressive mind. According to renowned Ethiopian historian Richard Pankhurst (Pankhurst, n.d.), typewriters entered into Ethiopia at the dawn of the last century but were originally used only by expatriates residing in the country. Pankhurst further stated that Emperor Mineelik was presented with an English-language typewriter by Robert P. Skinner, an American envoy, in 1903 after which the Emperor "immediately asked "Why can't we have an Amharic typewriter?""[1]

The development of an Ethiopic typewriter would take another two decades and start an age-old debate on the reform of the Ethiopic script. In contrast to the 26 Latin letters, each of which was given a separate key on Latin-letter typewriters, it was not practical to do the same for the Ethiopic characters because of their large number. The Ethiopic characters numbered as high as 276 excluding the twenty Ethiopic numerals. A watershed moment in the long history of Ethiopic, the encounter with the typewriter led many to wonder if Ethiopic was fit for technology. Kinife Meekaeil (2001 E.C.) argued that a strong challenge to the Ethiopic script came at the introduction of the typewriter to the nation. In fact, it was the advent of the typewriter that triggered the century-old debate on the size and complexity of the traditional Ethiopic writing system.

Mineelik's desire for an Ethiopic typewriter may have led him to entertain ideas for a new script, making him one of the first Ethiopians to attempt to tackle the problem in modern times. Demoz (1983) stated that a certain Meshesha Weriqei created a new script (**Figure 14.1**) that Mineelik announced and that the reasons

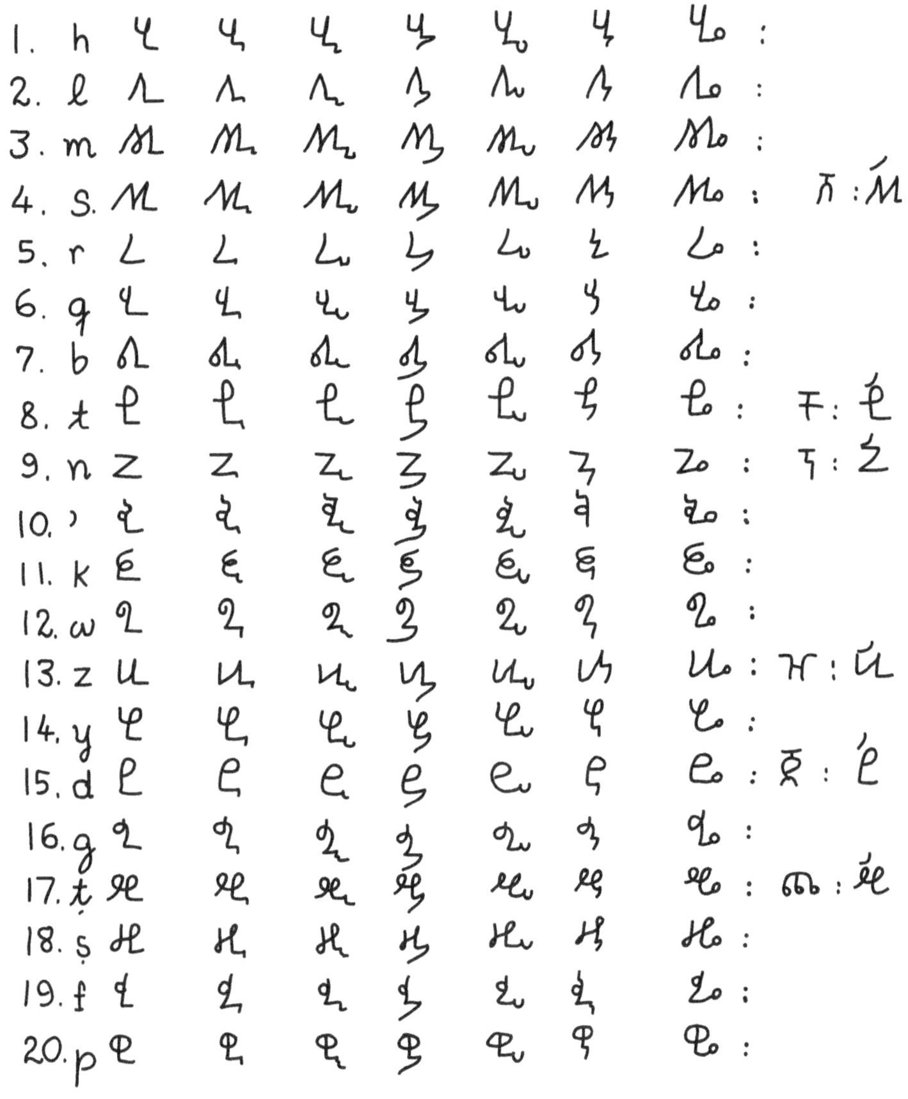

Figure 14.1: "The Menelik Syllabary." Original image by Musei Dekopei[1] as reproduced by Abraham Demoz in "Amharic Script Reform Efforts, Ethiopian Studies: Dedicated to Wolf Leslau on the Occasion of his 75th Birthday." November 14th, 1981, Otto Harrassowitz, 1983. Image traced over original.

for the creation of the new script were not provided (as cited in Kinife, 2009). Another reason for the desired orthographic reform was the inability to use the traditional Ethiopic script for telegraphic communication, which required a type of Morse code. However, it is not clear how Minileek's new script could be considered to be a significant improvement over the traditional script. Nevertheless, the said new script was never implemented and there are no known surviving documents with text in the script. Although it may be impossible to verify the reasons for Mineelik's new script, it is clear that the same diacritical marks were used in each vowelic order, which might be an effort to simplify the script.

The effort to reform the Ethiopic script that had begun shortly after the introduction of the typewriter to Ethiopia continued after the death of Mineelik. The following is a summary of the efforts to produce Ethiopic typewriters with or without associated alphabetic reform ideas in the decades before the Second Ethio-Italian War of 1935-36 as stated by Leslau (1953) and Kinife (2001 E.C. (c. 1994)):

- In 1916 E.C. (c. 1924), *Ato* Alemu Habite Meekaeil manufactured an Ethiopic typewriter, which was used by *Ras* Teferee Mekonnen (Teferi Mekonnen), before he was crowned emperor;
- In 1923 E.C. (c. 1931), *Mehanidees* Ayyana Birru manufactured an Ethiopic typewriter;
- In 1923 E.C. (c. 1931), a typewriter that was commissioned by Dr. Aleme Woriq and manufactured in England was presented;
- *Aleqa* Keedane Welid Kifilei published his reform of the Ethiopic characters that were proposed to be suitable both for Amharic and Giiz typewriters.

In the 20th century, numerous other scholars tried to come up with innovative ideas for a better writing system. The list included *Ato* Alemu Hayile Mariyam, *Ato* Ariaya Birru, *Bilata* Merisiei Hazen Welide Qeeriqos, *Liuul* Ras Immiru, *Ato* Meeleeon Neqiniq, *Ato* Haddees Alemayyehu, *Ato* Abebe Retta, *Ato* Zewidei Gebire Mariyam, *Ato* Seyifu Felleqe, *Ato* Samueil Terrefe, *Bilata* Welide Geeorigees, Dr. Abreham Demoz, *Ato* Tekile Mariyam Fanitayei, Dr. Amisalu Akileelu, *Ato* Liuul Segged Alemayyehu, *Metoaleqa* Yiggezu Bisirat, *Ato* Fanitu Beqqele and *Ato* Amanueil Abireham (Aberra Molla, n.d.). Molla (Molla, n.d.) stated that *Aleqa* Kidane Wolde Kiflie (c. 1862 – July 6, 1944), an Ethiopian theologian and linguist, was the first to present a proposal on how to adapt the typewriter for Ethiopic. The *aleqa* proposed the obsoletion of most of the Ethiopic alphasyllabic characters after keeping only a few of them to form an alphabet with consonants and vowels. The letterforms and phonemes of the consonants were adopted directly from the 1st order, while the vowels were from the vowelic (i.e. 2nd to 7th) orders of the character families ሀ, ወ, አ and የ. Molla further stated that the proposed consonants and vowels were thus to replace the traditional alphasyllabic characters phonetically. For example, the phonemes represented by the traditional character ሁ <hu> would now be represented by the letter combination ሀዩ with the two characters ሀ and ዩ read as "ሁ".[2]

Although imperfect, the *aleqa*'s proposal, which was never implemented, would have dramatically improved the Ethiopic writing system. Meanwhile, Ayyana Birru, who was educated in Ethiopia and Alexandria, Egypt, and who is credited for successfully adapting the typewriter for Ethiopic in 1923 E.C. (c. 1931), did

ሀ	ሁ	ሂ	ሃ	ሄ	ህ	ሆ	ከ	ኩ	ኪ	ካ	ኬ	ክ	ኮ
ለ	ሉ	ሊ	ላ	ሌ	ል	ሎ	ኸ	ኹ	ኺ	ኻ	ኼ	ኽ	ኾ
ሐ	ሑ	ሒ	ሓ	ሔ	ሕ	ሖ	ወ	ዉ	ዊ	ዋ	ዌ	ው	ዎ
መ	ሙ	ሚ	ማ	ሜ	ም	ሞ	ዐ	ዑ	ዒ	ዓ	ዔ	ዕ	ዖ
ሠ	ሡ	ሢ	ሣ	ሤ	ሥ	ሦ	ዘ	ዙ	ዚ	ዛ	ዜ	ዝ	ዞ
ረ	ሩ	ሪ	ራ	ሬ	ር	ሮ	ዠ	ዡ	ዢ	ዣ	ዤ	ዥ	ዦ
ሰ	ሱ	ሲ	ሳ	ሴ	ስ	ሶ	የ	ዩ	ዪ	ያ	ዬ	ይ	ዮ
ሸ	ሹ	ሺ	ሻ	ሼ	ሽ	ሾ	ደ	ዱ	ዲ	ዳ	ዴ	ድ	ዶ
ቀ	ቁ	ቂ	ቃ	ቄ	ቅ	ቆ	ጀ	ጁ	ጂ	ጃ	ጄ	ጅ	ጆ
ቐ	ቑ	ቒ	ቓ	ቔ	ቕ	ቖ	ገ	ጉ	ጊ	ጋ	ጌ	ግ	ጎ
በ	ቡ	ቢ	ባ	ቤ	ብ	ቦ	ጠ	ጡ	ጢ	ጣ	ጤ	ጥ	ጦ
ተ	ቱ	ቲ	ታ	ቴ	ት	ቶ	ጨ	ጩ	ጪ	ጫ	ጬ	ጭ	ጮ
ቸ	ቹ	ቺ	ቻ	ቼ	ች	ቾ	ጰ	ጱ	ጲ	ጳ	ጴ	ጵ	ጶ
ኀ	ኁ	ኂ	ኃ	ኄ	ኅ	ኆ	ጸ	ጹ	ጺ	ጻ	ጼ	ጽ	ጾ
ነ	ኑ	ኒ	ና	ኔ	ን	ኖ	ፀ	ፁ	ፂ	ፃ	ፄ	ፅ	ፆ
ኘ	ኙ	ኚ	ኛ	ኜ	ኝ	ኞ	ፈ	ፉ	ፊ	ፋ	ፌ	ፍ	ፎ
አ	ኡ	ኢ	ኣ	ኤ	እ	ኦ	ፐ	ፑ	ፒ	ፓ	ፔ	ፕ	ፖ

Figure 14.2: The *feedel* from an Ethiopic typewriter.

so by modifying the print heads of the typewriter to create a ligated version of the Ethiopic script. His invention of ligating or overstriking portions of a glyph to create the desired Ethiopic character was improved further, and Ethiopic typewriters were produced by the likes of Olivetti S.p.A., an Italian company which had an office in Addis Ababa during the imperial government (**Figure 14.2** shows the Ethiopic *feedel* typed using an Ethiopic typewriter). However, the desire for a better writing system had not stopped with the successful, albeit clumsy, adaptation of the typewriter especially since the Ethiopic typewriter remained a poor compromise between handwriting and the printing press. Wright (1964) observed that,

> No compensation is to be found in the Amharic typewriters so far manufactured; apart from the obvious advantage of providing duplicated copies, they have nothing to recommend them, being difficult to operate, and producing typescript that is extremely troublesome and confusing to read, as well ugly and characterless.[3]

Few in numbers and virtually inexistent in private possession, Ethiopic typewriters were used mostly by government agencies for official documents. Considered powerful weapons for the production of anti-government propaganda materials, the personal possession and smuggling of typewriters was a serious crime during the Derig regime, which was in power from 1974 until the end of the Ethiopian Civil War in 1991. Computers eventually replaced typewriters near the end of the 20th century.

Lost Century: A Summary of Previous Attempts to Reform Ethiopic

The first three-quarters of the 20th century saw the most proposals for and debates on the reform of the Ethiopic script.

As a sign of the importance given to the issue, Kinife (2001 E.C. (c. 1994)) stated that the now-defunct government-owned newspapers *Aimiro* and *Birihanina Selam* used to report on the various efforts to reform the script by a previous generation of scholars. The goal of most of these efforts had been the streamlining of the Ethiopic script by way of reducing the number of characters, or by the use of standard diacritic marks to be uniformly applied to each character in a given vowelic order, or both. Although not all scholars agreed on the extent of the reduction of characters or the way uniformity is achieved in a single vowelic order, most agreed on the elimination of most of the characters in the Ethiopic extension set. On the other hand, many argued for a full-fledged alphabet with consonants and vowels to be extracted from the script itself (similar to the proposal presented in this book). Except for some differences in the selection of the vowels and how they were to be applied to the seven vowel sounds, all of the proposed alphabets would have dramatically reduced the number of the Ethiopic characters. Kinife further stated that there was a committee set up to study and propose a reform of the Ethiopic writing system, which was active until it was disbanded following the Italian invasion (Second Ethio-Italian War) in 1935. It was Zewidei G. Medihin who initiated the reform movement again after the 1941 defeat of the Italians in a document titled *Beadees Siriaat Yetezegaje Feedel* (Proposed Reformed Script) by proposing a reform not too different from those presented before the war.

In 1940 E.C. (c. 1948) a collection of Ethiopic reform proposals was published in Addis Ababa in an Amharic booklet titled ፊደልን ፡ ማሻሻል (Reforming the Feedel). Following the publication of the booklet, a version of which may have been titled ለወጣቶች ፡ እድል ፡ ከትምሕርት ፡ ወዳጆች (For the Future of the Youth from Friends of Education), the reform movement picked up even more steam (Kinife, 2001 E.C.). Leslau (1953) stated that the booklet listed the proposals by Ras Immiru, *Ato* Abbebe Retta, *Bilatta* Merisiei Hazen Welide Qeeriqos, and Dr. F. C. Laubach; and discussed the reform of the script which had about 250 characters that complicated printing, made the manufacture of typewriters difficult, and posed challenges for the teaching-learning process. The proposals were introduced to the general public only after the arrival of Dr. F. C. Laubach in Ethiopia in 1947, who worked with the Ministry of Education at a time when the Ministry was studying the various reform ideas to facilitate education. Signed የትምህርት ፡ ወዳጆች (Friends of Education), the booklet was a culmination of the efforts of reformers and their supporters who wanted to create public awareness of the reform ideas. The following is a summary of the reforms introduced in the booklet, none of which has ever been implemented (Leslau, 1953):

The proposal by *Ras* Immiru (1892 – 1980):

- Replaced the traditional Ethiopic alphasyllabary with a set of consonants and vowels that would have almost made a truly alphabetic script.
- Proposed 31 consonants (ሀ, ለ, መ, ረ, ሰ, ሸ, ቀ, በ, ተ, ቸ, ነ, ኘ, አ, ከ, ወ, ዘ, ዠ, የ, ደ, ጀ, ገ, ጠ, ጨ, ጰ, ጸ, ፈ, ፐ, ቈ, ኈ, ኰ, and ጐ) using the 1st order letterforms and eliminated the alphasyllabic characters in the rest of the Ethiopic vowelic orders.

- Eliminated the characters ሠ, ሐ, ኀ, ዐ, and ፀ, which are redundant in Amharic phonology (apparently without consideration for the phonology of other Ethiopian languages, including Giiz).
- Used the አ family of characters for the proposed six vowels (ኡ, ኢ, ኣ, ኤ, እ, and ኦ), which compares to the seven basic vowel sounds required by Ethiopic grammar. The 1st order not allocated a vowel, the proposal makes no use of the *giiz* vowel አ. For example, the Ethiopic triliteral words ተመን <temen> (valuation), and እግሬ/እግር <igiree/igir> (leg) would be spelled as ተመንእ and እገእረኢ/እገእረእ, respectively.
- Considered the labiovelars ቈ, ኈ, ኰ, and ጐ like other consonants.
- Did not discuss diphthongs, such as ሟ.

<u>Option 1 of the proposal by Abbebe Retta:</u>

- Replaced the Traditional Ethiopic alphasyllabary with a set of consonants and vowels that would have almost made a truly alphabetic script.
- Proposed 21 consonants (ሀ, ለ, መ, ረ, ሰ, ቀ, በ, ተ, ነ, አ, ከ, ወ, ዘ, የ, ደ, ገ, ጠ, ጰ, ጸ, ፈ, and ፐ) using the 1st order letterforms and eliminated the alphasyllabic characters in the rest of the Ethiopic vowelic orders.
- Removed the prepalatals and affricates ሸ, ቸ, ኘ, ዠ, ጀ, and ጨ and, instead, proposed that a horizontal line be shown as a diacritical mark over each of their graphically similar counterparts ሰ, ተ, ነ, ዘ, ደ, and ጠ as follows: ሰ̄, ተ̄, ነ̄, ዘ̄, ደ̄, and ጠ̄.
- Eliminated the characters ሠ, ሐ, ኀ, ዐ, and ፀ, which are redundant in Amharic phonology (similar to Ras Immiru's proposal apparently without consideration for the phonology of other Ethiopian languages, including Giiz).
- Used the አ family of characters for the proposed six vowels (አ, ኡ, ኢ, ኣ, ኤ, and ኦ), which compares to the seven basic vowel sounds required by Ethiopic grammar. The 6th order not allocated a vowel, the proposal makes no use of the *sadis* vowel እ. For example, the Ethiopic triliteral words ተመን <temen> (valuation), and እግሬ/እግር <igiree/igir> (leg) would be spelled as ተአመአን and እገረኢ/እገረ, respectively.
- Removed the labiovelars ቈ, ኈ, ኰ, and ጐ and replaced each of them with a digraph made up of a non-labialized form of the character with the semivowel letter ወ as follows: ቀወ, ሀወ, ከወ, and ገወ.
- Did not discuss diphthongs, such as ሟ, and
- Used doubling of consonants to show gemination.

<u>Option 2 of the proposal by Abbebe Retta:</u>

- Kept the alphasyllabic nature of the traditional Ethiopic script, although it modified the vowel notations, which is in contrast to Option 1,
- Consisted of the same consonants in the 1st order as those proposed in Option 1,
- Except for the 1st order, the proposal applied the vowel marks uniformly

on all characters within an order. The uniformity was achieved by the use of the 1st order letterforms as base glyphs and then adding a diacritical mark that remained consistent within an order with each order having a unique diacritics. The following is an example of how the system works on the ሰ character family:

ሰ, ሱ, ሲ, ሳ, ሴ, ስ, and ሶ.

<u>The proposal by *Bilatta* Merisiei Hazen Welide Qeeriqos:</u>

- Called for the adoption of the Latin script while keeping the traditional Ethiopic script intact.
- Had a system of transliteration of the Ethiopic script to help with the adoption of the Latin script. The following equivalencies show the system proposed by the *bilatta*: *b* = በ, *d* = ደ, *f* = ፈ, *g* = ገ, *h* = ሀ ሐ and ኀ, *k* = ከ, *l* = ለ, *m* = መ, *n* = ነ, *p* = ፐ, *q* = ቀ, *r* = ረ, *s* = ሰ and ሠ, *t* = ተ, *w* = ወ, *y* = የ, and *z* = ዘ.
- Used diacritical marks to account for non-Latin sounds and extra vowels in Ethiopic. The circumflex (ˆ) is used over the Latin letters c, g, n, p, s, t, and z to transliterate the prepalatals and affricates ጨ, ጀ, ኘ, ጰ, ሸ, ቸ, and ዠ, respectively.
- Used the breve (˘) over the Latin letters *s* and *t* to translate the plosive characters ጸ and ጠ, respectively.
- The labiovelars ቈ, ኈ, ኰ, and ጐ are transliterated as *qu*, *hu*, *ku*, and *gu*, respectively.
- The seven Ethiopic vowels are transliterated in their traditional order as follows: e, u, i, a, é, ê, o.
- Used doubling of consonants to show gemination.

<u>The proposal by Dr. F. C. Laubach:</u>*

- Kept the alphasyllabic nature of the traditional Ethiopic script, although it modified the vowel notations.
- Kept all the consonants of the traditional Ethiopic script, although it was reported that some phonemes were confused.
- Except for the 1st order, the proposal applied the vowel marks uniformly on all characters within an order. The uniformity was achieved by the use of the 1st order letterforms as base glyphs and then adding a diacritical mark that remained consistent within an order, with each order having a unique diacritics. Perhaps the least logical proposal of all, the following is an example of how the system works on the ሰ character family:

  ሰ, ሱ, ሲ, ሳ, ሴ, ስ, and ሶ.

- Did not discuss diphthongs, such as ሟ.

* To my knowledge the only Ethiopic reform proposal by a person originally from a foreign country, Laubach's ideas seems to be the least practical because of the potential confusion that can arise between the 3rd and 5th order characters and the 4th and 6th order characters given the similarity of the diacritical marks in those orders.

Selomon Tesema (2012) listed the following historic works, among others, by reformers that discussed the need for the reform of the Ethiopic writing system:

- Aleqa Keedane Welid Kifilei. መዝገበ ፊደላት ሴማውያት (Encyclopedia of Semitic Scripts). Direi Dawa, 1926 E.C. (c. 1932),
- Ministry of Education & Arts. አዲስ የአማርኛ ፊደል (New [Ethiopic] Script). Addis Ababa, 1939 E.C. (c. 1947),
- Friends of Education. ፊደልን ማሻሻል (Reforming the Ethiopic Script). Addis Ababa, 1940 E.C. (c. 1948),
- የአማርኛ ፊደል ሕግን እንዲጠብቅ ለማድረግ የተዘጋጀ ሪፖርት (Report for the Standardization of the [Ethiopic] Script). *Ethiopian Studies Magazine*, Vol. 8, No. 1. Addis Ababa, 1962 E.C. (c. 1970), and
- ስለአማርኛ ፊደል መሻሻል ጥናትና ውሳኔ (Research Findings and Decisions on the Reform of the [Ethiopic] Script)" Addis Ababa, 1973 E.C. (c. 1981).

Selomon Tesema further noted that, as far back as the first half of the 20th century, reformers, among whom were scholars of the Ethiopian Orthodox Church, argued that the Ethiopic script had become "outdated, antiquated, archaic, ineffectual, and unsuited for the printing press as well as for efficiency."[4] The need for orthographic representation of gemination or consonant elongation was another area where reform was sought. *Abba* T. Mariyam Semiharay, who was one of the early 20th century Ethiopian intellectuals, had published a book by using special signs for marking gemination and the Ethiopic *sadis* vowel (Kinife, 2001 E.C.). Haddees Alemayyehu, one of Ethiopia's most celebrated novelists, also published books a few decades later with similar ideas for marking gemination, but his idea, like that of Mariyam's, was never adopted by anyone else.

The reform movements eventually led to the recognition of the need for action by the imperial government's Ministry of Education, which ordered the establishment of a committee to study and propose the required reform of the Ethiopic writing system from c. 1948 to c. 1951. Kinife stated that the committee was chaired by Abbebe Reta and had the following members who attended at least one of the five meetings held: Adees Alemayehu, *Bilata* Merisiei Hazen W. Qeeriqos, *Bilata* Welide Geeyorigees Welide Yohanis, Meeleeyon Neqiniq, Zewidei Gebire Medihin, Seyifu Felleqe, Kebbede Meekaeil, and Samueil Terrefe, who represented the Ethiopian Orthodox Church. In what he referred to as the third reform movement, Selomon Tesema (2012) stated that the third generation of reformers argued that the Ethiopic script was not suited for the typewriter, among other shortcomings, and that three reform ideas, including modification of the Ethiopic characters, were debated.

As was the case with previous reform movements, in the third reform movement, high-ranking government officials had aligned themselves to opposing sides of the reform debate which was said to be intense (Selomon Tesema, 2012). Selomon Tesema further stated that participants included Abbebe Retta (who was then deputy minister of health), Merisiei Hazen Welide Qiriqos (who was posted as the deputy minister of health in 1943 E.C.), *Bilatta* Zewidei Belayineh (who was then minister of education), *Ras* Immiru, *Ato* Mekonnin (who was head secretary of the Ministry of Education), Colonel Tamirat Yiggezu, and representatives from the Ethiopian Orthodox Church (Birhanu Diniqei, Yeneita Asires Yeneisew, and Menigisitu Lemma, who eventually became a celebrated writer). The following list summarizes the issues discussed and the recommendations made by the committee (Kinife, 2001 E.C.):

- That many years ago, reform proposals had been blocked by some interest groups because such reforms were seen as damaging to Ethiopian national heritage, culture, and religion;
- That government needed to pass laws and regulations for the proposed reforms to be implemented;
- That two types of scripts could be used in parallel—the reformed script for use by government and the general public and the traditional script for text in Giiz—the language for whom the script was originally developed;
- That whether or not, once enacted, the reform had to be phased in for a smooth transition or conversion to the new system and whether or not public campaigns to introduce the new script would be required;
- That other African nations had intention to use the Ethiopic script as long as the characters were simplified and followed logical rules;
- That students would take significantly less time to learn the simplified script and that anyone who had already learned how to read and write traditional Ethiopic would not have difficulty learning the proposed simplified script in a short time;
- That not only did many Ethiopian students and teachers welcomed the proposed reform, but also that foreigners found the proposed simplified script a lot easier for learning;
- That fewer letters were beneficial for typewriting as well as for using the writing system in general on a daily basis;
- That whether government must enact the proposed reform for it to become the law of the land or whether the public would be guided to familiarize themselves with the reformed script for eventual adoption of it without enactment;
- That the reform had been unnecessarily delayed and that a document containing ideas for the reform of the script had been lost and that enacting the reform would be the best course of action without necessarily denying the public some time to familiarize themselves with the reformed script;
- That the typeface of the *giiz* or 1st order characters (CORE CHARACTERS) should remain as they were since they were the original consonantal Ethiopic characters;
- That except three characters, each of the *kaiib* (2nd) order characters followed the same rule of having a horizontal stroke on the right side; and, therefore, the three characters that did not follow this rule should be modified so that they follow the rule;

- That except six characters, each of the *salis* (3rd) order characters followed the same rule of having a horizontal stroke on the foot of the right side; and, therefore, the six characters that did not follow this rule should be modified so that they follow the rule;
- That, as a group, the characters of the *rabiii* (4th) order were the second most irregular characters and, therefore, the creation of new rules to make them uniform was required but was postponed to a latter time along with the ones for the 6th order;
- That all *hamis* (5th) order characters used a small ring at the base of the right leg and should remain as they were;
- That, as a group, the characters of the *sadis* (6th) order were the most irregular of all and thus it was necessary to propose a horizontal stroke on the left side of each of the core characters; however, because of the possible technical challenges, the final proposal was postponed to a later time;
- That with some modifications, it was decided to keep the *sabiii* (7th) order characters; and
- That, finally, it was decided to review the technical details of the reform by assigning two members of the committee and that a further study was needed and the results of the study would be presented to Emperor Haile Selassie.

Additional recommendations passed by the committee are summarized as follows:

- That the typeface of the core characters (*giiz* order) of the Ethiopic script should remain as they are;
- That the typeface of the *kaiib* order characters would be based on the core characters and should have a horizontal stroke on the middle of the right side of each character (e.g. ቡ);
- That the typeface of the *salis* order characters should be based on the core characters and should have a horizontal stroke at the foot of the right side of each character (e.g. ቢ);
- That the typeface of the *rabiii* order characters should be based on the core characters and should have a horizontal stroke at the foot of the left side of each character (e.g. ቃ);
- That the typeface of the *hamis* order characters should be based on the core characters and should have a ring at the foot of the right side of each character (e.g. ቤ);
- That the typeface of the *sadis* order characters should be based on the core characters and should have a horizontal stroke at the middle of the left side of each character (e.g. ·በ);
- That the typeface of the *sabiii* order characters should be based on the core characters and should have a ring at the top of the right side of each character (e.g. ሆ);
- That the six redundant characters ሐ, ሠ, ኀ, ኸ, ዐ, and ጸ be eliminated; and
- That the Ethiopic extension set characters be eliminated in favour of what might resemble digraphs.

The committee's description of some of the benefits of the reform is summarized as follows:

- That fewer characters meant less time to learn the Ethiopic script;
- That the Ethiopic typewriter would be more efficient;
- That it would be easier and quicker for the printing press tasks (typesetting, editing, and manufacturing of movable types);
- That it would offer better spelling;
- That it would provide immense benefit for lexicography and alphabetical listing and searching of words; and
- That it would provide the possibility for other nations to adopt it.

Selomon Tesema (2012) stated that the generation of reformers that rose in the decade before the 1974 overthrow of the Imperial government argued for the reform of the Ethiopic writing system based on the issues that are mostly related to pedagogy and the heavy burden placed on teachers and students, which included:

- The large number of characters in the script,
- The use of redundant characters in the script (Amharic), and
- The lack of a method to mark gemination.

Selomon Tesema (2012) further stated that in his book የአማርኛ ፊደልን ስለማሻሻል የቀረበ ጥናት (Report on the Study for the Reform of the [Ethiopic] Script), Kebbede Beritelomeiwos had presented proposals for dealing with redundant characters similar to those used in Haddees Alemayyehu's novel *Fiqir Isike Meqabir* (1965). Selomon Tesema further stated that the decade between 1964 and 1974 saw a wave of publications reflective of the fourth reform movement. For example, articles on national newspapers (*Yezareiyitu Etiyopxiya*, *Meeyaziya* 3 and *Ginibot* 15, 1956 E.C. (c. 1964), and *Addees Zemen*, *Tahisas* 10 and *Meggabeet* 7, 1961 E.C.) reflected the rivalry between opposing camps of the reform divide.

Citing ስለአማርኛ ፊደል መሻሻል ጥናትና ውሳኔ (1973 E.C.), Selomon further stated that a committee whose members included Maitre Artist Afewerk Tekle, *Ato* Aseffa Leeben, *Ato* Abbebe Weriqei, *Ato* Habite Mariyam Mariqos, *Ato* Menigistu Lemma, *Ato* Tekile Xadeeq Mekureeya, *Ato* Seifu Metafereeya, Dr. Amsalu Akililu, Dr. Meriid W. Aregay, Dr. Birihanu Abbebe, and Dr. Gebireyesus Hayilu met at the Adama Ras Hotel in Nazireit (Adama), Ethiopia, from February 13 to 19, 1980, and passed a nine-point resolution on the issue of the Ethiopic writing system, including the issue of redundant characters and punctuation. To this day, none of the resolution points are known to the general public, let alone to be implemented.

In the early 2000's, the Ethiopian Languages Research Center (now Academy of Ethiopian Languages and Cultures), Ethiopia's equivalent to the *Académie française*, published an Ethiopic dictionary titled አማርኛ መዝገበ ቃላት (Haregeweyin Kebede et. al., 1993 E.C.), in which it proposed the reform of the Ethiopic writing system based solely on Amharic phonology. The proposed reforms, which were applied in the publication, are summarized as follows:

- Reduction of the Ethiopic characters to 28 rows of character sets for a total of 196 characters (28 x 7 = 196),
- Obsoletion of the redundant family of characters ሐ, ሠ, ኀ, ዐ, and ፀ in the Amharic language, and
- Restoration of the 1st order vowelic sounds of the characters ሀ and አ, which in the Amharic language, had traditionally been given the 4th order vowelic sound.

Here again, suffice it to say that none of the reform ideas are known to the general public, let alone to be implemented.

To my knowledge, the last published material proposing a reform of the Ethiopic script was presented in the Amharic book ብቸኛው አፍሪካዊ ፊደል፡- ተሻሽሎ የቀረበ አዲስ የኢትዮጵያ ሥርዓተ ፊደል ገበታና የንባብ መለማመጃ by Dr. Fiqirei Yoseif, which was published in Debire Zeyit (Beeshofitu) in 2001 E.C. (c. 2009).[5] DejeS ZeTewahedo (2009) stated that the author proposed the reduction of the Ethiopic characters and simplification of the vowelic orders. The core characters were reduced to 29 through the elimination of redundant characters, and the vowelic orders were simplified through the uniform application of a diacritical mark in each vowelic order. Fiqirei Yoseif's proposed reform is comparable to the proposals by Abbebe Retta (Option # 2) and Dr. F. C. Laubach published in the 1949 booklet ፊደልን ማሻሻል. DejeS ZeTewahedo (2009) stated that, the author proposed to mark gemination with a special sign and that the book contained text in the proposed script for a reading exercise. Apparently presented from the perspective of Amharic phonology only, the proposal was criticized by Ethiopian linguists for not accounting for characters needed in other Ethiopian languages, including Ethiocushitic and the other Ethiosemitic languages, and for other errors (DejeS ZeTewahedo, 2009).

Previous and Possible Future Criticisms for Reform

In presenting the proposed reform, it is imperative to discuss possible future criticisms and those that had previously been raised against the effort to reform the Ethiopic orthography. In the hundred years since efforts began to reform Ethiopic, scholars continued the debate on whether or not a reform of the alphabet was necessary and, if so, whether or not a minor or a major reform was appropriate. Unfortunately, none of the proposed improvements have ever been implemented to date but, at this point in its history, Ethiopia no longer seems to have the luxury to delay reform of its writing system any further. It might help to compare the difference between the traditional Ethiopic writing system and the proposed writing system, somewhat loosely, to the difference between the analog and digital worlds. The challenges of converting to digital systems had simply not enough magnitude to close the door for the wind of change that ushered in the digital age. As *Bilatta* Merisiei Hazen Welide Qeeriqos (1948 E.C.), one of the 20th century Ethiopian grammarians, argued in favour of the improvement of the Ethiopic script,

> ፊደል ፡ የቋንቋ ፡ መሣሪያ ፡ ነው፡፡ መሣሪያ ፡ በየጊዜው ፡ እንዲሻሻል ፡ እንዲሳል ፡ እንዲሰነገል ፤ ፊደልም ፡ እንደዚሁ ፡ ተሻሽሎ ፡ ሊታደስ ፡ የሚያስፈልግ ፡ ነው ፡፡ የአማርኛን ፡ ፊደል ፡ ለማሻሻል ፡ ከብዙ ፡ ሊቃውንት፡ ልዩ ፡ ልዩ ፡ አሳቦች ፡ ቀርበዋል ፡፡ የሁሉም ፡ አሳብ ፡ በአናጋሪ ፡ ፊደል (በዋየል) ፡ ይነገር ፡ በማለት ፡ የተባበረ፡ ሆኖአል ፡፡ መደቡ ፡

> ግዕዝ ፡ ወይም ፡ ሳድስ ፡ ሆኖ ፡ በአ ፡ ፊደል ፡ አናጋሪነት ፡ እንዲነበብ ፡ አሳብ ፡ ያቀረቡ፡ አሉ። ደግሞ ፡ በአ ፡ ፊደልና ፡ በተመደቡ ፡ በሌሎች ፡ ፊደላት ፡ አናጋሪነት ፡ እንዲነበብ ፡ የወሰኑ ፡ አሉ ። የሁሉም ፡ አሳብ ፡ የተመሰገነ ፡ ነው ። [6]
>
> A script is a tool for language. Just as tools need to be improved from time to time, scripts should also be improved as needed. Various ideas to improve the Ethiopic script have been presented by many scholars, all of whom recommended the use of separate vowels. There are those who recommended the use of the አ family of characters as the vowels for a script based on the *giiz* (1st order) or *sadis* (6th order) characters….These are all great ideas.

Dr. Bedilu Waqijira (2005 E.C.) argued that the call for the reform of the Ethiopic script, which had been raised by many scholars of past and present generations, was an effort to remove a weakness from our national heritage and help society take even more pride in the writing system but that it ought not to be seen as an effort to tarnish it. Dr. Bedilu Waqijira lamented Ethiopia's dilemma with regards to the reform of its script by stating that,

> ወደር የለሽ ጥንታዊ ስልጣኔያችን በእጃችን ያለ ዛሬያችንን አኮስሶ አስተሳሰባችንን ያለ ልክ ተጭኖታል:: ማንነታችንን የምንገልጸው በሱ ነው፤ የምንኮራው በሱ ነው:: ይህ ባልከፋ፤ ከፋቱ ጉድፉን ልንነቅስለት አለመድፈራችን ነው:: ጉድፉን ነቅስን ለመታደግ ይቅርና ስለ ጉድፉ ማውራት የሚያስቀስፍ ይመስለናል:: [7]
>
> Our ancient civilization—which has very few equals—has negatively influenced our thinking by making us pay little attention to our day, which is in our hands. We express our identity [in the Ethiopic script] and we take great pride in it—that is good, except that we have not been bold enough to remove its weakness. We think it is sacrilegious to discuss its weakness, let alone to rescue it from its weakness.

Criticism of the Reform in General

As the reform encompasses both grammar and orthography, critics may argue that the reform is too sweeping or too radical for the general public to accept it. However, both grammar and orthography are highly intertwined for Ethiopic and therefore significant improvement to one necessitates a similar level of improvement to the other. Secondly, the proposed grammar and orthography are much simpler and will inevitably be preferred over the traditional ones after the general public is introduced to them. Being highly phonemic, the traditional orthography does not encourage consistent spelling. Fluctuations in pronunciation and word derivation result in very few words having fixed spelling. Some consonants and vowels required for the reconstruction of the basic morphophonemic elements of words are often lost making the grammars of the languages mysterious for many. Phonemic spelling can hide morphological similarities between two or more words, which indicates the interdependency of grammar and orthography.

The Ethiopic writing system has been in continuous change since it was first devised thousands of years ago. One of the most recent change is the abandoning of the two-dot letter separator, which is replaced by white space similar to the conventional rules in the European orthographies. Despite having its own writing system for millennia, Ethiopia has had one of the least literate populations in the world. Moreover, in recent decades, some non-Ethiosemitic languages have opted out of the traditional Ethiopic writing system mentioning linguistic, pedagogical, and practical reasons, while Ethiopia continued to postpone its language reform.

Writing Speed

Critics could question, as they did in a previous generation, the efficiency of the proposed orthography on the speed of writing or typing as it uses at least two letters (a consonant and a vowel) to represent almost every phoneme in contrast to the traditional orthography, which uses a single alphasyllabic character. However, this argument does not stand to scrutiny with regards to both typing and handwriting. When typewriters were still in use in Ethiopia, it was said that the average skilled typist was able to type only about 15 to 20 words per minute on the Ethiopic typewriter (Shelemay as cited in Harvard University, 2011), which was slow compared to professional typists in the international arena who could type 50 to 80 words per minute. When typewriting using the traditional orthography, on average it takes more than two keystrokes to type a character (most keyboards require the use of only one keystroke for most of the characters in the 6th order of the main character set, but require at least two or three keystrokes for all other Ethiopic characters). With a writing system consisting of consonants and vowels as the proposed alphabet, typing of an equivalent phoneme or word will not require more keystrokes. It takes about 580 keystrokes to render the 245 traditional characters of the MAIN SET on the average computer keyboard, which provides a ratio of almost two and a half times as many keystrokes required for typing as the number of syllables rendered. The Ethiopic EXTENSION SET, on average, requires even more keystrokes. The proposed orthography can represent the syllables represented by the Ethiopic extension set characters with fewer or equal number of keystrokes but not by any more keystrokes (see Chapter 12).

The proposed orthography is even more beneficial for handwriting as it takes less time to write anything using only a total of seven vowels and 22 consonants, which compares to using hundreds of phonetic characters in the traditional orthography. It is known that all the characters of the traditional orthography have different shapes and many are complex (consider, for example, the characters ጆ ቾ ዀ ሜ ሟ ጮ ጬ ሼ ቯ ዮ ኸ and ኝ). My informal experiment shows that, on average, writing a paragraph legibly using the traditional script takes a little more time than writing the same paragraph using the proposed orthography with consonants and vowels. One reason may be that all the consonants of the proposed alphabets (with some exceptions) are taken directly from the 1st order of the Ethiopic script, which has the simplest shapes of the seven orders. It takes more effort to write characters in the 2nd, 3rd, 4th, 5th, 6th, and 7th orders, which are now replaced by vowels of simple shapes and characters in the 1st order. The second reason may be that the complexity of the traditional characters makes it almost impossible to create connected and cursive letters for speed and therefore result in poor handwriting. Wright (1964) lamented that,

> To-day, unfortunately, the handwriting of Ethiopians has deteriorated badly; compared with any good manuscript written before about 1750. ... As for the everyday handwriting of most Ethiopians, it is nearly always hideous. Good handwriting is rarely taught in schools, more attention being paid nowadays to the acquiring of a legible English hand than to the development of a shapely [Ethiopic] one. In consequence, it is most unusual to find among school children one who can write an [Ethiopic] script which is not virtually indecipherable and an offence to the eye. Higher education inevitably produces a still greater subservience to English writing and a further neglect of the [Ethiopic] script.[8]

Paper Space

Another criticism against a script with separate letters for consonants and vowels has been the perceived doubling of paper space needed to write text as compared to using the traditional script. This argument is not as correct as it seems. In a technological age where efficient communication is the key to success and where electronic media is becoming the primary mode of communication, there is little need to worry about paper space. Secondly, even if more paper space may be required to accommodate text in the proposed orthography, especially since we will continue to use the print media and handwriting for the foreseeable future, the benefits of the proposed orthography far outweighs the loss of additional paper space. Thirdly, while paper space will increase with the increased number of letters required to represent a given syllable, a doubling of paper space does not necessarily occur because, in a given page layout, the margins and the space between words and paragraphs will remain the same regardless of the type of script used. Therefore, the effect on the size of paper space from the use of a script with consonants and vowels will be marginal. My informal experiment with text in both the traditional and proposed orthographies shows that only about 25 percent more paper space is required for text in the proposed orthography of the same number of words and average font size to text in the traditional orthography on an A4 size page. In fact, it can even take lesser space as the font size for simpler letterforms can be made smaller and still be readable. Regardless of the size of additional space required for using a full-fledged alphabet, the loss of additional paper space would be an insignificant cost to pay to improve a writing system, which will have enormous benefits for the progress of society. By way of comparison, the proposed orthography uses, on average, about the same number of letters as English for a translated version of a sentence.

Loss of Access to Old Documents

Critics may argue that, with the introduction the proposed orthography, future generations will lose the ability to read and comprehend materials written in the traditional orthography. However, access to literature in the traditional Ethiopic orthography will not be lost because such text will always be a parallel version of text in the reformed Ethiopic since there will be significant phoneme-to-phoneme relationships. Given that all the letterforms of the consonants and vowels in the proposed orthography are directly adopted from the traditional Ethiopic script, users of Ethiopic will likely be able to read and comprehend old documents even with the most rudimentary training. As any Ethiopian who has ever used the Latin script to transcribe an Ethiopic word knows, the Ethiopic characters are romanized using Latin syllables made up of consonants and vowels. This reversible method is comparable to converting text from the traditional Ethiopic script to the consonants and vowels of the proposed Ethiopic script and vice versa. Moreover, in a technologically advanced generation, it will not be too far-fetched to imagine that Ethiopian innovators will soon develop computer software that quickly converts text from traditional Ethiopic to the proposed reformed Ethiopic. Already the technology that converts scanned images of text from old manuscripts into text format exists in today's world, and this will make the reform of the writing system all the more viable.

Sacred Heritage

An argument that was presented in a previous generation against the reform of the Ethiopic script was that the script is a sacred heritage received from our forefathers. Desita Tekile Welid (1970) described the problem of spelling inconsistencies, such as ሂሣብ, ሂሳብ, and ሒሳብ <hisab> (invoice, bill, or mathematics), even within the same text but, at the same time, rebuked those who suggested the deletion of redundant characters that add to the problem. Desita compared the reduction of the size of the Ethiopic script to the reduction of Ethiopian territory. However, while I believe that Ethiopians have the solemn responsibility to keep their heritage, what is important to determine is how to keep it. A new way of preserving the Ethiopic script from fading into irrelevance is urgently needed as the creeping assault from the English language and the Latin script has increased especially in recent decades. Not all heritages may need to be preserved in the same way, and the only way of preserving this particular heritage is to modernize it in keeping with the times. Perhaps one of the most important argument against keeping the traditional writing system may be the fact that many non-Semitic languages in Ethiopia have abandoned it altogether after the 1991 regime change because the writing system was not able to fulfill their specific orthographic needs. The difficulties for writing arising from the size and complexity of the traditional Ethiopic script, especially as compared to the Latin script, was reported at least as far back as 1840 by missionaries who translated parts of the Bible into Oromiffa (see Krapf and Isenberg, 1840).

As a nation, our use of the traditional alphabet is handicapping our writing system and our ability to develop a modern, world-class communication system that not only is good for communicating sophisticated information in science and technology but is also able to self-preserve. Unfortunately, those who argued against the reform of the Ethiopic script did not seem to take this fact into consideration and, therefore, this criticism may surface again. Some have even considered any reform of the Ethiopic script tantamount to sacrilege. However, since the ancient Ethiopic consonantal characters will not change, this position will not be justifiable. Moreover, as an ebugeeda (abugida), the traditional Ethiopic script itself is a reform on the previous consonant-only (abjad) script—ancient Ethiopic—which was in use during the Kingdom of Axum between the 1st and 4th centuries A.D. The fact that our forefathers dared to reform what was handed down to them by their forefathers is something that we all are proud of (imagine how difficult it would have been to read this book if it was written using consonants only, which would have been the case with the ancient Ethiopic script). The fourth-century reform was by far the most radical reform for Ethiopic because it produced alphasyllabic characters by fusing consonants and vowels. Our forefathers were wise enough to know when reform was needed and to act on it, which helped them develop a world-class writing system for their time. Since then Ethiopic had gone through other modifications, particularly since the use of Giiz declined as an official language. Tigirinya, Amharic, and other Ethiopian languages had been modifying the script in the last few centuries by adding characters to suit their needs. Those were latter day generations that acted when the need arose. Our generation will fail to honour our forefathers if we refuse to carry on the torch and reform the script in order to make it a world-class writing system for our time.

The Process of Conversion to the Proposed Orthography

If and when the respective authorities accept the proposed language reform, I recommend its implementation be carried out in phases. The phases may be planned for two- to five-year blocks of time. The phases will be based on the extent of the implementation of the reform. For example, in the first phase, Government could provide information to the public on the components of the proposed reform but not require anyone to abide by the changes yet. However, on subsequent phases, implementation can start slowly until, in the final phase, all legal communications are conducted using the proposed orthography. Once the schedule for the phasing is determined, Government will need to take the necessary steps for the success of the process. The following are the recommended phases:

Phase I: Introductory Phase

The first phase will require very little training or effort and will probably need to last a few months. In this phase, the traditional Ethiopic script will be retained, but, orthographically, the nucleus and the morphemes of word derivatives will be separated. Word separation will be a great start as it will help people to get used to the permanent separation of the root word, the prime pronouns, the prepositions, etc. However, as this is an introductory phase, implementation of the reform is entirely voluntary.

The following are recommended actions for Government to take in Phase I:

- Conduct illustrative campaigns through radio, television, newspapers, flyers, posters, and billboards until a certain level of public understanding of this phase of the reform is achieved;
- Register volunteers to help with this phase of the conversion;
- Sponsor the development of computer software and hardware that will support the new orthography;
- Initiate and fund the preparation of reference materials, such as dictionaries, within a short time;
- Start training of trainers who will be sent to selected schools, starting with elementary schools, across the country.

Phase II: Nominal Implementation

The second phase will see the nominal implementation of the proposed reform and will probably need to last for one or more years. In this phase, Government will require printed news media to include text in the new orthography beginning with at least one article of a specified length in each of their published materials in addition to all billboards and signage being required to use the proposed orthography alongside the traditional one. Moreover, textbooks for students in the lowest grades will introduce the proposed orthography, and the curriculum will be revised accordingly.

The following are recommended actions for Government to take in Phase II:

- Conduct illustrative campaigns through radio, television, newspapers, flyers, posters, and billboards until a certain level of public understanding of this phase of the reform is achieved.

- Facilitate the distribution of materials describing the details of the reform, such as printed copies of this book, to the public.
- Prepare textbooks and dictionaries in Amharic in preparation for the next phase (Phase III), which includes abolishing of English as the medium of instruction in Ethiopia.
- Prepare a curriculum for all levels of the school system for implementation in the next phase (Phase III), based on the proposed language reform.
- Train teachers in all levels of the school system so that they can teach their students according to planned phasing of the reform.
- Host national and regional literary competitions among high school students, for example, for a prize. Such literary competitions can outlive the deadline for complete conversion to the proposed orthography and will almost certainly have an enormous effect in reviving Ethiopian literature and ushering in a great literary culture in the country.
    - Regional literary competitions will require the use of the regional language—such as Tigirinya, Amharic, Oromiffa, or Somaleenya—and the proposed orthography.
    - National literary competitions will be held in Amharic, as the federal language, but competitors from each region will compete for the first spot for the region before passing to the national arena. While winners of the regional literary competitions should enter the national competition directly, the regional competitions will be separate from the national competition.

Phase III: Substantial Implementation

The third phase will see the substantial implementation of the proposed reform at the end of the period, which will probably need to last for three or more years. In this phase, Government will require all publicly distributed text, including all communications between government agencies, or between private agencies and government agencies, all educational materials, legal documents, product descriptions, business names, etc. to conform to the proposed orthography by the end of the phase.

The following are recommended actions for Government to take in Phase III:

- Help implement the proposed reform of the Ethiopic writing system in all schools across the country.
- Abolishing of English as the medium of instruction in all public schools, with the possible exception of some higher educational institutions where preparation of the relevant educational materials in Amharic may require more time.
- Implement the use of Amharic as the medium of instruction in all schools run by the federal Ministry of Education.
- Continue to train teachers at all levels of the education system to make them qualified for the reform with a higher level of qualification in this phase so

that they can handle the challenges of the shift to the reformed orthography.

- Initiate and sponsor the preparation of dictionaries and the development of technical terms to be used by industry and the general public alike in fulfillment of the language reform.
- Continue to sponsor national and regional literary competitions

No Further Delay: The Time for Action is Now

Ethiopian languages and the Ethiopic writing system are at a major crossroads today. Faced with the communication needs of a modern world, globalization and the threat of English's unchallenged expansion, today Ethiopia needs to implement a coordinated language reform like never before. From orthographic reforms to removing the choking hold of English in education and society, in general, policy makers should act quickly to reverse the deterioration of verbal and written communications in the nation. Perspicacious decisions need to be made to propel Ethiopia out of the ashes of poverty and backwardness and into the best place on earth with a world-class writing system and a modern, efficient culture of communication.

It is heartening to note that other nations also have implemented language and orthographic reforms (**Table 14.1**) for the same reason that they needed to remove communication impediments to the progress of society. The Atatürk Reforms of Turkey, which included language reform and were implemented in the 1920's by President Mustafa Kemal Atatürk—a great modernizer and the architect of modern Turkey—may be one of the most sweeping language reforms in history that saw the modernization of Turkey in the 20th century. The Turkish reform of the alphabet, in particular, was the culmination of efforts by various Turkish scholars starting in the mid 19th century, which provides an interesting comparison to the century-old effort by Ethiopian scholars to reform the Ethiopic script that began at the dawn of the last century.

In Ethiopia, despite a hundred years of several proposals for the reform of the Ethiopic writing system, nothing of importance has been implemented to improve written and spoken communication. In fact, almost none of the reform proposals of the last century or the new century—which includes proposals by the Ethiopian Languages Academy (c. 2000) for eliminating redundant characters, and by Dr. Fiqirei Yoseif (c. 2009) for eliminating redundant characters and applying uniform marks to the vowelic orders—are known to the public.

I urge the Ethiopian people and government to implement the proposed reforms as soon as possible. All great and useful reform ideas should be welcomed and encouraged to guarantee a strong and prosperous Ethiopia that will not only survive but thrive in a modern, 21st-century world. Ethiopia cannot and must not wait for another hundred years for a reform to happen.

Table 14.1: Some of the more successful language reforms in history[9]

REFORM TYPE	MAIN PROPONENT OR IMPLEMENTER OF THE REFORM	MOST RECENT REFORM
Belgian language reforms		1844,1864, 1946, 1996, 2006
Chinese language reforms		1920s
Chinese simplified characters		1956
Dutch language reforms		1883, 1934, 1947, 1996, 2006
Ethiopic orthographic reform	King Ezana	4th century
French language reforms	l'Académie Française.	1740, 1762, 1835, 1992
German language reform		1901/02
German orthographic reform		1996
Hebrew language reform	Eliezer Ben-Yehuda	1920s
Irish language reform		1940s
Japanese language reform		1946
Norwegian language reform		1907, 1917, 1929, 1938
Portuguese language reform		20th century
Somali language reform	President Siad Barre / Musa Haji Ismail Galal	1970s
Turkish language reform	President Mustafa Kemal Atatürk	1920s
Vietnamese language reform		20th century

PART VI

APPENDICES, ENDNOTES, AND MORE

Appendix A: The Derivatives of the Tigirinya Noun ድሙ

ድሙ
ድሙን

ትድሙ
ትድሙን
ዝድሙ
ዝድሙን

ደማሙ
ደማሙን

ታድሙ
ታድሙን
ዛድሙ
ዛድሙን

ዝድሞኹም
ዝድሙዓ
ዝድሙኣን
ዝድሙዑ
ዝድሞም

ዛድሞኹም
ዛድሙዓ
ዛድሙኣን
ዛድሙዑ
ዛድሞም

ድሞይ
ድሙና
ድሞኺ
ድሞኽን
ድሞኻ
ድሞኹም
ድሙዓ
ድሙኣን
ድሙዑ
ድሞም

ደማሙተይ
ደማሙና
ደማሙኺ
ደማሙኽን
ደማሙኻ
ደማሙኹም
ደማሙዓ
ደማሙተን
ደማሙቱ
ደማሙቶም

ትድሞይ
ትድሙና
ትድሞኺ
ትድሞኽን
ትድሞኻ
ትድሞኹም
ትድሙዓ
ትድሙኣን
ትድሙዑ
ትድሞም

ታድሞይ
ታድሙና
ታድሞኺ
ታድሞኽን
ታድሞኻ
ታድሞኹም
ታድሙዓ
ታድሙኣን
ታድሙዑ
ታድሞም

ዝድሞይ
ዝድሙና
ዝድሞኺ
ዝድሞኽን
ዝድሞኻ

ዛድሞይ
ዛድሙና
ዛድሞኺ
ዛድሞኽን
ዛድሞኻ

Appendix B: The Derivatives of the Amharic Noun ድመት

ድመት
ድመቶች
ድመቶቹ

ድመትም
ድመቶችም
ድመቶቹም

ድመትን
ድመቶችን
ድመቶቹን

ድመትንም
ድመቶችንም
ድመቶቹንም

ድመትና
ድመቶችና
ድመቶቹና

ድመትንና
ድመቶችንና
ድመቶቹንና

ድመቱ
ድመቱን
ድመቱንና
ድመቱና

የድመቱ
የድመቱን
የድመቱንና
የድመቱና

ድመቱም
ድመቱንም
የድመቱም
የድመቱንም

የድመት
የድመቶች
የድመቶቹ

የድመትም
የድመቶችም
የድመቶቹም

የድመትን
የድመቶችን
የድመቶቹን

የድመትንም
የድመቶችንም
የድመቶቹንም

የድመትና
የድመቶችና
የድመቶቹና

የድመትንና
የድመቶችንና
የድመቶቹንና

ድመቷ
ድመቷን
ድመቷንና
ድመቷና

የድመቷ
የድመቷን
የድመቷንና
የድመቷና

ድመቷም
ድመቷንም
የድመቷም
የድመቷንም

ድመቴ
ድመታችን
ድመትህ
ድመትሽ
ድመትዎ
ድመታችሁ
ድመቱ
ድመቷ
ድመታቸው

ድመቴም
ድመታችንም
ድመትህም
ድመትሽም
ድመትዎም
ድመታችሁም
ድመቱም
ድመቷም
ድመታቸውም

ድመቴን
ድመታችንን
ድመትህን
ድመትሽን
ድመትዎን
ድመታችሁን
ድመቱን
ድመቷን
ድመታቸውን

ድመቴንም
ድመታችንንም
ድመትህንም
ድመትሽንም
ድመትዎንም
ድመታችሁንም
ድመቱንም
ድመቷንም
ድመታቸውንም

ድመቶቼ
ድመቶቻችን
ድመቶችህ
ድመቶችሽ
ድመቶችዎ
ድመቶቻችሁ
ድመቶቹ
ድመቶቿ
ድመቶቻቸው

ድመቶቼም
ድመቶቻችንም
ድመቶችህም
ድመቶችሽም
ድመቶችዎም
ድመቶቻችሁም
ድመቶቹም
ድመቶቿም
ድመቶቻቸውም

ድመቶቼን
ድመቶቻችንን
ድመቶችህን
ድመቶችሽን
ድመቶችዎን
ድመቶቻችሁን
ድመቶቹን
ድመቶቿን
ድመቶቻቸውን

ድመቶቼንም
ድመቶቻችንንም
ድመቶችህንም
ድመቶችሽንም
ድመቶችዎንም
ድመቶቻችሁንም
ድመቶቹንም
ድመቶቿንም
ድመቶቻቸውንም

የድመቴ	የድመቶቼ	ድመቴና	ድመቶቼና
የድመታችን	የድመቶቻችን	ድመታችንና	ድመቶቻችንና
የድመትህ	የድመቶችህ	ድመትህና	ድመቶችህና
የድመትሽ	የድመቶችሽ	ድመትሽና	ድመቶችሽና
የድመትዎ	የድመቶችዎ	ድመትዎና	ድመቶችዎና
የድመታችሁ	የድመቶቻችሁ	ድመታችሁና	ድመቶቻችሁና
የድመቱ	የድመቶቹ	ድመቱና	ድመቶቹና
የድመቷ	የድመቶቿ	ድመቷና	ድመቶቿና
የድመታቸው	የድመቶቻቸው	ድመታቸውና	ድመቶቻቸውና
የድመቴም	የድመቶቼም	ድመቴንና	ድመቶቼንና
የድመታችንም	የድመቶቻችንም	ድመታችንንና	ድመቶቻችንንና
የድመትህም	የድመቶችህም	ድመትህንና	ድመቶችህንና
የድመትሽም	የድመቶችሽም	ድመትሽንና	ድመቶችሽንና
የድመትዎም	የድመቶችዎም	ድመትዎንና	ድመቶችዎንና
የድመታችሁም	የድመቶቻችሁም	ድመታችሁንና	ድመቶቻችሁንና
የድመቱም	የድመቶቹም	ድመቱንና	ድመቶቹንና
የድመቷም	የድመቶቿም	ድመቷንና	ድመቶቿንና
የድመታቸውም	የድመቶቻቸውም	ድመታቸውንና	ድመቶቻቸውንና
የድመቴን	የድመቶቼን	የድመቴና	የድመቶቼና
የድመታችንን	የድመቶቻችንን	የድመታችንና	የድመቶቻችንና
የድመትህን	የድመቶችህን	የድመትህና	የድመቶችህና
የድመትሽን	የድመቶችሽን	የድመትሽና	የድመቶችሽና
የድመትዎን	የድመቶችዎን	የድመትዎና	የድመቶችዎና
የድመታችሁን	የድመቶቻችሁን	የድመታችሁና	የድመቶቻችሁና
የድመቱን	የድመቶቹን	የድመቱና	የድመቶቹና
የድመቷን	የድመቶቿን	የድመቷና	የድመቶቿና
የድመታቸውን	የድመቶቻቸውን	የድመታቸውና	የድመቶቻቸውና
የድመቴንም	የድመቶቼንም	የድመቴንና	የድመቶቼንና
የድመታችንንም	የድመቶቻችንንም	የድመታችንንና	የድመቶቻችንንና
የድመትህንም	የድመቶችህንም	የድመትህንና	የድመቶችህንና
የድመትሽንም	የድመቶችሽንም	የድመትሽንና	የድመቶችሽንና
የድመትዎንም	የድመቶችዎንም	የድመትዎንና	የድመቶችዎንና
የድመታችሁንም	የድመቶቻችሁንም	የድመታችሁንና	የድመቶቻችሁንና
የድመቱንም	የድመቶቹንም	የድመቱንና	የድመቶቹንና
የድመቷንም	የድመቶቿንም	የድመቷንና	የድመቶቿንና
የድመታቸውንም	የድመቶቻቸውንም	የድመታቸውንና	የድመቶቻቸውንና

ያድሙቴ	ያችድሙቴ	በድሙቴም	በድሙቶቼም
ያድመታችን	ያችድመታችን	በድመታችንም	በድሙቶቻችንም
ያድሙትህ	ያችድሙትህ	በድሙትህም	በድሙቶችህም
ያድሙትሽ	ያችድሙትሽ	በድሙትሽም	በድሙቶችሽም
ያድሙትዎ	ያችድሙትዎ	በድሙትዎም	በድሙቶችዎም
ያድመታችሁ	ያችድመታችሁ	በድመታችሁም	በድሙቶቻችሁም
ያድሙቱ	ያችድሙቱ	በድሙቱም	በድሙቶቹም
ያድሙቷ	ያችድሙቷ	በድሙቷም	በድሙቶቿም
ያድመታቸው	ያችድመታቸው	በድመታቸውም	በድሙቶቻቸውም
ያድሙቴም	ያችድሙቴም	በድሙቴና	በድሙቶቼና
ያድመታችንም	ያችድመታችንም	በድመታችንና	በድሙቶቻችንና
ያድሙትህም	ያችድሙትህም	በድሙትህና	በድሙቶችህና
ያድሙትሽም	ያችድሙትሽም	በድሙትሽና	በድሙቶችሽና
ያድሙትዎም	ያችድሙትዎም	በድሙትዎና	በድሙቶችዎና
ያድመታችሁም	ያችድመታችሁም	በድመታችሁና	በድሙቶቻችሁና
ያድሙቱም	ያችድሙቱም	በድሙቱና	በድሙቶቹና
ያድሙቷም	ያችድሙቷም	በድሙቷና	በድሙቶቿና
ያድመታቸውም	ያችድመታቸውም	በድመታቸውና	በድሙቶቻቸውና
ያድሙቴና	ያችድሙቴና	ለድሙቴ	ለድሙቶቼ
ያድመታችንና	ያችድመታችንና	ለድመታችን	ለድሙቶቻችን
ያድሙትህና	ያችድሙትህና	ለድሙትህ	ለድሙቶችህ
ያድሙትሽና	ያችድሙትሽና	ለድሙትሽ	ለድሙቶችሽ
ያድሙትዎና	ያችድሙትዎና	ለድሙትዎ	ለድሙቶችዎ
ያድመታችሁና	ያችድመታችሁና	ለድመታችሁ	ለድሙቶቻችሁ
ያድሙቱና	ያችድሙቱና	ለድሙቱ	ለድሙቶቹ
ያድሙቷና	ያችድሙቷና	ለድሙቷ	ለድሙቶቿ
ያድመታቸውና	ያችድመታቸውና	ለድመታቸው	ለድሙቶቻቸው
በድሙቴ	በድሙቶቼ	ለድሙቴም	ለድሙቶቼም
በድመታችን	በድሙቶቻችን	ለድመታችንም	ለድሙቶቻችንም
በድሙትህ	በድሙቶችህ	ለድሙትህም	ለድሙቶችህም
በድሙትሽ	በድሙቶችሽ	ለድሙትሽም	ለድሙቶችሽም
በድሙትዎ	በድሙቶችዎ	ለድሙትዎም	ለድሙቶችዎም
በድመታችሁ	በድሙቶቻችሁ	ለድመታችሁም	ለድሙቶቻችሁም
በድሙቱ	በድሙቶቹ	ለድሙቱም	ለድሙቶቹም
በድሙቷ	በድሙቶቿ	ለድሙቷም	ለድሙቶቿም
በድመታቸው	በድሙቶቻቸው	ለድመታቸውም	ለድሙቶቻቸውም

ለድመቴና	ለድመቶቼና	ያለድመቴ	ያለድመቶቼ
ለድመታችንና	ለድመቶቻችንና	ያለድመታችን	ያለድመቶቻችን
ለድመትህና	ለድመቶችህና	ያለድመትህ	ያለድመቶችህ
ለድመትሽና	ለድመቶችሽና	ያለድመትሽ	ያለድመቶችሽ
ለድመትዎና	ለድመቶችዎና	ያለድመትዎ	ያለድመቶችዎ
ለድመታችሁና	ለድመቶቻችሁና	ያለድመታችሁ	ያለድመቶቻችሁ
ለድመቱና	ለድመቶቹና	ያለድመቱ	ያለድመቶቹ
ለድመቷና	ለድመቶቿና	ያለድመቷ	ያለድመቶቿ
ለድመታቸውና	ለድመቶቻቸውና	ያለድመታቸው	ያለድመቶቻቸው

ስለድመቴ	ስለድመቶቼ	ያለድመቴም	ያለድመቶቼም
ስለድመታችን	ስለድመቶቻችን	ያለድመታችንም	ያለድመቶቻችንም
ስለድመትህ	ስለድመቶችህ	ያለድመትህም	ያለድመቶችህም
ስለድመትሽ	ስለድመቶችሽ	ያለድመትሽም	ያለድመቶችሽም
ስለድመትዎ	ስለድመቶችዎ	ያለድመትዎም	ያለድመቶችዎም
ስለድመታችሁ	ስለድመቶቻችሁ	ያለድመታችሁም	ያለድመቶቻችሁም
ስለድመቱ	ስለድመቶቹ	ያለድመቱም	ያለድመቶቹም
ስለድመቷ	ስለድመቶቿ	ያለድመቷም	ያለድመቶቿም
ስለድመታቸው	ስለድመቶቻቸው	ያለድመታቸውም	ያለድመቶቻቸውም

ስለድመቴም	ስለድመቶቼም	ያለድመቴና	ያለድመቶቼና
ስለድመታችንም	ስለድመቶቻችንም	ያለድመታችንና	ያለድመቶቻችንና
ስለድመትህም	ስለድመቶችህም	ያለድመትህና	ያለድመቶችህና
ስለድመትሽም	ስለድመቶችሽም	ያለድመትሽና	ያለድመቶችሽና
ስለድመትዎም	ስለድመቶችዎም	ያለድመትዎና	ያለድመቶችዎና
ስለድመታችሁም	ስለድመቶቻችሁም	ያለድመታችሁና	ያለድመቶቻችሁና
ስለድመቱም	ስለድመቶቹም	ያለድመቱና	ያለድመቶቹና
ስለድመቷም	ስለድመቶቿም	ያለድመቷና	ያለድመቶቿና
ስለድመታቸውም	ስለድመቶቻቸውም	ያለድመታቸውና	ያለድመቶቻቸውና

ስለድመቴና	ስለድመቶቼና	እንደድመቴ	እንደድመቶቼ
ስለድመታችንና	ስለድመቶቻችንና	እንደድመታችን	እንደድመቶቻችን
ስለድመትህና	ስለድመቶችህና	እንደድመትህ	እንደድመቶችህ
ስለድመትሽና	ስለድመቶችሽና	እንደድመትሽ	እንደድመቶችሽ
ስለድመትዎና	ስለድመቶችዎና	እንደድመትዎ	እንደድመቶችዎ
ስለድመታችሁና	ስለድመቶቻችሁና	እንደድመታችሁ	እንደድመቶቻችሁ
ስለድመቱና	ስለድመቶቹና	እንደድመቱ	እንደድመቶቹ
ስለድመቷና	ስለድመቶቿና	እንደድመቷ	እንደድመቶቿ
ስለድመታቸውና	ስለድመቶቻቸውና	እንደድመታቸው	እንደድመቶቻቸው

እንደድመቴም	እንደድመቶቼም
እንደድመታችንም	እንደድመቶቻችንም
እንደድመትህም	እንደድመቶችህም
እንደድመትሽም	እንደድመቶችሽም
እንደድመትዎም	እንደድመቶችዎም
እንደድመታችሁም	እንደድመቶቻችሁም
እንደድመቱም	እንደድመቶቹም
እንደድመቷም	እንደድመቶቿም
እንደድመታቸውም	እንደድመቶቻቸውም

እንደድመቴና	እንደድመቶቼና
እንደድመታችንና	እንደድመቶቻችንና
እንደድመትህና	እንደድመቶችህና
እንደድመትሽና	እንደድመቶችሽና
እንደድመትዎና	እንደድመቶችዎና
እንደድመታችሁና	እንደድመቶቻችሁና
እንደድመቱና	እንደድመቶቹና
እንደድመቷና	እንደድመቶቿና
እንደድመታቸውና	እንደድመቶቻቸውና

Appendix C: The Derivatives of the Amharic Word ማጠብ

This appendix lists thousands of derivatives of the Amharic infinitive verb ማጠብ (to wash), without necessarily listing all possible derivatives, which I have estimated to number up to 50,000 (including those considered bad grammar). To save time and resources, I have shown square brackets where two or more of Amharic's subject personal pronouns and object personal pronouns need to be inserted. The numbers shown to the left of each derivative indicates the count within each group of derivatives by counting from the top left to the bottom right. For example, in the first group of derivatives below, there are a total of 32 derivatives, excluding 4 derivatives involving the 3rd person plural (3PP) pronoun (listed but not counted) and the 3rd person singular formal/polite (3PS-R) pronoun (not listed), which are spelled and pronounced the same as the derivatives of the 2nd person singular formal/polite (2PS-R) pronoun. However, the derivatives of the 3PP pronoun are counted in the second group of derivatives because it can take the same or a different object pronoun than the derivatives of the 2PS-R pronoun. In this group, there are a total of 189 derivatives. The count is based on at least 4 derivatives for each of the words listed. For example, አጠብሁ represents the following 8 derivatives:

	DERIVATIVE	SUBJECT PRONOUN	OBJECT PRONOUN
1	አጠብሁህ	1PS	2PSM
2	አጠብሁሽ	1PS	2PSF
3	አጠብኳችሁ	1PS	2PP
4	አጠብሁዎ	1PS	2PS-R
5	አጠብሁት	1PS	3PSM
6	አጠብኳት	1PS	3PSF
7	አጠብኳቸው	1PS	3PP
8	አጠብኳቸው	1PS	3PS-R

D1

1	አጠብሁ	9	ታጠብሁ	17	አሳጠብሁ	25	አስታጠብሁ
2	አጠብን	10	ታጠብን	18	አሳጠብን	26	አስታጠብን
3	አጠብህ	11	ታጠብህ	19	አሳጠብህ	27	አስታጠብህ
4	አጠብሽ	12	ታጠብሽ	20	አሳጠብች	28	አስታጠብሽ
5	አጠቡ	13	ታጠቡ	21	አሳጠቡ	29	አስታጠቡ
6	አጠባችሁ	14	ታጠባችሁ	22	አሳጠባችሁ	30	አስታጠባችሁ
7	አጠበ	15	ታጠበ	23	አሳጠበ	31	አስታጠበ
8	አጠበች	16	ታጠበች	24	አሳጠበች	32	አስታጠበች
-	አጠቡ	-	ታጠቡ	-	አሳጠቡ	-	አስታጠቡ

1-8	አጠብሁ[]	-	64-71	አሳጠብሁ[]	127-134 አስታጠብሁ[]
8-16	አጠብን[]	-	72-79	አሳጠብን[]	135-142 አስታጠብን[]
16-21	አጠብህ[]	-	80-84	አሳጠብህ[]	143-147 አስታጠብህ[]
21-26	አጠብሽ[]	-	85-89	አሳጠብች[]	148-152 አስታጠብሽ[]
16-31	አጠቡ[]	-	90-94	አሳጠቡ[]	153-157 አስታጠቡ[]
31-36	አጠባችሁ[]	-	95-99	አሳጠባችሁ[]	158-162 አስታጠባችሁ[]
36-45	አጠበ[]	-	100-108	አሳጠበ[]	163-171 አስታጠበ[]
45-54	አጠበች[]	-	109-117	አሳጠበች[]	172-180 አስታጠበች[]
54-63	አጠቡ[]	-	118-126	አሳጠቡ[]	181-189 አስታጠቡ[]

1	እያጠብሁ	9	እየታጠብሁ	17	እያሳጠብሁ	25	እያስታጠብሁ
2	እያጠብን	10	እየታጠብን	18	እያሳጠብን	26	እያስታጠብን
3	እያጠብህ	11	እየታጠብህ	19	እያሳጠብህ	27	እያስታጠብህ
4	እያጠብሽ	12	እየታጠብሽ	20	እያሳጠብሽ	28	እያስታጠብሽ
5	እያጠቡ	13	እየታጠቡ	21	እያሳጠቡ	29	እያስታጠቡ
6	እያጠባችሁ	14	እየታጠባችሁ	22	እያሳጠባችሁ	30	እያስታጠባችሁ
7	እያጠበ	15	እየታጠበ	23	እያሳጠበ	31	እያስታጠበ
8	እያጠበች	16	እየታጠበች	24	እያሳጠበች	32	እያስታጠበች
-	እያጠቡ	-	እየታጠቡ	-	እያሳጠቡ	-	እያስታጠቡ

1-8	እያጠብሁ[]	-	64-71	እያሳጠብሁ[]	127-134	እያስታጠብሁ[]
8-16	እያጠብን[]	-	72-79	እያሳጠብን[]	135-142	እያስታጠብን[]
16-21	እያጠብህ[]	-	80-84	እያሳጠብህ[]	143-147	እያስታጠብህ[]
21-26	እያጠብሽ[]	-	85-89	እያሳጠብሽ[]	148-152	እያስታጠብሽ[]
16-31	እያጠቡ[]	-	90-94	እያሳጠቡ[]	153-157	እያስታጠቡ[]
31-36	እያጠባችሁ[]	-	95-99	እያሳጠባችሁ[]	158-162	እያስታጠባችሁ[]
36-45	እያጠበ[]	-	100-108	እያሳጠበ[]	163-171	እያስታጠበ[]
45-54	እያጠበች[]	-	109-117	እያሳጠበች[]	172-180	እያስታጠበች[]
54-63	እያጠቡ[]	-	118-126	እያሳጠቡ[]	181-189	እያስታጠቡ[]

1	አላጠብሁ	9	አልታጠብሁ	17	አላሳጠብሁ	25	አላስታጠብሁ
2	አላጠብን	10	አልታጠብን	18	አላሳጠብን	26	አላስታጠብን
3	አላጠብህ	11	አልታጠብህ	19	አላሳጠብህ	27	አላስታጠብህ
4	አላጠብሽ	12	አልታጠብሽ	20	አላሳጠብሽ	28	አላስታጠብሽ
5	አላጠቡ	13	አልታጠቡ	21	አላሳጠቡ	29	አላስታጠቡ
6	አላጠባችሁ	14	አልታጠባችሁ	22	አላሳጠባችሁ	30	አላስታጠባችሁ
7	አላጠበ	15	አልታጠበ	23	አላሳጠበ	31	አላስታጠበ
8	አላጠበች	16	አልታጠበች	24	አላሳጠበች	32	አላስታጠበች
-	አላጠቡ	-	አልታጠቡ	-	አላሳጠቡ	-	አላስታጠቡ

1-8	አላጠብሁ[...]	-	64-71	አላሳጠብሁ[...]	127-134	አላስታጠብሁ[...]
8-16	አላጠብን[...]	-	72-79	አላሳጠብን[...]	135-142	አላስታጠብን[...]
16-21	አላጠብህ[...]	-	80-84	አላሳጠብህ[...]	143-147	አላስታጠብህ[...]
21-26	አላጠብሽ[...]	-	85-89	አላሳጠብሽ[...]	148-152	አላስታጠብሽ[...]
16-31	አላጠቡ[...]	-	90-94	አላሳጠቡ[...]	153-157	አላስታጠቡ[...]
31-36	አላጠባችሁ[...]	-	95-99	አላሳጠባችሁ[...]	158-162	አላስታጠባችሁ[...]
36-45	አላጠበ[...]	-	100-108	አላሳጠበ[...]	163-171	አላስታጠበ[...]
45-54	አላጠበች[...]	-	109-117	አላሳጠበች[...]	172-180	አላስታጠበች[...]
54-63	አላጠቡ[...]	-	118-126	አላሳጠቡ[...]	181-189	አላስታጠቡ[...]

1	አላጠብሁም	9	አልታጠብሁም	17	አላሳጠብሁም	25	አላስታጠብሁም
2	አላጠብንም	10	አልታጠብንም	18	አላሳጠብንም	26	አላስታጠብንም
3	አላጠብህም	11	አልታጠብህም	19	አላሳጠብህም	27	አላስታጠብህም
4	አላጠብሽም	12	አልታጠብሽም	20	አላሳጠብሽም	28	አላስታጠብሽም
5	አላጠቡም	13	አልታጠቡም	21	አላሳጠቡም	29	አላስታጠቡም
6	አላጠባችሁም	14	አልታጠባችሁም	22	አላሳጠባችሁም	30	አላስታጠባችሁም
7	አላጠበም	15	አልታጠበም	23	አላሳጠበም	31	አላስታጠበም
8	አላጠበችም	16	አልታጠበችም	24	አላሳጠበችም	32	አላስታጠበችም
-	አላጠቡም	-	አልታጠቡም	-	አላሳጠቡም	-	አላስታጠቡም

1-8	አላጠብሁ[...]ም		-	64-71	አላሳጠብሁ[...]ም	127-134	አላስታጠብሁ[...]ም
8-16	አላጠብን[...]ም		-	72-79	አላሳጠብን[...]ም	135-142	አላስታጠብን[...]ም
16-21	አላጠብህ[...]ም		-	80-84	አላሳጠብህ[...]ም	143-147	አላስታጠብህ[...]ም
21-26	አላጠብሽ[...]ም		-	85-89	አላሳጠብሽ[...]ም	148-152	አላስታጠብሽ[...]ም
16-31	አላጠቡ[...]ም		-	90-94	አላሳጠቡ[...]ም	153-157	አላስታጠቡ[...]ም
31-36	አላጠባችሁ[...]ም		-	95-99	አላሳጠባችሁ[...]ም	158-162	አላስታጠባችሁ[...]ም
36-45	አላጠበ[...]ም		-	100-108	አላሳጠበ[...]ም	163-171	አላስታጠበ[...]ም
45-54	አላጠበች[...]ም		-	109-117	አላሳጠበች[...]ም	172-180	አላስታጠበች[...]ም
54-63	አላጠቡ[...]ም		-	118-126	አላሳጠቡ[...]ም	181-189	አላስታጠቡ[...]ም

1-8	አጠብሁል[]	64-71	ታጠብሁል[]	127-134	አሳጠብሁል[]	190-197	አስታጠብሁል[]
8-16	አጠብንል[]	72-79	ታጠብንል[]	135-142	አሳጠብንል[]	198-205	አስታጠብንል[]
16-21	አጠብህል[]	80-84	ታጠብህል[]	143-147	አሳጠብህል[]	206-210	አስታጠብህል[]
21-26	አጠብሽል[]	85-89	ታጠብሽል[]	148-152	አሳጠብሽል[]	211-215	አስታጠብሽል[]
16-31	አጠቡል[]	90-94	ታጠቡል[]	153-157	አሳጠቡል[]	216-220	አስታጠቡል[]
31-36	አጠባችሁል[]	95-99	ታጠባችሁል[]	158-162	አሳጠባችሁል[]	221-225	አስታጠባችሁል[]
36-45	አጠበል[]	100-108	ታጠበል[]	163-171	አሳጠበል[]	226-234	አስታጠበል[]
45-54	አጠበችል[]	109-117	ታጠበችል[]	172-180	አሳጠበችል[]	234-243	አስታጠበችል[]
54-63	አጠቡል[]	118-126	ታጠቡል[]	181-189	አሳጠቡል[]	244-252	አስታጠቡል[]

1-8	እያጠብሁል[]	64-71	እየታጠብሁል[]	127-134	እያሳጠብሁል[]	190-197	እያስታጠብሁል[]
8-16	እያጠብንል[]	72-79	እየታጠብንል[]	135-142	እያሳጠብንል[]	198-205	እያስታጠብንል[]
16-21	እያጠብህል[]	80-84	እየታጠብህል[]	143-147	እያሳጠብህል[]	206-210	እያስታጠብህል[]
21-26	እያጠብሽል[]	85-89	እየታጠብሽል[]	148-152	እያሳጠብሽል[]	211-215	እያስታጠብሽል[]
16-31	እያጠቡል[]	90-94	እየታጠቡል[]	153-157	እያሳጠቡል[]	216-220	እያስታጠቡል[]
31-36	እያጠባችሁል[]	95-99	እየታጠባችሁል[]	158-162	እያሳጠባችሁል[]	221-225	እያስታጠባችሁል[]
36-45	እያጠበል[]	100-108	እየታጠበል[]	163-171	እያሳጠበል[]	226-234	እያስታጠበል[]
45-54	እያጠበችል[]	109-117	እየታጠበችል[]	172-180	እያሳጠበችል[]	234-243	እያስታጠበችል[]
54-63	እያጠቡል[]	118-126	እየታጠቡል[]	181-189	እያሳጠቡል[]	244-252	እያስታጠቡል[]

1-8	አላጡብሁል[]	64-71	አልታጡብሁል[]	127-134	አላሳጡብሁል[]	190-197	አላስታጡብሁል[]
8-16	አላጡብንል[]	72-79	አልታጡብንል[]	135-142	አላሳጡብንል[]	198-205	አላስታጡብንል[]
16-21	አላጡብህል[]	80-84	አልታጡብህል[]	143-147	አላሳጡብህል[]	206-210	አላስታጡብህል[]
21-26	አላጡብሽል[]	85-89	አልታጡብሽል[]	148-152	አላሳጡብችል[]	211-215	አላስታጡብሽል[]
16-31	አላጠቡል[]	90-94	አልታጠቡል[]	153-157	አላሳጠቡል[]	216-220	አላስታጠቡል[]
31-36	አላጠባችሁል[]	95-99	አልታጠባችሁል[]	158-162	አላሳጠባችሁል[]	221-225	አላስታጠባችሁል[]
36-45	አላጠበል[]	100-108	አልታጠበል[]	163-171	አላሳጠበል[]	226-234	አላስታጠበል[]
45-54	አላጠበችል[]	109-117	አልታጠበችል[]	172-180	አላሳጠበችል[]	234-243	አላስታጠበችል[]
54-63	አላጠቡል[]	118-126	አልታጠቡል[]	181-189	አላሳጠቡል[]	244-252	አላስታጠቡል[]

1-8	አላጡብሁል[]ም	64-71	አልታጡብሁል[]ም	127-134	አላሳጡብሁል[]ም	190-197	አላስታጡብሁል[]ም
8-16	አላጡብንል[]ም	72-79	አልታጡብንል[]ም	135-142	አላሳጡብንል[]ም	198-205	አላስታጡብንል[]ም
16-21	አላጡብህል[]ም	80-84	አልታጡብህል[]ም	143-147	አላሳጡብህል[]ም	206-210	አላስታጡብህል[]ም
21-26	አላጡብሽል[]ም	85-89	አልታጡብሽል[]ም	148-152	አላሳጡብችል[]ም	211-215	አላስታጡብሽል[]ም
16-31	አላጠቡል[]ም	90-94	አልታጠቡል[]ም	153-157	አላሳጠቡል[]ም	216-220	አላስታጠቡል[]ም
31-36	አላጠባችሁል[]ም	95-99	አልታጠባችሁል[]ም	158-162	አላሳጠባችሁል[]ም	221-225	አላስታጠባችሁል[]ም
36-45	አላጠበል[]ም	100-108	አልታጠበል[]ም	163-171	አላሳጠበል[]ም	226-234	አላስታጠበል[]ም
45-54	አላጠበችል[]ም	109-117	አልታጠበችል[]ም	172-180	አላሳጠበችል[]ም	234-243	አላስታጠበችል[]ም
54-63	አላጠቡል[]ም	118-126	አልታጠቡል[]ም	181-189	አላሳጠቡል[]ም	244-252	አላስታጠቡል[]ም

1-8	አጡብሁብ[]	64-71	ታጡብሁብ[]	127-134	አሳጡብሁብ[]	190-197	አስታጡብሁብ[]
8-16	አጡብንብ[]	72-79	ታጡብንብ[]	135-142	አሳጡብንብ[]	198-205	አስታጡብንብ[]
16-21	አጡብህብ[]	80-84	ታጡብህብ[]	143-147	አሳጡብህብ[]	206-210	አስታጡብህብ[]
21-26	አጡብሽብ[]	85-89	ታጡብሽብ[]	148-152	አሳጡብሽብ[]	211-215	አስታጡብሽብ[]
16-31	አጠቡብ[]	90-94	ታጠቡብ[]	153-157	አሳጠቡብ[]	216-220	አስታጠቡብ[]
31-36	አጠባችሁብ[]	95-99	ታጠባችሁብ[]	158-162	አሳጠባችሁብ[]	221-225	አስታጠባችሁብ[]
36-45	አጠበብ[]	100-108	ታጠበብ[]	163-171	አሳጠበብ[]	226-234	አስታጠበብ[]
45-54	አጠበችብ[]	109-117	ታጠበችብ[]	172-180	አሳጠበችብ[]	234-243	አስታጠበችብ[]
54-63	አጠቡብ[]	118-126	ታጠቡብ[]	181-189	አሳጠቡብ[]	244-252	አስታጠቡብ[]

1-8	እያጡብሁብ[]	64-71	እየታጡብሁብ[]	127-134	እያሳጡብሁብ[]	190-197	እያስታጡብሁብ[]
8-16	እያጡብንብ[]	72-79	እየታጡብንብ[]	135-142	እያሳጡብንብ[]	198-205	እያስታጡብንብ[]
16-21	እያጡብህብ[]	80-84	እየታጡብህብ[]	143-147	እያሳጡብህብ[]	206-210	እያስታጡብህብ[]
21-26	እያጡብሽብ[]	85-89	እየታጡብሽብ[]	148-152	እያሳጡብሽብ[]	211-215	እያስታጡብሽብ[]
16-31	እያጠቡብ[]	90-94	እየታጠቡብ[]	153-157	እያሳጠቡብ[]	216-220	እያስታጠቡብ[]
31-36	እያጠባችሁብ[]	95-99	እየታጠባችሁብ[]	158-162	እያሳጠባችሁብ[]	221-225	እያስታጠባችሁብ[]
36-45	እያጠበብ[]	100-108	እየታጠበብ[]	163-171	እያሳጠበብ[]	226-234	እያስታጠበብ[]
45-54	እያጠበችብ[]	109-117	እየታጠበችብ[]	172-180	እያሳጠበችብ[]	234-243	እያስታጠበችብ[]
54-63	እያጠቡብ[]	118-126	እየታጠቡብ[]	181-189	እያሳጠቡብ[]	244-252	እያስታጠቡብ[]

1-8	አላጠብሁብ[]	64-71	አልታጠብሁብ[]	127-134	አላሳጠብሁብ[]	190-197	አላስታጠብሁብ[]
8-16	አላጠብንብ[]	72-79	አልታጠብንብ[]	135-142	አላሳጠብንብ[]	198-205	አላስታጠብንብ[]
16-21	አላጠብህብ[]	80-84	አልታጠብህብ[]	143-147	አላሳጠብህብ[]	206-210	አላስታጠብህብ[]
21-26	አላጠብሽብ[]	85-89	አልታጠብሽብ[]	148-152	አላሳጠብሽብ[]	211-215	አላስታጠብሽብ[]
16-31	አላጠቡብ[]	90-94	አልታጠቡብ[]	153-157	አላሳጠቡብ[]	216-220	አላስታጠቡብ[]
31-36	አላጠባችሁብ[]	95-99	አልታጠባችሁብ[]	158-162	አላሳጠባችሁብ[]	221-225	አላስታጠባችሁብ[]
36-45	አላጠበብ[]	100-108	አልታጠበብ[]	163-171	አላሳጠበብ[]	226-234	አላስታጠበብ[]
45-54	አላጠበችብ[]	109-117	አልታጠበችብ[]	172-180	አላሳጠበችብ[]	234-243	አላስታጠበችብ[]
54-63	አላጠቡብ[]	118-126	አልታጠቡብ[]	181-189	አላሳጠቡብ[]	244-252	አላስታጠቡብ[]

1	ባጠብሁ	9	በታጠብሁ	17	ባሳጠብሁ	25	ባስታጠብሁ
2	ባጠብን	10	በታጠብን	18	ባሳጠብን	26	ባስታጠብን
3	ባጠብህ	11	በታጠብህ	19	ባሳጠብህ	27	ባስታጠብህ
4	ባጠብሽ	12	በታጠብሽ	20	ባሳጠብሽ	28	ባስታጠብሽ
5	ባጠቡ	13	በታጠቡ	21	ባሳጠቡ	29	ባስታጠቡ
6	ባጠባችሁ	14	በታጠባችሁ	22	ባሳጠባችሁ	30	ባስታጠባችሁ
7	ባጠበ	15	በታጠበ	23	ባሳጠበ	31	ባስታጠበ
8	ባጠበች	16	በታጠበች	24	ባሳጠበች	32	ባስታጠበች
	ባጠቡ	-	በታጠቡ	-	ባሳጠቡ	-	ባስታጠቡ

1-8	ባጠብሁ[]		-	64-71	ባሳጠብሁ[]	127-134	ባስታጠብሁ[]
8-16	ባጠብን[]		-	72-79	ባሳጠብን[]	135-142	ባስታጠብን[]
16-21	ባጠብህ[]		-	80-84	ባሳጠብህ[]	143-147	ባስታጠብህ[]
21-26	ባጠብሽ[]		-	85-89	ባሳጠብሽ[]	148-152	ባስታጠብሽ[]
16-31	ባጠቡ[]		-	90-94	ባሳጠቡ[]	153-157	ባስታጠቡ[]
31-36	ባጠባችሁ[]		-	95-99	ባሳጠባችሁ[]	158-162	ባስታጠባችሁ[]
36-45	ባጠበ[]		-	100-108	ባሳጠበ[]	163-171	ባስታጠበ[]
45-54	ባጠበች[]		-	109-117	ባሳጠበች[]	172-180	ባስታጠበች[]
54-63	ባጠቡ[]		-	118-126	ባሳጠቡ[]	181-189	ባስታጠቡ[]

1	ባላጠብሁ	9	ባልታጠብሁ	17	ባላሳጠብሁ	25	ባላስታጠብሁ
2	ባላጠብን	10	ባልታጠብን	18	ባላሳጠብን	26	ባላስታጠብን
3	ባላጠብህ	11	ባልታጠብህ	19	ባላሳጠብህ	27	ባላስታጠብህ
4	ባላጠብሽ	12	በልታጠብሽ	20	ባላሳጠብሽ	28	ባላስታጠብሽ
5	ባላጠቡ	13	በልታጠቡ	21	ባላሳጠቡ	29	ባላስታጠቡ
6	ባላጠባችሁ	14	በልታጠባችሁ	22	ባላሳጠባችሁ	30	ባላስታጠባችሁ
7	ባላጠበ	15	በልታጠበ	23	ባላሳጠበ	31	ባላስታጠበ
8	ባላጠበች	16	በልታጠበች	24	ባላሳጠበች	32	ባላስታጠበች
	ባላጠቡ	-	በልታጠቡ	-	ባላሳጠቡ	-	ባላስታጠቡ

1-8	ባላጣብሁ[]	-	64-71	ባላሳጣብሁ[]	127-134	ባላስታጣብሁ[]
8-16	ባላጣብን[]	-	72-79	ባላሳጣብን[]	135-142	ባላስታጣብን[]
16-21	ባላጣብህ[]	-	80-84	ባላሳጣብህ[]	143-147	ባላስታጣብህ[]
21-26	ባላጣብሽ[]	-	85-89	ባላሳጣብሽ[]	148-152	ባላስታጣብሽ[]
16-31	ባላጣቡ[]	-	90-94	ባላሳጣቡ[]	153-157	ባላስታጣቡ[]
31-36	ባላጣባችሁ[]	-	95-99	ባላሳጣባችሁ[]	158-162	ባላስታጣባችሁ[]
36-45	ባላጣበ[]	-	100-108	ባላሳጣበ[]	163-171	ባላስታጣበ[]
45-54	ባላጣበች[]	-	109-117	ባላሳጣበች[]	172-180	ባላስታጣበች[]
54-63	ባላጣቡ[]	-	118-126	ባላሳጣቡ[]	181-189	ባላስታጣቡ[]

1-8	ባጣብሁል[]	-	64-71	ባሳጣብሁል[]	127-134	ባስታጣብሁል[]
8-16	ባጣብንል[]	-	72-79	ባሳጣብንል[]	135-142	ባስታጣብንል[]
16-21	ባጣብህል[]	-	80-84	ባሳጣብህል[]	143-147	ባስታጣብህል[]
21-26	ባጣብሽል[]	-	85-89	ባሳጣብሽል[]	148-152	ባስታጣብሽል[]
16-31	ባጣቡል[]	-	90-94	ባሳጣቡል[]	153-157	ባስታጣቡል[]
31-36	ባጣባችሁል[]	-	95-99	ባሳጣባችሁል[]	158-162	ባስታጣባችሁል[]
36-45	ባጣበል[]	-	100-108	ባሳጣበል[]	163-171	ባስታጣበል[]
45-54	ባጣበችል[]	-	109-117	ባሳጣበችል[]	172-180	ባስታጣበችል[]
54-63	ባጣቡል[]	-	118-126	ባሳጣቡል[]	181-189	ባስታጣቡል[]

1-8	ባላጣብሁል[]	-	64-71	ባላሳጣብሁል[]	127-134	ባላስታጣብሁል[]
8-16	ባላጣብንል[]	-	72-79	ባላሳጣብንል[]	135-142	ባላስታጣብንል[]
16-21	ባላጣብህል[]	-	80-84	ባላሳጣብህል[]	143-147	ባላስታጣብህል[]
21-26	ባላጣብሽል[]	-	85-89	ባላሳጣብሽል[]	148-152	ባላስታጣብሽል[]
16-31	ባላጣቡል[]	-	90-94	ባላሳጣቡል[]	153-157	ባላስታጣቡል[]
31-36	ባላጣባችሁል[]	-	95-99	ባላሳጣባችሁል[]	158-162	ባላስታጣባችሁል[]
36-45	ባላጣበል[]	-	100-108	ባላሳጣበል[]	163-171	ባላስታጣበል[]
45-54	ባላጣበችል[]	-	109-117	ባላሳጣበችል[]	172-180	ባላስታጣበችል[]
54-63	ባላጣቡል[]	-	118-126	ባላሳጣቡል[]	181-189	ባላስታጣቡል[]

1-8	ባጣብሁብ[]	-	64-71	ባሳጣብሁብ[]	127-134	ባስታጣብሁል[]
8-16	ባጣብንብ[]	-	72-79	ባሳጣብንብ[]	135-142	ባስታጣብንል[]
16-21	ባጣብህብ[]	-	80-84	ባሳጣብህብ[]	143-147	ባስታጣብህል[]
21-26	ባጣብሽብ[]	-	85-89	ባሳጣብሽብ[]	148-152	ባስታጣብሽል[]
16-31	ባጣቡብ[]	-	90-94	ባሳጣቡብ[]	153-157	ባስታጣቡል[]
31-36	ባጣባችሁብ[]	-	95-99	ባሳጣባችሁብ[]	158-162	ባስታጣባችሁል[]
36-45	ባጣበብ[]	-	100-108	ባሳጣበብ[]	163-171	ባስታጣበል[]
45-54	ባጣበችብ[]	-	109-117	ባሳጣበችብ[]	172-180	ባስታጣበችል[]
54-63	ባጣቡብ[]	-	118-126	ባሳጣቡብ[]	181-189	ባስታጣቡል[]

ባላጠብሁብ[]		ባላሳጠብሁብ[]	
ባላጠብንብ[]		ባላሳጠብንብ[]	
ባላጠብህብ[]		ባላሳጠብህብ[]	
ባላጠብሽብ[]		ባላሳጠብሽብ[]	
ባላጠቡብ[]		ባላሳጠቡብ[]	
ባላጠባችሁብ[]		ባላሳጠባችሁብ[]	
ባላጠበብ[]		ባላሳጠበብ[]	-
ባላጠበችብ[]		ባላሳጠበችብ[]	
ባላጠቡብ[]		ባላሳጠቡብ[]	

እንዳጠብሁ	እንደታጠብሁ	እንዳሳጠብሁ	እንዳስታጠብሁ
እንዳጠብን	እንደታጠብን	እንዳሳጠብን	እንዳስታጠብን
እንዳጠብህ	እንደታጠብህ	እንዳሳጠብህ	እንዳስታጠብህ
እንዳጠብሽ	እንደታጠብሽ	እንዳሳጠብሽ	እንዳስታጠብሽ
እንዳጠቡ	እንደታጠቡ	እንዳሳጠቡ	እንዳስታጠቡ
እንዳጠባችሁ	እንደታጠባችሁ	እንዳሳጠባችሁ	እንዳስታጠባችሁ
እንዳጠበ	እንደታጠበ	እንዳሳጠበ	እንዳስታጠበ
እንዳጠበች	እንደታጠበች	እንዳሳጠበች	እንዳስታጠበች
እንዳጠቡ	እንደታጠቡ	እንዳሳጠቡ	እንዳስታጠቡ

እንዳላጠብሁ	እንዳልታጠብሁ	እንዳላሳጠብሁ	እንዳላስታጠብሁ
እንዳላጠብን	እንዳልታጠብን	እንዳላሳጠብን	እንዳላስታጠብን
እንዳላጠብህ	እንዳልታጠብህ	እንዳላሳጠብህ	እንዳላስታጠብህ
እንዳላጠብሽ	እንዳልታጠብሽ	እንዳላሳጠብሽ	እንዳላስታጠብሽ
እንዳላጠቡ	እንዳልታጠቡ	እንዳላሳጠቡ	እንዳላስታጠቡ
እንዳላጠባችሁ	እንዳልታጠባችሁ	እንዳላሳጠባችሁ	እንዳላስታጠባችሁ
እንዳላጠበ	እንዳልታጠበ	እንዳላሳጠበ	እንዳላስታጠበ
እንዳላጠበች	እንዳልታጠበች	እንዳላሳጠበች	እንዳላስታጠበች
እንዳላጠቡ	እንዳልታጠቡ	እንዳላሳጠቡ	እንዳላስታጠቡ

እንዳጠብሁል[]		እንዳሳጠብሁል[]	እንዳስታጠብሁል[]
እንዳጠብንል[]		እንዳሳጠብንል[]	እንዳስታጠብንል[]
እንዳጠብህል[]		እንዳሳጠብህል[]	እንዳስታጠብህል[]
እንዳጠብሽል[]		እንዳሳጠብሽል[]	
እንዳጠቡል[]		እንዳሳጠቡል[]	እንዳስታጠቡል[]
እንዳጠባችሁል[]		እንዳሳጠባችሁል[]	እንዳስታጠባችሁል[]
እንዳጠበል[]		እንዳሳጠበል[]	እንዳስታጠበል[]
እንዳጠበችል[]		እንዳሳጠበችል[]	እንዳስታጠበችል[]
እንዳጠቡል[]		እንዳሳጠቡል[]	እንዳስታጠቡል[]

	እንዳላጠብሁል[]		እንዳላሳጠብሁል[]	እንዳላስታጠብሁል[]
	እንዳላጠብንል[]		እንዳላሳጠብንል[]	እንዳላስታጠብንል[]
	እንዳላጠብህል[]		እንዳላሳጠብህል[]	እንዳላስታጠብህል[]
	እንዳላጠብሽል[]		እንዳላሳጠብሽል[]	
	እንዳላጠቡል[]		እንዳላሳጠቡል[]	እንዳላስታጠቡል[]
	እንዳላጠባችሁል[]		እንዳላሳጠባችሁል[]	እንዳላስታጠባችሁል[]
	እንዳላጠበል[]		እንዳላሳጠበል[]	እንዳላስታጠበል[]
	እንዳላጠበችል[]		እንዳላሳጠበችል[]	እንዳላስታጠበችል[]
	እንዳላጠቡል[]		እንዳላሳጠቡል[]	እንዳላስታጠቡል[]
	እንዳጠብሁብ[]		እንዳሳጠብሁብ[]	
	እንዳጠብንብ[]		እንዳሳጠብንብ[]	
	እንዳጠብህብ[]		እንዳሳጠብህብ[]	
	እንዳጠብሽብ[]		እንዳሳጠብሽብ[]	
	እንዳጠቡብ[]		እንዳሳጠቡብ[]	-
	እንዳጠባችሁብ[]		እንዳሳጠባችሁብ[]	
	እንዳጠበብ[]		እንዳሳጠበብ[]	
	እንዳጠበችብ[]		እንዳሳጠበችብ[]	
	እንዳጠቡብ[]		እንዳሳጠቡብ[]	
	እንዳላጠብሁብ[]		እንዳላሳጠብሁብ[]	
	እንዳላጠብንብ[]		እንዳላሳጠብንብ[]	
	እንዳላጠብህብ[]		እንዳላሳጠብህብ[]	
	እንዳላጠብሽብ[]		እንዳላሳጠብሽብ[]	
	እንዳላጠቡብ[]		እንዳላሳጠቡብ[]	
	እንዳላጠባችሁብ[]		እንዳላሳጠባችሁብ[]	
	እንዳላጠበብ[]		እንዳላሳጠበብ[]	
	እንዳላጠበችብ[]		እንዳላሳጠበችብ[]	
	እንዳላጠቡብ[]		እንዳላሳጠቡብ[]	
D2	አጥቤ	ታጥቤ	አሳጥቤ	አስታጥቤ
	አጥበን	ታጥበን	አሳጥበን	አስታጥበን
	አጥበህ	ታጥበህ	አሳጥበህ	አስታጥበህ
	አጥበሽ	ታጥበሽ	አሳጥበሽ	አስታጥበሽ
	አጥበው	ታጥበው	አሳጥበው	አስታጥበው*
	አጥባችሁ	ታጥባችሁ	አሳጥባችሁ	አስታጥባችሁ
	አጥቦ	ታጥቦ	አሳጥቦ	አስታጥቦ
	አጥባ	ታጥባ	አሳጥባ	አስታጥባ
	አጥበው	ታጥበው	አሳጥበው	አስታጥበው*

አጥቤያለሁ	ታጥቤያለሁ	አሳጥቤያለሁ	አስታጥቤያለሁ
አጥበናል	ታጥበናል	አሳጥበናል	አስታጥበናል
አጥበሃል	ታጥበሃል	አሳጥበሃል	አስታጥበሃል
አጥበሻል	ታጥበሻል	አሳጥበሻል	አስታጥበሻል
አጥበዋል	ታጥበዋል	አሳጥበዋል	አስታጥበዋል*
አጥባችኋል	ታጥባችኋል	አሳጥባችኋል	አስታጥባችኋል
አጥቧል	ታጥቧል	አሳጥቧል	አስታጥቧል
አጥባለች	ታጥባለች	አሳጥባለች	አስታጥባለች
አጥበዋል	ታጥበዋል	አሳጥበዋል	አስታጥበዋል*
አጥቤል[]	ታጥቤል[]	አሳጥቤል[]	አስታጥቤል[]
አጥበንል[]	ታጥበንል[]	አሳጥበንል[]	አስታጥበንል[]
አጥበህል[]	ታጥበህል[]	አሳጥበህል[]	አስታጥበህል[]
አጥበሽል[]	ታጥበሽል[]	አሳጥበሽል[]	አስታጥበሽል[]
አጥበውል[]	ታጥበውል[]	አሳጥበውል[]	አስታጥበውል[]*
አጥባችሁል[]	ታጥባችሁል[]	አሳጥባችሁል[]	አስታጥባችሁል[]
አጥቦል[]	ታጥቦል[]	አሳጥቦል[]	አስታጥቦል[]
አጥባል[]	ታጥባል[]	አሳጥባል[]	አስታጥባል[]
አጥበውል[]	ታጥበውል[]	አሳጥበውል[]	አስታጥበውል[]*
አጥቤል[]አለሁ	ታጥቤል[]አለሁ	አሳጥቤል[]አለሁ	አስታጥቤል[]አለሁ
አጥበንል[]አል	ታጥበንል[]አል	አሳጥበንል[]አል	አስታጥበንል[]አል
አጥበህል[]አል	ታጥበህል[]አል	አሳጥበህል[]አል	አስታጥበህል[]አል
አጥበሽል[]አል	ታጥበሽል[]አል	አሳጥበሽል[]አል	አስታጥበሽል[]አል
አጥበውል[]አል	ታጥበውል[]አል	አሳጥበውል[]አል	አስታጥበውል[]አል*
አጥባችሁል[]አል	ታጥባችሁል[]አል	አሳጥባችሁል[]አል	አስታጥባችሁል[]አል
አጥቦል[]አል	ታጥቦል[]አል	አሳጥቦል[]አል	አስታጥቦል[]አል
አጥባል[]አለች	ታጥባል[]አለች	አሳጥባል[]አለች	አስታጥባል[]አለች
አጥበውል[]አል	ታጥበውል[]አል	አሳጥበውል[]አል	አስታጥበውል[]አል*
አጥቤብ[]	ታጥቤብ[]	አሳጥቤብ[]	አስታጥቤብ[]
አጥበንብ[]	ታጥበንብ[]	አሳጥበንብ[]	አስታጥበንብ[]
አጥበህብ[]	ታጥበህብ[]	አሳጥበህብ[]	አስታጥበህብ[]
አጥበሽብ[]	ታጥበሽብ[]	አሳጥበሽብ[]	አስታጥበሽብ[]
አጥበውብ[]	ታጥበውብ[]	አሳጥበውብ[]	አስታጥበውብ[]*
አጥባችሁብ[]	ታጥባችሁብ[]	አሳጥባችሁብ[]	አስታጥባችሁብ[]
አጥቦብ[]	ታጥቦብ[]	አሳጥቦብ[]	አስታጥቦብ[]
አጥባብ[]	ታጥባብ[]	አሳጥባብ[]	አስታጥባብ[]
አጥበውብ[]	ታጥበውብ[]	አሳጥበውብ[]	አስታጥበውብ[]*

	አጥቤብ[]አለሁ	ታጥቤብ[]አለሁ	አሳጥቤብ[]አለሁ	አስታጥቤብ[]አለሁ
	አጥበንብ[]አል	ታጥበንብ[]አል	አሳጥበንብ[]አል	አስታጥበንብ[]አል
	አጥበህብ[]አል	ታጥበህብ[]አል	አሳጥበህብ[]አል	አስታጥበህብ[]አል
	አጥበሽብ[]አል	ታጥበሽብ[]አል	አሳጥበሽብ[]አል	አስታጥበሽብ[]አል
	አጥበውብ[]አል	ታጥበውብ[]አል	አሳጥበውብ[]አል	አስታጥበውብ[]አል*
	አጥባችሁብ[]አል	ታጥባችሁብ[]አል	አሳጥባችሁብ[]አል	አስታጥባችሁብ[]አል
	አጥቦብ[]አል	ታጥቦብ[]አል	አሳጥቦብ[]አል	አስታጥቦብ[]አል
	አጥባብ[]አለች	ታጥባብ[]አለች	አሳጥባብ[]አለች	አስታጥባብ[]አለች
	አጥበውብ[]አል	ታጥበውብ[]አል	አሳጥበውብ[]አል	አስታጥበውብ[]አል*
D3	አጥብ	እታጠብ	አሳጥብ	አስታጥብ
	እናጥብ	እንታጠብ	እናሳጥብ	እናስታጥብ
	ታጥብ	ትታጠብ	ታሳጥብ	ታስታጥብ**
	ታጥቢ	ትታጠቢ	ታሳጥቢ	ታስታጥቢ
	ያጥቡ	ይታጠቡ	ያሳጥቡ	ያስታጥቡ*
	ታጥቡ	ትታጠቡ	ታሳጥቡ	ታስታጥቡ
	ያጥብ	ይታጠብ	ያሳጥብ	ያስታጥብ
	ታጥብ	ትታጠብ	ታሳጥብ	ታስታጥብ**
	ያጥቡ	ይታጠቡ	ያሳጥቡ	ያስታጥቡ*
	አላጥብ	አልታጠብ	አላሳጥብ	አላስታጥብ
	አናጥብ	አንታጠብ	አናሳጥብ	አናስታጥብ
	አታጥብ	አትታጠብ	አታሳጥብ	አታስታጥብ**
	አታጥቢ	አትታጠቢ	አታሳጥቢ	አታስታጥቢ
	አያጥቡ	አይታጠቡ	አያሳጥቡ	አያስታጥቡ*
	አታጥቡ	አትታጠቡ	አታሳጥቡ	አታስታጥቡ
	አያጥብ	አይታጠብ	አያሳጥብ	አያስታጥብ
	አታጥብ	አትታጠብ	አታሳጥብ	አታስታጥብ**
	አያጥቡ	አይታጠቡ	አያሳጥቡ	አያስታጥቡ*
	አጥባለሁ	እታጠባለሁ	አሳጥባለሁ	አስታጥባለሁ
	እናጥባለን	እንታጠባለን	እናሳጥባለን	እናስታጥባለን
	ታጥባለህ	ትታጠባለህ	ታሳጥባለህ	ታስታጥባለህ
	ታጥቢያለሽ	ትታጠቢያለሽ	ታሳጥቢያለሽ	ታስታጥቢያለሽ
	ያጥባሉ	ይታጠባሉ	ያሳጥባሉ	ያስታጥባሉ*
	ታጥባላችሁ	ትታጠባላችሁ	ታሳጥባላችሁ	ታስታጥባላችሁ
	ያጥባል	ይታጠባል	ያሳጥባል	ያስታጥባል
	ታጥባለች	ትታጠባለች	ታሳጥባለች	ታስታጥባለች
	ያጥባሉ	ይታጠባሉ	ያሳጥባሉ	ያስታጥባሉ*

ላጥብ	ልታጠብ	ላሳጥብ	ላስታጥብ
ልናጥብ	ልንታጠብ	ልናሳጥብ	ልናስታጥብ
ልታጥብ	ልትታጠብ	ልታሳጥብ	ልታስታጥብ**
ልታጥቢ	ልትታጠቢ	ልታሳጥቢ	ልታስታጥቢ
ሊያጥቡ	ሊታጠቡ	ሊያሳጥቡ	ሊያስታጥቡ*
ልታጥቡ	ልትታጠቡ	ልታሳጥቡ	ልታስታጥቡ
ሊያጥብ	ሊታጠብ	ሊያሳጥብ	ሊያስታጥብ
ልታጥብ	ልትታጠብ	ልታሳጥብ	ልታስታጥብ**
ሊያጥቡ	ሊታጠቡ	ሊያሳጥቡ	ሊያስታጥቡ*
ሳጥብ	ስታጠብ	ሳሳጥብ	ሳስታጥብ
ስናጥብ	ስንታጠብ	ስናሳጥብ	ስናስታጥብ
ስታጥብ	ስትታጠብ	ስታሳጥብ	ስታስታጥብ**
ስታጥቢ	ስትታጠቢ	ስታሳጥቢ	ስታስታጥቢ
ሲያጥቡ	ሲታጠቡ	ሲያሳጥቡ	ሲያስታጥቡ*
ስታጥቡ	ስትታጠቡ	ስታሳጥቡ	ስታስታጥቡ
ሲያጥብ	ሲታጠብ	ሲያሳጥብ	ሲያስታጥብ
ስታጥብ	ስትታጠብ	ስታሳጥብ	ስታስታጥብ**
ሲያጥቡ	ሲታጠቡ	ሲያሳጥቡ	ሲያስታጥቡ*
ባጥብ	ብታጠብ	ባሳጥብ	ባስታጥብ
ብናጥብ	ብንታጠብ	ብናሳጥብ	ብናስታጥብ
ብታጥብ	ብትታጠብ	ብታሳጥብ	ብታስታጥብ**
ብታጥቢ	ብትታጠቢ	ብታሳጥቢ	ብታስታጥቢ
ቢያጥቡ	ቢታጠቡ	ቢያሳጥቡ	ቢያስታጥቡ*
ብታጥቡ	ብትታጠቡ	ብታሳጥቡ	ብታስታጥቡ
ቢያጥብ	ቢታጠብ	ቢያሳጥብ	ቢያስታጥብ
ብታጥብ	ብትታጠብ	ብታሳጥብ	ብታስታጥብ**
ቢያጥቡ	ቢታጠቡ	ቢያሳጥቡ	ቢያስታጥቡ*
እንዳጥብ	እንድታጠብ	እንዳሳጥብ	እንዳስታጥብ
እንድናጥብ	እንድንታጠብ	እንድናሳጥብ	እንድናስታጥብ
እንድታጥብ	እንድትታጠብ	እንድታሳጥብ	እንድታስታጥብ**
እንድታጥቢ	እንድትታጠቢ	እንድታሳጥቢ	እንድታስታጥቢ
እንዲያጥቡ	እንዲታጠቡ	እንዲያሳጥቡ	እንዲያስታጥቡ*
እንድታጥቡ	እንድትታጠቡ	እንድታሳጥቡ	እንድታስታጥቡ
እንዲያጥብ	እንዲታጠብ	እንዲያሳጥብ	እንዲያስታጥብ
እንድታጥብ	እንድትታጠብ	እንድታሳጥብ	እንድታስታጥብ**
እንዲያጥቡ	እንዲታጠቡ	እንዲያሳጥቡ	እንዲያስታጥቡ*

የማጥብ	የምታጠብ	የማሳጥብ	የማስታጥብ
የምናጥብ	የምንታጠብ	የምናሳጥብ	የምናስታጥብ
የምታጥብ	የምትታጠብ	የምታሳጥብ	የምታስታጥብ**
የምታጥቢ	የምትታጠቢ	የምታሳጥቢ	የምታስታጥቢ
የሚያጥቡ	የሚታጠቡ	የሚያሳጥቡ	የሚያስታጥቡ
የምታጥቡ	የምትታጠቡ	የምታሳጥቡ	የምታስታጥቡ
የሚያጥብ	የሚታጠብ	የሚያሳጥብ	የሚያስታጥብ
የምታጥብ	የምትታጠብ	የምታሳጥብ	የምታስታጥብ**
የሚያጥቡ	የሚታጠቡ	የሚያሳጥቡ	የሚያስታጥቡ*
አጥብል[]	እታጠብል[]	አሳጥብል[]	አስታጥብል[]
እናጥብል[]	እንታጠብል[]	እናሳጥብል[]	እናስታጥብል[]
ታጥብል[]	ትታጠብል[]	ታሳጥብል[]	ታስታጥብል[]**
ታጥቢል[]	ትታጠቢል[]	ታሳጥቢል[]	ታስታጥቢል[]
ያጥቡል[]	ይታጠቡል[]	ያሳጥቡል[]	ያስታጥቡል[]*
ታጥቡል[]	ትታጠቡል[]	ታሳጥቡል[]	ታስታጥቡል[]
ያጥብል[]	ይታጠብል[]	ያሳጥብል[]	ያስታጥብል[]
ታጥብል[]	ትታጠብል[]	ታሳጥብል[]	ታስታጥብል[]**
ያጥቡል[]	ይታጠቡል[]	ያሳጥቡል[]	ያስታጥቡል[]*
አጥብል[]ለሁ	እታጠብል[]ለሁ	አሳጥብል[]ለሁ	አስታጥብል[]ለሁ
እናጥብል[]ለን	እንታጠብል[]ለን	እናሳጥብል[]ለን	እናስታጥብል[]ለን
ታጥብል[]ለህ	ትታጠብል[]ለህ	ታሳጥብል[]ለህ	ታስታጥብል[]ለህ
ታጥቢል[]ለሽ	ትታጠቢል[]ለሽ	ታሳጥቢል[]ለሽ	ታስታጥቢል[]ለሽ
ያጥቡል[]ል	ይታጠቡል[]ል	ያሳጥቡል[]ል	ያስታጥቡል[]ል*
ታጥቡል[]ላችሁ	ትታጠቡል[]ላችሁ	ታሳጥቡል[]ላችሁ	ታስታጥቡል[]ላችሁ
ያጥብል[]ል	ይታጠብል[]ል	ያሳጥብል[]ል	ያስታጥብል[]ል
ታጥብል[]ለች	ትታጠብል[]ለች	ታሳጥብል[]ለች	ታስታጥብል[]ለች
ያጥቡል[]ል	ይታጠቡል[]ል	ያሳጥቡል[]ል	ያስታጥቡል[]ል*
አጥብብ[]	እታጠብብ[]	አሳጥብብ[]	አስታጥብብ[]
እናጥብብ[]	እንታጠብብ[]	እናሳጥብብ[]	እናስታጥብብ[]
ታጥብብ[]	ትታጠብብ[]	ታሳጥብብ[]	ታስታጥብብ[]**
ታጥቢብ[]	ትታጠቢብ[]	ታሳጥቢብ[]	ታስታጥቢብ[]
ያጥቡብ[]	ይታጠቡብ[]	ያሳጥቡብ[]	ያስታጥቡብ[]*
ታጥቡብ[]	ትታጠቡብ[]	ታሳጥቡብ[]	ታስታጥቡብ[]
ያጥብብ[]	ይታጠብብ[]	ያሳጥብብ[]	ያስታጥብብ[]
ታጥብብ[]	ትታጠብብ[]	ታሳጥብብ[]	ታስታጥብብ[]**
ያጥቡብ[]	ይታጠቡብ[]	ያሳጥቡብ[]	ያስታጥቡብ[]*

አጥብብ[]ለሁ	እታጠብብ[]ለሁ	አሳጥብብ[]ለሁ	አስታጥብብ[]ለሁ
እናጥብብ[]ለን	እንታጠብብ[]ለን	እናሳጥብብ[]ለን	እናስታጥብብ[]ለን
ታጥብብ[]ለህ	ትታጠብብ[]ለህ	ታሳጥብብ[]ለህ	ታስታጥብብ[]ለህ
ታጥቢብ[]ለሽ	ትታጠቢብ[]ለሽ	ታሳጥቢብ[]ለሽ	ታስታጥቢብ[]ለሽ
ያጥቡብ[]ል	ይታጠቡብ[]ል	ያሳጥቡብ[]ል	ያስታጥቡብ[]ል*
ታጥቡብ[]ላችሁ	ትታጠቡብ[]ላችሁ	ታሳጥቡብ[]ላችሁ	ታስታጥቡብ[]ላችሁ
ያጥብብ[]ል	ይታጠብብ[]ል	ያሳጥብብ[]ል	ያስታጥብብ[]ል
ታጥብብ[]ለች	ትታጠብብ[]ለች	ታሳጥብብ[]ለች	ታስታጥብብ[]ለች
ያጥቡብ[]ል	ይታጠቡብ[]ል	ያሳጥቡብ[]ል	ያስታጥቡብ[]ል*

የማጥብል[]	የምታጠብል[]	የማሳጥብል[]	የማስታጥብል[]
የምናጥብል[]	የምንታጠብል[]	የምናሳጥብል[]	የምናስታጥብል[]
የምታጥብል[]	የምትታጠብል[]	የምታሳጥብል[]	የምታስታጥብል[]**
የምታጥቢል[]	የምትታጠቢል[]	የምታሳጥቢል[]	የምታስታጥቢል[]
የሚያጥቡል[]	የሚታጠቡል[]	የሚያሳጥቡል[]	የሚያስታጥቡል[]*
የምታጥቡል[]	የምትታጠቡል[]	የምታሳጥቡል[]	የምታስታጥቡል[]
የሚያጥብል[]	የሚታጠብል[]	የሚያሳጥብል[]	የሚያስታጥብል[]
የምታጥብል[]	የምትታጠብል[]	የምታሳጥብል[]	የምታስታጥብል[]**
የሚያጥቡል[]	የሚታጠቡል[]	የሚያሳጥቡል[]	የሚያስታጥቡል[]*

የማጥብብ[]	የምታጠብብ[]	የማሳጥብብ[]	የማስታጥብብ[]
የምናጥብብ[]	የምንታጠብብ[]	የምናሳጥብብ[]	የምናስታጥብብ[]
የምታጥብብ[]	የምትታጠብብ[]	የምታሳጥብብ[]	የምታስታጥብብ[]**
የምታጥቢብ[]	የምትታጠቢብ[]	የምታሳጥቢብ[]	የምታስታጥቢብ[]
የሚያጥቡብ[]	የሚታጠቡብ[]	የሚያሳጥቡብ[]	የሚያስታጥቡብ[]*
የምታጥቡብ[]	የምትታጠቡብ[]	የምታሳጥቡብ[]	የምታስታጥቡብ[]
የሚያጥብብ[]	የሚታጠብብ[]	የሚያሳጥብብ[]	የሚያስታጥብብ[]
የምታጥብብ[]	የምትታጠብብ[]	የምታሳጥብ ብ[]	የምታስታጥብብ[]**
የሚያጥቡብ[]	የሚታጠቡ ብ[]	የሚያሳጥቡብ[]	የሚያስታጥቡብ[]*

እንዳጥብል[]	እንድታጠብል[]	እንዳሳጥብል[]	እንዳስታጥብል[]
እንድናጥብል[]	እንድንታጠብል[]	እንድናሳጥብል[]	እንድናስታጥብል[]
እንድታጥብል[]	እንድትታጠብል[]	እንድታሳጥብል[]	እንድታስታጥብል[]**
እንድታጥቢል[]	እንድትታጠቢል[]	እንድታሳጥቢል[]	እንድታስታጥቢል[]
እንዲያጥቡል[]	እንዲታጠቡል[]	እንዲያሳጥቡል[]	እንዲያስታጥቡል[]*
እንድታጥቡል[]	እንድትታጠቡል[]	እንድታሳጥቡል[]	እንድታስታጥቡል[]
እንዲያጥብል[]	እንዲታጠብል[]	እንዲያሳጥብል[]	እንዲያስታጥብል[]
እንድታጥብል[]	እንድትታጠብል[]	እንድታሳጥብል[]	እንድታስታጥብል[]**
እንዲያጥቡል[]	እንዲታጠቡል[]	እንዲያሳጥቡል[]	እንዲያስታጥቡል[]*

እንዳጥብብ[]	እንድታጠብብ[]	እንዳሳጥብብ[]	እንዳስታጥብብ[]
እንድናጥብብ[]	እንድንታጠብብ[]	እንድናሳጥብብ[]	እንድናስታጥብብ[]
እንድታጥብብ[]	እንድትታጠብብ[]	እንድታሳጥብብ[]	እንድታስታጥብብ[]**
እንድታጥቢብ[]	እንድትታጠቢብ[]	እንድታሳጥቢብ[]	እንድታስታጥቢብ[]
እንዲያጥቡብ[]	እንዲታጠቡብ[]	እንዲያሳጥቡብ[]	እንዲያስታጥቡብ[]*
እንድታጥቡብ[]	እንድትታጠቡብ[]	እንድታሳጥቡብ[]	እንድታስታጥቡብ[]
እንዲያጥብብ[]	እንዲታጠብብ[]	እንዲያሳጥብብ[]	እንዲያስታጥብብ[]
እንድታጥብብ[]	እንድትታጠብብ[]	እንድታሳጥብብ[]	እንድታስታጥብብ[]**
እንዲያጥቡብ[]	እንዲታጠቡብ[]	እንዲያሳጥቡብ[]	እንዲያስታጥቡብ[]*

ባጥብል[]	ብታጠብል[]	ባሳጥብል[]	ባስታጥብል[]
ብናጥብል[]	ብንታጠብል[]	ብናሳጥብል[]	ብናስታጥብል[]
ብታጥብል[]	ብትታጠብል[]	ብታሳጥብል[]	ብታስታጥብል[]**
ብታጥቢል[]	ብትታጠቢል[]	ብታሳጥቢል[]	ብታስታጥቢል[]
ቢያጥቡል[]	ቢታጠቡል[]	ቢያሳጥቡል[]	ቢያስታጥቡል[]*
ብታጥቡል[]	ብትታጠቡል[]	ብታሳጥቡል[]	ብታስታጥቡል[]
ቢያጥብል[]	ቢታጠብል[]	ቢያሳጥብል[]	ቢያስታጥብል[]
ብታጥብል[]	ብትታጠብል[]	ብታሳጥብል[]	ብታስታጥብል[]**
ቢያጥቡል[]	ቢታጠቡል[]	ቢያሳጥቡል[]	ቢያስታጥቡል[]*

ባጥብብ[]	ብታጠብብ[]	ባሳጥብብ[]	ባስታጥብብ[]
ብናጥብብ[]	ብንታጠብብ[]	ብናሳጥብብ[]	ብናስታጥብብ[]
ብታጥብብ[]	ብትታጠብብ[]	ብታሳጥብብ[]	ብታስታጥብብ[]**
ብታጥቢብ[]	ብትታጠቢብ[]	ብታሳጥቢብ[]	ብታስታጥቢብ[]
ቢያጥቡብ[]	ቢታጠቡብ[]	ቢያሳጥቡብ[]	ቢያስታጥቡብ[]*
ብታጥቡብ[]	ብትታጠቡብ[]	ብታሳጥቡብ[]	ብታስታጥቡብ[]
ቢያጥብብ[]	ቢታጠብብ[]	ቢያሳጥብብ[]	ቢያስታጥብብ[]
ብታጥብብ[]	ብትታጠብብ[]	ብታሳጥብብ[]	ብታስታጥብብ[]**
ቢያጥቡብ[]	ቢታጠቡብ[]	ቢያሳጥቡብ[]	ቢያስታጥቡብ[]*

ሳጥብል[]	ስታጠብል[]	ሳሳጥብል[]	ሳስታጥብል[]
ስናጥብል[]	ስንታጠብል[]	ስናሳጥብል[]	ስናስታጥብል[]
ስታጥብል[]	ስትታጠብል[]	ስታሳጥብል[]	ስታስታጥብል[]**
ስታጥቢል[]	ስትታጠቢል[]	ስታሳጥቢል[]	ስታስታጥቢል[]
ሲያጥቡል[]	ሲታጠቡል[]	ሲያሳጥቡል[]	ሲያስታጥቡል[]*
ስታጥቡል[]	ስትታጠቡል[]	ስታሳጥቡል[]	ስታስታጥቡል[]
ሲያጥብል[]	ሲታጠብል[]	ሲያሳጥብል[]	ሲያስታጥብል[]
ስታጥብል[]	ስትታጠብል[]	ስታሳጥብል[]	ስታስታጥብል[]**
ሲያጥቡል[]	ሲታጠቡል[]	ሲያሳጥቡል[]	ሲያስታጥቡል[]*

ሳጥብብ[]	ስታጠብብ[]	ሳሳጥብብ[]	ሳስታጥብብ[]
ስናጥብብ[]	ስንታጠብብ[]	ስናሳጥብብ[]	ስናስታጥብብ[]
ስታጥብብ[]	ስትታጠብብ[]	ስታሳጥብብ[]	ስታስታጥብብ[]**
ስታጥቢብ[]	ስትታጠቢብ[]	ስታሳጥቢብ[]	ስታስታጥቢብ[]
ሲያጥቡብ[]	ሲታጠቡብ[]	ሲያሳጥቡብ[]	ሲያስታጥቡብ[]*
ስታጥቡብ[]	ስትታጠቡብ[]	ስታሳጥቡብ[]	ስታስታጥቡብ[]
ሲያጥብብ[]	ሲታጠብብ[]	ሲያሳጥብብ[]	ሲያስታጥብብ[]
ስታጥብብ[]	ስትታጠብብ[]	ስታሳጥብብ[]	ስታስታጥብብ[]**
ሲያጥቡብ[]	ሲታጠቡብ[]	ሲያሳጥቡብ[]	ሲያስታጥቡብ[]*

ላጥብል[]	ልታጠብል[]	ላሳጥብል[]	ላስታጥብል[]
ልናጥብል[]	ልንታጠብል[]	ልናሳጥብል[]	ልናስታጥብል[]
ልታጥብል[]	ልትታጠብል[]	ልታሳጥብል[]	ልታስታጥብል[]**
ልታጥቢል[]	ልትታጠቢል[]	ልታሳጥቢል[]	ልታስታጥቢል[]
ሊያጥቡል[]	ሊታጠቡል[]	ሊያሳጥቡል[]	ሊያስታጥቡል[]*
ልታጥቡል[]	ልትታጠቡል[]	ልታሳጥቡል[]	ልታስታጥቡል[]
ሊያጥብል[]	ሊታጠብል[]	ሊያሳጥብል[]	ሊያስታጥብል[]
ልታጥብል[]	ልትታጠብል[]	ልታሳጥብል[]	ልታስታጥብል[]**
ሊያጥቡል[]	ሊታጠቡል[]	ሊያሳጥቡል[]	ሊያስታጥቡል[]*

ላጥብብ[]	ልታጠብብ[]	ላሳጥብብ[]	ላስታጥብብ[]
ልናጥብብ[]	ልንታጠብብ[]	ልናሳጥብብ[]	ልናስታጥብብ[]
ልታጥብብ[]	ልትታጠብብ[]	ልታሳጥብብ[]	ልታስታጥብብ[]**
ልታጥቢብ[]	ልትታጠቢብ[]	ልታሳጥቢብ[]	ልታስታጥቢብ[]
ሊያጥቡብ[]	ሊታጠቡብ[]	ሊያሳጥቡብ[]	ሊያስታጥቡብ[]*
ልታጥቡብ[]	ልትታጠቡብ[]	ልታሳጥቡብ[]	ልታስታጥቡብ[]
ሊያጥብብ[]	ሊታጠብብ[]	ሊያሳጥብብ[]	ሊያስታጥብብ[]
ልታጥብብ[]	ልትታጠብብ[]	ልታሳጥብብ[]	ልታስታጥብብ[]**
ሊያጥቡብ[]	ሊታጠቡብ[]	ሊያሳጥቡብ[]	ሊያስታጥቡብ[]*

ላላጥብ	ላልታጠብ	ላላሳጥብ	ላላስታጥብ
ላናጥብ	ላንታጠብ	ላናሳጥብ	ላናስታጥብ
ላታጥብ	ላትታጠብ	ላታሳጥብ	ላታስታጥብ**
ላታጥቢ	ላትታጠቢ	ላታሳጥቢ	ላታስታጥቢ
ላያጥቡ	ላይታጠቡ	ላያሳጥቡ	ላያስታጥቡ*
ላታጥቡ	ላትታጠቡ	ላታሳጥቡ	ላታስታጥቡ
ላያጥብ	ላይታጠብ	ላያሳጥብ	ላያስታጥብ
ላታጥብ	ላትታጠብ	ላታሳጥብ	ላታስታጥብ**
ላያጥቡ	ላይታጠቡ	ላያሳጥቡ	ላያስታጥቡ*

ሳላጥብ	ሳልታጠብ	ሳላሳጥብ	ሳላስታጥብ
ሳናጥብ	ሳንታጠብ	ሳናሳጥብ	ሳናስታጥብ
ሳታጥብ	ሳትታጠብ	ሳታሳጥብ	ሳታስታጥብ**
ሳታጥቢ	ሳትታጠቢ	ሳታሳጥቢ	ሳታስታጥቢ
ሳያጥቡ	ሳይታጠቡ	ሳያሳጥቡ	ሳያስታጥቡ*
ሳታጥቡ	ሳትታጠቡ	ሳታሳጥቡ	ሳታስታጥቡ
ሳያጥብ	ሳይታጠብ	ሳያሳጥብ	ሳያስታጥብ
ሳታጥብ	ሳትታጠብ	ሳታሳጥብ	ሳታስታጥብ**
ሳያጥቡ	ሳይታጠቡ	ሳያሳጥቡ	ሳያስታጥቡ*

ባላጥብ	ባልታጠብ	ባላሳጥብ	ሳላስታጥብ
ባናጥብ	ባንታጠብ	ባናሳጥብ	ሳናስታጥብ
ባታጥብ	ባትታጠብ	ባታሳጥብ	ሳታስታጥብ**
ባታጥቢ	ባትታጠቢ	ባታሳጥቢ	ሳታስታጥቢ
ባያጥቡ	ባይታጠቡ	ባያሳጥቡ	ሳያስታጥቡ*
ባታጥቡ	ባትታጠቡ	ባታሳጥቡ	ሳታስታጥቡ
ባያጥብ	ባይታጠብ	ባያሳጥብ	ሳያስታጥብ
ባታጥብ	ባትታጠብ	ባታሳጥብ	ሳታስታጥብ**
ባያጥቡ	ባይታጠቡ	ባያሳጥቡ	ሳያስታጥቡ*

እንዳላጥብ	እንዳልታጠብ	እንዳላሳጥብ	እንዳላስታጥብ
እንዳናጥብ	እንዳንታጠብ	እንዳናሳጥብ	እንዳናስታጥብ
እንዳታጥብ	እንዳትታጠብ	እንዳታሳጥብ	እንዳታስታጥብ**
እንዳታጥቢ	እንዳትታጠቢ	እንዳታሳጥቢ	እንዳታስታጥቢ
እንዳያጥቡ	እንዳይታጠቡ	እንዳያሳጥቡ	እንዳያስታጥቡ*
እንዳታጥቡ	እንዳትታጠቡ	እንዳታሳጥቡ	እንዳታስታጥቡ
እንዳያጥብ	እንዳይታጠብ	እንዳያሳጥብ	እንዳያስታጥብ
እንዳታጥብ	እንዳትታጠብ	እንዳታሳጥብ	እንዳታስታጥብ**
እንዳያጥቡ	እንዳይታጠቡ	እንዳያሳጥቡ	እንዳያስታጥቡ*

የማላጥብ	የማልታጠብ	የማላሳጥብ	የማላስታጥብ
የማናጥብ	የማንታጠብ	የማናሳጥብ	የማናስታጥብ
የማታጥብ	የማትታጠብ	የማታሳጥብ	የማታስታጥብ**
የማታጥቢ	የማትታጠቢ	የማታሳጥቢ	የማታስታጥቢ
የማያጥቡ	የማይታጠቡ	የማያሳጥቡ	የማያስታጥቡ*
የማታጥቡ	የማትታጠቡ	የማታሳጥቡ	የማታስታጥቡ
የማያጥብ	የማይታጠብ	የማያሳጥብ	የማያስታጥብ
የማታጥብ	የማትታጠብ	የማታሳጥብ	የማታስታጥብ**
የማያጥቡ	የማይታጠቡ	የማያሳጥቡ	የማያስታጥቡ*

አላጥብል[]	አልታጠብል[]	አላሳጥብል[]	አላስታጥብል[]
አናጥብል[]	አንታጠብል[]	አናሳጥብል[]	አናስታጥብል[]
አታጥብል[]	አትታጠብል[]	አታሳጥብል[]	አታስታጥብል[]**
አታጥቢል[]	አትታጠቢል[]	አታሳጥቢል[]	አታስታጥቢል[]
አያጥቡል[]	አይታጠቡል[]	አያሳጥቡል[]	አያስታጥቡል[]*
አታጥቡል[]	አትታጠቡል[]	አታሳጥቡል[]	አታስታጥቡል[]
አያጥብል[]	አይታጠብል[]	አያሳጥብል[]	አያስታጥብል[]
አታጥብል[]	አትታጠብል[]	አታሳጥብል[]	አታስታጥብል[]**
አያጥቡል[]	አይታጠቡል[]	አያሳጥቡል[]	አያስታጥቡል[]*
አላጥብብ[]	አልታጠብብ[]	አላሳጥብብ[]	አላስታጥብብ[]
አናጥብብ[]	አንታጠብብ[]	አናሳጥብብ[]	አናስታጥብብ[]
አታጥብብ[]	አትታጠብብ[]	አታሳጥብብ[]	አታስታጥብብ[]**
አታጥቢብ[]	አትታጠቢብ[]	አታሳጥቢብ[]	አታስታጥቢብ[]
አያጥቡብ[]	አይታጠቡብ[]	አያሳጥቡብ[]	አያስታጥቡብ[]*
አታጥቡብ[]	አትታጠቡብ[]	አታሳጥቡብ[]	አታስታጥቡብ[]
አያጥብብ[]	አይታጠብብ[]	አያሳጥብብ[]	አያስታጥብብ[]
አታጥብብ[]	አትታጠብብ[]	አታሳጥብብ[]	አታስታጥብብ[]**
አያጥቡብ[]	አይታጠቡብ[]	አያሳጥቡብ[]	አያስታጥቡብ[]*
የማላጥብል[]	የማልታጠብል[]	የማላሳጥብል[]	የማላስታጥብል[]
የማናጥብል[]	የማንታጠብል[]	የማናሳጥብል[]	የማናስታጥብል[]
የማታጥብል[]	የማትታጠብል[]	የማታሳጥብል[]	የማታስታጥብል[]**
የማታጥቢል[]	የማትታጠቢል[]	የማታሳጥቢል[]	የማታስታጥቢል[]
የማያጥቡል[]	የማይታጠቡል[]	የማያሳጥቡል[]	የማያስታጥቡል[]*
የማታጥቡል[]	የማትታጠቡል[]	የማታሳጥቡል[]	የማታስታጥቡል[]
የማያጥብል[]	የማይታጠብል[]	የማያሳጥብል[]	የማያስታጥብል[]
የማታጥብል[]	የማትታጠብል[]	የማታሳጥብል[]	የማታስታጥብል[]**
የማያጥቡል[]	የማይታጠቡል[]	የማያሳጥቡል[]	የማያስታጥቡል[]*
የማላጥብብ[]	የማልታጠብብ[]	የማላሳጥብብ[]	የማላስታጥብብ[]
የማናጥብብ[]	የማንታጠብብ[]	የማናሳጥብብ[]	የማናስታጥብብ[]
የማታጥብብ[]	የማትታጠብብ[]	የማታሳጥብብ[]	የማታስታጥብብ[]**
የማታጥቢብ[]	የማትታጠቢብ[]	የማታሳጥቢብ[]	የማታስታጥቢብ[]
የማያጥቡብ[]	የማይታጠቡብ[]	የማያሳጥቡብ[]	የማያስታጥቡብ[]*
የማታጥቡብ[]	የማትታጠቡብ[]	የማታሳጥቡብ[]	የማታስታጥቡብ[]
የማያጥብብ[]	የማይታጠብብ[]	የማያሳጥብብ[]	የማያስታጥብብ[]
የማታጥብብ[]	የማትታጠብብ[]	የማታሳጥብብ[]	የማታስታጥብብ[]**
የማያጥቡብ[]	የማይታጠቡብ[]	የማያሳጥቡብ[]	የማያስታጥቡብ[]*

እንዳላጥብል[]	እንዳልታጠብል[]	እንዳላሳጥብል[]	እንዳላስታጥብል[]
እንዳናጥብል[]	እንዳንታጠብል[]	እንዳናሳጥብል[]	እንዳናስታጥብል[]
እንዳታጥብል[]	እንዳትታጠብል[]	እንዳታሳጥብል[]	እንዳታስታጥብል[]**
እንዳታጥቢል[]	እንዳትታጠቢል[]	እንዳታሳጥቢል[]	እንዳታስታጥቢል[]
እንዳያጥቡል[]	እንዳይታጠቡል[]	እንዳያሳጥቡል[]	እንዳያስታጥቡል[]*
እንዳታጥቡል[]	እንዳትታጠቡል[]	እንዳታሳጥቡል[]	እንዳታስታጥቡል[]
እንዳያጥብል[]	እንዳይታጠብል[]	እንዳያሳጥብል[]	እንዳያስታጥብል[]
እንዳታጥብል[]	እንዳትታጠብል[]	እንዳታሳጥብል[]	እንዳታስታጥብል[]**
እንዳያጥቡል[]	እንዳይታጠቡል[]	እንዳያሳጥቡል[]	እንዳያስታጥቡል[]*

እንዳላጥብብ[]	እንዳልታጠብብ[]	እንዳላሳጥብብ[]	እንዳላስታጥብብ[]
እንዳናጥብብ[]	እንዳንታጠብብ[]	እንዳናሳጥብብ[]	እንዳናስታጥብብ[]
እንዳታጥብብ[]	እንዳትታጠብብ[]	እንዳታሳጥብብ[]	እንዳታስታጥብብ[]**
እንዳታጥቢብ[]	እንዳትታጠቢብ[]	እንዳታሳጥቢብ[]	እንዳታስታጥቢብ[]
እንዳያጥቡብ[]	እንዳይታጠቡብ[]	እንዳያሳጥቡብ[]	እንዳያስታጥቡብ[]*
እንዳታጥቡብ[]	እንዳትታጠቡብ[]	እንዳታሳጥቡብ[]	እንዳታስታጥቡብ[]
እንዳያጥብብ[]	እንዳይታጠብብ[]	እንዳያሳጥብብ[]	እንዳያስታጥብብ[]
እንዳታጥብብ[]	እንዳትታጠብብ[]	እንዳታሳጥብብ[]	እንዳታስታጥብብ[]**
እንዳያጥቡብ[]	እንዳይታጠቡብ[]	እንዳያሳጥቡብ[]	እንዳያስታጥቡብ[]*

ባላጥብል[]	ባልታጠብል[]	ባላሳጥብል[]	ባላስታጥብል[]
ባናጥብል[]	ባንታጠብል[]	ባናሳጥብል[]	ባናስታጥብል[]
ባታጥብል[]	ባትታጠብል[]	ባታሳጥብል[]	ባታስታጥብል[]**
ባታጥቢል[]	ባትታጠቢል[]	ባታሳጥቢል[]	ባታስታጥቢል[]
ባያጥቡል[]	ባይታጠቡል[]	ባያሳጥቡል[]	ባያስታጥቡል[]*
ባታጥቡል[]	ባትታጠቡል[]	ባታሳጥቡል[]	ባታስታጥቡል[]
ባያጥብል[]	ባይታጠብል[]	ባያሳጥብል[]	ባያስታጥብል[]
ባታጥብል[]	ባትታጠብል[]	ባታሳጥብል[]	ባታስታጥብል[]**
ባያጥቡል[]	ባይታጠቡል[]	ባያሳጥቡል[]	ባያስታጥቡል[]*

ባላጥብብ[]	ባልታጠብብ[]	ባላሳጥብብ[]	ባላስታጥብብ[]
ባናጥብብ[]	ባንታጠብብ[]	ባናሳጥብብ[]	ባናስታጥብብ[]
ባታጥብብ[]	ባትታጠብብ[]	ባታሳጥብብ[]	ባታስታጥብብ[]**
ባታጥቢብ[]	ባትታጠቢብ[]	ባታሳጥቢብ[]	ባታስታጥቢብ[]
ባያጥቡብ[]	ባይታጠቡብ[]	ባያሳጥቡብ[]	ባያስታጥቡብ[]*
ባታጥቡብ[]	ባትታጠቡብ[]	ባታሳጥቡብ[]	ባታስታጥቡብ[]
ባያጥብብ[]	ባይታጠብብ[]	ባያሳጥብብ[]	ባያስታጥብብ[]
ባታጥብብ[]	ባትታጠብብ[]	ባታሳጥብብ[]	ባታስታጥብብ[]**
ባያጥቡብ[]	ባይታጠቡብ[]	ባያሳጥቡብ[]	ባያስታጥቡብ[]*

ሳላጥብል[]
ሳናጥብል[]
ሳታጥብል[]
ሳታጥቢል[]
ሳያጥቡል[]
ሳታጥቡል[]
ሳያጥብል[]
ሳታጥብል[]
ሳያጥቡል[]

ሳልታጠብል[]
ሳንታጠብል[]
ሳትታጠብል[]
ሳትታጠቢል[]
ሳይታጠቡል[]
ሳትታጠቡል[]
ሳይታጠብል[]
ሳትታጠብል[]
ሳይታጠቡል[]

ሳላሳጥብል[]
ሳናሳጥብል[]
ሳታሳጥብል[]
ሳታሳጥቢል[]
ሳያሳጥቡል[]
ሳታሳጥቡል[]
ሳያሳጥብል[]
ሳታሳጥብል[]
ሳያሳጥቡል[]

ሳላስታጥብል[]
ሳናስታጥብል[]
ሳታስታጥብል[]**
ሳታስታጥቢል[]
ሳያስታጥቡል[]*
ሳታስታጥቡል[]
ሳያስታጥብል[]
ሳታስታጥብል[]**
ሳያስታጥቡል[]*

ሳላጥብብ[]
ሳናጥብብ[]
ሳታጥብብ[]
ሳታጥቢብ[]
ሳያጥቡብ[]
ሳታጥቡብ[]
ሳያጥብብ[]
ሳታጥብብ[]
ሳያጥቡብ[]

ሳልታጠብብ[]
ሳንታጠብብ[]
ሳትታጠብብ[]
ሳትታጠቢብ[]
ሳይታጠቡብ[]
ሳትታጠቡብ[]
ሳይታጠብብ[]
ሳትታጠብብ[]
ሳይታጠቡብ[]

ሳላሳጥብብ[]
ሳናሳጥብብ[]
ሳታሳጥብብ[]
ሳታሳጥቢብ[]
ሳያሳጥቡብ[]
ሳታሳጥቡብ[]
ሳያሳጥብብ[]
ሳታሳጥብብ[]
ሳያሳጥቡብ[]

ሳላስታጥብብ[]
ሳናስታጥብብ[]
ሳታስታጥብብ[]**
ሳታስታጥቢብ[]
ሳያስታጥቡብ[]*
ሳታስታጥቡብ[]
ሳያስታጥብብ[]
ሳታስታጥብብ[]**
ሳያስታጥቡብ[]*

ላላጥብል[]
ላናጥብል[]
ላታጥብል[]
ላታጥቢል[]
ላያጥቡል[]
ላታጥቡል[]
ላያጥብል[]
ላታጥብል[]
ላያጥቡል[]

ላልታጠብል[]
ላንታጠብል[]
ላትታጠብል[]
ላትታጠቢል[]
ላይታጠቡል[]
ላትታጠቡል[]
ላይታጠብል[]
ላትታጠብል[]
ላይታጠቡል[]

ላላሳጥብል[]
ላናሳጥብል[]
ላታሳጥብል[]
ላታሳጥቢል[]
ላያሳጥቡል[]
ላታሳጥቡል[]
ላያሳጥብል[]
ላታሳጥብል[]
ላያሳጥቡል[]

ላላስታጥብል[]
ላናስታጥብል[]
ላታስታጥብል[]**
ላታስታጥቢል[]
ላያስታጥቡል[]*
ላታስታጥቡል[]
ላያስታጥብል[]
ላታስታጥብል[]**
ላያስታጥቡል[]*

ላላጥብብ[]
ላናጥብብ[]
ላታጥብብ[]
ላታጥቢብ[]
ላያጥቡብ[]
ላታጥቡብ[]
ላያጥብብ[]
ላታጥብብ[]
ላያጥቡብ[]

ላልታጠብብ[]
ላንታጠብብ[]
ላትታጠብብ[]
ላትታጠቢብ[]
ላይታጠቡብ[]
ላትታጠቡብ[]
ላይታጠብብ[]
ላትታጠብብ[]
ላይታጠቡብ[]

ላላሳጥብብ[]
ላናሳጥብብ[]
ላታሳጥብብ[]
ላታሳጥቢብ[]
ላያሳጥቡብ[]
ላታሳጥቡብ[]
ላያሳጥብብ[]
ላታሳጥብብ[]
ላያሳጥቡብ[]

ላላስታጥብብ[]
ላናስታጥብብ[]
ላታስታጥብብ[]**
ላታስታጥቢብ[]
ላያስታጥቡብ[]*
ላታስታጥቡብ[]
ላያስታጥብብ[]
ላታስታጥብብ[]**
ላያስታጥቡብ[]*

እንደማጥብ	እንደምታጠብ	እንደማሳጥብ	እንደማስታጥብ
እንደምናጥብ	እንደምንታጠብ	እንደምናሳጥብ	እንደምናስታጥብ
እንደምታጥብ	እንደምትታጠብ	እንደምታሳጥብ	እንደምታስታጥብ**
እንደምታጥቢ	እንደምትታጠቢ	እንደምታሳጥቢ	እንደምታስታጥቢ
እንደሚያጥቡ	እንደሚይታጠቡ	እንደሚያሳጥቡ	እንደሚያስታጥቡ*
እንደምታጥቡ	እንደምትታጠቡ	እንደምታሳጥቡ	እንደምታስታጥቡ
እንደሚያጥብ	እንደሚይታጠብ	እንደሚያሳጥብ	እንደሚያስታጥብ
እንደምታጥብ	እንደምትታጠብ	እንደምታሳጥብ	እንደምታስታጥብ**
እንደሚያጥቡ	እንደሚይታጠቡ	እንደሚያሳጥቡ	እንደሚያስታጥቡ*

እንደማላጥብ	እንደማልታጠብ	እንደማላሳጥብ	እንደማላስታጥብ
እንደማናጥብ	እንደማንታጠብ	እንደማናሳጥብ	እንደማናስታጥብ
እንደማታጥብ	እንደማትታጠብ	እንደማታሳጥብ	እንደማታስታጥብ**
እንደማታጥቢ	እንደማትታጠቢ	እንደማታሳጥቢ	እንደማታስታጥቢ
እንደማያጥቡ	እንደማይታጠቡ	እንደማያሳጥቡ	እንደማያስታጥቡ*
እንደማታጥቡ	እንደማትታጠቡ	እንደማታሳጥቡ	እንደማታስታጥቡ
እንደማያጥብ	እንደማይታጠብ	እንደማያሳጥብ	እንደማያስታጥብ
እንደማታጥብ	እንደማትታጠብ	እንደማታሳጥብ	እንደማታስታጥብ**
እንደማያጥቡ	እንደማይታጠቡ	እንደማያሳጥቡ	እንደማያስታጥቡ*

እንደማጥብል[]	እንደምታጠብል[]	እንደማሳጥብል[]	እንደማስታጥብል[]
እንደምናጥብል[]	እንደምንታጠብል[]	እንደምናሳጥብል[]	እንደምናስታጥብል[]
እንደምታጥብል[]	እንደምትታጠብል[]	እንደምታሳጥብል[]	እንደምታስታጥብል[]**
እንደምታጥቢል[]	እንደምትታጠቢል[]	እንደምታሳጥቢል[]	እንደምታስታጥቢል[]
እንደሚያጥቡል[]	እንደሚይታጠቡል[]	እንደሚያሳጥቡል[]	እንደሚያስታጥቡል[]*
እንደምታጥቡል[]	እንደምትታጠቡል[]	እንደምታሳጥቡል[]	እንደምታስታጥቡል[]
እንደሚያጥብል[]	እንደሚይታጠብል[]	እንደሚያሳጥብል[]	እንደሚያስታጥብል[]
እንደምታጥብል[]	እንደምትታጠብል[]	እንደምታሳጥብል[]	እንደምታስታጥብል[]**
እንደሚያጥቡል[]	እንደሚይታጠቡል[]	እንደሚያሳጥቡል[]	እንደሚያስታጥቡል[]*

እንደማላጥብል[]	እንደማልታጠብል[]	እንደማላሳጥብል[]	እንደማላስታጥብል[]
እንደማናጥብል[]	እንደማንታጠብል[]	እንደማናሳጥብል[]	እንደማናስታጥብል[]
እንደማታጥብል[]	እንደማትታጠብል[]	እንደማታሳጥብል[]	እንደማታስታጥብል[]**
እንደማታጥቢል[]	እንደማትታጠቢል[]	እንደማታሳጥቢል[]	እንደማታስታጥቢል[]
እንደማያጥቡል[]	እንደማይታጠቡል[]	እንደማያሳጥቡል[]	እንደማያስታጥቡል[]*
እንደማታጥቡል[]	እንደማትታጠቡል[]	እንደማታሳጥቡል[]	እንደማታስታጥቡል[]
እንደማያጥብል[]	እንደማይታጠብል[]	እንደማያሳጥብል[]	እንደማያስታጥብል[]
እንደማታጥብል[]	እንደማትታጠብል[]	እንደማታሳጥብል[]	እንደማታስታጥብል[]**
እንደማያጥቡል[]	እንደማይታጠቡል[]	እንደማያሳጥቡል[]	እንደማያስታጥቡል[]*

	እንደማጥብብ[]	እንደምታጠብብ[]	እንደማሳጥብብ[]	እንደማስታጥብብ[]
	እንደምናጥብብ[]	እንደምንታጠብብ[]	እንደምናሳጥብብ[]	እንደምናስታጥብብ[]
	እንደምታጥብብ[]	እንደምትታጠብብ[]	እንደምታሳጥብብ[]	እንደምታስታጥብብ[]**
	እንደምታጥቢብ[]	እንደምትታጠቢብ[]	እንደምታሳጥቢብ[]	እንደምታስታጥቢብ[]
	እንደሚያጥቡብ[]	እንደሚይታጠቡብ[]	እንደሚያሳጥቡብ[]	እንደሚያስታጥቡብ[]*
	እንደምታጥቡብ[]	እንደምትታጠቡብ[]	እንደምታሳጥቡብ[]	እንደምታስታጥቡብ[]
	እንደሚያጥብብ[]	እንደሚይታጠብብ[]	እንደሚያሳጥብብ[]	እንደሚያስታጥብብ[]
	እንደምታጥብብ[]	እንደምትታጠብብ[]	እንደምታሳጥብብ[]	እንደምታስታጥብብ[]**
	እንደሚያጥቡብ[]	እንደሚይታጠቡብ[]	እንደሚያሳጥቡብ[]	እንደሚያስታጥቡብ[]*
	እንደማላጥብብ[]	እንደማልታጠብብ[]	እንደማላሳጥብብ[]	እንደማላስታጥብብ[]
	እንደማናጥብብ[]	እንደማንታጠብብ[]	እንደማናሳጥብብ[]	እንደማናስታጥብብ[]
	እንደማታጥብብ[]	እንደማትታጠብብ[]	እንደማታሳጥብብ[]	እንደማታስታጥብብ[]
	እንደማታጥቢብ[]	እንደማትታጠቢብ[]	እንደማታሳጥቢብ[]	እንደማታስታጥቢብ[]
	እንደማያጥቡብ[]	እንደማይታጠቡብ[]	እንደማያሳጥቡብ[]	እንደማያስታጥቡብ[]
	እንደማታጥቡብ[]	እንደማትታጠቡብ[]	እንደማታሳጥቡብ[]	እንደማታስታጥቡብ[]
	እንደማያጥብብ[]	እንደማይታጠብብ[]	እንደማያሳጥብብ[]	እንደማያስታጥብብ[]
	እንደማታጥብብ[]	እንደማትታጠብብ[]	እንደማታሳጥብብ[]	እንደማታስታጥብብ[]
	እንደማያጥቡብ[]	እንደማይታጠቡብ[]	እንደማያሳጥቡብ[]	እንደማያስታጥቡብ[]
D4	ልጠብ	ልታጠብ	ላሳጥብ	ላስታጥብ
	እንጠብ	እንታጠብ	እናሳጥብ	እናስታጥብ
	እጠብ	ታጠብ	አሳጥብ	አስታጥብ
	እጠቢ	ታጠቢ	አሳጥቢ	አስታጥቢ
	ይጠቡ	ይታጠቡ	ያሳጥቡ	ያስታጥቡ*
	እጠቡ	ታጠቡ	አሳጥቡ	አስታጥቡ
	ይጠብ	ይታጠብ	ያሳጥብ	ያስታጥብ
	ትጠብ	ትታጠብ	ታሳጥብ	ታስታጥብ
	ይጠቡ	ይታጠቡ	ያሳጥቡ	ያስታጥቡ*
	አልጠብ	አልታጠብ	አላሳጥብ	አላስታጥብ
	አንጠብ	አንታጠብ	አናሳጥብ	አናስታጥብ
	አትጠብ	አትታጠብ	አታሳጥብ	አታስታጥብ**
	አትጠቢ	አትታጠቢ	አታሳጥቢ	አታስታጥቢ
	አይጠቡ	አይታጠቡ	አያሳጥቡ	አያስታጥቡ*
	አትጠቡ	አትታጠቡ	አታሳጥቡ	አታስታጥቡ
	አይጠብ	አይታጠብ	አያሳጥብ	አያስታጥብ
	አትጠብ	አትታጠብ	አታሳጥብ	አታስታጥብ**
	አይጠቡ	አይታጠቡ	አያሳጥቡ	አያስታጥቡ*

ልጠብል[]	ልታጠብል[]	ላሳጥብል[]	ላስታጥብል[]
እንጠብል[]	እንታጠብል[]	እናሳጥብል[]	እናስታጥብል[]
እጠብል[]	ታጠብል[]	አሳጥብል[]	አስታጥብል[]
እጠቢል[]	ታጠቢል[]	አሳጥቢል[]	አስታጥቢል[]
ይጠቡል[]	ይታጠቡል[]	ያሳጥቡል[]	ያስታጥቡል[]*
እጠቡል[]	ታጠቡል[]	አሳጥቡል[]	አስታጥቡል[]
ይጠብል[]	ይታጠብል[]	ያሳጥብል[]	ያስታጥብል[]
ትጠብል[]	ትታጠብል[]	ታሳጥብል[]	ታስታጥብል[]
ይጠቡል[]	ይታጠቡል[]	ያሳጥቡል[]	ያስታጥቡል[]*
አልጠብል[]	አልታጠብል[]	አላሳጥብል[]	አላስታጥብል[]
አንጠብል[]	አንታጠብል[]	አናሳጥብል[]	አናስታጥብል[]
አትጠብል[]	አትታጠብል[]	አታሳጥብል[]	አታስታጥብል[]**
አትጠቢል[]	አትታጠቢል[]	አታሳጥቢል[]	አታስታጥቢል[]
አይጠቡል[]	አይታጠቡል[]	አያሳጥቡል[]	አያስታጥቡል[]*
አትጠቡል[]	አትታጠቡል[]	አታሳጥቡል[]	አታስታጥቡል[]
አይጠብል[]	አይታጠብል[]	አያሳጥብል[]	አያስታጥብል[]
አትጠብል[]	አትታጠብል[]	አታሳጥብል[]	አታስታጥብል[]**
አይጠቡል[]	አይታጠቡል[]	አያሳጥቡል[]	አያስታጥቡል[]*
ልጠብብ[]	ልታጠብብ[]	ላሳጥብብ[]	ላስታጥብብ[]
እንጠብብ[]	እንታጠብብ[]	እናሳጥብብ[]	እናስታጥብብ[]
እጠብብ[]	ታጠብብ[]	አሳጥብል[]	አስታጥብብ[]
እጠቢብ[]	ታጠቢብ[]	አሳጥቢብ[]	አስታጥቢብ[]
ይጠቡብ[]	ይታጠቡብ[]	ያሳጥቡብ[]	ያስታጥቡብ[]*
እጠቡብ[]	ታጠቡብ[]	አሳጥቡብ[]	አስታጥቡብ[]
ይጠብብ[]	ይታጠብብ[]	ያሳጥብብ[]	ያስታጥብብ[]
ትጠብብ[]	ትታጠብብ[]	ታሳጥብብ[]	ታስታጥብብ[]
ይጠቡብ[]	ይታጠቡብ[]	ያሳጥቡብ[]	ያስታጥቡብ[]*
አልጠብብ[]	አልታጠብብ[]	አላሳጥብብ[]	አላስታጥብብ[]
አንጠብብ[]	አንታጠብብ[]	አናሳጥብብ[]	አናስታጥብብ[]
አትጠብብ[]	አትታጠብብ[]	አታሳጥብብ[]	አታስታጥብብ[]**
አትጠቢብ[]	አትታጠቢብ[]	አታሳጥቢብ[]	አታስታጥቢብ[]
አይጠቡብ[]	አይታጠቡብ[]	አያሳጥቡብ[]	አያስታጥቡብ[]*
አትጠቡብ[]	አትታጠቡብ[]	አታሳጥቡብ[]	አታስታጥቡብ[]
አይጠብብ[]	አይታጠብብ[]	አያሳጥብብ[]	አያስታጥብብ[]
አትጠብብ[]	አትታጠብብ[]	አታሳጥብብ[]	አታስታጥብብ[]**
አይጠቡብ[]	አይታጠቡብ[]	አያሳጥቡብ[]	አያስታጥቡብ[]*

Appendix D: Some Formal, Informal, and Slang Expressions in Tigirinya and Amharic

Note: Amharic seems to have more informal and slang expressions than Tigirinya. Where a Tigirinya expression is of interest, it is shown to the left of a vertical bar (|) before an Amharic expressions.

ENGLISH	FORMAL (ድዕbqወq)	INFORMAL (qbqወq)	SLANG (ɯobocόʒ̃ʒ̃q)
	ቃoʂoɑ	ቃoʂόɑρ፣ ቃoʂʂoɑ nόho ρ	qʒόtop | ቃόʂʂόɑ	
	ቃommq፣ nόɯόmnnόt	ʒόʂʂqt	
	ቃoʂoɑ | mόʒόt፣ no ቃoʂʂoɑ o ʜoɑoʒqt	- | ʂόcρ	
	ʒόɯɯόhoʒόtq (ʒόɯɯόhoɑtq/ʒόɯɯόhόʒόtq	ʒόɯɯόhqtq	
		όhohq	እንትን
[formal way of referring to a person]	[qʒόtotq]	[qʒόŧotq (qʒόŧqtq/qʒόtotq)]	[አንቺታ (when used for a male)]
already	ʂόcρ	-	አሬዲ | አሬዲ
Americans	qɑqcqhqωqqʒ		ኣሜሪካኖች
arm	hόʒόʂ		እጅ
baby	υόɵqʒ, όʒόnρቃoቃόhq		
beautiful	ɑόhόhoόό | ωόn	ቃρʒόʂρ	
beggar	ዴo όʒq nόmq	hoɑqʒ̃	
body	ɯoωόʒot, qhqh	ɔohq	
calamity / disaster	ɑoqt		
child	nόhqttqʒq	hόʂ̃	
church			ቸርች
customer, patron	qɑqh | ʂoʒόnoʒ̃ʒ̃q		
driver	ɔoʒqυυq ɑohqʒq | qñόhocόhqcq		ሾፌር
etcetera	ωoʜotocobo (ω፡ʜ፡t)	ɔohoɑoho | ɑόʒqɑόʒ	
false	υqɯot	υυqɯρt | ωόñot	ፉገራ, ቁጭጩ
flag	ɯoʒόʂoቃqhqɑq	-	ባንዲራ
floor	ωhh | ωhh	-	መሬት

foot	ɱnqɑqɑq | ɱnqɑqɑq		እግሬ | እግር
friend	ϖoʠqʠ / ɔoqʠʠ	ɔoqʠʠoʠʠq	ነፍሴ
good	ɑoʜòʜqɑ / ɑqʜoɓqq	ɱòco	ደንበኛ, ኣሪፍ, ቆንጆ
half	ɔoɑqɯ / ɔòɑqɦ	ɔòɑqɦ	
hand	qqʠ | òʠʠ		
leg	òɔòcq | òɔòc		
many/much	nòʜo		መአት
marriage	tòʠqc	ɔqnòŧq / ɯρɯòt ɔoʜʜòŧq	
Media	ɑocqʜonòtq ʋʋqɓɓqɦ		
method	ʜqʠq		ሲስተም
naked / nakedness	òòcòɸqɿ | òcòɸqɿ: òcòɸqɿoɯòɔq /	cqɸɸot | cqɸot / cqɸotòɿɿot	
newborn	ነoΠ		
please	ònqʜʜ ρ / qŧŧòʋo	ònqʜʜ ʋò / ɦò	በናትህ / ሽ / ኣችሁ
please	noʠʠq ʜq/ʜq/ʜoɑ/ʜòɿ		
pregnant	ɿoɓòɯomoc	òcòɔoʜ	
security guard	ɱònnoɸq / ʜon	ʜonoʠʠq	– | ዘቡልቄ
shoe	ɯqòɿq | ɑomnnqɑqq		ጫማ | ጫማ
small/little	qɿoɯòttoʠq	tòɿɿòɦ	ጥንጥ
some part of a whole	ʜoɓqʜ	–	ግማሽ
storey	ʠocònq | ʠocòn	ፎቅ | ፎቅ	
substitute	ɑòttòʜ	ɓoɿòtq	
time	ɔòʜq | ɔòʜq (ɔqʜq)		ሰዓት
toddler	[ʋòɵqɿ-ʜòʠ] / qʠqɔq		ፈልፈላ
vehicle	toɦòʜocòʜqcq	ɑòʜqɿq	
wealthy	nqʜoɵoɔɔq	ʋqnòtqɑ	ሞጃ
you (SSM(P))	òcòɯòρ	qɿòto / qɿòŧq / qɿòto	
young lady	ʜòʠqɔocoʠ	ɯqt ʜòʠ	
young man	[ϖoɿòʠqɔocoʠ]	ϖoɿòʠ ʜòʠ	

Appendix E: Examples of Wrong Use of Active-Intransitive Verbs in Tigirinya

WRONG EXPRESSIONS	CORRECT EXPRESSIONS	REMARKS
ሞይቑኒ	ᏣᎠρqቃ ɋ q ɋ	
ቆይሩኒ	ቐρqc ɋ q ɋ	
ከቢዱኒ	ነq q ɋ ከonnqջ q o፡፡	
ደኺሙኒ	ՁከυqᏣ ɋ q ɋ	
መሲሉኒ	ነq q ɋ ᏣoωqԿ o፡፡	
ይኣኽለኒ	ነq q ɋ όq qከόԿ q o፡፡	
ኮይኑኒ	ነq q ɋ όq ከρ३ q o፡፡	
ኣጋጢሙኒ	ነq q ɋ ɔomqᏣ o፡፡	
ጥዒሙኒ	ነq q ɋ mόqqᏣ o፡፡	
ሓጺሩኒ	ነq q ɋ υυqθqc o፡፡	
ሰልቹይኒ	ՈoԿό王 q ɋ ρ፡፡	
ይስመዐኒ	ቶιωόᏣᏣόό ρ q ɋ፡፡	
ይረኣየኒ	ነό q ɋ όq ccόqջ q o፡፡	
ጠምዩኒ		
ጸምዩኒ		
ሒሹኒ		

Appendix F: Examples of Wrong Use of Active-Intransitive Verbs in Amharic

WRONG EXPRESSIONS	CORRECT EXPRESSIONS	REMARKS
ሞቀኝ	ꝏρq̣ф q̣ q q̣	
በረደኝ	ꝏρq̣c q̣ q q̣	
ከበደኝ	ነq q q̣ ነoกกq̣ą q o::	
ደከመኝ	ꝏρq̣c q̣ q q̣	
መሰለኝ		
ይበቃኛል	ho o̍ʒq̣ กoфq ʒoꝏ	
ሆነኝ	ho̍ነነ q̣ ʒoꝏ/υρʒ o	
ኣጋጠመኝ	ho o̍ʒq̣ ɔommoꝏ o	
ጣፈጠኝ		
ኣጠረኝ		
ወብቀኝ	ꝉo ꝏoกกoф υo::	
ይሰማኛል		
ይታየኛል	Πo o̍ʒq̣ o̍q tqɐ qh::	
ሰለቸኝ	Πohoŧŧo υo to̍::	

Appendix G: Examples of Wrong Use of Passive-Intransitive Verbs – Amharic

WRONG EXPRESSIONS	CORRECT EXPRESSIONS	REMARKS
ራበኝ	†o cqn uo::	
ጠማኝ	†o moαqαqq uo::	
ገረመኝ	†o ɔoccoαq uo::	
ተሻለኝ	†o ῆqh uo:: / †o ƅoωωow uo::	
ደነቀኝ	†o ʠo϶϶oȸ uo	
ጨነቀኝ	†o mno϶϶oȸ uo::	
ደበረኝ	†o ʠonnoc uo::	
ከፋኝ	†o ɦoƅƅq uo::	
መረረኝ	†o αqqccoc uo:: / Ꮁo ό϶q, αqocqcq ϶oω::	
ጣፈጠኝ		
ቸገረኝ		
አሞኛል		

Endnotes

PART I: INTRODUCTION

Chapter 1: Introduction

Sources of epigraphs in written order:

Gibbon, Edward. *The History of the Decline and Fall of the Roman Empire, Esq: Volume the Fourth*. London: Printed for A. Strahan; and T. Cadell, 1788. p. 617.

"Toast Remarks by President Obama and Prime Minister Hailemariam Desalegn of Ethiopia at State Dinner." *The White House*. The White House, 27 July 2015. Web. 28 July 2015.

1. Stringer, Chris. "Human Evolution: Out of Ethiopia." *Nature* 423 (2013): 692-95. Print.

   In 2015, Dr Zeresenay Alemseged, senior curator of anthropology at the California Academy of Sciences, said "we have the evidence that homo sapiens indeed emerged in Ethiopia" as quoted by Smith (2015). (Smith, David. "Obama Meets Lucy, 'the Grandmother of Humanity,' during Ethiopia Visit." *The Guardian*. Guardian News and Media, 27 July 2015. Web. 27 July 2015.)

2. The chronology of the Zagwe dynasty, which was previously though to have began soon after the decline of Axum in the 12th century (the decline of Axum has now been revised to centuries earlier) has been contentious among historians. For a discussion on the controversy, see Phillipson (2014), p. 228.

3. For discussions on how the Derig regime deliberately exacerbated the 1984 famine, see Young, 1997: 129-134.

4. See, for example:

   Bughin, Jacques, et el. "Lions on the Move II: Realizing the Potential of Africa's Economies." *McKinsey Global Institute*. McKinsey & Company. 2016. PDF.

   Kushkush, Isma'il. "Ethiopia, Long Mired in Poverty, Rides an Economic Boom." *The New York Times*. The New York Times, 03 Mar. 2015. Web. 05 July 2016.

   According to Smith, 2014, "[t]o be in Ethiopia is to witness an economic miracle" since the "country has enjoyed close to double-digit growth for a decade" as exemplified by a study that "found it was creating millionaires faster than anywhere else on the continent" and that Addis' streets "reverberate with hammering from construction workers as the concrete skeletons of new towers and a light rail project rise into the crane-dotted sky,"--some of the signs that support the government's goal of becoming a middle-income country by 2025. (Smith, David. "Ethiopia, 30 Years after the Famine." *The Guardian*. Guardian News and Media, 22 Oct. 2014. Web. 20 July 2015.)

   For more information on Ethiopia's progress on the MDG, see: Government of the Federal Democratic Republic of Ethiopia and UNCT. National Planning Commission and UNDP. *Millennium Development Goals Report 2014: Assessment of Ethiopia's Progress towards the MDGs.* Addis Ababa: National Planning Commission and UNDP, 2015. PDF.

5. See, for example, Smith, 2013: (Smith, David. "Ethiopia Hailed as 'African Lion' with Fastest Creation of Millionaires." *The Guardian*. Guardian News and Media, 04 Dec. 2013. Web. 04 Dec. 2013.) And, Kushkush, 2015: (Kushkush, Isma'il. "Ethiopia, Long Mired in Poverty, Rides an Economic Boom." *The New York Times.* The New York Times, 03 Mar. 2015. Web. 05 July 2016.) For a similar expression, see Dori, 2014: (Dori, Dereje Feyissa. "Ethiopia's 'African Tiger' Leaps towards Middle Income | Dereje Feyissa Dori." The Guardian. Guardian News and Media, 22 Oct. 2014. Web. 23 Oct. 2014.)

6. For example, in 2009, in an unprecedented move, the African Union designated Prime Minister Meles Zenawi in unison as the lead negotiator to represent the continent to the 2009 United Nations Climate Change Conference in Copenhagen. (Harsch, Ernest. "Climate Deal: Hard Work Lies Ahead." *UN News Center*. UN, Jan. 2010. Web. 08 July 2013.)

7. See, for example, Beckhusen, 2015: (Beckhusen, Robert. "Ethiopia Spends Very Little Money on Its Military—And It Works." *War Is Boring*. War Is Boring, 10 Mar. 2015. Web. 15 Oct. 2015.) Covering the news April 19, 2015 of the brutal murder of civilian expatriate Ethiopians in Libya by the barbaric jihadist group Islamic State, Fortin (2015) noted that "[w]ith its formidable military and pervasive intelligence network, Ethiopia is [...] a linchpin of stability in the volatile Horn of Africa." (Fortin, Jacey. "Grief Mixes With Anger Over Christian Ethiopian Deaths."

The New York Times. The New York Times, 22 Apr. 2015. Web. 22 Apr. 2015.) As of April 30, 2016, Ethiopia's total contribution of police, military experts, and troops to the United Nations peacekeeping operations is the largest in the world according to UN figures. ("Troop and Police Contributors. United Nations Peacekeeping." *UN News Center*. UN, 30 Apr. 2016. Web. 08 July 2016.)

8. The following is an excerpt from material provided by the White House on remarks made by United States President Barack Obama at a September 25, 2014 bilateral meeting with Prime Minister Haile Mariam: "When I spoke previously at the Africa Summit about some of the bright spots and progress that we're seeing in Africa, I think there's no better example than what has been happening in Ethiopia -- one of the fastest-growing economies in the world. We have seen enormous progress in a country that once had great difficulty feeding itself. It's now not only leading the pack in terms of agricultural production in the region, but will soon be an exporter potentially not just of agriculture, but also power because of the development that's been taking place there.... And [when it comes to peacekeeping] it turns out that Ethiopia may be one of the best in the world -- one of the largest contributors of peacekeeping; one of the most effective fighting forces when it comes to being placed in some very difficult situations and helping to resolve conflicts. So Ethiopia has been not only a leader economically in the continent, but also when it comes to security and trying to resolve some of the longstanding conflicts there..." ("Remarks by President Obama and Prime Minister Desalegn of Ethiopia Before Bilateral Meeting." *The White House*. The White House, 25 Sept. 2014. Web. 26 Sept. 2014.)
9. For example, Jeffrey (2014) quoted Yvo de Boer, director general of Global Green Growth Institute, an international organisation advocating for economic growth through environmental sustainability, as saying, "Ethiopians can give answers whereas often in industrialised countries people aren't sure what to do...Ethiopians should be asked." (Jeffrey, James. "Ethiopia Shows Developing World How to Make a Green Economy Prosper." *Inter Press Service*. Inter Press Service, 16 Oct. 2014. Web. 23 Oct. 2014.)
10. Hamlin, Kevin, Ilya Gridneff, and William Davison. "Ethiopia Becomes China's China in Search for Cheap Labor." *Bloomberg.com*. Bloomberg, 22 July 2014. Web. 29 Oct. 2014.
11. Lewis, M. Paul, Gary F. Simons, and Charles D. Fennig (eds.). 2016. *Ethnologue: Languages of the World, Nineteenth edition*. Dallas, Texas: SIL International. Online version: http://www.ethnologue.com.
12. See, for example, Baye Yimam. *Yeamarinya Sewasiw. [Amharic Grammar]*. Rev. ed. Addis Ababa, 2000 [E.C.] pp. xxi & xxvi.
13. For more discussion on this issue, which I shall refer to as the Ethiopian language crisis, refer to Chapters 5 and 13.
14. See, for example, Snetsehay Assefa, 2015: (Assefa, Snetsehay. "Amharic, Not Just For Ethiopians." *Addis Fortune*. Independent News & Media, 11 Jan. 2015. Web. 11 Jan. 2015.)
15. For example, Peterson (2015) stated that "Ethiopians do respect foreigners who learn their complicated languages and attempt to fathom the wax and gold of their culture." (Peterson, Stephen. *Public Finance and Economic Growth in Developing Countries: Lessons from Ethiopia's Reforms*. New York, New York: Routledge, 2015. P. 9.) Very few native speakers of Ethiopian languages, particularly Amharic, know much about grammar, let alone to use correct grammar (Chapter 5: Overview of Language Crisis and Miscommunication in Ethiopia).
16. Dillmann, August. *Ethiopic Grammar*. Rev. Carl Bezold. Trans. James A. Crichton. Second ed. Eugene: Wipf & Stock, 2005. Print. p. 3
17. Kitchen, A., C. Ehret, S. Assefa, and C. J. Mulligan. "Bayesian Phylogenetic Analysis of Semitic Languages Identifies an Early Bronze Age Origin of Semitic in the Near East." *Proceedings of the Royal Society B: Biological Sciences* 276.1668 (2009): 2703-710. Web. 03 Mar. 2015.
18. "Aksum." *UNESCO World Heritage Centre*. UNESCO, n.d. Web. 28 Sept. 2014.
19. For example, Andah and et al (1993) stated that in the late second and early first millennium BC there were contacts between Ethiopian and Arabian people across the Red Sea each of them possibly having separate cultural and ethnic identity. (Andah, Bassey and et al. *The Archaeology of Africa: Food, Metals and Towns*. New York, London: Routledge, 1993. p 612.) And UNESCO World Heritage Centre stated that between around the second millennium B.C and the 4th century A.D, there were immigrants from southern Arabia into ancient Ethiopia. ("Aksum." *UNESCO World Heritage Centre*. UNESCO, n.d. Web. 28 Sept. 2014.)
20. Hetzron, Robert. *The Semitic Languages*. New York: Routledge, 1997. Print. p. 242

21. In an SBS radio interview, Girma Demeke, an Ethiopianist, said that Emperor Yohhannis used Amharic extensively and worked to promote it. ("Interview with Dr. Girma Awgichew Demeke Pt 2." Interview. YouTube. *SBS Amharic Radio*, 31 Mar. 2013. Web. 03 Dec. 2015.)
22. Lewis, M. Paul, Gary F. Simons, and Charles D. Fennig (eds.). 2016. *Ethnologue: Languages of the World, Nineteenth edition.* Dallas, Texas: SIL International. Online version: http://www.ethnologue.com.
23. The number of Tigirinya speakers in Tigiray is calculated by extrapolating the information provided by the 2007 Population and Housing Census Report (Central Statistics Agency) using an average population growth rate of 2.6% (World Bank). The number of Tigirinya speakers in Eritrea is based on various sources, including: World Population Prospects: The 2015 Revision. *United Nations, Department of Economic and Social Affairs, Population Division.* July 2015.
24. From data provided by Ethnologue: (Lewis, M. Paul, Gary F. Simons, and Charles D. Fennig (eds.). 2016. *Ethnologue: Languages of the World, Nineteenth edition.* Dallas, Texas: SIL International. Online version: http://www.ethnologue.com.)
25. The number of Amharic speakers in Ethiopia is calculated by extrapolating the information provided by the 2007 Population and Housing Census Report (Central Statistics Agency) using an average population growth rate for Ethiopia of 2.6% (World Bank).
26. The number of L2 speakers for Amharic is extrapolated from data provided by Ethnologue: (Lewis, M. Paul, Gary F. Simons, and Charles D. Fennig (eds.). 2016. *Ethnologue: Languages of the World, Nineteenth edition.* Dallas, Texas: SIL International. Online version: http://www.ethnologue.com.)
27. Bright, William. "What's the Difference between Speech and Writing?" *Linguistic Society of America.* Linguistic Society of America, n.d. Web. 29 July 2015.
28. Ullman, Berthold L. *Ancient Writing and Its Influence: Introd. by Julian Brown.* Cambridge, MA: MIT, 1969. Print. p. 4.
29. Ibid. p. 4.
30. Coulmas, Florian. *The Writing Systems of the World.* Oxford, UK: B. Blackwell, 1989. Print. p. 3.
31. Dye, Melody. "The Advantages of Being Helpless." *Scientific American.* Scientific American, 09 Feb. 2010. Web. 28 July 2012.
32. My translation of the Amharic by Desita Tekile Welid. *Adees Yamarinya Mezigebe Qalat [New Amharic Dictionary].* Addis Ababa, 1970. Print. Note.
33. My translation of an Amharic article by Kibirom (2013) on The Reporter website: (http://www.ethiopianreporter.com/index.php/politics/item/3077). 13 Sept. 2013.
34. Rymer, Russ. "Vanishing Languages." *National Geographic.* National Geographic Magazine, July 2012. Web. 25 Aug. 2013.
35. See, for example, National Geographic: "Enduring Voices: Disappearing Languages." *National Geographic.* National Geographic, n.d. Web. 25 Aug. 2013
36. Yacob, Daniel. "Ethiopic at the End of the 20th Century." *International Journal of Ethiopian Studies* 2.1/2 (2005): 121-40. PDF. p. 121.
37. Tekile-Welid, Desita. *Adees Yamarinya Mezigebe Qalat. [New Amharic Dictionary].* Addis Ababa, Artistic Printers: 1970. N.p.
38. Baye Yimam. *Yeamarinya Sewasiw. [Amharic Grammar].* Rev. ed. Addis Ababa, 2000 [E.C.] P. xxvii.
39. Baye Yimam. *Yeamarinya Sewasiw. [Amharic Grammar].* Rev. ed. Addis Ababa, 2000 [E.C.] pp. xxi & xxvi.
40. Ibid

Chapter 2: The Ethiopic Script: An Introduction

Source of epigraph:

Alberge, Dalya. "Archaeologists Strike Gold in Quest to Find Queen of Sheba's Wealth." *The Guardian.* Guardian News and Media, 12 Feb. 2012. Web. 12 Feb. 2013.

1. Fattovich, Rodolfo, "Akkälä Guzay" in Uhlig, Siegbert, ed. *Encyclopaedia Aethiopica: A-C.* Wiesbaden: Otto Harrassowitz KG, 2003, p. 169
2. See, for example:

   Lepage, Claude, and Jacques Mercier. *Les Églises Historiques Du Tigray: Art Éthiopien = Ethiopian Art: The Ancient Churches of Tigrai.* Paris: ERC, 2005. Print.

   Munro-Hay, Stuart. *Aksum: An African Civilisation of Late Antiquity.* (1991): 1-227. PDF.

   Phillipson, David W. *Foundations of an African Civilization: Aksum & the Northern Horn, 1000 BC - AD 1300.* Addis Ababa: Addis Ababa University Press, 2014. Print.
3. Hetzron, Robert. *The Semitic Languages.* New York: Routledge, 1997. Print. p. 24
4. See, for example, Wright (1964: 12)

5. Hetzron, Robert. *The Semitic Languages.* New York: Routledge, 1997. Print. p. 24.

6. Housed in a monastery near Aadiwa, Tigiray, one of the Garima (Gereema) Gospels, Gereema 2—named after Abba Gereema, the revered monk who is believed to have written it—is the oldest illustrated Christian manuscript in the world dating back to 390 A.D. (Bailey, 2013) and one of the first translations of the Bible into Giiz. Bailey noted that the illustrations indicate a "school of painting in sub-Saharan Africa that may have been responsible for the earliest Christian paintings in manuscripts" in the world. (Bailey, Martin. "Research Uncovers Lost African School of Painting." *The Art Newspaper.* The Art Newspaper, 20 Dec. 2013. Web. 08 Oct. 2016.)

7. See, for example, Leslau (1979): (Leslau, Wolf. *Etymological Dictionary of Gurage (Ethiopic).* Wiesbaden: O. Harrassowitz, 1979. Print. p. xiv.)

8. "Tigrinya." *UCLA Language Materials Project: Language Profile.* UCLA International Institute, Center for World Languages, n.d. Web. 09 Jan. 2015.

9. Leslau, Wolf. *Introductory Grammar of Amharic.* Otto Harrassowitz, Wiesbaden. 2000. Print. p. xv.

10. The sound represented by the character family ኸ <kh> is also shared by Amharic. However, for all intents and purposes, modern Amharic (or at least South Central Amharic) no longer uses it with the exception of some words like መኸር. Also refer to Kebede et. al. (1993 E.C.) አማርኛ መዝገበ ቃላት *Amarinya Mezigebe Qalat.* Ethiopian Languages Research Center. Addis Ababa University. Addis Ababa, A.A. P. xiv.

11. Published by the German Marcellus Silber in 1513 in Rome, *Psalterium David et cantica aliqua in lingua Chaldea* (David's Psalter and Song of Songs in the [Giiz] Language) was the first Ethiopic book published by a printing press. The text has been reproduced in this book using the modern Noto Sans Ethiopic font by closely matching the original punctuation and spacing between words. Figure 7.3 shows a reproduced and desaturated copy of the original text.

12. Lambdin (1978)

13. Julie D. Allen ... [et al.]. (October 2014) The Unicode Standard, Version 7.0 – Core Specification. Unicode Consortium. P. 696.

14. See also Honeyman (1952, pp. 136, 141).

15. See, for example, Honeyman (1952).

16. Julie D. Allen ... [et al.]. (October 2014) The Unicode Standard, Version 7.0 – Core Specification. Unicode Consortium. P. 704.

PART II: OVERVIEW OF THE ETHIOPIC PROBLEMS AND THE CONCEPT OF MODULARIZATION

Chapter 3: Overview of Ethiopic Grammatical and Orthographic Problems

Sources of epigraphs in written order:

My translation of the Amharic by Desita Tekile Welid. *Adees Yamarinya Mezigebe Qalat [New Amharic Dictionary].* Artistic Printers. Addis Ababa, 1970. Print. Note.

Peterson, Stephen. *Public Finance and Economic Growth in Developing Countries: Lessons from Ethiopia's Reforms.* New York, New York: Routledge, 2015. P. 9.

Some attribute this quote to Walter J. West.

1. Haregeweyin Kebede et. al. አማርኛ መዝገበ ቃላት *Amarinya Mezigebe Qalat.* Addis Ababa: Addis Ababa University, Ethiopian Languages Research Center, 1993 E.C. (c. 2001) p. iv.

2. Ge/E Gorifu. *Gitximeetat Hagerey: Quaniqua Tigirinya Nimimiibal Itexabhife [National Poems: Published for the Development of Tigirinya].* (N.d.). p. 2.

3. Beckett, Chris. "The Secret World of Ethiopian Poetry – The Missing Slate." *The Missing Slate.* Low Key/ Slate Publications, 28 Mar. 2016. Web. 25 July 2016.

4. In the last 100 years, this had generated debate among scholars to revise the alphabet and many scholarly studies and reform ideas had been presented to no effect (refer to Chapter 14). The reform is long due and this generation cannot afford to postpone it yet again.

5. The transliteration shown does not take into account the proposed de-synthesization discussed in Chapter 4. For the proposed standard transliteration, refer to Chapter 9: Proposed Standard System for the Romanization of Ethiopic.

6. Most, though not all, of the 'Base' characters shown are part of the ancient consonantal Ethiopic script. Most of the characters shown from the 2nd to the 7th orders were added in the 4th century during the reign of King Ezana. Each of the characters in the 'Type 1 Extension Set' is a fusion of a consonant and two vowels and many are created in modern times. Almost all of the characters in the 'Type 2 Extension Set' are new having been added into Ethiopic in the last few decades and with the exception of the ቨ <v> family of characters, all are exclusively used for languages other than Giiz, Tigirinya, and Amharic.

7. Cowley, R. "The Standardisation of Amharic Spelling." *Journal of Ethiopian Studies* 5.2 (1967): 1-8. PDF. p. 1.

8. Wright, Stephen. "The Transliteration of Amharic." *Journal of Ethiopian Studies* 2.1 (1964): p. 1. PDF.
9. "Tigrinya Keyboard Map." *Geezexperience.com.* N.p., n.d. Web. 29 Oct. 2015.
   It was because I was unable to find a word that I was trying to look up on an Ethiopic dictionary that I started to study the problem of spelling and eventually publish my findings with my proposed solutions in this book.
10. Asker, Lars, et al. *Applying Machine Learning to Amharic Text Classification.* Stockholm University and Swedish Institute of Computer Science, n.d. PDF. p. none.
11. Leslau, Wolf. *English-Amharic Context Dictionary.* Louvain: Imprimerie Orientaliste, 1973. P. xii.
12. Ibid. P. xii.
13. An example of an extreme scenario of poor reading skill was observed on an Ethiopian state television during the Amharic translation of a speech by Egyptian President Abdel-Fattah el-Sisi. Sisi was addressing the Ethiopian parliament on March 25, 2015, and the event was being broadcast live with a translator's voice over the president's voice. In what was unmistakably a reading from a written translation of the president's speech (the president read his speech in Arabic), the translator routinely stumbled on words, repeated half-finished words, and strangely seemed that the translator was not familiar with the Ethiopic script. Although, it should have been possible for the station to find a more skillful person to read the translated document, the fact that any person working in the newsroom of a national television should have such a low level of reading skill is indicative of a more structural failure in the education system, and probably not merely an individual person's failure.
14. Madessa, Amanuel Hirpa. *Probabilistic Information Retrieval System for Amharic Language.* MSc. Thesis. Addis Ababa: Addis Ababa University Institutional Repository, 2012. PDF. p. 33.

Chapter 4: Overview of Ethiopic Morphology and Proposed Modularization

Note on epigraph:

Ethiopians' lamentation of the death of their hero Emperor Yohannis (Yohannes) IV, who was mortally wounded in 1889 while defending his country against the invading Sudanese Mahdist army. The Ethiopic text, which is in the traditional Ethiopic script, is my de-synthesized and geminated version of the original poem. My translation that follows tries to preserve the original message without being too literal.

1. Blair, John G. *Modular America: Cross-cultural Perspectives on the Emergence of an American Way.* New York: Greenwood, 1988. Print. p. 125.
2. Fisseha, Yonas. *Development of Stemming Algorithm for Tigrigna Text.* Addis Ababa: Addis Ababa University Institutional Repository, 2011. PDF. p. 27.
3. Berhe, Hailay Beyene. *Design and Development of Tigrigna Search Engine.* MSc. Thesis. Addis Ababa: Addis Ababa University Institutional Repository, 2013. PDF. p. 26.
4. The romanization used here is the one I proposed for the traditional orthography, which transliterates all pre-reform Ethiopic text 'as is' without accounting for gemination and de-synthesization in order to be true to the original text (refer to Chapter 9).

Chapter 5: Overview of Language Crisis and Miscommunication in Ethiopia

Note on epigraph:

Although there are stark differences between the causes of the problems the UK parliamentarians addressed in their 2009 report on bad use of official language and the language problems in Ethiopia, the end result is the same: miscommunication. Whereas the problem with language use in UK is deliberate use of language by politicians to obscure the messages in their speeches and official communiqués, the problem in Ethiopia is continuing deterioration of Ethiopian languages in their capacity to act as effective means of communication because of lack of a strong literary culture, poor or inexistent language policy, and the damaging effects of the use of English as the official medium of instruction in the nation.

1. "Dr Tedros Adhanom Visit to Denmark." YouTube. Ethiopian Embassy in Sweden, 06 Dec. 2014. Web. 06 Dec. 2014.
2. Yigizaw, Aniteneh. *Yeameireeka wid lij Maya Angelou* [America's beloved daughter Maya Angelou]. Adees Adimas. 23 *Ginibot* 2006 E.C., 750th ed.: 17+.
3. Weriqu, Geitahun. "*Obama siledeimokirasee alitenageremin* [Did Obama not speak about democracy]?" Reeporiter. Addis Ababa. Reeporiter, 02 Aug. 2015. Web. 08 Aug. 2015.
4. Abebe, Menigisitu. "*Yezewideetu hosipeetal leefit sew gedele* [The Zewideetu hospital elevator killed a person]." Adees Adimas. Addis Ababa. Adees Adimas, 28 Mar. 2015. Web. 05 Apr. 2015.

5. "TORONTO 9th Ethiopian Nations, Nationalities & Peoples Day Celebration." YouTube. Wedi Gud-Bahri, 14 Dec. 2014. Web. 19 Dec. 2014.

6. Abebe, Menigisitu. "*Yezewideetu hosipeetal leefit sew gedele* [The Zewideetu hospital elevator killed a person]." Adees Adimas. Addis Ababa. Adees Adimas, 28 Mar. 2015. Web. 05 Apr. 2015.

7. Ghelawdewos Araia. *Language for whose Audience in the Ethiopian context? A Message to PM Hailemariam Desalegn.* Hamden, CT: Institute of Development & Education for Africa Inc., 2013. PDF. p. 1-3.

8. To learn more about the near failure of the education system in Ethiopia due to the negative effect of the use of English as the medium of instruction in the country from middle school to tertiary education, refer to: Negash, Tekeste. *Education in Ethiopia: From Crisis to Brink of Collapse.* Uppsala: Nordic Africa Institute. 2006. PDF.

9. Abebe, Menigisitu. "*Yezewideetu hosipeetal leefit sew gedele* [The Zewideetu hospital elevator killed a person]." Adees Adimas. Addis Ababa. Adees Adimas, 28 Mar. 2015. Web. 05 Apr. 2015.

10. "Background." *Entoto Observatory and Research Center.* Entoto Observatory and Research Center. Web. 27 Dec. 2015

11. Gebeyaw, Abebayehu. "*Adees Abeba Adama dires heida tasitedadiralec malet ayidelem [It does not mean that Addis Ababa will administer [sic.] going [sic.] as far as Adama].*" Adees Adimas. Addis Ababa. Adees Adimas, 26 Apr. 2014. Web. 28 Apr. 2014.

PART III: PROPOSED ORTHOGRAPHIC REFORMS

Chapter 6: *Hiddasei* Giiz: Proposed Alphabetic Reform

Sources of epigraphs in their written order:

Hammond, Jenny. *Sweeter Than Honey: Ethiopian Women and Revolution Testimonies of Tigrayan Women.* Trenton: Red Sea, 1990. Print. P. 11.

Demoz (1983) as cited by Yacob, Daniel, and Yitna Firdyiwek in "System for Ethiopic Representation in ASCII (SERA)." *Media Ethiopia.* N.p., n.d. Web. 15 Jan. 2016.

1. Amin, Salim, and Chip Duncan. "Tigray: Then and Now." YouTube. *Camerapix-Duncan Group Production / ONE,* 1 Nov. 2011. Web. 30 Oct. 2014.

2. Eric Michael Weisenmiller. *"A Study of the Readability of On-Screen Text (Doctoral Dissertation),"* Virginia Polytechnic Institute and State University. Blacksburg, Virginia. July 1999. p. 37.

3. The International System of Units (SI), Bureau International des Poids et Mesures, 8th edition 2006, p. 121.

Chapter 7: *Hiddasei* Giiz: Proposed Typographic Reform

Sources of epigraphs in their written order:

Bringhurst, Robert. *The Elements of Typographic Style.* 3rd ed. Hartley & Marks, 2004. Print.

1. See, also: Nosnitsin, 2012. p. 7.

2. The 1513 Ethiopic psalter is the first Ethiopic book to come out of the printing press, not including earlier materials from woodblock printing. Sources:

   Wright, Stephen. "Book and Manuscript Collections in Ethiopia." *Journal of Ethiopian Studies* 2.1 (1964): p. 15. PDF.

   "The Ethiopic Psalter of 1513." *King's Collections: Online Exhibitions.* Web. 13 Sept. 2015.

3. "What Is A Font?" *Design With FontForge.* FontForge, n.d. Web. 14 Oct. 2015.

4. For example, in a 1986 radio interview, Fesseha Atlaw, who developed what is believed to be the first Ethiopic word processor in 1985, stated that in comparison to the Latin script, it was difficult to computerize the Ethiopic script because of (1) the large number of characters in the script, (2) the complicated shapes of the Ethiopic letterforms with varying widths and heights, and (3) due to various ways of marking the hidden vowels even within the same vowelic order. (Source: https://www.facebook.com/Ethiopic.Software/videos/1769037979993982).

5. I refer to these fonts as King Ezana family of fonts since their typeface dates back centuries and since the seven vowelic orders were established following the reform of the script during Ezana's reign.

Chapter 8: *Hiddasei* Giiz: Other Proposed Orthographic Reforms

Notes on epigraphs in their written order:

A Tigirinya proverb with an unknown originator pointing out the challenges with identifying the characters of the vocalized Ethiopic script by names because each of the characters is without a letter name other than the sound it represents.

The Ethiopic text is my version of a poem by Poet Laureate Tsegaye Gabre- Medhin (1936 – 2006), perhaps the greatest Ethiopian poet in history, in the proposed Ethiopic orthography. My translation that follows tries to preserve the original message without being too literal.

1. In the 20th century, some attempts were made to show gemination on Ethiopic text but never received popular acceptance. In his Amharic grammar book *Yamarinya Siwasiw* (1948 (E.C)), Bilata Merisiei Hazen Welide Qeeriqos stated that he had wanted to show gemination by placing a marker above every germinated character but was unable to get the typeface cut in time for the printing of the book. The 1965 Amharic classic *Fiqir Isike Meqabir* (Love Till the Grave) by one of Ethiopia's most celebrated novelists, Haddees Alemayyehu, showed gemination by placing two dots above every character that was geminated. However, his method was not universally accepted. A 1989 E.C. (c. 1997) Tigirinya-Tigirinya dictionary by the Ethiopian Institute of Languages also showed double dots above germinated characters, although such a system is seen virtually nowhere else.
2. Romanization of proposed Ethiopic digraphs shall follow similar rules for gemination by doubling the second letter. Similarly, Roman letter digraphs proposed to transliterate unique Ethiopic phonemes shall be geminated by doubling the second letter of each digraph. For more on gemination and romanization of Ethiopic, refer to Chapter 9: Proposed Standard Romanization of Ethiopic.
3. Proposed Roman letter digraphs and Ethiopic digraphs may not necessarily have components that are individually direct equivalents between the two scripts. For example, the Roman letter digraphs tx and cx, which are proposed for the transliteration of the Ethiopic letter ጠ and the Ethiopic digraph ጠሰ, respectively, are not directly equivalent to the corresponding Ethiopic letters. Each digraph shall be considered as made up of independent letters for the purpose of alphabetizing.
4. In 2012, I was talking to a friend who was learning Amharic as his second language from one of his family member who was of Ethiopian ancestry. He used a certain Amharic word in his conversation, which was not intelligible to me because of the way the word was pronounced. Unfortunately, he was unable to spell the word for me because the Ethiopic alphabet is vocalized and would only provide the same phonetic value as the phonemes of the word. It is easy to see how such difficulty in communication can affect a nation with 80 languages and dialects in the daily sociopolitical and economic activities of citizens.
5. Peter T. Daniles in Kaye (1991) provides a skeptical, if unbalanced, analysis of the origins of the Ethiopic letter names, arguing that the Ethiopic letter names were adapted from Hebrew sources centuries after Ethiopic was developed. However, this argument seems incorrect given the fact that the script was used for centuries before it became vocalized, which makes it inconceivable that it could have been used without some way of identifying each letter by a name. (Alan S. Kaye. (1991). *Semitic Studies: in honor of Wolf Leslau on the occasion of his 85th birthday*. Wiesbaden: Harrassowitz, Volume 1, pp 281ff.)
6. For a previous proposal for a Morse Code for Ethiopic, refer to Paz, Israel, and Hailemariam Dersso (undated) who proposed the first Morse Code for Ethiopic sometime in the years before the 1974 overthrow of the Haile Selassie government.
7. Meshesha, Million, and C. V. Jawahar. *"Optical Character Recognition of Amharic Documents."* Diss. Center for Visual Information Technology, International Institute of Information Technology. Hyderabad, India. Undated. Print.

PART IV: OTHER PROPOSED STANDARDS FOR ETHIOPIC

Chapter 9: Proposed Standard System for the Romanization of Ethiopic

Note on epigraph:

The Gentleman's Magazine coverage of the arrival of the Rosetta Stone in England, 1802.

1. Wright, Stephen. "The Transliteration of Amharic." *Journal of Ethiopian Studies* 2.1 (1964): 1-10. PDF. p. 5.
2. Johann Potken (ca. 1470 – ca. 1525), who prepared the book, stubbornly thought that he was dealing with the Chaldean language, rather than a distinct language called Giiz. Although he studied Giiz and became proficient enough to publish the book in Giiz, to him, Giiz was none other than the Chaldean language.
3. Wright, Stephen. "The Transliteration of Amharic." *Journal of Ethiopian Studies* 2.1 (1964): p. 2. PDF.
4. Adapted from: *Romanization System for Tigrinya: BGN/*

PCGN 2007 System. United States BGN and United Kingdom PCGN. Nov. 2015. PDF.

5. Adapted from: *Romanization System for Amharic: BGN/PCGN 1967 System*. United States BGN and United Kingdom PCGN. Nov. 2015. PDF.
6. For example, refer to the romanization method employed by Siegbert Uhlig, et al. (eds.) (2003). Encyclopaedia Aethiopica, Vol. 1: A-C. Wiesbaden: Harrassowitz Verlag.
7. Firdyiwek, Yitna, and Daniel Yaqob. "The System for Ethiopic Representation in ASCII." (1997): p. 2. PDF.
8. Allen, Julie D., et al. *The Unicode Standard Version 7.0 – Core Specification*. Mountain View: Unicode Consortium, 2014. Print.
9. Wright, Stephen. "The Transliteration of Amharic." *Journal of Ethiopian Studies* 2.1 (1964): pp. 1, 2. PDF.
10. For vowel lengthening in Ethiocushitic languages, particularly in Oromiffa, and its romanization, refer to Chapter 13.

Chapter 10: Proposed Standard System of Giizization

Note on epigraph:

My translation of a poetic prelude in *Adees Yamarinya Mezigebe Qalat [New Amharic Dictionary]* by Desta Tekile Welid. Addis Ababa: Artistic Printers, 1970. Print

Chapter 11: Proposed Giizization of Numerical Terms

Notes on epigraphs in order of their appearance:

A Tigirinya proverb with an unknown originator noting that things do not always work as planned in an imperfect world.

An Amharic proverb with an unknown originator noting the benefits of sharing responsibilities in society.

1. Numeric table adapted from "Ge'ez Script." Wikipedia. Wikimedia Foundation. Web. 24 May 2013.
2. See Tekile-Welid, Desita (1970). p. 17.
3. "A Look at Ethiopic Numerals." *The Ge'ez Frontier Foundation's Data Archive*. The Ge'ez Frontier Foundation, 2014. Web. 14 Oct. 2013.

Chapter 12: Proposed Standardization of the Ethiopic Keyboard

Sources on epigraphs in their written order:

Emperor Minileek (Menelik) made the comment after receiving an English typewriter as a gift from an American diplomat in 1903. Source: Pankhurst, Richard, Dr. "Innovation and Opposition to Change in Ethiopian History: 'Why Can't We Have an Amharic Typewriter?'- Menelik." Web log post. *Link Ethiopia*. Link Ethiopia. Web. 27 Feb. 2014

"Ethiopia Journal: Addresses." *Carpe Cakem! A Scrapbook of Thoughts on Arts, Culture and the Christian Life*. N.p., 26 Oct. 2011. Web. 29 Sept. 2015.

1. Johann Potken, who published the Ethiopic Psalter, stubbornly thought that he was dealing with the Chaldean language, rather than Giiz, a separate language. Although he studied Giiz, to him, Giiz was nothing other than a version of the Chaldean language. Sources:

   "The Ethiopic Psalter of 1513." *King's Collections: Online Exhibitions*. Web. 13 Sept. 2015.

   Wright, Stephen. "Book and Manuscript Collections in Ethiopia." *Journal of Ethiopian Studies* 2.1 (1964): p. 15. PDF.
2. Demoz (1983) stated that a certain Meshesha Weriqei created a new script that Emperor Minileek announced but that the reasons for the creation of the new script was not stated (as cited in Kinife, 2009).
3. "Olivetti Diaspron 82 Amharic Language Manual Typewriter." *Collection of Historical Scientific Instruments*. Harvard University. Web. 05 Apr. 2016.
4. Various sources, including the following:

   "Conversation with Yitna Firdyiwek." Telephone interview. Jun. 2016.

   "Conversation with Fesseha Atlaw." Telephone interview. Sep. 2016.

   "Legends of Ethiopic Computing." *Abyssinia Gateway*. N.p., n.d. Web. 01 May 2016.

   "Computerizing Ethiopia: A Conversation With Daniel Admassie." *Abyssinia Gateway*. N.p., n.d. Web. 01 May 2016.

   "From DOS to Dashen: A Conversation with Fesseha Atlaw." *Abyssinia Gateway*. N.p., n.d. Web. 01 May 2016.
5. "Conversation with Dr. Aberra Molla." Telephone interview. Feb. 2015.

6. Snetsehay Assefa and Bereket Getaneh. "Local App Developers Thrive." *Addis Fortune*. Independent News & Media, 14 Dec. 2014. Web. 02 Jan. 2015.
7. Ayele, Guenet. "Methodology - Amharic Computer." *Ethiopass.visascol.com*. Visascol - Ethiopass, n.d. Web. 18 Sept. 2016.
8. Molla, Aberra. Ethiopic Character Entry. Aberra Molla, assignee. Patent US20090179778 A1. Published 16 July 2009. Web. 10 Feb. 2015.

PART V: THE ROLE OF GOVERNMENT

Chapter 13: More on the Ethiopian Language Crisis and Recommended Solutions

Sources on epigraphs in their written order:

Article 5 of the 1995 Constitution of the Federal Democratic Republic of Ethiopia.

My transcription and translation of radio interview given by Prof. Tekeste Negash. Audio source: "Interview with Prof Tekeste Negash - Pt 1 - SBS Amharic." *YouTube*. SBS Amharic Radio, 30 Oct. 2014. Web. 11 Nov. 2014.

1. Bishaw, Alemayehu, and Jon Lasser. "Education in Ethiopia: Past, Present and Future Prospects." *African Nebula* 5 (2012): 1-17. PDF. 05 May 2014. p. 56.
2. Wright, Stephen. "Book and Manuscript Collections in Ethiopia." *Journal of Ethiopian Studies* 2.1 (1964): p. 16. PDF.
3. Bishaw, Alemayehu, and Jon Lasser. "Education in Ethiopia: Past, Present and Future Prospects." *African Nebula* 5 (2012): 1-17. PDF. 05 May 2014. p. 56.
4. "Interview with Prof Tekeste Negash - Pt 1 - SBS Amharic." *YouTube*. SBS Amharic Radio, 30 Oct. 2014. Web. 11 Nov. 2014.
5. Negash, Tekeste. *Education in Ethiopia: From Crisis to Brink of Collapse*. Uppsala: Nordic Africa Institute, 2006. Print. p. 33.
6. Ibid. p. 8.
7. Ibid. p. 21.
8. Ibid. p. 32.
9. Ojo, B. J., and Nneka Umera-Okeke. *English Pronunciation Errors: A Case Study of Amhara and Oromia Regions of Ethiopia*. N.d. PDF. p. 161. (Unpublished.)
10. 2007 Population and Housing Census
11. The little known Academy of Ethiopian Languages and Cultures has had several different names since its establishment in 1968 in a typical fashion for an Ethiopian institution/organization adding to its obscurity. First set up under the auspices of the then Ministry of Education and Arts with a national mandate, today the academy is under Addis Ababa University and is said to be carrying out its mandates autonomously. Endowing it with constitutional powers to protect and nurture Ethiopian languages (along with a sticky name) will no doubt go a long way in ensuring a better future of Ethiopian languages.
12. "Self-Made Translators." *Addis Fortune*. Independent News & Media, 07 Dec. 2015. Web. 22 Dec. 2015.
13. For more information on the European effort for machine translation between pairs of European languages, consult the EuroMatrixPlus website (www.euromatrixplus.net)

Chapter 14: The Politics of Reform: Previous Efforts for and Opposition to Language Reform

Sources on epigraphs in their written order:

Pankhurst, Richard, Dr. "Innovation and Opposition to Change in Ethiopian History: The Coming of the Radio, and Developments in the Field of Currency, Education, and Public Health." Web log post. *Link Ethiopia*. Link Ethiopia. Web. 27 Feb. 2014.

Kidanewelid Tekilei. "[Untitled.]" Letter to the editor. *Semina Weriq*. Vol. 2. 1988. 13. PDF. Ser. 4.

"Ethiopian Standards." *Ethiopian Standards Agency*. Web. 06 Oct. 2016.

1. Pankhurst, Richard. ""Why Can't We Have an Amharic Typewriter?"- Menelik | Link Ethiopia." Link Ethiopia. Link Ethiopia. Web. 7 July 2014.
2. Molla, Aberra. "Engineer Ayana Birru." *Ethiopian Computers & Software*. Ethiopian Computers & Software. Web. 22 Jan. 2013.
3. Wright, Stephen. "The Transliteration of Amharic." *Journal of Ethiopian Studies* 2.1 (1964): p. 3. PDF.
4. Selomon Tesema. "የፊደል ጣጣና የአምስቱ ትውልድ ውዝግብ! (The Problems of the *Feedel* and the Controversy [That Lasted] Five Generation[s]!" *Change!* 05 Dec. 2012. Web. 23 Sept. 2016.
5. Having not read the book, most of the information I have about the work is from the following source: ZeTewahedo, DejeS. """ብቸኛው አፍሪካዊ ፊደል" (The Sole African Alphabet) የተሰኘው በዶክተር ፍቅሬ ዮሴፍ የተዘጋጀው

መጽሐፍ." ደጀ ሰላም *Deje Selam*: 22 Feb. 2009. Web. 13 Oct. 2016.

6. Bilatta Merisiei Hazen Welide Qeeriqos. *Beaddees Siriat Yetesenada Yamarinya Siwasiw (A New Approach to Amharic Grammar)*. Addis Ababa: Artistic Printing, 1948 E.C. (c. 1956). Print.

7. Bedilu Waqijira. "የአጻጻፍ ሥርዓታችንን ስለማሻሻል (About Reforming Our Writing System)." Addis Times. 2005 E.C. (c. 2012). Vol. 1, No. 6. p. 26.

8. Wright, Stephen. "The Transliteration of Amharic." *Journal of Ethiopian Studies* 2.1 (1964): p. 3.

9. "Language Reform." *Wikipedia*. Wikimedia Foundation. Web. 20 Sept. 2014. And other sources.

Acknowledgment

Born in Komibolica in the then province of Wello and raised in Addis Ababa speaking Amharic as my first language, I was able to learn Tigirinya as a second language from my parents. I remember how my late father Tewolde Medhin Kahssay (1944 – 2015) was consistent and systematic in his effort to teach me his ancestral language, which has critically helped me to cover Tigirinya as much as Amharic in this proposal for language reform for Ethiopia. Thanks, Dad! Your effort has paid off!

My deepest gratitude goes to my wife Misrak and our precious daughter Eliana. Enormously time-consuming, the development of this book has been a great burden to my family. I am eternally indebted to my wife who lovingly took care of the house chores day in and day out to give me the time I needed to work on this book. I have spent many nights researching and writing to produce this book—often abandoning or relegating many of my responsibilities at home. My daughter, who was born within a year of my starting the research work into what eventually became this publication, was born and raised in a home with an absent-minded dad. Thanks, Eliana, for putting up with me while I worked on this book!

I would like to acknowledge my friend Eyasu Teklu for introducing me to the www.good-amharic-books.com website, which has electronic versions of books of all kind in Ethiopian languages. My appreciation to my friend Samuel Tewolde who provided me with Tigirinya language materials and, as a native Tigirinya speaker, helped me decipher some of the Tigirinya personal pronouns many of which have alternative forms. I would also like to thank my friend Marshet Gossaye for providing me with Tigirinya, Amharic, and Oromiffa language materials that I needed.

Thanks are in order for Ato Fesseha Atlaw, one of the towering figures in the computerization of Ethiopic, for reviewing and helping edit a section in this book in addition to taking the time for a phone conversation with me. As well, thanks are in order for Yitna Firdyiwek of the University of Virginia and Dr. Aberra Molla, noted Ethiopian scientist and developer of Ethiopic software, for taking the time for a phone discussion with me and providing me with valuable information on the history of the computerization of Ethiopic. I am grateful to Prof. Ephraim Isaac of Harvard University for taking the time to respond to my questions related to the Ethiopic script.

I am thankful to Katie Sambrook and King's College London for kindly granting me permission to reproduce in this book images from the 1513 Ethiopic Psalter *Psalterium David et cantica aliqua in lingua Chaldea [Giiz]*, which is part of King's collection. As well, I am thankful to Sara M. Frankel and Harvard University's Collection of Historical Scientific Instruments for kindly granting me permission to reproduce in this book photos from their collection of a 1950's Ethiopic typewriter.

I am indebted to many people who have worked hard for the development of Ethiopic and whom I have met only through their works, including those who have provided historical information, from whose contributions I have benefited as cited where appropriate. Among them is Kinife Meekaeil, whose work with regards to the history of the efforts made by various Ethiopian scholars to reform the Ethiopic script in the past hundred years has been very beneficial to me. I should also mention my friends Begashaw Mekonnen, Binora Dado, and Peter Apswoude for their encouragement and moral support for which I am very thankful.

In some ways, this book may be considered as a work in progress, especially because many of the reform ideas presented in it are the first of their kind for Ethiopia and the work for the improvement of language use in Ethiopia has only begun. Primarily, my intended audience are Ethiopian policy makers who have the authority and solemn responsibility to protect and develop Ethiopian languages. However, I believe that scholars, especially those in the areas of Ethio-Semitic and Ethio-Cushitic languages, and Ethiopians, in general, will find this book exceptionally useful. All comments will be appreciated and acknowledged when and where appropriate.

Works Cited

Abraham, Kinfe. *Ethiopia: From Bullets to the Ballot Box (The Bumpy Road to Democracy and the Political Economy of Transition).* Lawrenceville: The Red Sea Press Inc, 1994. Print.

Allen, Julie D., et al. *The Unicode Standard, Version 7.0 – Core Specification.* Mountain View: Unicode Consortium, 2014. PDF.

Amsalu Aklilu. *Amharic-English Dictionary.* Addis Ababa: Kuraz Publishing Agency, 1980 E.C. (c. 1988). Print.

Andah, Bassey, et al. *The Archaeology of Africa: Food, Metals and Towns.* New York, London: Routledge, 1993. Print.

Aregay, Merid W, Donald Crummey, Gideon Goldenberg, Paolo Marrassini, Siegbert Uhlig, Ewald Wagner and, Baye Yimam. *Encyclopaedia Aethiopica: Volume 1: A-C.* Wiesbaden: Harrassowitz Verlag, 2003. Print.

Armbruster, C. H. *Initia Amharica; an Introduction to Spoken Amharic.* Part I: Grammar. Cambridge: University Press, 1908. Print.

Asker, Lars, et al. *Applying Machine Learning to Amharic Text Classification.* Stockholm University and Swedish Institute of Computer Science, n.d. PDF.

Aspen, Harald, Birhanu Teferra, Shiferaw Bekele, and Svein Ege. *Research in Ethiopian Studies: Selected Papers of the 16th International Conference of Ethiopian Studies, Trondheim July 2007.* Wiesbaden: Harrassowitz, 2010. Print.

Ayele, Guenet. "Methodology - Amharic Computer." *Ethiopass.visascol.com.* Visascol - Ethiopass, n.d. Web. 18 Sept. 2016.

Bausi, Alessandro, Siegbert Uhlig, Baye Yimam, Donald Crummey, and Gianfranco Fiaccadori. *Encyclopaedia Aethiopica. Supplementa, Addenda Et Corrigenda, Maps, Index.* Wiesbaden: Harrassowitz, 2014. Print.

Bayei Yimam. *Yeamarinya Sewasiw. [Amharic Grammar].* Rev. ed. ባየ ይማም። የአማርኛ ሰዋሰው። የተሻሻለ ሁለተኛ እትም። Addis Ababa: Commerical Printers, 2000 E.C. (c. 2008). Print.

Berhe, Hailay Beyene. *Design and Development of Tigrigna Search Engine.* MSc. Thesis. Addis Ababa University Institutional Repository, 2013. PDF.

Bishaw, Alemayehu, and Jon Lasser. "Education in Ethiopia: Past, Present and Future Prospects." *African Nebula* 5 (2012): 1-17. PDF.

Bilatta Merisiei Hazen Welide Qeeriqos. ብላታ መርስኤ ሀዘን ወልደ ቂርቆስ። በአዲስ ስርአት የተሰናዳ ያማርኛ ሰዋሰው። *Beaddees Siriat Yetesenada Yamarinya Siwasiw (A New Approach to Amharic Grammar).* Addis Ababa: Artistic Printing, 1948 E.C. (c. 1956). Print.

Blair, John G. *Modular America: Cross-cultural Perspectives on the Emergence of an American Way.* New York: Greenwood, 1988. Print.

Bringhurst, Robert. *The Elements of Typographic Style.* 3rd ed. Hartley & Marks, 2004. Print.

Coulmas, Florian. *The Writing Systems of the World.* Oxford, UK: B. Blackwell, 1989. Print.

Cowley, R. "The Standardisation of Amharic Spelling." *Journal of Ethiopian Studies* 5.2 (1967): 1-8. PDF.

Dalby, Andrew. *Dictionary of Languages: The Definitive Reference to More than 400 Languages.* Columbia University Press. Revised edition. 2004.

Daniels, Peter T., and Bright, William. *The World's Writing Systems*. New York, Oxford: Oxford University Press, 1996.

——. "Fundamentals of Grammatology." *Journal of the American Oriental Society* 110.4 (1990): 727-31. PDF.

Desie Qeleb. *Tinisaei Giiz. The Revival of Geez.* ደሴ ቀለብ። ትንሳኤ ግእዝ። Addis Ababa: Ethiopian Orthodox Church, Sunday Schools Department, 2002 E.C. (c. 2010). Print.

Desita Tekile-Welid. *Adees Yamarinya Mezigebe Qalat. [New Amharic Dictionary].* ደስታ ተክለወልድ። አዲስ ያማርኛ መዝገበ ቃላት። Addis Ababa: Artistic Printers, 1970. Print.

Dillmann, August, Carl Bezold, and James A. Crichton. *Ethiopic Grammar*. London: Williams & Norgate, 1907. Print.

Durban, Chris. *Interpreting Getting it Right: A guide to buying interpreting services.* Alexandria: American Translators Association, 2011. Print.

Felici, Jim. *The Complete Manual of Typography: A Guide to Setting Perfect Type*. 2nd ed. Berkeley: Peachpit, 2011. Print.

Firdyiwek, Yitna, and Daniel Yaqob. *The System for Ethiopic Representation in ASCII*. 1997: p. 2. PDF.

Fisseha, Yonas. *Development of Stemming Algorithm for Tigrigna Text.* Addis Ababa: Addis Ababa University Institutional Repository, 2011. PDF.

Fromkin, Victoria, Robert Rodman, Nina Hyams, and Kirsten M. Hummel. *An Introduction to Language*. 3rd Canadian ed. Toronto: Thomson/Nelson, 2006. Print.

Getahun Amare. *The English-Amharic Idioms Dictionary*. Addis Ababa: Tambek International, 1986 E.C. (c. 1994). Print.

Ghelawdewos Araia. *Language for whose Audience in the Ethiopian context? A Message to PM Hailemariam Desalegn*. Hamden, CT: Institute of Development & Education for Africa Inc., 2013. PDF. p. 1-3.

Goldenberg, Gideon. *Semitic Languages: Features, Structures, Relations, Processes*. Oxford: Oxford University Press, 2012. Print.

Griefenow-Mewis, Catherine. *On Results of the Reform in Ethiopia's Language and Education Policies*. Wiesbaden: Otto Harrassowitz GmbH & Co. KG, 2009. Print.

Hammond, Jenny. *Sweeter Than Honey: Ethiopian Women and Revolution Testimonies of Tigrayan Women*. Trenton: Red Sea, 1990. Print.

Haregeweyin Kebede, et al. አማርኛ መዝገበ ቃላት *Amarinya Mezigebe Qalat. [Amharic Dictionary]*. Addis Ababa: Ethiopian Languages Research Center, Addis Ababa University, 1993 E.C. (c. 2001). Print.

Heine, Bernd, and Derek Nurse. *African Languages: An Introduction*. Cambridge: Cambridge University Press, 2000. Print.

Hetzron, Robert. *The Semitic Languages*. New York: Routledge, 1997. Print.

Hinsene Mekuria. *English – Oromo – Amharic Dictionary*. 5th ed. Addis Ababa: Commercial Printing Enterprise, 2010. Print.

Honeyman, A. M. "The Letter-Order of the Semitic Alphabets in Africa and the Near East." *Africa: Journal of the International African Institute* 22.2 (1952): 136-47. PDF.

Hooker, J. T. *Reading the Past: Ancient Writing from Cuneiform to the Alphabet*. Berkeley: U of California/British Museum, 1990. Print.

Hornus, Jérémie. *The Ethiopic Writing System: A Typographic Approach*. Diss. University of

Reading. *Issuu.* 2014. Web. 10 Sept. 2016.

Isenberg, Rev. Charles William. *Dictionary of the Amharic Language.* London: The Church Missionary Society, 1841. Print.

Janson, Tore. *The History of Languages: An Introduction.* Oxford: Oxford University Press, 2012. Print.

Johanson, Donald, and Blake Edgar. *From Lucy to Language.* (Revised, Updated and Expanded). New York: Simon & Schuster, 2006. Print.

Kahssay, Lou, and Wongel Gebeyehu. *Let's Discover Abyssinia: Amharic Alphabet Book.* Toronto: 2006. Print.

Kaye, Alan S. *Semitic Studies: In Honor of Wolf Leslau on the Occasion of His 85th Birthday.* Vol. 1. Wiesbaden: Harrassowitz, 1991. Print.

Kinife Meekaeil. "ስለ አማርኛ ፊደል መሻሻል የተደረጉ ጥናቶች መዘርዝር። (A List of Studies Made to Reform the [Ethiopic] Script)." Melbourne. 2001 E.C. (c. 1994). PDF.

Kitchen, Andrew, Christopher Ehret, et al. 2009. "Bayesian phylogenetic analysis of Semitic languages identifies an Early Bronze Age origin of Semitic in the Near East." *Proceedings of the Royal Society B: Biological Sciences* 276 no. 1665 (June 22)

Krapf, J.L., and C.W. Isenberg. *An Imperfect Outline of the Elements of the Galla Language.* London: Church Missionary Society, 1840. Print.

Lambdin, Thomas O. *Introduction to Classical Ethiopic (Ge'ez),* Harvard Semitic Studies 24. Winona Lake: Eisenbrauns, 2006.

Leslau, Wolf. *English-Amharic Context Dictionary.* Louvain: Imprimerie Orientaliste, 1973. Print.

——. *Introductory Grammar of Amharic.* Otto Harrassowitz, Wiesbaden. 2000. Print.

——. "La Réforme De L'alphabet Éthiopien." *Rassegna Di Studi Etiopici* 12 (1953): 96-106. PDF.

——. "The Present State of Ethiopic Linguistics." *Journal of Near Eastern Studies* 5.3 (1946): 215-29. PDF.

Madessa, Amanuel Hirpa. *Probabilistic Information Retrieval System for Amharic Language.* MSc. Thesis. Addis Ababa: Addis Ababa University Institutional Repository, 2012. PDF.

Martin, Henri-Jean. Transl. by Lydia G. Cochrane. *The History and Power of Writing.* Chicago. University Of Chicago Press. 1995.

Mason, John. *Tigrinya Grammar.* Lawrenceville, NJ. The Red Press Inc. 1996.

Mesifin Lisanu. *Yeamarinya Mexihheite-Qalat.* Addis Ababa: Artistic Printers, 1952 E.C. (1960).

Molla, Aberra. "Engineer Ayana Birru." *Ethiopian Computers & Software.* Ethiopian Computers & Software. Web.

Molla, Aberra. "The Ethiopic Alphabet." *Ethiopian Computers & Software.* Ethiopian Computers & Software. Web.

Nakanishi, Akira. *Writing Systems of the World.* Tuttle Publishing. 1980.

Negash, Tekeste. *Education in Ethiopia: From Crisis to Brink of Collapse.* Uppsala: Nordic Africa Institute. 2006. PDF.

Nosnitsin, Denis. "Ethiopian Manuscripts and Ethiopian Manuscript Studies: A Brief Overview and Evaluation." *Gazette Du Livre Médiéval* 58.1 (2012): 1-16. PDF.

Ojo, B. J., and Nneka Umera-Okeke. *English Pronunciation Errors: A Case Study of Ambara and Oromia Regions of Ethiopia.* N.d. PDF. p160 - 176. (Unpublished.)

"Olivetti Diaspron 82 Amharic Language Manual Typewriter." Collection of Historical Scientific Instruments. Harvard University. Web. 05 Apr. 2016.

Owens, Jonathan. *A Grammar of Harar Oromo (Northeastern Ethiopia).* Hamburg: Buske. Helmut Buske Verlag Hamburg. 1985.

Phillipson, David W. *Foundations of an African Civilisation: Aksum & the Northern Horn, 1000 BC – AD 1300.* Addis Ababa: Addis Ababa University Press, 2014. Print.

Prah, Kwesi Kwaa. ""No Country Can Make Progress on the Basis of a Borrowed Language"." Interview. *eLearning Africa.* eLearning Africa, 2013. Web.

Robinson, Andrew. *The Story of Writing: Alphabets, Hieroglyphs & Pictograms.* 2nd edition. London, UK. Thames & Hudson. 2007.

Sampson, Geoffrey. *Writing Systems: A Linguistic Introduction.* Stanford, CA. Stanford University Press. 1985.

Selomon Tesema. "የፊደል ጣጣና የአምስቱ ትውልድ ውዝግብ! (The Problems of the *Feedel* and the Controversy [That Lasted] Five Generation[s]!" *Change!* 05 Dec. 2012. Web. 23 Sept. 2016.

Spencer, John H. *Ethiopia at Bay: A Personal Account of the Haile Selassie Years.* Tsehai Publishers. 2006. Print.

Tekhesite Tekhile, Danieil Mehharee, Xehayinesh Gebire- Yowihanis, et. al. *Mezigebe Qalat Tigirinya Bitigirinya.* Addis Ababa, Ethiopia. Ethiopian Languages Academy, Tigirinya Division. 1989 E.C. (c. 1997).

Terrefe Raswork. *Design of Amharic Teleprinter (Teletype).* Addis Ababa, c. 1966. 9-15. PDF.

"The Ethiopic Psalter of 1513." *King's Collections: Online Exhibitions.* Web. 13 Sept. 2015.

Ullendorff, Edward. "Studies in the Ethiopic Syllabary." *Africa: Journal of the International African Institute* 21.3 (1951): 207-17. PDF.

Ullman, Berthold L. *Ancient Writing and Its Influence: Introd. by Julian Brown.* Cambridge, MA: MIT, 1969. Print.

Wodajo, Mulugeta. "Postwar Reform in Ethiopian Education." *Comparative Education Review* 2.3 (1959): 24-30. PDF.

Wright, Stephen. "Book and Manuscript Collections in Ethiopia." *Journal of Ethiopian Studies* 2.1 (1964): 11-24. PDF.

——. "The Transliteration of Amharic." *Journal of Ethiopian Studies* 2.1 (1964): 1-10. PDF.

Yacob, Daniel. "Ethiopic at the End of the 20th Century." *International Journal of Ethiopian Studies* 2.1/2 (2005): 121-40. PDF.

Young, John. *Peasant Revolution in Ethiopia: The Tigray People's Liberation Front, 1975-1991.* Cambridge: Cambridge UP, 1997. Print.

ZeTewahedo, DejeS. """ብቸኛው አፍሪካዊ ፊደል" (The Sole African Alphabet) የተሰኘው በዶክተር ፍቅሬ ዮሴፍ የተዘጋጀው መጽሐፍ." ደጀ ሰላም *Deje Selam*: 22 Feb. 2009. Web. 13 Oct. 2016.

Index

F

G

H

V

W

Y

Z

www.ingramcontent.com/pod-product-compliance
Lightning Source LLC
Chambersburg PA
CBHW081416230426
43668CB00016B/2248
9780995091108